FIRST CITY

EARLY AMERICAN STUDIES

Daniel K. Richter, Director,
McNeil Center for Early American Studies,
Series Editor

Exploring neglected aspects of our colonial, revolutionary, and early national history and culture, Early American Studies reinterprets familiar themes and events in fresh ways. Interdisciplinary in character, and with a special emphasis on the period from about 1600 to 1850, the series is published in partnership with the McNeil Center for Early American Studies.

A complete list of books in the series is available from the publisher.

FIRST CITY

Philadelphia and the Forging of Historical Memory

GARY B. NASH

PENN

University of Pennsylvania Press

PHILADELPHIA

Printed in the United States of America on acid-free paper

10 9 8 7 6 5 4 3 2 1

Published by
University of Pennsylvania Press
Philadelphia, Pennsylvania 19104-4011
Text design by Dean Bornstein

Library of Congress Cataloging-in-Publication Data
Nash, Gary B.
First City: Philadelphia and the forging of historical memory / Gary B. Nash
p. cm. (Early American studies)
ISBN 0-8122-3630-0 (alk. paper)
Includes bibliographical references and index.
1. Historic preservation—Pennsylvania—Philadelphia (Pa.)—History. 2. Memory—Social aspects—Pennsylvania—Philadelphia. 3. Philadelphia (Pa.)—History. 4. Philadelphia (Pa.)—Historiography. 5. Philadelphia (Pa.)—History—Societies, etc. I. Title. II. Series
F158.3 .N37 2001
974.8′11′0072073—dc21 2001047082

For Carol and John
Clarke and Gwen

CONTENTS

INTRODUCTION: MAKING HISTORY MATTER

"Truth is shaped strictly by the needs of those who wish to receive it."
— Russell Banks, *Cloudsplitter* (1996)

"Men of literary tastes . . . are always apt to overlook the working classes and to confine the records they make of their own time, in great degree, to the habits and fortunes of their own associates. . . . This has made it nearly impossible to discern the very real influence their character and condition has had on the fortune and fate of the nation."
— Frederick Law Olmsted, *A Journey in the Seaboard Slave States* (1859)

As many Americans know, the two most important documents in the history of the United States, the Declaration of Independence and the Constitution of 1787, were drafted and signed at the State House in Philadelphia, now Independence Hall. The city was also the site of the first American paper mill, hospital, medical college, subscription library, street lighting, scientific and intellectual society, bank, and government mint. The city served on and off as the official capital of the country until 1800. Today, we remember less about the significance of Philadelphia to the history of the nation than the record shows. But even the memories lodged in the public mind cannot be taken for granted, and they are far from complete. Indeed, the Philadelphia story could have been written another way; in fact, it has been rewritten many times. At the beginning of the twenty-first century, the unearthing of Philadelphia's past is a thriving business. Today, the long look backward by historians is renovating the public recollection of the city's past.

Remembering Philadelphia's bygone days existed from the beginning, as soon as a mother told her children a story about olden times or a father reminded his offspring of his arrival in Penn's woods. But for a long time the city's history was passed only informally from one generation to another. No biography of Philadelphia's founder appeared for almost a century after his death. No city history appeared until Philadelphia was on the verge of celebrating its 150th birthday. Not until Jefferson and Madison had retired from their presidencies did Philadelphians witness the advent of calculated, organized memory-making.

In 1816, just after the Treaty of Ghent ended the War of 1812, Pennsylvania's legislators eyed the venerable State House building in Philadelphia, where the Declaration of Independence and U.S. Constitution had been signed. Razing the building and selling the land for commercial development in the fast-growing, forward-looking city seemed like a practical idea, for the state government had moved to Harrisburg seventeen years before and legislators knew that tax-shy citizens would appreciate how the sale of the property could underwrite the costs of a new capitol building on the banks of the Susquehanna. Sentimental attachment to the site of the nation's birth did not figure much in the legislature's planning because the public itself was indifferent to preserving what would later become a national icon. Even the Liberty Bell seemed nothing more than a rusty relic. As a later preservationist commented ruefully, the old bell was not thought worth mentioning in the plan to raze the State House, "but left to be sold as old lumber within the walls and rafters of Independence Hall."[1]

As early as 1802, Pennsylvania's General Assembly had considered selling the State House, the Liberty Bell included, while dividing into building lots the parklike expanse familiarly called the State House Yard. The city of Philadelphia itself had secured state permission in 1812 for demolishing the piazzas and wing buildings that gave Independence Hall, still called the Pennsylvania State House, its distinctive character. The city promptly erected office space that "created a Chestnut Street facade in the character of a Philadelphia rowhouse development."[2]

Obliterating old buildings was for many Americans a way of freeing themselves from the tyranny of forerunners—what Thoreau would call a "purifying destruction."[3] The home of Philadelphia's most famous figure, Benjamin Franklin, was treated as anything but hallowed space. In 1802, twelve years after Printer Ben died, Franklin's daughter and her husband converted the home where so many national and international figures had met during the Revolutionary era into a boardinghouse. Then they demolished the house entirely in 1812 to prepare the site for division into small urban building lots. Philadelphians' memory of Franklin had waned so rapidly by this time that lagging sales of an earthenware figurine of America's "universal man" convinced the manufacturer to pep up the trade by relabeling Franklin's image "George Washington."[4]

Unexpectedly, the close call with plans to obliterate Independence Hall kindled reverence for places associated with the American Revolution. William Duane, publisher of the newspaper founded by Benjamin Franklin Bache, Franklin's grandson, campaigned in 1816 that "in Pennsylvania, under the *Gothic mist of ignorance and vice*, by which it is now governed— everything is to be *pulled down.*" The building where the Declaration of Independence "was deliberated and determined," he thundered, should be venerated "as a monument of that splendid event; but this is not the spirit of the rulers of Pennsylvania now—the *state house must be sold*— for every thing now in political affairs is *barter and sale!*"[5] Duane's outcry led the state to sell the building to the city of Philadelphia for $70,000 before it fell under the gavel. However, even as the negotiation proceeded, the city removed much of the original pine paneling of the Assembly Room where the Founding Fathers signed the Declaration of Independence. Eager to modernize the building for

FIGURE 1. John Trumbull, *The Declaration of Independence, 4 July 1776*, oil, 1818, Yale University. Trumbull's painting, which gained him fame, shows the pine paneling removed in 1816. He deplored "the spirit of innovation [that] laid unhallowed hands upon [Independence Hall] and violated its venerable walls by 'modern improvement,' as it is called."

office use, the city sold pieces of the paneling as souvenirs (Figure 1). Well in advance of the public, one candidate for county commissioner made this sale an election issue, vowing to stop the defacement.

By June 1818, when Philadelphia finally took possession of Independence Hall from the state, its citizens awakened to the importance of saving historic buildings as treasured symbols of American history. In the same month, an old friend—indeed the Quaker city's founder—introduced them to another use of the past. Readers of the *Philadelphia Union* found advice from William Penn, dead for almost a century, on one of the burning issues of the day. In a series of articles, Penn had returned, at least in spirit, to comment benevolently on the proposal to transport free African Americans back to Africa. The recently formed American Colonization Society had turned this proposal into a national debate, and here in the pages of the *Union* (actually, in heaven) was Penn discussing the matter with two lately deceased black leaders: Absalom Jones, minister of Philadelphia's St. Thomas's African Episcopal Church for nearly a quarter century, and Paul Cuffe, merchant and ship captain in New Bedford, Massachusetts, and one of the nation's few black Quakers.

In their "dialogues on the African colony," Penn, Jones, and Cuffe debated the matter warmly. The man putting words into their mouths was Robert Finley, president of

FIGURE 2. Raphaelle Peale, *Portrait of Absalom Jones*, oil, 1810, Delaware Art Museum. Raphaelle Peale, the son of Charles Willson Peale, painted sixty-four-year-old Absalom Jones in 1810. Jones's master brought him to Philadelphia as a slave at age sixteen, and the dutiful servant was able to purchase his wife's freedom shortly after marrying her in 1770. But his master would not permit Jones's own self-purchase until 1784. Eight years later he founded Philadelphia's first independent black church.

Princeton Theological Seminary and publicist of the American Colonization Society. Finley's design was to sway black opinion in Philadelphia. He knew, as did everyone in the city, that African Americans had thronged Richard Allen's Mother Bethel Church on Sixth Street near Pine just a year before to discuss repatriation to Africa. Before a packed house, several black leaders had supported voluntary immigration to Africa. They agreed with the reasoning of white patrons of the free black community that congealed white racism would never allow free blacks to succeed in the United States, that repatriated black Christians would have a chance to convert millions of heathen Africans to the true religion, and that several million repatriated blacks might create a new outlet for American goods. But ordinary black Philadelphians, knowing that the American Colonization Society had enlisted prominent southern slaveholders and politicians who called free blacks "a dangerous and useless part of the community," nearly brought down the walls of Mother Bethel with shouts of "No!" when the question was put about who favored repatriation.

In their celestial discussion, Absalom Jones firmly rejected repatriation as a deportation scheme designed to squelch efforts to abolish slavery (Figure 2). Paul Cuffe dissented. Reminding Penn and Jones that he had taken a boatload of free blacks to Sierra Leone only a few years before he died, Cuffe explained that the plan was "one of the most beneficent that human genius could have devised." Jones remained unconvinced. Penn, father of religious and ethnic toleration, promised to consult George Washington, also in heaven since his death nineteen years before. Reporting back, Penn vouchsafed that the Pater Patriae warmly endorsed colonization of free blacks for their own good. Cuffe chimed in that the racial prejudice of white Americans was intractable, leaving Africa as the only viable choice. Jones still doubted that whites wished to do a great good for a people they hated. But Penn and Cuffe persisted. Finally, swallowing his doubts that whatever pleased slavemasters could benefit free blacks, Jones acceded: "My objections have been refuted; my scruples vanquished. And all my doubts satisfied. Heaven speed the undertaking!"[6]

What Philadelphia's black community made of Reverend Finley's enlistment of Philadelphia's long-deceased founder to convince them to pack their bags, leave the city, and head home to Africa cannot be recovered from extant documents. But in both deed and word, black Philadelphians certainly regarded Finley's imaginary dialogues as the work of a pillager of the past who put deceased heroes, black and white, on the side of the American Colonization Society. After the *Union* ran Finley's "Dialogues on African Colonization," they remonstrated in 1818 and 1819 against the Colonization Society. They spoke more compellingly with their feet when the society sent the first two ships to establish the colony of Liberia in 1819 and 1820. Of about 10,000 free blacks in Philadelphia, only twenty-two embarked. New recruitment campaigns in 1823 and 1824 for Liberia-bound ships failed miserably, netting only another handful of black Philadelphians.

In 1824, only six years after the crumbling State House began its metamorphosis to the Independence Hall shrine and black Philadelphians rejected Finley's manipulation of William Penn's and Absalom Jones's views on colonization, the city entered a new era of historical consciousness in which restoring collective memory of the past came to be seen as an urgent matter. The arrival on September 28, 1824 of the Marquis de Lafayette, hero of the American Revolution and surrogate son of the childless George Washington, became a galvanizing moment. Invited by Congress to return to the United States, the aging Lafayette toured every corner of the country, inspiring grand receptions, massive parades, civic celebrations, and monument raising for thirteen months. No city outdid Philadelphia. Ten thousand troops assembled to be reviewed by him; visiting crowds

FIGURE 3. *General LaFayette's arrival at Independence Hall Philad\a Sep\t 28th 1824*, Winterthur Museum. The Germantown Print Works produced the most spectacular souvenirs of the Lafayette celebrations: printed linen handkerchiefs. The one shown here depicts architect William Strickland's massive stage-prop ceremonial arch, based on the Septimus Severus Arch in Rome. Workers erected it across the street from Independence Hall (missing its cupola, which had rotted badly and been torn down). A balloon begins its ascent as six white horses draw Lafayette through the arch in a decked-out barouche.

strained the capacity of local inns and taverns; the price of some commodities doubled; deputations from outlying areas vied for a chance to meet the hero, accompanied by his son George Washington Lafayette; children from scores of schools were brought before him for his blessing (Figure 3).[7]

Fervor in Philadelphia far outlasted Lafayette's seven-day visit. Two weeks after his departure for points south, the *Saturday Evening Post* reported that "We wrap our bodies in La Fayette coats during the day, and repose between La Fayette blankets at night. . . . We have La Fayette bread, La Fayette butter, La Fayette beef, and La Fayette vegetables . . . Even the ladies distinguish their *proper* from *common* kisses, under the title '*La Fayette smooches*.'"[8] Entrepreneurs scrambled to put Lafayette's image on whatever appeared to have commercial potential—snuffboxes, cravats, brandy flasks, white kid gloves, pitchers, glasses, and gewgaws. The flesh-and-blood Lafayette might never return, but Philadelphians could cherish his memory through souvenirs of the week-long celebration. Suddenly, they began to see that while history is *about* the past, it is *for* the future.

The anticipation of Lafayette's visit brought renewed attention to Independence Hall as an icon associated with the American Revolution. "Through word and image," historian Charlene Mires explains, "Lafayette's visit redefined the State House as a significant bridge between past and present."[9] Choosing the east room of the State House as the proper place to receive Lafayette, Philadelphia officials commissioned the redecoration of the now shabby chamber. This produced a room more handsomely furnished than it had been when the delegates to the Second Continental Congress signed the Declaration of Independence. But enhancing the memory of the "glorious cause" seemed fitting at a time when Philadelphia's leaders were worrying about a noble era slipping away in the memory of a new generation.[10]

Lafayette brilliantly refocused attention on the virtue and heroism of the revolutionary generation in a way that kindled Philadelphians' reverence for historic sites that could be transformed into sacred spaces. After the mayor of Philadelphia welcomed Lafayette to "this hallowed Hall" (the east room of the State House), Lafayette drove home the point: "Here within these sacred walls . . . was boldly declared the independence of these United States. Here, sir, was planned the formation of our virtuous, brave, revolutionary army and the providential inspiration received that gave the command of it to our beloved, matchless Washington."[11] From this point on, the usage "State House" changed to "Independence Hall." One of the last living links to the Revolution, Lafayette was instrumental in hurrying the old State House along its way to becoming a national shrine.

The power of buildings and civic observances to connect the present with the past, becoming manifest during Lafayette's visit, resurfaced two years later, in 1826, as city leaders prepared for the fiftieth anniversary of the Declaration of Independence. Especially moved to action was a group of patrician Philadelphians who banded together for a dinner in the house that William Penn had occupied during his last sojourn in Philadelphia, from 1699 to 1701. By the 1820s, Penn's house had been converted into Doyle's Hotel, but this did not diminish the enthusiasm of an august group, many of them the great-great-grandchildren of Penn's compatriots, from setting a new agenda for using the past for present purposes. "A new current of feeling seems to have set in," one of the dinner participants wrote, and emotions were stoked by the dinner address of the aged Peter Du Ponceau, who had come to America with Lafayette to fight for liberty's cause. At the time president of the American Philosophical Society, Du Ponceau gave an address "full of the fire of the patriot and the taste of the scholar." He reminded his friends that "there is a love of country which has a hallowed cast, from commingling thankfulness for blessings with the memory of the mighty dead. . . . We are among those who believe there is inspiration in these things, and our creed is that a man who can tread over the ashes of the dead with indifference, and contemplate the deeds of other times without emotion, cannot be a patriot or hero."[12]

From this dinner, beginning with festiveness and ending with a sense of mission, came the founding of the Historical Society of Pennsylvania. Although it was not the first Philadelphia institution to collect manuscripts, books, and artifacts that could preserve memory of the past or use it to refurbish the present, the Historical Society would slowly emerge as the largest, most important, and most influential. Already the Library Company of Philadelphia, the American Philosophical Society, and the Athenaeum of Philadelphia were in the business of preserving the past, but now the Historical Society began to assume a central place among institutions devoted to warding off historical amnesia.

The four events between 1816 and 1826—saving Independence Hall, arguing over the Colonization Society's plans to repatriate African Americans, celebrating Lafayette's visit, and founding the Historical Society of Pennsylvania—focused the attention of many Philadelphians on history's value and history's power. After this formative decade, the process of constructing a web of memory never ceased. Engaging the passion of an increasing number of leaders and becoming the mission of a growing number of institutions, remembering Philadelphia would become in time a thriving enterprise. But, as we will see, this was far from an easy task, made all the more complicated by the fact that Philadelphians, in their growing diversity, came to understand that memory-making was neither a value-free and politically sanitized matter nor a mental activity promising everyone the same rewards. As soon as people began to see that the shaping of Philadelphia's past was a partisan activity, involving a certain silencing of the city's history, the process of remembering Philadelphia became a contested matter—and has remained so ever since.

I was inspired to write this book after my involvement with an exhibition—Visions and Revisions: Finding Philadelphia's Past—that opened in November 1989 at the Historical Society of Pennsylvania. Working on the exhibit obliged me to confront many of the issues examined here, especially the ongoing process of rediscovering and redefining American history—in this case the history of Philadelphia and the surrounding region. Behind every element of the book, as with the exhibit, lies the belief that historical societies, like art museums, are not dispassionate and impartial venues but rather institutions that carry out, however subtly, ideological, cultural, and politically informed agendas. The exhibition traced the city's fascinating history from before the arrival of William Penn's first Quaker settlers to the early twentieth century. Its creators strove to convey a new appreciation of how people of widely diverse origins, of all classes and conditions, came to Philadelphia, lived there, and contributed to its making. We wanted viewers to understand what it was like to live in the city during different eras, in the midst of the swirl of change brought about by revolution, industrialization, mass immigration, religious awakenings, civil war, and more. Through artifacts and words, we attempted to show how Philadelphians, in all their variety, experienced and influenced the course of urban life during times of growth and times of depression, moments of celebration and moments of crisis, eras of confidence and eras of confusion. We aimed to convey something of what it was like in different eras to be child or adult, female or male, black or white, immigrant or native-born, of great or slender means, of different religious commitments. In short, the intention of the exhibit was to introduce readers to a Philadelphia they barely knew.[13]

First City: Philadelphia and the Forging of Historical Memory, while exploring chapters of Philadelphia history that have been reworked and enriched by talented historians of this generation, makes no claim to comprehensiveness. Rather, it treats the city synoptically in a series of era-based chapters, where particular elements of social and cultural history are provided within a framework of economic and political history. With no attempt to provide exhaustive detail, I take special pains in throwing light on the role that heretofore relatively anonymous groups in urban society—women, racial and religious minorities, and laboring people—have played in shaping the city's history. In doing so, I join others in attempting to restore to memory lost chapters of the city's history.

To fix our gaze downward is somewhat at odds with history's gatekeepers of earlier generations. For the founders of the Historical Society of Pennsylvania and the city's other cultural institutions, the great change-makers were men like William Penn, the founder; James Logan, the statesman and scientist; Benjamin Franklin, the diplomat, civic improver, publisher, scientist, and statesman; and a panoply of revolutionary heroes from Washington and Jefferson to Adams and Dickinson. Great men made history; ordinary people followed their lead. Hence remembering the past in heroic, almost providential, terms was an exercise in stabilizing society and legitimating order, authority, and status. Looking backward for inspiration to great leaders could provide balance in times of bewildering change, friction, and outright conflict.

This vision of history's uses, dominant everywhere in the world for many centuries, has been called by J. H. Plumb "confirmatory history"—a "narration of events of particular people, nations or communities in order to justify authority, to create confidence and to secure stability."[14] Certainly this was the vision of the early nineteenth-century founders of historical societies in the United States. John Fanning Watson, Philadelphia's first chronicler writing before the Civil War, lamented the passing of "our former golden age of moderation and virtue" and was sickened at the effects of "foreign influence," which made it impossible for anyone living in an immigrant-filled city such as New York or Philadelphia to "claim [it] to be an *American* city."[15] Even in a society that regarded its democratic institutions and egalitarian ethos as nearly unique, written history in the United States, as elsewhere, was the personal property of those with political, social, religious, and economic authority. As the Haitian historian Michel-Rolph Trouillot puts it, "Lived inequalities yield unequal historical power."[16]

But in the past few decades we have seen a flowering of an American history sensitive to gender, race, religion, and class, which is to say, a democratized history. In no small part, this has happened because the old guild of historians has yielded to a much more diverse set of practitioners. With new questions to carry to the sources and new stories to tell, people who previously had slender claims to be the custodians of the past have found their voices. This redistribution of the property in history has offended many people, including some academic historians, because they miss what they remember as a more coherent, worshipful, and annealing rendition of the past. Yet the explosion of historical knowledge has invigorated history and increased its popularity. People who find in accounts of the past figures like themselves—alike in color or class, religion or region, sex or social situation—naturally find history more satisfying than when it is simply organized around a triumphalist version of the past in which the occupants of the national pantheon, representing a very narrow slice of society, get most of the play. Narratives of glory will always have a market, but human empathy with less than oversized figures, as much in history as in literature, has created a market as well. Moreover, only an inclusive history can overcome the defeatist notion that the past was inevitably determined. This is particularly fitting in an open and generally optimistic society that prizes the autonomy of the individual. If the history we are making today is subject to human will, or what historians call human agency, then yesterday's history must have been fluid and unpredictable rather than moving along some predetermined course. If history did not unfold inevitably in Philadelphia, then surely a great many people must have been significant actors in the unfolding. Such a consciousness of a complex and contingent past quickens people to the idea that they too can contribute to a different future. If presented inclusively, history has a powerful potential to impart a sense of individuality, of the possibilities of choice, of the human capacity for both good and evil.

Woven into this history of Philadelphia is a second theme: how certain Philadelphians in the past wanted to *remember* the city's history and how contests over managing and manipulating historical memory arose. "In history," writes Trouillot, "power begins at the source," as the production of historical materials begins with historical actors of yore and proceeds with those who follow to assemble and preserve these materials.[17] Accordingly, this is the story of how museums, libraries, and historical societies, beginning in the late eighteenth century, became instrumental in transmitting historical memory from one generation to another by collecting, preserving, and exhibiting what they regarded as the stuff of history. But how did these institutional trustees decide what counted as a historical object or a source worth preserving? Such decision-making, as we shall see, has usually been inconsistent, sometimes full of contradictions, and often incapable of controlling the flow of historical materials coming "over the transom." What has remained constant is the belief that history matters. Continuously under negotiation, inside boardrooms and outside in the community at large, has been a set of questions: What constitutes history? How is historical memory cultivated, perpetuated, deflected, and overturned? What do we need to know about the past, and who is entitled to reconstruct it? How does the past help us make sense of the present? Who has the authority to answer these questions?

By exploring the values and dispositions of Philadelphia's collecting and exhibiting institutions, I hope to explain what the leaders of Philadelphia's cultural agencies had in mind as they went about the work of gathering materials that would preserve the past; how the city's cultural institutions constructed their relations with audiences, appealing to some while discouraging others; how they positioned themselves as authoritative custodians of the past and decorated authors of master narratives; how their audiences absorbed or resisted the memories of the past that their cultural leaders wanted to inscribe on the public mind; and how those outside the select circle of history's guardians contested official commemorations and constructed alternative remembrances of the past.

Readers will find that this book is much more about attempts to cultivate historical memory than about how well these endeavors succeeded. As we know from a sprawling literature on how *individual* memory operates—the work of psychologists, brain researchers, oral historians, and sociologists—remembering the past is an imperfect, incomplete, ever-shifting, and fragile matter. Short-term and long-term personal memory operates very differently in the mind of the ordinary individual, and individual historical memory is an equally fickle affair. Assaying *public* memory—collective understanding of the past—is even harder. Every generation or so, a survey shows that most Americans know almost nothing about the past. Even large proportions of high school students, having just studied American history, get confused about whether the American Revolution preceded or followed the Civil War. In 2000 Congress committed $50 million to cure an abysmal recollection of the nation's past (according to a study that differs little from a similar assessment conducted in 1940) without an intelligent discussion of how history has been taught in the past, without a consideration about how the management of memory has been roundly contested, and without a moment's thought about how the average citizen will use a memory of the past—which memory?—to bring about specific outcomes in the world's largest democracy. Nor have researchers been able to reach firm conclusions about exactly how memory is implanted: By school textbooks? By movies, radio, and television? By tales told by elders around the dining room table? By Colonial Williamsburg, Sturbridge Village, Plimoth Plantation, Valley Forge, and hundreds of other historic sites? By historical novels and popular biographies? Or by Disneyland? My objective in this book is to explore how institutional elites, often challenged by Philadelphians far beneath them in social station, tried to cultivate historical memory. But the task of determining exactly *what* was remembered in a populous, diverse, and changing Philadelphia awaits another historian who has at hand a methodology not yet invented.

This is a Philadelphia story as it unfolds over more than two centuries. No city's history is the same as any other's, and certainly none is quite like Philadelphia's. But William Penn's "green country town" is a particularly appropriate place to study the contest over historical memory because the city was so closely associated with the nation's founding, revolution, and nation building, all rich subjects for historical memory. In addition, memory-making in Philadelphia is unusually fascinating because it has been complicated by the city's rich variety of ethnic, racial, and religious groups, often mutually antagonistic, often remembering the past differently. Fitting the pacifist and influential Quakers, the largest and most important free black population in post-revolutionary America, and the nineteenth-century waves of Irish Catholics and eastern European Jews into a unified and unifying history has been an exquisite challenge for myth-makers at the city's elite institutions.

While Philadelphia has its own narrative and its own fascinating cast of storytellers, remembering history is not unique to Philadelphia. It is shared by every community that produces, consumes, and markets history.[18] Therefore, this book presumes to provide a model for examining the process of memory-making: how particular people with vested power reconstructed the past through collecting, narrating, and interpreting; how that history was presented to the public; and how individuals and groups outside the circle of cultural arbiters tried to gain a claim on the past by resisting "official" truth and telling different stories. As in most other cities, deep inequalities in how Philadelphia society functioned were paralleled by inequalities in the official historical narratives. But in the Quaker city, as in other communities, the mantle of legitimacy could not prevent subordinate storytellers from trying to break through layers of silence. Not all the world is Philadelphia, but in every site of human habitation the process of constructing memory has proceeded in ways this study hopes to make clear.[19]

In the pages that follow, the reader will find an abundance of images. I have chosen them with three purposes in mind. Some of the images are chosen because they evoke a sense of the character and rhythm of urban life in different eras in ways that often elude textual materials. Others convey how Philadelphia imprinted itself on the minds of artists, lithographers, and photographers, who turned their impressions into collectible views of the city, whimsical or sardonic scenes meant to entertain, or frankly propagandistic vehicles commissioned by those exercising one kind of power or another. Finally, still other images depict a variety of sources, drawn from material culture as well as paper-based archives, that have helped historians in recent years to uncover chapters of Philadelphia's hidden past. Taken together, the range of images is also meant to carry forward the message of what it means to collect the documentary, artifactual, and artistic records of the past. I have paid more than casual attention to the captions accompanying the images, because it is here that I tell much of the story about how and when a particular piece of the past found its way to a collecting institution. Part of that account is about the vagaries as well as the priorities that explain just what the scholar or curious citizen, in search of a piece of the past, can find today when entering the doors of the Library Company, the Athenaeum, the Historical Society, the Atwater Kent Museum of Philadelphia History, the Philadelphia Museum of Art, and a host of other institutions. Every institution has collecting priorities and policies, which have changed over time, but assembling historical materials has depended at least as much on what appears on one's doorstep as on what one chooses to collect.

Just as people have seen their history through different lenses—depending on who they are, their reasons for consulting historical accounts, and what experiences, ideas, and values they bring to the act of looking backward—every article of material culture and every scrap of written language is susceptible to variant interpretations. The meaning of the Declaration of Independence and the intention of its authors are argued as strenuously today as two hundred years ago. Chairs, dolls, samplers, trade cards, paintings, lithographs—even photographs—all speak to us in a variety of ways, and their meaning and value to the collector or curator change with time, sometimes dramatically. Some of the artifacts portrayed in the following pages, such as the image of Washington on a pitcher or a Civil War battle scene, were created at particular historic moments to influence the way people thought about the past. Others—a tall-case clock or a decorated fireman's parade helmet—were not created for pedagogic or political use but have enabled historians and curators in our own times to recapture parts of the past otherwise undisclosed in textual materials. With this in mind, the meaty caption accompanying each illustration is meant to lean on the ingenuity of Philadelphia's quintessential eighteenth-century citizen, Benjamin Franklin. Printer Ben invented bifocal glasses for people who needed their vision adjusted so they could see the world clearly in both short and long perspectives. In this book, I am engaged in something similar—asking readers to gaze bifocally, sometimes trifocally, in order to see the past as it was experienced differently by Philadelphians of various stations in life; to see how our understanding of bygone eras depends partly on what historical materials were collected, preserved, and exhibited; to look at artifacts, documents, and paintings from different angles of vision. The text of what follows ought to make some sense without the illustrations, and the illustrations, without text, should give new perspectives on the past. But word and image, like pie and ice cream, are meant to be savored together.

Chapter 1

PIECES OF THE COLONIAL PAST

Pennsylvania was the product of Quaker beliefs and aspirations, and Philadelphia became its pulsebeat on the banks of the Delaware River. "I have obtained [Pennsylvania] that an example may be set up to the nations," wrote William Penn, its founder, in 1681.[1] Penn hoped that his colony of diverse settlers would show a strife-ridden world a new formula for living. Adept promoter as well as revered defender of persecuted Quakers, he attracted settlers from England, Ireland, Wales, and continental Europe with policies of religious toleration, pacifism, and fair treatment for all.

But the fertile Delaware River valley where Penn was to plant his "seed of a nation" already had inhabitants. For at least 12,000 years before Penn and the Quakers arrived, the area had been inhabited by distant ancestors of the Lenape (later to be called Delaware). Europeans had encountered the Lenape at least as early as 1609, when the Dutch sailed into Delaware Bay, and more intensely after 1624, when a small group of Dutch settlers occupied Burlington Island in the Delaware River. Over the next half century the Dutch, Finnish, Swedish, and English settlers traded and mingled with the Lenape. Thus, Penn built his colony amid small settlements of both native and intruding peoples. Penn may never have realized that his open-door policy toward a variety of immigrants would undermine the peaceful Indian relations he vowed to put into effect (see Figure 4).

Every society must fabricate and sustain creation stories, and nearly everyone craves knowledge about his or her beginnings—those who came first, those who blazed the trails, those who did great deeds. No sooner was the colony well established than it began, like most successful enterprises, to remember itself in selective ways. From the first, the urge in Philadelphia to collect historical materials, documents, and objects relating to William Penn, the early Quakers, and the original inhabitants assumed a special, almost holy importance. Philadelphia's first collecting institutions, the Library Company of Philadelphia and the American Philosophical Society, were initially dedicated to gathering "useful knowledge," the term used in the formal title of each, rather than historical materials. But these two endeavors soon merged.

"Constructive buying and generous giving" marked the Library Company's collecting from its founding at the hand of Benjamin Franklin in 1731, when the colony had existed for fifty years and the recently arrived printer was only twenty-five years old. Within nine years, the library's growth prompted a move to the west wing of the State House.

Already it had more than 600 volumes. The germ of the library's historical holdings came in 1755, when its purchasing agent in London shipped as a present a group of rare early accounts of the colony's founding. By 1769, the collection moved to more spacious quarters on the second floor of nearby Carpenters' Hall. In 1784, just after the American Revolution, the Library Company became the first Philadelphia institution to acquire by purchase primary source materials relating to American history.[2]

From its founding in 1743 until the very end of the eighteenth century, the Philosophical Society, also a creature of the relentlessly ingenious Franklin, was less aggressive in collecting. It passively received books, artifacts, and learned papers but had no active policy of acquiring or purchasing anything. Primarily, it was an early-day think tank whose members read papers and invited people from near and far to expand the common knowledge. Only in 1797 did the Philosophical Society evince much interest in history, by creating a committee on "the antiquities of North America." With Thomas Jefferson serving as its president, the society began soliciting material: natural history specimens, including mammoth skeletons; sketches and reports on the remains of ancient Indian fortifications and earthworks; and data on the languages, customs, and character of American Indians. In 1801-3 the society spent money for the first time, to purchase books and manuscripts from the sale of Benjamin Franklin's library, broken up by his daughter and her husband. This was the foundation of what would become a mighty Franklin collection. Eight years later, in 1811, Peter Stephen Du Ponceau, who had come from France in 1777 to fight with the Americans against the British and became America's most eminent lawyer on international law, proposed the systematic acquisition of historical documents. Philadelphia's involvement in the War of 1812 probably delayed action on this initiative, but in 1815 the society created a Committee on History, Moral Science, and General Literature, charged with forming "a collection of original documents, such as official and private letters, Indian treaties, ancient records, ancient maps" that would "throw light on the History of the United States, but more particularly of this state . . . for the public benefit."[3]

At first glance, it is surprising that the American Philosophical Society was so interested in Native Americans; its members were more interested in Indians than in William Penn, the Quakers, or even the American Revolution. Much of this interest stemmed from Jefferson's fascination with Indian languages and customs and the enthusiasm of Philadelphia doctors such as Benjamin Rush and Benjamin Smith Barton, who believed Indian languages held the key to solving the mysteries of Indian origins and Indian natural remedies. The astounding linguistic prowess of Du Ponceau also sharpened interest in Native Americans. Steadily, the American Philosophical Society gathered historical materials: a memoir of Chief Ouachita contributed by Jefferson in 1803; observations of the Choctaw, Cherokee, and Chickasaw nations in the same year; and Lenape grammars, notes, and essays contributed by two Moravian missionaries, John Gottlieb Heckewelder and David Zeisberger, both of whom lived with the Indians for years. Also, between 1820 and 1825, though nobody proposed acquiring materials relating to the American Revolution, came important papers from two stalwarts of "the spirit of '76": Virginia's

Richard Henry Lee and Rhode Island's Nathanael Greene, one of Washington's most trusted generals.

Though the Philosophical Society had begun gathering historical materials by fits and starts, it lost its mainspring, Peter Du Ponceau, to his law practice and linguistic research by about 1820. But four years later Lafayette's triumphant arrival in Philadelphia inspired the forming of the Historical Society of Pennsylvania. Its leaders did not intend to compete with or eclipse the Philosophical Society, but this is what gradually happened. The Philosophical Society lost the momentum Du Ponceau had created and would not regain it for the rest of the nineteenth century. Especially a casualty was the Committee on History. Although the Philosophical Society received a large collection of Benjamin Franklin papers in 1840, the history committee was never very successful in acquiring historical materials and abandoned its interest in local, regional, or even national history. But filling that vacuum was the Library Company—under the energetic leadership of John Jay Smith, the great-grandson of Penn's trusted agent James Logan—and the budding Historical Society.

To some extent, the leaders of the Philosophical Society, the Library Company, and the Historical Society in the first third of the nineteenth century were part of an interlocking, history-minded club. The powerful lawyer William Rawle and Joseph Parker Norris, for many years the president of the Bank of Pennsylvania, were involved in all three institutions; others, such as Du Ponceau, Zachariah Poulson, William Meredith, and Caspar Wistar, were involved in two of the "big three." Notwithstanding these interconnections, the three institutions acquired different characters. After its reorganization in 1769, the Philosophical Society's self-selected membership was primarily composed of weighty intellectuals—men of science, literature, linguistics, medicine, law, and philosophy—who were selected nationally and internationally. They presented carefully wrought learned papers to the society and desultorily passed along what others put in their hands. Physical and mathematical sciences, along with American Indian linguistics, had been their greatest strengths, with history "but a graft upon an uncongenial trunk."[4] The Historical Society of Pennsylvania, from the beginning, was very different. It was composed almost entirely of local residents, many of whom were related and traced their families back to early settlers; it grew by internal nomination of new members, ensuring that it would be a gentleman's club; it made the collection of historical materials its singular priority; it was policy driven rather than intellectually thirsty; it created an aloofness that kept the unwashed away; and it was self-conscious about cultivating a reverence for particular aspects of the past in order to counteract the acids its members saw eating at their community.

Somewhat similarly, Library Company leaders shared a reverence for the past and a consummate love of family connections. No one exemplified this more than its librarian from 1829 to 1851, John Jay Smith, whose many-branched family counted scores of relatives descended from William Penn's cadre of Quaker "first purchasers." But the Library Company was a subscription institution that by 1774, according to one account, attracted "twenty tradesmen" for each "person of distinction and fortune."[5] Its doors were open to all, with a rule, followed to the present day, that "any civil person" could use the books unless the person had "to be awakened twice" or showed "any evidence of 'pulex irritans' [fleas]."[6] For this reason its collections needed to be broad and latitudinarian. Thus, long before the Historical Society was founded, the Library Company had established its openness to all religious groups, political parties, and social classes, knowing that if it meant to be a civic institution it could not afford to shut out any part of its constituency.

William Penn: Man, Family, Community

The founders of the Historical Society of Pennsylvania were far more focused on William Penn and the early Quakers than on the Native Americans whom the Philosophical Society had found so fascinating. At the dinner meeting that led to the founding of the Historical Society, Du Ponceau memorialized "a great man—the purest and noblest law giver that the annals of history can produce. His administration was the only golden age which did not belong to fable."[7] Of course Du Ponceau was operating in the realm of fable or legend with these words, but it is understandable that his encomium to Penn resonated with the small gathered group, since five of the seven Historical Society founders were descended from old Philadelphia Quaker families. Also, in the 1820s, as these well-to-do urbanites looked about them, they trembled at the character of their rapidly changing city. Rowdy gangs—Death-fetchers, Bloodtubs, and Hyenas—spilled through Philadelphia's streets. Workers and servants no longer deferred to their betters as the Historical Society founders imagined had happened in the colonial period. Penn's "greene country towne," the town of their grandparents and great-grandparents, had become a sprawling, turbulent, heterogeneous city in the early stages of industrialization. The founders hoped that by selecting and collecting the right historical materials—books, manuscripts, and artifacts—they could restore a collective memory that might nurture unity and order as people reflected on a less trammeled, more virtuous, and less materialistic past.

To this end, the Historical Society founders proposed to form an "ample library" of books and historical documents and a "cabinet" (or small room) for the preservation and display of historical artifacts. Working behind the scenes was John Fanning Watson, a banker, amateur historian, and one of the earliest collectors of American material culture. For several years, Watson had been gathering materials for the first history of Philadelphia, which he would publish in 1830, and his most important confidant in this was John Jay Smith, who would shortly become the Library Company's librarian. Both Pennsylvania Brahmins, Watson and Smith loathed the forces unleashed by immigration, industrialization, and democratization. In Watson's nostalgic conception, a historical society might spread the values of genteel culture and impart a shared sense of identity among Philadelphians who, in the boisterous 1820s, seemed to be pulling in every direction while forgetting their precious heritage.

FIGURE 4. Francis Place, side by side chalk drawings of Hannah Callowhill Penn and William Penn, HSP. Place, a London limner, captured the couple at about the time of their marriage in 1696, when Hannah was twenty-five and William fifty-one. Seven children came from this marriage. No other portraits of Penn or his wife are known to have been executed. By the mid-eighteenth century, some wealthy Quakers had given up the idea of portraits as signs of vanity and commissioned oil paintings. The Historical Society acquired the crayon portraits in 1957 at a London auction.

Objects, paintings, manuscripts, and pamphlets relating to William Penn and the early Quaker immigrants—what Watson liked to call "the dust of perished matter"—became the most important type of material that the Historical Society's founders collected. Thus, from its inception, the Historical Society was not simply a neutral gathering place for valuable historical materials but an institution for carrying out certain political and ideological responsibilities, as its founders understood them. In this way, they made a heroic figure of Penn, ignoring many episodes of the founder's often troubled life and the contentiousness in early Philadelphia that stretched the patience of both Penn and the governors he appointed after he returned to England. Veneration for Penn and early leaders such as James Logan and Isaac Norris flowed naturally from their reading of the past, because they wished to cultivate the memory of a society in which each person knew his or her rank and deferred to those above. The society of their dreams was also one in which change occurred because of the wisdom and work of great leaders. Great men made history; ordinary people followed their lead.[8]

Many of the first objects collected by the Historical Society were treasured because of their connection—real or purported—to Penn and the early Quakers. The very first acquisition, in 1825, was a medal, based on an original ivory relief portrait carved by a London friend of Penn in 1720. The medal, which was struck for the important Barclay family of Quakers in London about 1731, is inscribed: "By Deeds of Peace / Pennsylvania / Settled / 1681." This inscription was meant to remind all of the founding vision of a pacifist utopia. In 1827, Thomas I. Wharton, one of the society's founders and a descendant of an early prominent Quaker family, donated a pewter shaving basin, revered because it was supposed to have been used by Penn. Much later, the Penn family cradle, Penn's silver and tortoise shell razor and case, and Penn's Bible found their way to the society's collections. Everything connected to Penn took on an aura of virtue, and the Historical Society became the unofficial attic of Penn relics. Only a few choice Penn items went elsewhere, such as the founder's William and Mary secretary desk, which wandered from owner to owner after the American Revolution, when it was sold from Pennsbury Manor, Penn's country seat, on the upper Delaware River. Finally, it fell into the hands of the Library Company's mid-nineteenth-century librarian, John Jay Smith, who gave it to the company in 1873.

In cultivating collective memory, paintings have an unusual power to evoke the past, especially portraits of heroic figures or paintings of battlefield scenes. But the Quaker leaders of the Historical Society were hoist on their own petard because the Society of Friends was morally opposed to extravagance and hence regarded portraits as self-indulgent and ostentatious. Battlefield scenes were not simply tainted but repugnant to their pacifist principles. In contrast with Puritan Boston, where scores of merchants and ministers had their portraits painted, Quaker Philadelphia in its presumed golden age left a scant visual record of its iconic figures. Hence, the Historical Society's first painting, acquired in 1833, was of the young William Penn sumptuously attired in armor. Painted in oil about 1770 after an original executed in 1666, when Penn was twenty-two years old, the portrait displayed the founder clad in the trappings of the English ruling class. One year later, the rebellious young Penn shed his armor and joined the Society of Friends, its members widely regarded in England at this time as dangerously radical for their refusal to serve in the militia, their liberality toward women in religious affairs, and their rejection of hierarchy in churchly and worldly affairs. For more than a century, the Historical Society could display only the armored Penn of his pre-Quaker years. A more peace-loving rendition of Penn, a chalk drawing by Francis Place rendered about 1696 (Figure 4) that shows the founder in middle age, was not acquired until 1957.

The provenance of artifacts often establishes their value in the eyes of collecting institutions. But institutions often get more or less than they anticipated. Sometimes research conducted long after the acquisition of a particular artifact proves its provenance to have been wrongly assigned; and changing notions of what is important frequently reestablish the value of what has been determined to be a fraud. All of this is true in the case of the "Laetitia Penn" doll. A gift to the Historical Society in 1960, the gessoed and painted wood-body doll with glass eyes, fiber hair, and dress of various fabrics over pa-

FIGURE 5. William Penn gateleg table, PMA. This drop-leaf table, probably brought from England along with much other furniture to furnish Penn's manor house at Pennsbury, was a marker of high status in England in the late 1600s. Private collectors own much of the furniture brought across the Atlantic to Philadelphia, and individual pieces associated with early settlers, especially the famous, have acquired special symbolic significance. New techniques for analyzing furniture have unmasked previously treasured pieces, showing them to have been wrongly identified or so altered that they do not reflect the craftsmanship and aesthetics of the period.

per was thought to have been carried to America by Laetitia Penn, the founder's hoydenish twenty-one-year-old daughter, who accompanied him to Philadelphia when he returned to the colony in 1699. A letter written in 1865 makes just this claim. For some time the Historical Society had no reason to question the doll's authenticity and prized it as a genuine Penn family artifact. However, recent analysis of the style of dress and the construction and painting of the body places the manufacture of the doll more likely in the middle third of the eighteenth century. Seventeenth-century wooden dolls tend to have larger heads in relation to the body than the "Laetitia Penn" doll has, and earlier dolls rarely have the painted lower eyelines of the Penn doll. The Penn doll is very similar to the well-documented "Mary Jenkins" doll, brought from England to New York in 1745. Although it is disappointing that the doll now appears to be unconnected to

William and Laetitia Penn, it has taken on new value as a fine example of a rare plaything and as a record of styles in the early Georgian period.

Many of the early Penn objects collected by the Historical Society reflect the tension between Penn the aristocrat, proprietor, and country gentleman and Penn the Quaker visionary and civil libertarian. Penn's Quakerism did not keep him from building a magnificent estate at Pennsbury, Philadelphia's first country seat, or staffing it with servants and slaves, some of whom rowed him down the Delaware River for meetings in Philadelphia. Penn owned a number of slaves and freed several during his lifetime. It was probably indicative of the deep financial difficulties he was in at the end of his life, when he had to mortgage his colony to pay his debts, that he amended an earlier will freeing his slaves and instead bequeathed them to his heirs. Along with indentured servants, these slaves provided the workforce at Pennsbury and at Penn's townhouse in Philadelphia.

If owning slaves speaks of conflicting tendencies in Penn, so do the accouterments of life he assembled for his brief periods in Philadelphia. Penn's large, fashionable gateleg table (Figure 5), along with much other high-end furniture, jars with his repeated counsel in published essays for simplicity in dress and household possessions. He insisted to his second wife that "lowness as well as plainness" were important parts of his character. Yet, as the son of a wealthy English admiral and courtier and as a man who inhabited a world of privilege and power, he was accustomed to the strident display of costly caned chairs, four-wheeled coaches, silver settings, and other signifiers of a gentleman's life.[9]

The Penn family was also of great interest to the early collectors of the Library Company and the Historical Society, because family itself was at the heart of the world they wished to remember and perpetuate. Though not acquired until much later, Penn's letters to his three children from his first marriage, written as he was departing London for Philadelphia in 1682, were a treasure to the Society, for they revealed Penn as a devout Christian, an advocate of education, and a loving father. Such interest in the Penn family remains unabated, but of some 2,600 Penn documents that have survived, only 75 are private family letters. The vast collection of Penn Papers acquired by the Historical Society in 1870 at a London auction had been sadly pillaged, and it is possible that family papers, as Mary Maples Dunn has suggested, "were the special target of wanton destruction," possibly by "a disgruntled, illegitimate, and disinherited member of the family."[10]

With the meteoric rise of women's history in the last generation, the women connected to Penn have attracted much interest recently. Penn's second wife, Hannah Callowhill Penn, is of special significance. Hannah married William in 1696, accompanied him to Philadelphia on his second trip in 1699, and bore seven children. After Penn's debilitating stroke in 1712, Hannah and her advisors managed the founder's tangled legal and business affairs until his death six years later. As acting proprietor of Pennsylvania, Hannah Penn wielded more political power than any other colonial woman. One governor, William Keith, expressed his resentment at receiving "instructions from a woman" shortly before Hannah dismissed him.

Launching a Colony

By the time Penn and his fellow Quakers reached Pennsylvania in the early 1680s, more than a dozen English colonies existed in North America and the West Indies. But Penn and his followers were determined to establish a unique colony free of the violence, corruption, and intolerance that were widespread on both sides of the Atlantic.

When Penn received his grant for Pennsylvania, the Society of Friends had begun to leave behind the radical beginnings that had made them objects of scorn and brutal treatment by the English authorities and had brought from such a Puritan stalwart as Cotton Mather the charge that the Quakers were "the chokeweed of Christianity." The greater autonomy allowed women in religious affairs made Quakers suspect in the eyes of most of their Christian contemporaries. Especially troubling to those who defended gender hierarchy was how female Quaker "ministering Friends" or "Publishers of the Truth" fanned out across the Atlantic world, traveling unattended by husbands, fathers, or brothers. A seventeenth-century painting mocked Quakers for their radical ways, depicting a woman preaching to a gathering of urinating dogs and grotesque Quakers groping lewdly.[11]

Pennsylvania never entirely lived up to its visionary founding principles, but nowhere else in the hemisphere where Europeans were colonizing did there exist such substantial toleration for religious and ethnic differences and such relatively peaceful relations with Native American groups. Most European visitors were astounded at what had been achieved. Peter Kalm, a Swedish visitor, wrote in 1750: "Everyone who acknowledges God to be the Creator . . . and teaches or undertakes nothing against the state or against the common peace, is at liberty to settle, stay, and carry on his trade here, be his religious principles ever so strange." This would have pleased Penn, who had written: "I deplore two principles in religion: obedience upon authority without conviction and destroying them that differ with me for Christ's sake."[12]

Much of Penn's life from 1680 to 1686 revolved around attracting settlers and working out the framework of government for his colony. King Charles II had granted Penn extensive powers to govern the province in 1681, but the proprietor had to win the consent of his settlers in order to achieve a peaceful and just society. Building a colony was also a business proposition, one that could not succeed without vigorous promotion. Launching a colony was hugely expensive. Penn later calculated that he spent almost £12,000 (about $2.5 million today) in the first two years alone to obtain his patent from the king and promote his colony. He was not ashamed to say that he wanted some return on his investment. "Though I desire to extend religious freedom," he wrote in 1681, "yet I want some recompense for my trouble."[13]

Penn's attempts to create a utopia in the wilderness had all the elements of mythmaking, and it is no surprise that his efforts attracted the attention of collecting institutions. Although the Library Company had less than a burning interest in collecting Penn material for more than a century after its founding, partly because Penn's separately published essays were out of print for a long time and biographies of Penn did not appear until the early nineteenth century, the Historical Society from the outset was an avid collector of anything related to the launching of Pennsylvania. That interest has never abated. In its first year, the Historical Society asked the Philosophical Society to make a donation of its manuscript papers on the early history of Pennsylvania. Especially important were the rough minutes of the Provincial Council covering the period from 1693 to 1717. But the Philosophical Society brusquely denied the request, although it allowed the Historical Society's curator, Samuel Hazard, to publish the minutes a few years later.

Of special interest have been materials that documented the early promotion of Pennsylvania and the drafting of early laws and frames of government. From the late 1820s, the Historical Society negotiated with the descendants of James Logan, whose extensive correspondence with William Penn and his widow, Hannah Penn, provides the richest source of material on the early affairs of Pennsylvania. Negotiations with the Logan family went on through most of the nineteenth century, and this mother lode of manuscripts gradually reached the society. Descendants of other proprietary officials who had Penn correspondence, records, and documents also made gifts to the society, and some of its members began copying letters between Penn and the English government deposited in the Public Record Office in London.

But the biggest breakthrough came when a massive collection of Penn papers became available in 1870. The papers had been bought a year before for wastepaper from the house of Granville Penn, a grandson of William Penn who had been made an honorary member of the Historical Society in 1833. In one of those hairbreadth escapes from dispersion or destruction that has crippled historical reconstructions, a book dealer, recognizing their value, bought the papers, catalogued them, and offered them for sale. For about £555, an agent of the Historical Society purchased the largest part of the papers, which represent the heart of the society's holdings of the Penn Papers. Totaling more than twenty thousand documents, they include Penn's cash books, journals, letter books, receipt books, and commonplace books as well as hundreds of documents concerning Indian relations, the long boundary dispute with the proprietor of Maryland, Lord Baltimore, and many other aspects of colonial Pennsylvania history. Rich additions to the Penn material have been made in the early twentieth century by gift, and a huge addition—the correspondence between Penn and two of his most trusted officials in Pennsylvania in the years immediately after he left the colony in 1684—would come in the 1980s from the descendants of Benjamin Chew, another of the most important colonial officials of Pennsylvania. The five-volume edition of the most important papers and essays of William Penn prepared in the 1980s is built on these various collections (although the editors located hundreds of other items scattered throughout the world).

In promoting his colony Penn relied on two kinds of documents: vivid descriptions of the land and of the terms of settlement, and maps of the region. Penn wasted no time on the former, issuing *Some Account of the Province of Pennsylvania in America* in London in 1681. In this suitably optimistic account, he described what he had never seen: a land on the same

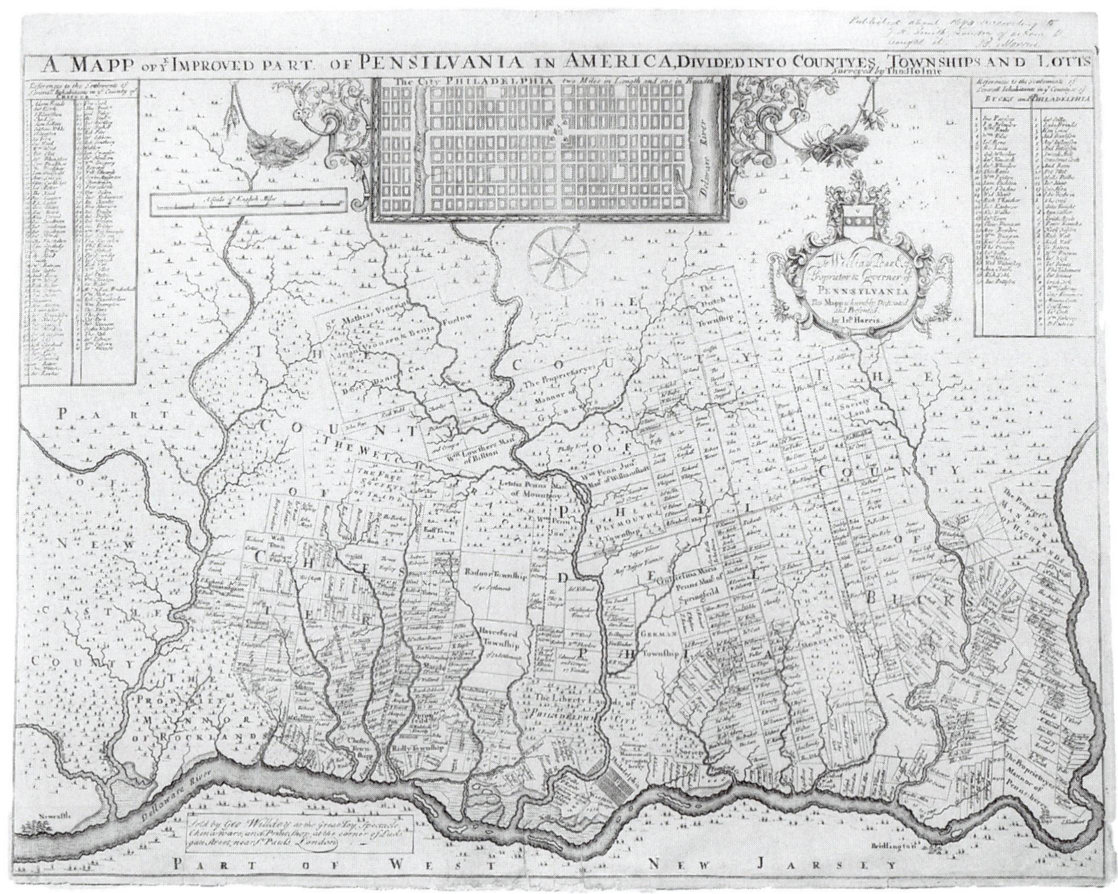

FIGURE 6. Thomas Holme, *A Mapp of the Improved Part of Pensilvania in America, Divided into Countyes, Townships and Lotts*, 1687, LCP. Nothing could serve Penn better than a map showing the rapid settlement of his "sylvan woods." He requested such a work in 1684 from his surveyor-general, Thomas Holme, and finally received it three years later. Its London engravers, using six copper plates, pleased Penn, the real estate promoter, greatly. Penn's manor land, at the bend of the Delaware River, shows in the lower right corner, and that of his daughter, Laetitia Penn, near the middle on the east bank of the Schuylkill River in the lower center.

latitude as Naples, Italy or Montpelier, France with fertile soil, fish-filled rivers, and wildlife in abundance. Here was a place for industrious farmers and urban artisans—all those who were "clogged and oppress'd about a Livelyhood," all the "younger Brothers of small Inheritances"—and for servants, who were promised fifty acres of good land after their term of servitude was over.

Many promotional tracts would flow from Penn's hand over the next few years, but a map of Pennsylvania proved harder to obtain. The proprietor sent his friend Thomas Holme to survey eastern Pennsylvania, and along with him went John Ladd, whose surveying instruments ended up in the Chicago Historical Society, which donated them to the Historical Society of Pennsylvania just 300 years after Ladd arrived on the Delaware. Holme and Ladd worked for five years surveying the site of Philadelphia and the original counties of Philadelphia, Bucks, and Chester. After Penn returned to London, he called again and again for the map. "All cry out, where is your map, what no map of your Settlements?" he wrote in September 1686 to Holme.[14] Finally it came the following year—a monumental map (Figure 6) showing the land granted to 670 early settlers, with some tracts of land left unlabeled because of disputed land titles. It was quickly engraved on six plates and sold by Quaker booksellers in London.

Penn's attempts to draft a frame of government were no less difficult. How did one devise a system of government that guaranteed a more just, peaceful, and equal society? Penn could do nothing by decree, and even the extensive powers granted him in his charter from the king were only as good as his settlers' willingness to accept them. Like all utopia builders, Penn had to consult, cajole, and compromise in constructing his "frame of government." Many interested parties advised and lobbied Penn in organizing the civil system under which colonists would live. Penn published an early version in London in 1681, one of twenty drafts of the Frame of Government finally hammered out the next year. But to his dismay, a ratifying convention, meeting at Chester in December 1682, shortly after Penn arrived in his colony, rejected the document because it gave too much power to the governor and council and too little to the elected assembly. It was hardly the golden age that the founders of the Historical Society remembered and wanted fellow Philadelphians to recall.

Pacifism and Indian Relations

". . . the king of the Countrey where I live, hath given unto me a great Province therein, but I desire to enjoy it with your Love and Consent, that we may always live together as Neighbours and friends."[15] In this single sentence, written to Lenape chiefs of the Delaware Valley, Penn dissociated himself from nearly two hundred years of violent European colonization in the Americas. He imagined colonization without conquest in the sylvan woods granted by his king, though no precedent for this existed.

The Historical Society did not have the scholarly interest in the Indian languages, customs, and human traits held by American Philosophical Society members. However, Historical Society leaders were deeply invested in preserving the writings and artifacts related to Indian-white relations. Just treatment of the Indians and the covenant of friendship Penn established with them gave Quakers historical legitimacy earned by no other aspect of their lives. Also, Penn's amity with the Indians stood in sharp contrast to the forcible sending of the Five Civilized Nations west along the "trail of tears" in the 1830s and the blood-drenched Indian wars west of the Mississippi River a generation later. Cultivating the memory of the founder's uniqueness in Indian relations also gave the Society of Friends missionary work among western Indian nations throughout the nineteenth century a special resonance. The Philosophical Society publicized its ethnological and philological studies of Indians, while the Historical Society capitalized on the Quaker treatment of Indians. The lesson was not lost on President Ulysses S. Grant, who in 1869, seeking to reform the government's treatment of western Native Americans, appointed Friends to direct the effort. Among those sent to the Great Plains were Samuel M. Janney, biographer of William Penn and author of other histories of the Quakers.

Within its first decade, the Historical Society acquired important Indian materials, including some of the writings of John Heckewelder, the Moravian missionary who had translated three Indian languages into English. Penn's 1681 manuscript letter, "To the Kings of the Indians," was a more poignant and usable piece. In it, Penn assured the Lenape of his good intentions and promised that the colony would have no walled forts, the symbols of interracial conflict to the north and south. " . . . the great God . . . hath made us not to devoure and destroy one an other but live Soberly and kindly together in the world . . . I have great love and regard towards you, and I desire to Winn and gain your love & friendship by a kind, just and peaceable life."[16] Penn also intended that such assurances would instill confidence in prospective settlers, who knew from reports published in England that up and down the Atlantic seaboard, from Maine to South Carolina, a devastating series of Indian wars had been fought just a few years before. Published in London in 1681, the manuscript letter would not be donated to the Historical Society until 1891, a year after the Wounded Knee Massacre ended the Great Plains Indian wars.

Other treasured acquisitions could solidify remembrance of the Quakers' attempt to show that, by disavowing violence and practicing fair dealing, people of different cultures could live together. The deed from the Lenape for approximately one hundred square miles of present-day Bucks County, negotiated by Penn's deputy William Markham in the summer of 1682, was not acquired until 1867, but it was frequently displayed to refresh the public's memory of Quaker benevolence and fair play. Signed with marks by twelve Indian leaders, it is the first known written agreement in Pennsylvania between native people and Penn's agents. There is more than a little irony in the fact that among the trade goods Markham agreed to exchange for the vast tract of land were guns and liquor. Markham was unaware that four of the Lenape chiefs had earlier sold a portion of this same tract to New York's governor, Edmund Andros. Like other American Indian leaders, the Lenape chiefs did not view a deed as a complete surrender of land but rather as permission for white newcomers to use the land and live there with indigenous people.

Historians and anthropologists have pointed out that the peaceful relations between the Quakers and Lenape lasting throughout Penn's lifetime were not simply the triumph of pacifist ideology. Much to the advantage of Quaker farmers seeking fertile land, the Delaware River valley may have been the least dense region of indigenous settlement along the Atlantic coastal plain. In addition, the semi-nomadic Lenape population had been sharply reduced by diseases brought by Dutch, Swedish, Finnish, and English settlers who preceded the Quakers. By the time the Quakers arrived, the Lenape popula-

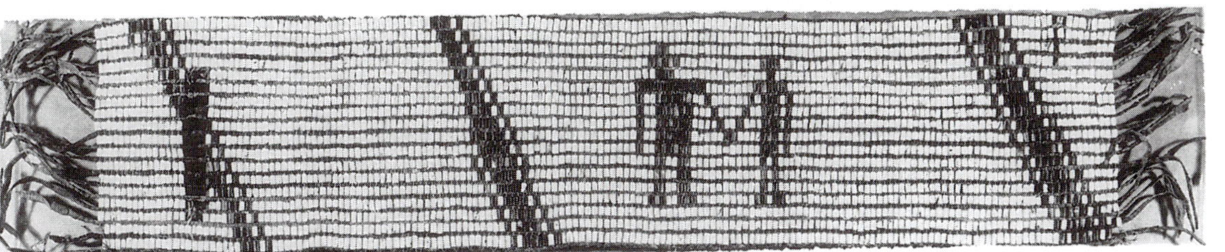

FIGURE 7. Great Belt of Wampum, HSP. The famous belt, fashioned from quahog shell beads and leather, shows a European with a broad hat, typical of Quaker garb, clasping hands with a Native American. At Philadelphia's 1864 Great Central Fair to raise money for wounded Civil War soldiers, the Wampum Belt was conspicuously displayed in the creation of a "William Penn Parlor" along with a cup said to have been presented to Penn by a Lenape chief at the Shackamaxon treaty gathering.

tion had been halved by three smallpox epidemics that struck the tribe between 1620 and 1670. Also favoring the Quaker peace policy was the unusually unwarlike ways of the Lenape themselves. Yet historians have not been able to refute the reverent Lenape view of Penn, carefully recorded at the end of the founder's life. In 1720, Indians reminded William Keith, Pennsylvania's governor appointed by Penn's widow, of their great love for Penn, who had promised at the first meeting with Indian chiefs "so much love and friendship, that he would not call them brothers, because brothers might differ; nor children, because they might offend and require correction; but he would reckon them as one body, one blood, one heart, and one head."[17]

These words were recalled at a meeting of the Historical Society in 1859, when John Granville Penn, the great-grandson of the founder, presented a handsome belt of wampum to the Society. Just as for Europeans a deed finalized a land exchange, the wampum belt for Indians signified a sealed agreement. Indians and Europeans also used simple shell beads or wampum (literally, "white string") as a medium of exchange. The wampum belt (Figure 7) is the Historical Society's most famous and asked-about possession because it reverberates hauntingly in the public consciousness as a reminder of what might have been in the tragic history of European exploitation of native peoples. Today, when peace studies programs have replaced military history, most school textbooks include an illustration of this famous wampum belt.

Acquiring the wampum belt occasioned unusual excitement at the Historical Society. Regarded as "one of the jewels in our cabinet of curios," as a later society president expressed it, its value "historically and sentimentally" was nearly unsurpassed. When John Granville Penn came from London to Philadelphia to contribute what would become a nearly holy relic and explain at length its authenticity, Historical Society leaders spared no ceremony to sanctify the icon, even though an earlier inquiry cast doubt that Penn ever met with Lenape chiefs to conclude a treaty of peace. Even an ex-president, Martin Van Buren, was enlisted to send a letter, and his words could not have been better chosen to evoke the spirit of an earlier day. The gift of the wampum belt, wrote Van Buren, "secures to Pennsylvania an historical monument of peculiar value" and vouches for Penn's "own noble resolution, taken at the outset, and never departed from, to found his Commonwealth 'on deeds of peace.'" The founder's great-grandson then gave what seemed an unassailable account of how the Penn family had acquired the belt and how it had remained in the family for nearly two hundred years. His great-grandfather, he related, had pressed a roll of parchment pledging a treaty of friendship into the hands of the chief sachem and implored him and other attending chiefs to "preserve it carefully for three generations, that their children might know what had passed between them, just as if he [Penn] had remained to repeat it." Solemnly, the Indians reciprocated, "according to their national custom," by giving Penn the wampum belt "with the record of a treaty of peace and friendship woven in its centre."[18]

Though modern scholars have searched hard, no proof has been found that the peace treaty meeting took place. It is even possible that the Belt of Wampum was made after William Penn's death in 1717. The belt depicts a portly European (presumably Penn) clasping hands with an American Indian, but in 1682 Penn was not portly at all; he was athletic enough to run races with some of the young Lenape men. Yet this modern-day sleuthing, while inconvenient for continuing to tell a story nearly as venerable as that of the landing at Plymouth Rock, has not tarnished the belt's iconic status. People create legends to preserve essential truths as they understand them, and nothing has served Quaker values better (now widely shared in the post-Cold War era in the case of their peace testimony) than the touching gift of the wampum belt to Penn. Penn did carry through on his extraordinary promise in his letter to the Indian kings in 1681 by creating a mechanism for resolving any disputes between the settlers and the Lenape. "[I]f in any thing any shall offend you or your People," he promised, "you shall have a full and Speedy Satisfaction for the same by an equall number of honest men on both sides."[19] Such intercultural arbitration, also implemented in the West Jersey colony across the Delaware River, though only briefly, was unprecedented.

If the Lenape did not string shells into a ceremonial wampum belt in 1682, the impulse to do so may not have been far from their intentions. Whatever the case, the early Historical Society councillors—and a great many non-Quakers since—have drawn tremendous sustenance from the wampum belt fable. Granville Penn certainly believed that a treaty of friendship was drawn up at Shackamaxon (present-day Kensington) just after Penn's arrival in the fall of 1682 and that it had been sealed by the great Belt of Wampum. He cited as authority Thomas Clarkson's 1813 *Memoirs of the Private and Public Life of William Penn* and many documents mentioning the "old first treaties of friendship." If the treaty of friendship meeting never occurred and the wampum belt was made many years later, we can appreciate how history is manipulated to fit the sensibilities of those living many years after a supposed event. Historians of public memory have mostly castigated the management of remembrance because the preservationist movement of the last century foisted many fables on an unsuspecting public. But the origins of the wampum belt legend, while doubtless reflecting the desire of nineteenth-century leaders to glorify as benign a previous Philadelphia elite from which they were descended,

FIGURE 8. Benjamin West, *Penn's Treaty with the Indians*, oil, 1771, PAFA. West's painting, commissioned by Thomas Penn, son of Pennsylvania's founder, almost immediately attracted attention: in 1773 a London publisher of engravings announced a 19-by-24-inch copy for 15 shillings. The painting was copied by engravers in Italy, Germany, France, and Mexico as well as England, Scotland, and Ireland. The emotional appeal of the painting was noted a generation later by leading Quaker abolitionist Thomas Clarkson, who claimed that an engraved copy was the only piece of art found in the houses of most Quakers.

were buried deep in the hope of perpetuating the Quakers' pacifist principles that had led to intercultural cooperation in a world of intercultural conflict.

Benjamin West, one of Pennsylvania's most famous painters and the first American-born painter to gain international fame, did his part to seal the memory of the Shackamaxon treaty of friendship meeting, even if it never took place. Just four years before the outbreak of the American Revolution, West painted what was to become one of the most widely reproduced paintings of a scene from American history (Figure 8). Europeans loved it because it showed them what Indians looked like, how they carried their babies, and how they dressed. But for Quakers on both sides of the Atlantic, West's painting depicting Penn's meeting with the Lenape became a symbol of the Quaker influence in American history and a reminder of the Quaker yearning for a peaceful world. In the early 1890s, plans were afoot among Quaker peace activists to place a copy in every Pennsylvania schoolhouse.

Living in England, West did not record history; he created it—or relied on an oral tradition of a "league of friendship," if not a specific peace treaty. Relying on descriptions of Penn as an old man, West made him look older than thirty-eight, his age in 1682. He

FIGURE 9. Jigsaw puzzle of Penn's Treaty with the Indians, LCP. Jigsaw puzzles were a favorite card table game in nineteenth-century middle- and upper-class homes, so children probably gained more cognizance of the Penn treaty legend this way than from their school books. The Library Company dates the puzzle to about 1850 but has no record of how it was acquired.

depicted Indian and Quaker clothing of the late 1700s, rather than the 1680s, and the buildings he depicted in Shackamaxon had not yet been built in 1682. Indians would not have carried weapons to a treaty meeting. A twentieth-century Quaker family legend alleges that the Indian mother with cradle-board baby is a likeness of West's wife. The stately elm tree at Shackamaxon Creek, however, was real and when it fell many years later, in 1810, pieces of it were considered as good as gold.[20]

Whatever its limitations as an accurate portrayal of Indian and early settler life near Philadelphia in 1682, West's treaty painting probably influenced public memory more than any other artistic work except portraits of George Washington. It had to swim against the tide of westward migration as the idea of Manifest Destiny suffused popular feeling and made a virtue of fighting Indians. But by the 1850s manufacturers of household goods were using it on dishes, bed and window curtains, whiskey glasses, bed quilts, hand-painted trays, lamp shades, and jigsaw puzzles (Figure 9). American lithographers pumped a steady stream of copies into the market throughout the nineteenth century, including early copies by Currier and Ives, sometimes giving the treaty date in 1661. A Philadelphia member of the Historical Society purchased West's famous painting in 1851 and allowed it to be exhibited at the city's Great Central Fair in 1864. Millions viewed it at the Columbian Exposition in 1893 in Chicago, where it was part of the Quaker-led Universal Peace Union exhibit.

The promise of a new era of intercultural comity lasted through Penn's lifetime, but by the 1730s Penn's open-door immigration policy had filled Pennsylvania with Scots-Irish and German immigrants who did not subscribe to Quaker pacifism and who hungered for land to the west of the largely Quaker settlements, lands still in the possession of native peoples.

Ironically, James Logan, Penn's most trusted official from 1699 to the founder's death in 1717, became a central figure in a new era of abrasive relations with the Lenape and other tribes. In 1735, when he was the colony's largest land speculator, Logan produced what he alleged was a copy of an old deed signed in 1686 that ceded a huge area between the Lehigh and Delaware rivers to Penn. Although the Lenape chiefs challenged the validity of the document, allegedly copied from an original that Logan could not produce, the Indian leaders succumbed to the combined pressure of the Pennsylvanians and their Iroquois allies who held sway over the Lenape. Two years after the chiefs signed a confirmation of the alleged 1686 deed, Logan arranged to "walk off" the bounds of the Indian deed, which granted Penn's heirs all the land from a specified point in Bucks County westward as far as a man could walk in a day and a half. Tishcohan (Figure 10) was one of the Lenape chiefs who learned to his dismay of the colonists' trickery: two of Penn's sons sent scouting parties through the woods to blaze a trail so that three specially trained woodsmen could average nearly four miles an hour in order to extend the Penns' claim almost sixty miles into Delaware territory, or twice as far as anticipated by the Indian chiefs. This became known as the "Walking Purchase." The voluminous papers of James Logan began reaching the Historical Society by 1840 and continued to arrive as late as 1984. Logan was so long lived and his interests so diverse—he was Pennsylvania's first polymath—that his paper trail can be followed not only in the trove of his papers at the Historical Society but also in the collections of the Library Company, the Pennsylvania State Archives, the Philadelphia City Archives, and the American Philosophical Society.

By the mid-eighteenth century, Penn's peaceful Indian policy was in tatters. The Seven Years' War all but shattered it as the French and their Indian allies attacked Pennsylvania's western settlements and set the frontier aflame. Philadelphia Quaker leaders quickly formed the Friendly Association for Regaining and Preserving Peace with the Indians by Pacific Measures in order to maintain the support of the Delaware (the term subsequently used for the Lenape)—an effort based not only on the hope of avoiding violence but also on the desire to maintain the Quakers' lucrative trade with the Indians. To this end, Quaker leaders refreshed Indian memory by distributing to Indian sachems silver peace medals harking back to the William Penn era. From Quaker silversmith shops came large medals with King George II gracing one side and a Quaker and an Indian the other. The Quaker—William Penn—is shown extending a winged peace pipe across a campfire to an Indian who accepts the offer. Struck in 1757, the peace medal was the first of its kind made in the English colonies. In this cagy use of history Quaker sil-

FIGURE 10. Gustavus Hesselius, *Tishcohan*, oil, 1735, HSP. Tishcohan was one of the signators to the Walking Purchase deed. Hesselius (1682-1755) was a Swedish immigrant and Philadelphia's only painter of note during the colonial period. Even the lack of competition did not give him full employment because most Quakers were still averse to displaying vanity through commissioning portraits and not enough affluent non-Quakers were available. Hesselius dressed Tishcohan with a trade blanket, a chipmunk-skin tobacco pouch with a leather thong, and a clay pipe of European manufacture.

versmiths soon produced other silver symbols of peace: brooches, arm bracelets, pendants, and crosses.

By the end of the Seven Years' War in 1763, Quakers were under heavy attack in their own colony for their Indian peace policy, which, frontiersmen charged, drenched their farms with blood. In late 1763, Scots-Irish farmers from Paxton Creek, to become known as "the Paxton Boys," massacred friendly and defenseless Conestoga Indians at Lancaster (where Penn had visited with Lenape leaders in 1700) and then marched to Philadelphia to demand that the legislative assembly protect the frontier (Figure 11). Franklin wrote

FIGURE 11. *The Paxton Expedition, Inscribed to the Author of the Farce*, LCP. This cartoon, distributed in 1764, is the first internal view of Philadelphia. The Court House at the center, built in 1707 on High (Market) Street, was the scene of annual voting for assemblymen. Voters mounted the stairs to cast their ballots in the central doorway. The scene shows Philadelphians, with cannons and shouldered muskets, preparing to repel the advancing Paxton Boys. At the left is the Greater Meeting House, erected in 1754.

a strongly worded pamphlet condemning the "white savages" for their unconscionable behavior, turning the election of 1764 into a scurrilous war of words. One part of the Quakers' "Holy Experiment" was coming to an end.[21]

From the Lancaster Massacre and the Paxton Boys' march on Philadelphia came America's first political cartoons. Along with a barrage of election pamphlets, these cartoons helped politicize eligible voters. In the colony's most heated election, Franklin lost his assembly seat—the only time he was to lose a political contest.

This deep fissure in late colonial society attracted the attention of the Library Company, which began collecting political pamphlets related to the Paxton Boys' expedition and also a barrage of pamphlets leading up to the ferocious Philadelphia election of 1764. When the Stamp Act crisis in 1765 ignited intense argument over new British regulations, the Library Company gathered pamphlets sparked by the debate. Proud of this collecting policy, Franklin wrote in 1771 that libraries such as the one he founded "made the common tradesmen and farmers as intelligent as most gentlemen from other countries, and perhaps have contributed in some degree to the stand so generally made throughout the colonies in defence of their privileges."[22] Over the waning years of the colonial era, the Library Company acquired a run of Philadelphia's first newspaper, the *American Weekly Mercury*, many new scientific treatises and works of political thought, and museum objects such as fauna preserved in spirits, antique coins, fossils, Eskimo parkas, tanned buffalo skins, and a woman's hand taken from an Egyptian mummy. But the Library Company's special importance was in collecting printed materials related to every aspect of English and American life.

A Mixed Multitude

From the beginning, Penn's colony attracted settlers from many parts of Europe, including many who had already sojourned in other West Indian or North American colonies. Speaking many languages and practicing many religions, they represented part of a tremendous worldwide redistribution of British, European, and African peoples, and their arrival gave early Pennsylvania a mélange of tongues, complexions, and religious beliefs. Penn tried to build a bedrock of tolerance to support this diverse population. He never entirely succeeded, but while prejudice and tensions sometimes flared into name-calling and near violence, Pennsylvania was spared the seething ethnic and religious hostilities that wracked Europe and many North American colonies in the seventeenth century.[23]

The collections of the Historical Society, Library Company, and Philosophical Society came to include rich evidence of Pennsylvania's patchwork of cultures. Though most of these institutions' leaders were alarmed by the late nineteenth-century wave of immigrants from southern and eastern Europe, they still paid some attention to the region's colonial ethnic past. Swedes were the first Europeans to live in what was to become Pennsylvania. Some fifty of them came to the Delaware Valley in 1638, and from that first experience came journals and drawings that provided a basis for Tomas Campanius Holm to write in Swedish what would later be translated as *A Short Description of New Sweden*. Published in Stockholm in 1702, Holm's *Short Description* includes the earliest known pictures of the Lenape—in family groups, trading with Swedish settlers, battling other Indians, and burying their dead.

The Swedes' arrival gave the Lenape their first experience with European intruders, and the contacts were bittersweet. The Indians welcomed trade, and the Swedes symbolized their peaceful intentions by translating Martin Luther's writings into a volume in the Lenape language or in a trade pidgin. Philadelphia's American Swedish Historical Museum, founded in 1926, and built with funding from wealthy Swedish-American industrialists, holds a copy of the book. But as in so many other cases of European-Indian contact, trade was often accompanied by mistrust and violence. It was also almost always accompanied by the exchange of culture. One vivid example of this is an infantry helmet, probably made in Sweden in the early seventeenth century, that became a prized possession of an Indian who was found buried with it near the Susquehanna River in Lancaster County. How it found its way to the Historical Society is unknown, a phantom gift that came "over the transom," in the parlance of curators.

The Swedish influence in Pennsylvania waned after the arrival of the English. The descendants of the initial Swedish settlers were not numerous, and Philadelphia's cultural arbiters wanted the master narrative to begin with the English. But Gloria Dei, the "Old

Swedes Church" in Philadelphia, became a revered sanctuary for people of many national origins. Its minister, Andreas Hesselius, was the brother of the colony's premier colonial painter.

Far more numerous than the Swedes—in fact, the most numerous of all immigrant groups to early Pennsylvania—were the Germans. Some 80,000 poured into Pennsylvania during the colonial era, most of them fleeing "God's three arrows"—famine, war, and pestilence—in their homelands along the Rhine. Although most of them moved through Philadelphia to take up farming, hundreds stayed in Pennsylvania's commercial center, taking up positions as artisans, innkeepers, printers, merchants, and clergymen.[24]

To Pennsylvania came Germans of many types, and they were among the earliest immigrants recruited by Penn, who had traveled through the Netherlands and the Rhineland and published his promotional tracts in German as well as English. Some of the earliest German settlers, like Johannes Kelpius, were pietists, seeking in Pennsylvania a refuge where they could put themselves beyond the scorn and abuse of their neighbors. In 1694, Kelpius led a settlement of some forty German pietists who purchased land in Germantown and became industrious members of that community. Christopher Witt's ink drawing of the mystic Kelpius, done about 1705 and purchased by the Historical Society 177 years later, may be the first portrait rendered in Pennsylvania.

Following the Peace of Utrecht in 1714, ending a series of Anglo-French wars that hampered immigration, German sojourners to Pennsylvania poured ashore. More numerous than the pietists were the Moravians, whose main settlement was in Bethlehem. Like the Quakers, the Moravians dressed conservatively, garbing themselves in grays and browns and avoiding ruffles or other evidences of vanity. Unlike the Quakers, who wished for peace with native peoples but had no desire to convert them to Quakerism, the Moravians were among the most fervent missionaries to the Indians.

Though Pennsylvania became dotted with pietistic German communities, the most numerous of the German immigrants were the industrious farmers and artisans of the more worldly Lutheran and German Reformed churches. Settling in the western parts of Bucks and Chester Counties and more thickly in Lancaster, York, and Berks Counties, they left behind a tradition of folk craftsmanship and art that is immensely popular today. The painted furniture German artisans produced shows how the culture of the homeland could persist when transplanted to an environment that did not despise or attack cultural diversity. The painted chest (Figure 12) was often the most important storage item found in rural southeastern Pennsylvania households well into the nineteenth century. Holding clothing, linens, bedding, and even tools and food, it was frequently used as well for seating or as a table surface. The chests, to be found in every German household, were highly individualized with carving, inlay, and painting. They played a key role in each family's migration. Many were inscribed with the name of the owner, thus marking a chest as the personal property of the immigrant and signifying how humble peasants began to see themselves as individuals. Many owners pasted their *taufschein* (baptismal certificate) inside the lid of the chest.[25]

The Historical Society, Philosophical Society, and Library Company had few mem-

FIGURE 12. Pennsylvania German painted chest over drawers, 1775, Mercer Museum. This chest was inscribed with its owner's name, Christina Hegern, and the date of its making, 1775. Public memory of the past is shaped—and skewed—by the kinds of objects that have survived. Common utilitarian household objects were seldom prized (often they simply wore out), and their owners or descendants usually discarded them. Now that interest in common folk has greatly increased, chests of this kind are precious, and entire museum exhibitions have been dedicated to this material culture, such as a 1999 exhibit at the Philadelphia Museum of Art that brought together an array of decorative as well as fine arts that gave the public the fullest picture yet of early Pennsylvania craftsmanship and aesthetic taste.

bers of German descent in the early years, partly because most German Americans lived in the counties west of Philadelphia and also because Philadelphia's Germans had a thriving historical and literary society of their own, founded in 1763. Therefore, the collecting of material relating to Pennsylvania Germans did not figure prominently in the minds of the city's collecting institutions at first. The Historical Society in 1882 received a rich collection of manuscripts, illustrated hymn books, German language pamphlets, and records of the Ephrata Cloister collected by Abraham H. Cassel, a descendant of Pennsylvania's most famous German printer of the colonial era—Christopher Sauer. In 1904, the Library Company acquired a collection of about one thousand German imprints, including some 150 from the press of Sauer, including the first Bible printed in German in North America. Already, the Philadelphia Museum of Art, founded in 1877, had been gathering a few examples of German American pottery and then, by the early twentieth century, systematically began acquiring pieces from regional dealers who purchased them from rural homesteads. The public's interest in German American folkways had been whetted in the 1864 Great Central Fair where a recreated Pennsylvania-German kitchen, with a huge banner reading "Grant's Up To Schnitz," captivated visitors. Philadelphia's German-Americans built on this interest two decades later with a massive bicentennial celebration of the first arrival of German immigrants in 1683. But not until 1926, when DuPont beneficence allowed the Museum of Art to install a kitchen and bedroom from a German American miller's house, did the public have regular access to the aesthetic taste and craftsmanship of the state's largest ethnic group.

Although cultural persistence was a hallmark of Pennsylvania's German communities—and has led to the production of hugely marketable ironware, pottery, and fabrics along the tourist routes in Lancaster, York, and Berks Counties today—it was from the beginning mixed with cultural adaptation. This was evident in some German newspapers that circulated in Philadelphia and the surrounding counties; the two-column, two-language format accommodated settlers of differing degrees of acculturation and provided an early form of bilingual education. No complete runs of these newspapers exist, which speaks to the limited eighteenth- and nineteenth-century vision of collecting institutions. As late as 1869, when James Rush left today's equivalent of $20 million to the Library Company of Philadelphia, he wagged his finger, so to speak, in his bequest, directing that the library *not* collect to amuse the public and therefore shun "mind-tainting reviews, controversial politics, scribblings of poetry and prose, biographies of unknown names, nor for those teachers of disjointed thinking, the daily newspapers, except, perhaps for reference to support . . . the authentic date of an event."[26] Widely shared among cultural leaders, Rush's vision of what was valuable and therefore collectible facilitated the obliteration of parts of the past that historians now strain to recapture.

Like the Germans, the Scots-Irish found in Pennsylvania a place of refuge, especially from economic privation. Also, like the Germans, most were unable to pay the fare across the Atlantic, and so they came as indentured servants. The term of service was four to seven years, during which time the servant surrendered his or her labor and the fruits of it entirely to the master. The indentured servant's rights, more liberal in Pennsylvania than in many colonies, were spelled out in written contracts that have filtered into the collections of many institutions. Often the servant was to receive a few pounds and, if lucky, two suits of clothes, one of them new, and perhaps a few tools. Such a grubstake was for many the beginning of the slow climb toward economic security.

The Scots-Irish left behind no body of vernacular furniture, such as in the case of the Germans, and until recently the leaders of collecting institutions were little concerned with collecting evidence of ordinary immigrants' lives. Not until the Balch Institute for Ethnic Studies was founded in 1971 did Philadelphia have an institution focused on immigration history and ethnic heritage, and the materials it has gathered largely pertain to the immigrant experience since the mid-nineteenth century. Hence, the early history of the Scots-Irish, one of Philadelphia's largest immigrant groups, is poorly documented. Only from the fragmentary records and artifacts of immigrant societies can partial stories be recovered. The medal of the Society of the Friendly Sons of St. Patrick, a mutual aid organization founded in 1771 for men of direct Irish descent, is one such rare item.

Besides the Germans and Scots-Irish, many other groups came to Philadelphia seeking a place of renewal. The Welsh and the French Huguenots made substantial contri-

An Account of the Births and Burials in the United Churches of CHRIST CHURCH and ST. PETER'S in PHILADELPHIA, by MATTHEW WHITEHEAD and JOHN ORMROD, Clerks, and JOSEPH DOLBY and GEORGE STOKES, Sextons, from DECEMBER 25, 1791, to DECEMBER 25, 1792.

Viz. Chriſtenings,	Males,	93	Burials,	Males,	61
	Females,	87		Females,	64
		180			125

Difference of Chriſtenings and Burials in *Chriſt Church* and *St. Peter's*, between this Year and laſt.

Chriſtenings Increaſed, 30—Burials Decreaſed, 58

Buried under one Year,	18	From thirty to forty,	14
From one to three,	21	to fifty,	16
to five,	3	to ſixty,	11
to ten,	4	to ſeventy,	9
to twenty,	8	to eighty,	5
to thirty,	12	to ninety,	5

The Diſeaſes and Caſualties this Year in *Chriſt Church* and *St. Peter's*.

Apoplexy,	1	Old Age,	3
Child-bed,	2	Purging and Vomiting,	9
Conſumption,	3	Purging,	1
Dropſy,	5	Palſy,	1
Decay,	53	Putrid Fever,	1
Fits,	10	Pleuriſy,	3
Fever,	10	Sore-throat,	2
Flux,	1	Small-pox,	2
Gout,	2	Scalded,	1
Hives,	2	Suddenly,	1
Killed,	2	Teeth and Worms,	3
Mortification,	2	Worms,	1
Nervous Fever,	5		

St. PAUL'S Church.

Baptiſms, 145, Increaſed, 28— Burials, 40, Increaſed 6

ROMAN CATHOLIC Churches.

St. MARY'S.

Baptiſms,	348	Increaſed,	20
Burials,	141	Increaſed,	15

HOLY TRINITY.

Baptiſms,	47	Decreaſed,	5
Burials,	13	Decreaſed,	21

Chriſtenings Increaſed or Decreaſed.

Swedes,	52	Increaſed,	11
German Lutherans,	440	Increaſed,	13
Ditto Reformed,	201	Increaſed,	85
Firſt Preſbyterians,	54	Decreaſed,	7
Second ditto,	76	Increaſed,	3
Third ditto,	65		
Scotch ditto,	26	Decreaſed,	14
The Aſſociate Church,	8		
Moravians,	7	Increaſed,	4
Methodiſts,	80	Increaſed,	35
Baptiſts,	32	Decreaſed,	1
Jews or Hebrew Church,	4	Increaſed,	2

Burials Increaſed or Decreaſed.

Swedes,	24	Increaſed,	2
German Lutherans,	185	Decreaſed,	2
Ditto Reformed,	73	Decreaſed,	43
The people called *Quakers*,	139	Decreaſed,	26
Firſt Preſbyterians,	37	Increaſed,	7
Second ditto,	61	Increaſed,	11
Third ditto,	43	Decreaſed,	5
Scotch ditto,	8	Decreaſed,	10
The Aſſociate Church,	6	Increaſed,	1
Moravians,	2	Decreaſed,	4
Society of *Free Quakers*,	15	Decreaſed,	9
Methodiſts,	30	Increaſed,	6
Baptiſts,	20	Increaſed,	3
Jews or Hebrew Church,	2	Increaſed,	1

Burials in the STRANGER'S GROUND.

Whites,	134	Increaſed,	4
Blacks,	67	Decreaſed,	3

Chriſtenings this Year,	1765	Increaſed,	13
Burials ditto,	1165	Decreaſed,	125

Alſo Mr. JOHN HUTTON, Departed this Life, December 19, Aged 108 Years and 4 Months.

134 / 67 / 201   965 / 311 / 676   1165 / 1135 / 30

FIGURE 13. Mortality bill, 1793, LCP. Mortality bills not only are an important source for studying the growth of churches in Philadelphia, but they have allowed demographic historians to chart the fertility and mortality rates in the city. For an era when municipal recording of vital statistics was unknown, the mortality bills have become a key source for reconstructing the dynamics of population growth in colonial Philadelphia.

butions to the city's life. So did non-Quaker English immigrants and many others who had first arrived at way stations in the West Indies or other parts of British North America. Church records have partly illuminated the lives of some of these people of the colonial period. Occasionally, these records were lost to fire through church arson or accident, but some found their way into the Historical Society or Philosophical Society collections because a famous Philadelphian, whose descendants left his papers to one of these institutions, was a treasurer or other officer of a particular church. As early as 1870, the Historical Society purchased a 1740 deed from Thomas Penn to Nathan Levy, the first Jew known to have settled in Pennsylvania, for land on which to establish a sanctified Jewish cemetery, which still survives. From one of Philadelphia's oldest Jewish families, the Gratzes, came Simon Gratz, one of the country's most avid collectors of Americana. Serving as a councillor and vice president of the Historical Society in the early twentieth century, he began giving most of his huge collection of nearly 60,000 manuscript letters and prints, rich in Jewish materials, to the Historical Society during World War I.

Of all the artifacts that have reached across the generations to speak of Philadelphia's polyglot nature, the simplest and yet most revealing are the mortality bills (Figure 13), first issued by the city's Anglican churches in the 1740s. Published annually, they detailed the births and deaths recorded in each of the city's congregations. Such mortality bills were common in England in the eighteenth century, but their Philadelphia counterparts may have been inspired by the Anglicans' desire to show how their congregations were growing more rapidly than those of other churches. If so, they would have lost their purpose by the late eighteenth century, when the one in Figure 13 was published, because by then the Methodist and Baptist churches were the fastest growing in the city.

Another group joining the human mosaic in early Philadelphia was the Africans, and they came, of course, not as immigrants but as involuntary laborers carried across the Atlantic under appalling conditions. Though small in number, they contributed much to the physical and cultural development of the seaport town and colonial capital.

Africans were in Philadelphia almost from the beginning. The Dutch had brought slaves with them to the Delaware Valley long before Penn and the Quakers arrived. But their number was vastly augmented in November 1684, when the *Isabella*, out of Bristol, England, sailed up the Delaware River with 150 Africans in chains. It does not comport well with the usual picture of the early pacifist settlers that they assembled on the newly built wharves and bid avidly to purchase these arrivals. At the outset of their "Holy Experiment," the pacifist Quakers had ensnared themselves in a troublesome institution. In an infant community with about 1,000 persons, these Africans immediately became central to the labor force that did the work of clearing trees and brush and erecting crude houses. This marked the beginning of the extensive intermingling of white and black Philadelphians that has continued ever since.[27]

Though the interest in Penn and his compatriots was a logical priority for Library Company or Historical Society leaders, Quakers' early involvement in slavery—as slave traders and slave owners—was decidedly not. The Library Company directors of the

FIGURE 14. *Portrait of Black Alice*, engraving, 1803, frontispiece in *Eccentric Biography; or Memoirs of Remarkable Female Characters, Ancient and Modern*, LCP. Because the compiler of *Eccentric Biography* arranged the entries alphabetically, readers encountered Alice first, to be followed by Joan of Arc. The Library Company acquired a copy of *Eccentric Biography* in 1832 from the peculiar artist James Cox in one of the shrewdest moves ever made by one of its librarians. Living alone with his dog and macaw, Cox scraped money together for years to buy books, accumulating a six-thousand-volume library. John Jay Smith, the Library Company's librarian, convinced Cox to sell his books for an annuity of $400. Cox died two years later, and the Library Company happily absorbed his fabulous collection.

early nineteenth century and Historical Society founders *were* interested in African Americans as objects of white reformers' zeal because many of these leaders were part of the Quaker-led antislavery movement. This explains the society's subscription from the beginning to the *African Observer*, an abolitionist journal edited by the Quaker Enoch Lewis. But Africans in Philadelphia were not themselves seen as fit subjects for commemorating the past or even as a valuable part of urban society. Their first newspapers, including the African Methodist Episcopal Church's *Christian Recorder*, published in Philadelphia, were never collected. John Fanning Watson, the city's leading annalist, was fearful of the large free black community. A devout Methodist, he hated the way black Methodists were, as he saw it, "corrupting" Sunday services through exuberant music, dancing, and noisy exhortation; he hated even more, as he explained in his book *Methodist Error* (1819), that white Methodists were adopting black Methodist churchly enthusiasm. Independent black churches, which were sprinkled throughout the city and became focal points of the black community, were a big mistake, in Watson's view. "Their aspirings and little vanities," he sneered in his 1830s *Annals of Philadelphia*, "have been rapidly growing since they got those separate churches." In his youth, he explained, "they were much humbler, more esteemed in their places, and more useful to themselves and others."[28]

Yet even if the topic of Philadelphia's deep engagement in slavery and the history of its victims lay outside the historical imagination of Library Company and Historical Society patrons, sometimes sheer inquisitiveness got the better of them. For example, during years of collecting material for his history of Philadelphia, Watson conducted oral interviews that yielded nuggets treasured by present-day historians of African Americans. One ancient informant described how, before the American Revolution, slaves divided into "numerous little squads" on Sundays and holidays, "dancing after the manner of their several nations in Africa, and speaking and singing in their native dialects." In these few words, we have the rarest of evidence of African cultural retention and continued ethnic identity among enslaved people cast up on the shores of the Delaware.

Though Watson had little respect for most black Philadelphians, he would have had great esteem for Black Alice, one of Philadelphia's most respected oral historians (Figure 14). She was probably the daughter of two of the 150 Africans sold at dockside in Philadelphia in 1684. Reputedly born in 1686, she lived to 116 years of age. Like an African *griot*—a story teller—she became a repository of historical information and was sound of mind until the very end of her life in 1802. In her advanced years she recalled life as a young slave, when Philadelphia was a wilderness where Indians hunted for game. She remembered the original wood structure of Christ Church, where she worshiped, built in 1695 with a low ceiling that she could touch with raised hands. She also recounted meeting William Penn and lighting the pipe of the man who, like most Quakers in this period, did not find Quaker beliefs and slaveholding incompatible. For many years she tended Dunk's Ferry, crossing the Delaware River north of the city, where she collected the tolls for her master. "Her conversation became peculiarly interesting, especially to the immediate descendants of the first settlers, of whose ancestors she often related acceptable anecdotes," reported an account of her in 1804. "Many respectable persons called to see her, who were all pleased with her innocent cheerfulness, and that dignified deportment, for which (though a slave and uninstructed) she was ever remarkable."[29]

Hidden treasures relating to African American history are often to be found in the materials that early collectors coveted for entirely different reasons, particularly in the manuscripts and records of wealthy white Philadelphians. After all, these residents were the slave traders and slave owners and often, in the aftermath of emancipation, the patrons of free black churches and organizations. Evidence that 150 Africans were brought to the city in 1684 is buried in a letter in the Penn Papers acquired in 1870; there a merchant describes to Penn, now back in England, how most of the hard money brought by the settlers of 1682-83 went down the Delaware River in the *Isabella*, having been exchanged for Africans. Similarly, when the Historical Society acquired by gift and purchase a huge trove of Chew family papers, it knew it could open windows on one of early Pennsylvania's most powerful families. But the Chew papers also included important information on how Chew sold Richard Allen's family to Stokely Sturgis, a farmer living near the Chew's Kent County, Delaware plantation, thus establishing the place where Allen came of age, obtained his freedom through self-purchase, and became a founding father in his own right—of the African Methodist Episcopal Church.

Only fragments of evidence of how slavery functioned in early Philadelphia can be found in the city's collecting institutions. But the head harness made of iron and copper (Figure 15) tells a story that is fleetingly documented in printed sources, that African slaves were shackled to prevent their escape and were harnessed with a bell that would proclaim any attempt at escape. If Philadelphia's Liberty Bell is our national icon for celebrating freedom, this rare item reminds us that other bells were cast to *prevent* freedom in a city where the slave population had reached nearly 1,500 by the 1760s and where the

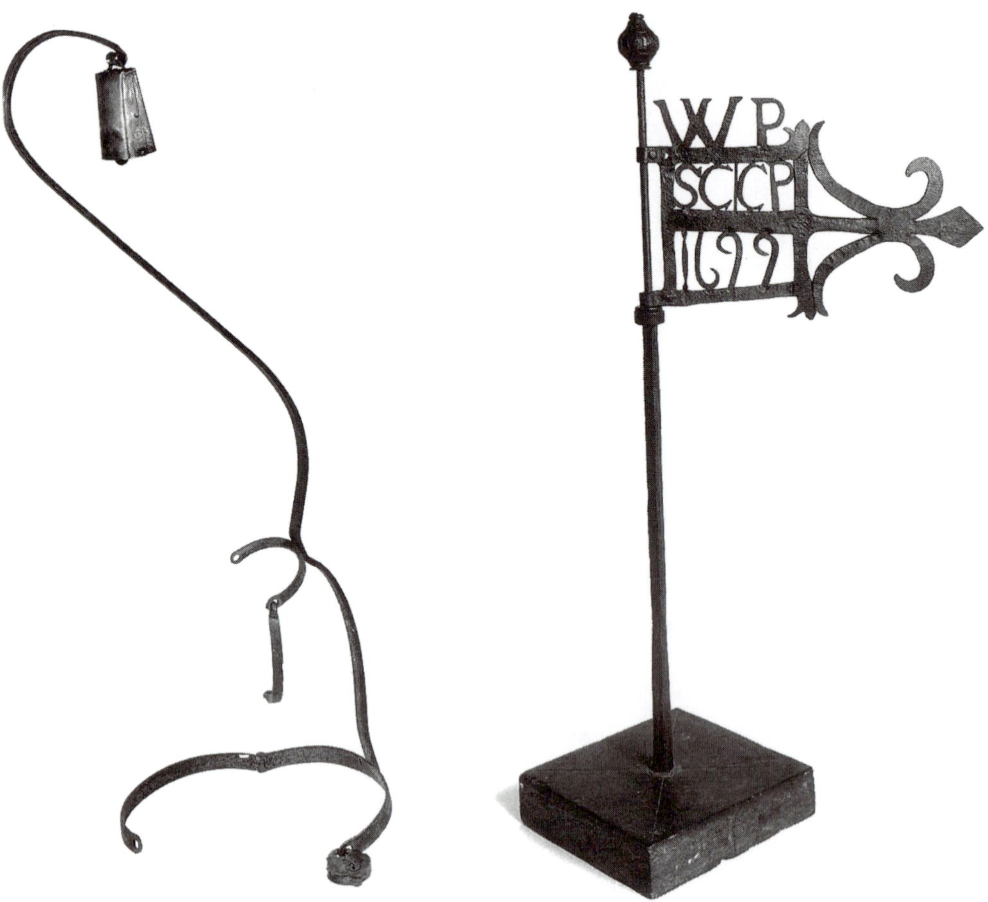

FIGURE 15. Slave head harness and weathervane, HSP. Philadelphia blacksmiths and other metalworkers are noted for fashioning artistic weathervanes of the type shown here, bearing the initials of William Penn and two of his business partners, Caleb Pusey and Samuel Carpenter, at a Chester County grain mill. The same artisan often turned his hand to the production of slave harnesses, chains, and shackles, but these items were rarely thought of as collectibles until recent years. The weathervane was given to the Historical Society in 1863.

proportion of families that owned slaves was not much different from that in Maryland or Virginia.

Although not collected because they would shed light on the African American experience, newspapers have become vital veins of ore much exploited by today's historians of black America. Because they regularly carried advertisements for the sale of slaves, both by slave traders with recently imported men and women for auction and by individual slave owners who were weary of a truculent slave or strapped for money, newspapers provide fascinating detail on slaves' physical appearance, linguistic ability, dress, temperament, and much else. The runaway slave ads—thousands of them—spanning nearly a century, from the first publication of the *Pennsylvania Gazette* in 1729, are a running if highly fragmentary story of the black campaign to destroy slavery by stealing themselves away.[30]

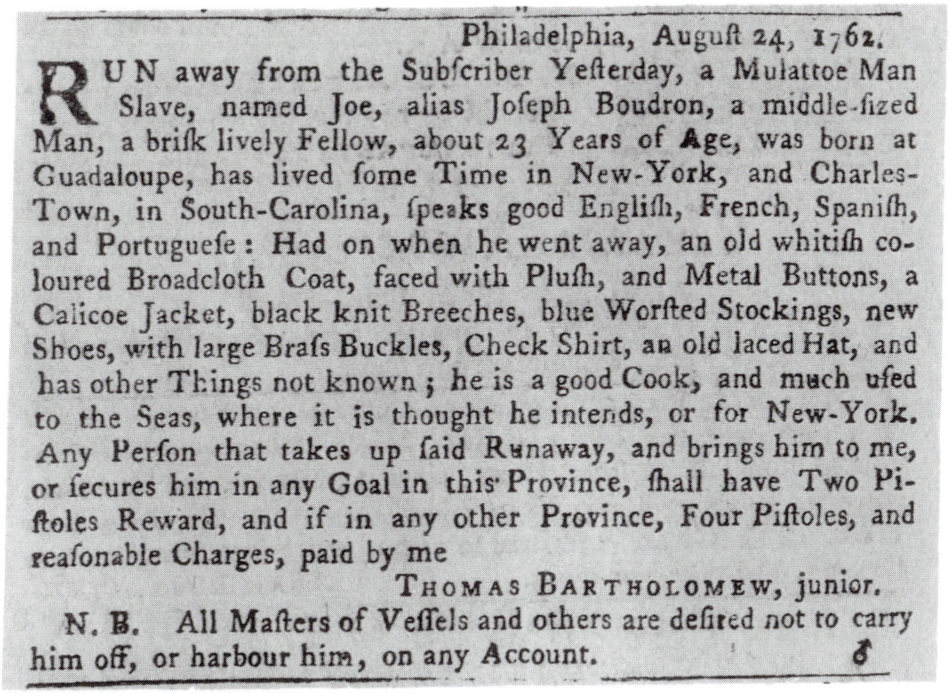

Philadelphia, Auguſt 24, 1762.

RUN away from the Subſcriber Yeſterday, a Mulattoe Man Slave, named Joe, alias Joſeph Boudron, a middle-ſized Man, a briſk lively Fellow, about 23 Years of Age, was born at Guadaloupe, has lived ſome Time in New-York, and Charles-Town, in South-Carolina, ſpeaks good Engliſh, French, Spaniſh, and Portugueſe: Had on when he went away, an old whitiſh coloured Broadcloth Coat, faced with Pluſh, and Metal Buttons, a Calicoe Jacket, black knit Breeches, blue Worſted Stockings, new Shoes, with large Braſs Buckles, Check Shirt, an old laced Hat, and has other Things not known; he is a good Cook, and much uſed to the Seas, where it is thought he intends, or for New-York. Any Perſon that takes up ſaid Runaway, and brings him to me, or ſecures him in any Goal in this Province, ſhall have Two Piſtoles Reward, and if in any other Province, Four Piſtoles, and reaſonable Charges, paid by me

THOMAS BARTHOLOMEW, junior.

N. B. All Maſters of Veſſels and others are deſired not to carry him off, or harbour him, on any Account.

FIGURE 16. Slave advertisement, *Pennsylvania Gazette*, August 26, 1762, HSP. Of all the sources on early slavery, the slave advertisements are the richest for showing individual Africans acting of and for themselves—negotiating the terrain during freedom flights, inventing new identities as a way of disguising their slave status, seeking out spouses, children, parents, and friends.

Some runaway slave ads provide examples of the opportunities to derive multiple meanings buried in pieces of the past collected by the Historical Society, the Philosophical Society, and the Library Company. The advertisement for a slave named Joe, by his master Thomas Bartholomew, in the *Pennsylvania Gazette* on August 26, 1762, is a case in point (Figure 16). At first glance, the ad seems to indicate simply Bartholomew's desire to reclaim his human property as well as Joe's resistance to bondage: "Run away from the Subscriber Yesterday, a Mulattoe Man Slave, named Joe, alias Joseph Boudron, a brisk lively Fellow." But careful attention to the ad's language tells us more. Joe was not satisfied with a shortened forename—the usual slave owner's assignment of a half-name signifying the slave's demeaned status. The "brisk lively Fellow" presumed to call himself Joseph Boudron, not Joe, probably choosing a surname derived from a previous experience with a French master or a European parent in Guadeloupe, the place of his birth according to the ad. The advertisement also reveals the mulatto slave's linguistic abilities: "speaks good English, French, Spanish, and Portuguese," indicating that this twenty-three-year-old man was among the city's most accomplished linguists. The ad also tells us about the slave's cosmopolitanism and knowledge of geography, having lived in the French West Indies, New York, and Charleston, a "good Cook," and "much used to the Seas."

Holding enslaved Africans in a society committed to peaceful relations was only one of the difficulties and tensions inherent in the business of founding colonies. For the visionary Penn, much frustration and disappointment attended his attempts to manage his colony from England. Yet the diversity encouraged by his peace testimony and policy of toleration, though it spawned strain and bitter words, allowed Pennsylvanians to think of community in a new way, as a collection of people whose welfare depended on ignoring their differences or, at least, tolerating them rather than fighting over them. In Philadelphia, Jewish merchants, German innkeepers, English craftsmen, French Huguenot shopkeepers, Scots-Irish sea captains and sailors, and enslaved Africans all mingled closely. Though certain groups such as the Germans, Scots-Irish, and Africans preserved some of their distinctive folkways rather than adopt wholesale the ways of the English majority, most Philadelphians embraced the idea of religious toleration and ethnic diversity, helping to make the colony a model for people in other areas. For Africans, Philadelphia was no city of brotherly love, but at least it was a city where, almost from the beginning, there were *some* who pricked the conscience of those who dealt in human flesh.

Chapter 2

RECALLING A COMMERCIAL SEAPORT

Between the time William Penn left his colony in 1701 after his second visit and the outbreak of disputes with Great Britain in 1764 that would lead to the American Revolution, Philadelphia became the largest commercial center in English-speaking America. Penn's liberal immigration policy encouraged rapid development of the region, and along with natural increase this drove Pennsylvania's population upward from a mere 18,000 in 1700 to about 220,000 in 1765. The urbanized Philadelphia region grew from about 2,200 in 1700 to 19,000 in 1760, and then to about 30,000 as the Revolution erupted in 1775. Around 1720, a little-known painter named Peter Cooper caught the bucolic nature of the sleepy riverfront town of the early eighteenth century (Figure 17), carved out of forests, with its two rude Quaker meetinghouses, a few primitive wharves, and streets extending only several blocks from the Delaware River.

When William Penn's son Thomas Penn commissioned George Heap to draw a panoramic view of Philadelphia thirty years later, artisans, merchants, mariners, and ordinary laborers—many of the latter indentured or enslaved—transformed Philadelphia into one of the English empire's prize overseas capitals (Figure 18). Although Heap's panorama is not strictly accurate—it exaggerates the height of public buildings and presents the curved waterfront as a straight line—it does not overstate the importance of maritime commerce to Philadelphia's economy. Approximately seventy wharves and twelve shipyards dotted the area shown, graphic evidence that Philadelphia had grown mightily by becoming the entrepôt that imported manufactured goods for a thriving region and exported foodstuffs, wood products, furs, and other commodities throughout the Atlantic basin. Many Philadelphians would have agreed with Lord Adam Gordon, a British colonel who fought in the Seven Years' War. Visiting Philadelphia in 1765, he called it "a great and noble city" and "one of the wonders of the world."

To the leaders of Philadelphia's cultural institutions, looking back from the nineteenth century, the prerevolutionary city was a marvelous success. Some modern planners, developers, and city dwellers have tried to recreate the imagined charm of Philadelphia in the mid-eighteenth century. Visitors to Cliveden in Germantown, the stately home of the Chew family, the restored Powel House on Third Street, the recreation of the Georgian drawing rooms of wealthy Philadelphia merchants at the Philadelphia Museum of Art, or the Henry Francis du Pont Winterthur Museum outside

FIGURE 17. Peter Cooper, *The South East Prospect of the City of Philadelphia*, c. 1720, LCP. Cooper's *Southeast Prospect* is thought to be the oldest surviving painting of a North American city. Cooper took liberties. The Quaker meeting houses, identified by key numbers, had no pinnacles, which would have offended Quaker values. Nor did the Court House, identified as #18, have a tower as depicted by the artist. Cooper's eight-foot-long painting on canvas was sent to London in 1744. In a fine example of the vagaries of collecting, it was discovered 113 years later in a London curiosity shop. The member of Parliament who found it took it to the American minister to the Court of St. James, Philadelphia-born George Mifflin Dallas, who gave it to the Library Company.

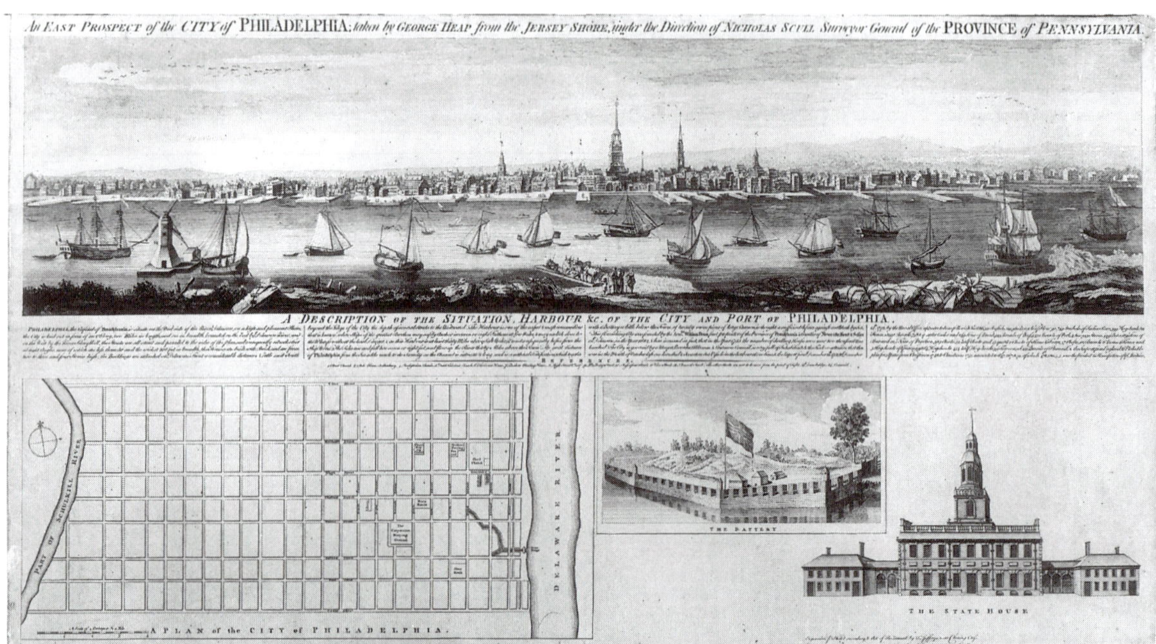

FIGURE 18. Scull and Heap, *An East Prospect of the City of Philadelphia*, engraving, 1756, LCP. William Penn's son Thomas commissioned an engraved view of Philadelphia to boast about the city's rapid growth and to stimulate further immigration and investment. The four plates constituting the view (only one is shown here) were engraved in London because of Philadelphia's chronic lack of engravers before the 1790s. The scene encompassed almost a mile and a half of the city's waterfront. The Delaware River here fairly boils with merchantmen riding on stylized waves.

Wilmington, Delaware, are appropriately dazzled by the restrained gentility of early Philadelphia aristocrats. But they are not seeing prerevolutionary Philadelphia, only the Georgian grandeur of a very small fraction of even the upper class.[1]

Today's historians view the bustling city through several lenses. In one light, it was a thriving shipping center where *some* merchants and officials built gracious houses and *some* artisans, like Benjamin Franklin, followed the way to wealth through industriousness, sobriety, and excellent craftsmanship. But another city can also be seen: one whose economic growth, spurred by population explosion and war contracting, made it a city of economic instability, of exploited indentured and slave labor, of a growing gap between the top and bottom of society that led to the emergence of an impoverished class. This underside of commercial development is not well documented in the city's early historical collections because the leaders of cultural agencies in the nineteenth century were not interested in the lives of the lower classes. However, historians have explored this side of the city's history through later acquisitions of the Historical Society, the Library Company, and more recently founded institutions such as the Atwater Kent Museum of Philadelphia History and the Balch Institute for Ethnic Studies. But most important has been the Archives of the City of Philadelphia, which by mandate systematically preserved such invaluable sources as vagrancy dockets, almshouse admission books and minutes, tax lists, deed and mortgage books, and probate records with inventories of personal possessions upon the death of the rich, the poor, and those in between (Figure 19).

Wheels of Commerce

Philadelphia's merchants and shopkeepers, whose records are abundant in the Historical Society's collections, became legendary. Dozens of colonial merchants were memorialized in street names—Shippen, Willing, Pemberton, Norris, Powel, and many more. These were the merchants who reached inland to tap the Indian fur trade and to gather the produce of the fertile rolling farmlands watered by the Delaware and Schuylkill rivers. They dispatched their ships to Africa, Europe, the West Indies, and—by 1785—to China. The wharves jutting into the Delaware River and the dense settlement for several miles along the river clearly displayed Philadelphia's "vigorous spirit of enterprise," as one merchant called it.[2]

Philadelphia's merchants established their fortunes by transporting the agricultural products of the hinterland—beef, pork, wheat, corn, and lumber—to wood- and food-hungry parts of the flourishing British empire. In the early decades of settlement, many business transactions took the form of barter, the direct exchange of goods and services. More complicated transactions became common in the 1700s, involving letters of credit, bills of exchange, and specie, or money in coin. An innovation was paper money, first issued in Pennsylvania in 1723 to help ease the city's earliest severe recession.

Not every merchant made a fortune, and taken together merchants did not form a cohesive group. A study in the 1980s shows that the city had about 320 merchants in the

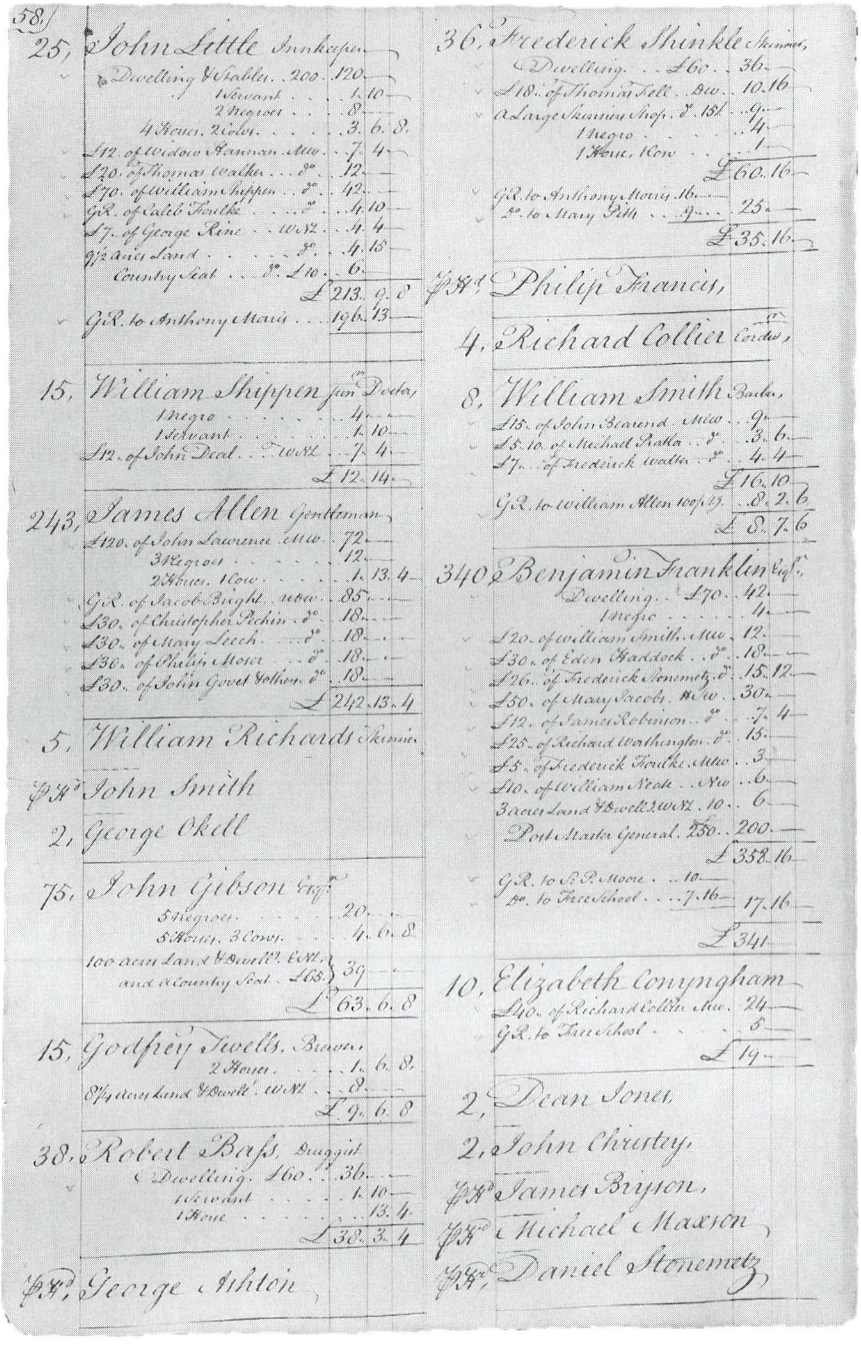

FIGURE 19. Pages of 1772 Philadelphia tax list, HSP. Until social historians in the 1970s began to use tax lists such as this one, the extent of slavery in colonial Philadelphia was discussed only impressionistically, if at all. The left page of the list shown here gives Benjamin Franklin's assessment for one slave but not for three others he took with him to London. The right page includes many of Franklin's neighbors who owned slaves, listed along with horses and cows as chattel

5, William Thorne Schoolmaster

3, Benjamin Humphreys Smith

ᵽH. Joseph Trimble,

ᵽH. Thomas Hood,

275, John Ross Esqr.
Dwelling .... £150. 90.
3 Negroes ... 12.
3 Horses, 1 Cow ... 2. 6. 8
£8. of Henry Cratz ... Mlw. 4. 16
£8. of Mary O'Hara ... do. 4. 16
£8. of Frederick Paul ... do. 4. 16
£8. of Susannah Powell ... do. 4. 16
£85. of John Bayard .. H.W. 51
£60. of Ann Bayard ... do. 36
£16. of William Todd .. Mlw. 9. 12
£6. of Edmund Shultz .. do. 3. 12
£40. of James Nevil .. W.N.L. 24
a Lot on Arch & 5th Street .. N.W. 9
50 Acres Land & Dwellg. Ext. £25. 15
50 Acres & Country Seat .. do. 20
40 Acres Land .... in Oxford. 3. 5
£ 294. 19. 8
G.R. to Anthony Morris ... 4
Do. to Rawle's Estate ... 6
Do. to Sarah Parker ... 2. 5
Do. to William Coates ... 8 20. 5
£ 274. 14. 8

215, John Lawrence Esqr.
3 Negroes ... 12
2 Horses ... 1. 6. 8
£140. of David Franks .. N.W. 84
£35. of Robert Gray ... do. 21
£9. of Daniel Weaver .. Mlw. 5. 8
£30. a New House ... do. 18
12 Acres Meadow .. Moyamensing 10. 16
Assistant Judge .. £100. 80
£232. 10. 8
G.R. to Philip Kearney .. 9
Do. to Richard Wells & Co. 9. 12 18. 12
£ 213. 18. 8

9, And for Philip Kearney's Estate
G.R. of John Lawrence .. Ext. 9

2, Tristram Heyler Baker,

3, William Roberts Carpenter

2 James Alexander Smith,

ᵽH. William Sheafe, } Merchts.
ᵽH. Lawrence Sickle

61.

118, Daniel Williams Merchant
Dwelling ... £75 .. 45
3 Negroes ... 12
2 Horses, 1 Cow ... 1. 13. 4
G.R. of John Lawrence .. Mlw. 20
£20. Store in his own Possession Cw. 12
£14 .. of Sundry Tenants ... do. 8. 8
8 Acres and Country Seat .. W.N.L. 6
£8. of William Wells ... do. 4. 16
£6. of William Keen ... Ext. 3. 12
£113. 9. 4
G.R. to Alex Boyer ... 6
Do. to Propr. 34 ... 2. 8 8. 8
And For £105. 1. 4

29, Eleanor Moode's Estate
£48. of William Crispin ... W.W. 28. 16

ᵽH. John Pryor.
And for his Father's Estate
45, £12. of Thomas Pugh ... Dw. 7. 4
Vacant Lot on Walnut Street . do. 3
£18. of Joseph Bowne ... do. 10. 16
a Shop in Dock ward ... £5 .. 3
a Lot .. in Southwark ... £3 .. 1. 16
14 Acres Land ... in W.N.L. 7
£12. of Jacob Rich .. Lower Dublin 7. 4
£9. of Bastian Miller. Germantown 5. 8
£45. 8

ᵽH. Benjamin Davis

2, William Facundus Staymaker,

31, Henry Funk, Innkeeper,
1 Negro ... 4
1 Horse ... 13. 4
£45. of Philip Edenburn. Bristol. 27
£31. 13. 4

5, George Rineholt Book Binder

4, Henry Deberiere Gunsmith

5, Jacob Kimley Shopkeeper,

3, William Kinley,

Daniel Clymer Attorney
1 Horse ... 13. 4
£36. of Richard Peters . H.W. 21. 12
Head & Estate £2. 5. £ 22. 5. 4

3, George Boots Cordwainer

property. Merchant Daniel Williams and gentlemen John Ross and John Lawrence owned three slaves each, along with much Philadelphia property rented out. Innkeeper Henry Funk owned one. Probate records for several thousand prerevolutionary Philadelphians confirm that slavery was extensively practiced in the City of Brotherly Love.

FIGURE 20. W. L. Breton, *The London Coffee House*, Watson, *Annals* (1830), LCP. Merchants bringing slaves to Philadelphia usually auctioned them at the London Coffee House at Front and High (Market) Streets. When Thomas Paine arrived in 1774, he boarded in a building looking down on the slave auctions. Offended by what he saw, he wrote one of his first essays, attacking the slave trade and the use of slaves.

early 1770s, and that fully 85 percent of them were not part of the city's social elite, itself sharply split between Quakers and Anglicans. Only half owned a horse, and most lived in cramped housing not much different from that of a successful furniture maker or silversmith.[3] All were part of an intensely competitive milieu, and all faced uncertain markets, unpredictable storms at sea, and frequent periods of war when they could speculate in disrupted overseas markets to their advantage or plummet into bankruptcy. No merchant could sit in his countinghouse and count on anything.

Between the merchant importer and the consumer stood the shopkeeper. Philadelphia had hundreds of them, and female entrepreneurs were numerous, especially as retailers of imported luxury wares. Catering to a thirst for British goods, part of the surging consumer demand throughout the world rimming the Atlantic Ocean, women shopkeepers became leading arbiters of taste. We are so accustomed to thinking of eighteenth-century women as guardians of domestic life, largely restricting themselves to the private realm, that it takes an adjustment of our angle of vision to appreciate that entrepreneurship flourished among single women and widows, especially after about 1750. As purveyors of British wares, women shopkeepers were drawn into the political sphere after 1764, when new British policies led to heated campaigns for nonimportation.[4]

The ships dispatched from the city wharves laden with wheat, wood, and meat often returned with human cargo: Irish and German indentured servants and Africans enslaved in places such as Senegambia, Angola, and Dahomey. The slave trade was especially active during the Seven Years' War (1756–63), when the flow of white indentured servants from Ireland and Germany stopped. Many account books of eighteenth-century merchants acquired over the years by the Historical Society show the sale of a shipload of newly arrived Africans, sometimes with entries showing the expenses incurred in "going after Negroes" or "taking up Negroes"—clues to how desperate Africans bolted into the wilderness after a torturous long voyage across the Atlantic, into Delaware Bay, and up the Delaware River (Figure 20). Neither the Historical Society nor any other institution collected materials that would interpret the experience from the viewpoint of the enslaved Africans, and indeed accounts of this kind were set down only rarely. But newspapers bristled with advertisements for slave sales and runaway slaves and servants, an important source of revenue for newspaper publishers such as Benjamin Franklin. In the absence of much material in the papers of Philadelphia's slave-importing merchants, the newspaper slave ads have been nearly the most valuable source of information on the experience of slaves and indentured servants.[5]

Beyond quickening the slave trade, the Seven Years' War, like most colonial wars, provided a special opportunity for war contractors, merchants prominent among them. The privateer was another such agent. Licensed by the government to prey on enemy shipping, an intrepid ship captain could leapfrog to the top of society if luck came his way. Such a man was Philadelphia's John Macpherson, who snared eighteen French vessels on a single voyage in 1758. So vast was Macpherson's haul that five years later he could afford to pour £14,000 sterling into building Mount Pleasant, his 160-acre estate outside the city (now Fairmount Park) to which this son of a Scottish immigrant soon retired in Georgian splendor. When John Adams saw Macpherson's Mount Pleasant, he called it "the most elegant country seat in the Northern colonies."[6]

In the 1760s, those profiting the most from the Seven Years' War initiated the first era of the construction of country seats within a day's journey from the city. The country house or mansion afforded the opportunity to retreat from urban disease, heat, and hubbub; it was also a place to display wealth and status. About fifteen years after Macpherson built Mount Pleasant, a visitor to Philadelphia observed that "the country round Philadelphia is . . . finely interspersed with genteel country seats, fields, and orchards, for several miles around, and along both the rivers for a good many miles."[7] Still, only about forty merchants owned a country seat by 1770, and many of the residences were hardly more than what today would serve as a summer cottage.

A Philadelphia merchant was no better than the ships he sent to sea and the sailors who manned them. Indeed, many merchants were ship captains as well or trained their sons as ship captains plying the Atlantic trade routes. Indispensable to Philadelphia's commercial economy, mariners and dockside laborers composed about 10 percent of all working males. The crews of many blue-water vessels included African Americans and occasionally Native Americans. Historians have often classified mariners as unskilled laborers, but no ship captain or vessel owner would have entrusted his seagoing property to "unskilled" hands. The lives of deep-sea sailors (and other Philadelphians at the bottom of the social scale) are sadly elusive, but historians have traced them in recent years in tax lists, deeds, poorhouse records, church marriage and baptism entries, and probate records, where inventories of the goods left at death have survived for some. Best recorded in printed materials are the lives and adventures of the pirates, some of whom lived in Philadelphia in the city's early years.

A romanticized picture of blue-water sailors clouds our picture of maritime reality. For example, the Seven Years' War seemingly brought flush times for mariners because the privateering boom put a premium on the seaman's labor. As early as 1756, one merchant was writing about the "Scarsity of seamen as Most of them are gone privateering."[8] Yet few of the fortune seekers realized their dreams. Privateering crews distributed their booty according to rank, and usually half the shares went to the ship's financial backers. The rest was distributed according to position, with the lowly cabin boys getting one-half to three-quarters of one share. Many privateersmen came home empty-handed, and many went to a watery grave because the already hazardous life at sea became even more hazardous. The main rewards went to the owner-investors, the officers, and the maritime artisans ashore. As a result of the rush to scoop up enemy riches from an English-dominated sea, it was they who received unparalleled wages while enjoying safe billets.

Mercantile wealth created colonial Philadelphia, although personal fortunes were as often made in real estate and the social elite probably had more gentlemen of inherited wealth than active merchants. The merchants' and shopkeepers' wealth also made the trades hum because much of the money earned by importers, exporters, and retailers was money spent on house construction or home furnishings. The building boom during and after the Seven Years' War nearly doubled the number of houses in the city between 1760 and 1777—from 2,969 to 5,470. This required the labor and skills of an army of house carpenters, glaziers, painters, stonecutters, masons, sawyers, and ordinary laborers. That several dozen city merchants were contracting for elegant new houses in and outside the city explains the need for a Philadelphia edition of *The British Architect, or The Builder's Treasury of Staircases*.

We often associate the design of colonial America's more elaborate buildings with cultivated amateur architects such as Thomas Jefferson or Philadelphia's lesser known Dr. John Kearsley, who designed Christ Church, built in 1727. But the subscription list for the 1775 Philadelphia edition of *The British Architect* tells a different story. The original 181 "encouragers" of the first architectural publication in North America included only two gentlemen and two merchants but 62 master builders, 111 house carpenters, two painters, and two plasterers. Such information about the history of early building has become the absorbing interest of the Athenaeum of Philadelphia. Founded in 1814 as a subscription library, it has now become the nation's most important repository of early American architectural history with extensive holdings of architectural drawings and books as well as material on fine furniture and the decorative arts.

All but forgotten to public memory about the humming commercial city on the Delaware in the colonial era are the enslaved Africans and free blacks. These two groups were indubitably important to the workings of commerce and the city's rapid expansion in the decades preceding the American Revolution. Close to fifteen hundred slaves lived with masters in the city in 1767, when nearly one of every six households contained at least one slave. Some of them moved ships, often going to sea with the sea captain who owned them; more moved goods, at dockside as stevedores or through the streets as wagon drivers. Others toiled in ropewalks, saw pits, shipyards, and tanneries, all connected to the fitting out of ships. Still others worked alongside masters in the shops of blacksmiths, blockmakers, and coopers. In every such instance they contributed to the turning of the wheels of commerce. Those who were domestic servants, including most of the enslaved women, contributed indirectly to the commercial success of white city dwellers by making life more comfortable for their masters and mistresses in kitchens, nurseries, stables, and taverns.[9]

The post-World War II restoration of Philadelphia's old commercial center of the eighteenth century has whisked slave history aside as cleanly as did the creation of Colonial Williamsburg in the 1930s, when the Rockefeller fantasy of eighteenth-century Virginia life took form. Anyone visiting Franklin Court today, ambling through the courtyard where the print shop, post office, and Venturi steel outline of the Franklin home recall the heyday of Printer Ben's fame, will see no evidence that Franklin acquired four slaves in the 1750s—Peter, Jemima, King, and Othello. Not a trace of John Cadwalader's seven slaves can be found in Nicholas Wainwright's *Colonial Grandeur in Philadelphia: The House and Furniture of General John Cadwalader* (1964). Careful attention by the author to the building and lavish furnishing of the house on Second Street makes this book the finest account of the mid-century Georgian efflorescence in colonial Philadelphia, yet it shrouds the details of how the Cadwalader mansion was partially built by enslaved labor and carefully cared for by his retinue of slaves. Visitors to Cliveden, now a property of the National Trust for Historic Preservation, will learn a lot about its builder, Benjamin Chew, attorney general and provincial councillor of Pennsylvania. But they will learn little about the dozens of slaves employed by Chew at Cliveden and on his Kent County, Delaware plantation, including the family of Richard Allen, who would found the African Methodist Episcopal Church. John Dickinson is etched in public memory as the "Pen man of the Revolution" for his famous protest pamphlet *Letters from a Farmer in Pennsylvania* (1768), but he is forgotten as the owner of about fifty-five slaves on the eve of the Revolution. Yet none of these famous white men could have ascended so high within the city's rising commercial sector of the mid-eighteenth century without the advantage provided by unpaid laborers—the silent, shadowy figures of the seaport's history.

Artisans and Artisanry

While planning his colony in London, Penn realized the importance of attracting skilled craftsmen to Pennsylvania, and in this he succeeded. By 1690, about 120 craftsmen were practicing their trades in the city. Eighty years later, on the eve of the Revolution, about half of Philadelphia's households were headed by craftsmen—or "leather- apron men," as they called themselves. The craftsmen took pride in their skills, knowing them to be indispensable to the community. They believed in the dignity of laboring with one's hands and regarded their skills, to be passed on to apprentices and journeymen, as a form of property. "The humblest workman thinks nobly of his trade" went the French saying in the eighteenth century, and it applied equally in Philadelphia.[10]

The dignity conferred by craft labor had its basis not only in the Protestant concept of calling, which held that in God's eyes the mason was as worthy as the merchant, but also in the awareness that no community could exist without the products of its dexterous artisans. Craft skill represented indispensable knowledge, and upon that knowledge rested a claim to a certain authority in the community. Moreover, craft skill was a form of capital, nonmaterial to be sure but at least as important as cash or real estate. Artisans invested their skill in products, and these handcrafted objects, to the craftsman's way of thinking, always bore his personal stamp and therefore, in an indirect way, were his possessions.

Conditions in North America fostered a corollary attitude that intensified this belief in the dignity of labor. In the seaboard cities, the incentives for industriousness went beyond a search for "a decent competency," as the phrase went in this era, because the availability of land and the persistent shortage of labor produced a more fluid social structure than in Europe. Penn's open-door policy and the liberal terms for purchasing land brought a rich array of skilled artisans to the Delaware, and in the early decades many forged ahead. The *Bristol Factor* that landed at Chester in October 1681, a year before Penn arrived and even before Philadelphia was laid out, brought Cesar Ghiselin, an eighteen-year-old silversmith who prospered; Thomas Wharton, a tailor whose sons would become important merchants; Nehemiah Allen, a cooper whose business thrived; Josiah Carpenter, a brewer who became a large landowner; Thomas Paschall, a pewterer who made a small fortune; and Abraham Hooper, a cabinetmaker who could hardly keep up with the demand for his furniture. In this single ship arrived the core of the artisan and commercial enterprises of the early decade. Each established a family that prospered.

Such generally favorable conditions encouraged unremitting labor as men found they could rise from journeyman to master more swiftly than in the German Palatinate, Ulster, or East Anglia. One result of the new attitude toward industriousness was the abandonment in Philadelphia and other cities of "St. Monday," the English artisan's habit of taking Monday as well as Sunday off from work. If more work meant only lower daily wages, as was often the case in England, where a surplus of labor existed, then a shorter workweek made perfect sense. But in the seaboard towns of colonial America, where labor was often in short supply, St. Monday fell victim to the conviction that laboring people, by the steady application of their skills, could raise themselves above the ruck.[11]

Working in their small shops, Philadelphia's diversified artisans created fine silver holloware, exquisitely carved furniture, and much more. Seen from one perspective, these artifacts are a tribute to the good taste of the wealthy families who commissioned

FIGURE 21. Iron stoveplate with German inscription, 1741, PMA. Pennsylvania's rich reserves of iron ore made possible a flourishing iron industry that demonstrated craft traditions, cultural preferences, and American ingenuity. This stove plate, forged at Durham Furnace in Bucks County, displays an inscription in German that translates as "Cain killed his brother Abel." Many other stove plates told moral stories. One with a war and peace motif shows two grenadiers with guns facing off while two short bearded men with broad-brimmed hats shake hands. Another portrays a family quarrel inspired by the devil himself where husband and wife, encouraged by their children, trade blows. Benjamin Franklin fused two fireplace traditions—English and German. His "New Invented Pennsylvania Fireplace" of 1744 combined the German tradition of cast iron heating stoves and the English tradition of open fireplaces with iron firebacks to protect the masonry and throw heat into the room. Franklin's fireplace—widely copied down to the present day—fitted an open-fronted stove into a fireplace opening.

them. But seen from another, they become a lasting reminder of the imagination and skill of the craftsmen who created them.

Philadelphia's many craftsmen produced articles on demand for urban customers, then called "bespoke work," but they produced as well for the entire Delaware River valley. For example, a Philadelphia blacksmith or cabinetmaker was intimately tied to the countryside surrounding the city not only because of the demand for his handicrafts but also because that is where he got the materials for fabricating his products. The stove plate shown in Figure 21 was made from ore refined in one of the thirty-nine furnaces

FIGURE 22. William Russell Birch, *Preparation for War to defend Commerce*, engraving, LCP. Though this scene of Joshua Humphreys's shipyard in Southwark was captured in about 1799, shipbuilding had not changed since before the Revolution. The frigate *Philadelphia* is under construction. Workmen at the top of the scaffolding use ropes and pulleys to lift a curved beam aboard the ship's prow. In the background is Gloria Dei Swedish Lutheran Church. Birch's engravings were commercially successful, but buyers of this one probably prized it for the rustic scene and patriotic overtones, not the representations of artisans' work.

and forges that operated in Philadelphia's hinterland. These operations drew heavily on slave and indentured servant labor for the incessant work of cutting timber and making charcoal.

Many Philadelphia artisans worked in small shops with only a few other craftsmen, and they prided themselves on fashioning their product, whether pewter bowl, ladder-back chair, or suit of clothes, from beginning to end. But some artisanal activities required the cooperative labor of many different craftsmen. The most important and complicated involved the construction of ships and buildings. Among the artisans involved in building and outfitting a vessel were ship carpenters, caulkers, wood carvers, painters, mastmakers, sailmakers, ropemakers, blacksmiths, gunsmiths, glassmakers, instrument makers, and ship chandlers. The products of these construction craftsmen's hands were hardly collectible, and the endless impulse to modernize has wiped away almost all traces of the eighteenth-century ropewalks and shipbuilding sites, so documenting the work of such craftsmen is difficult. In the background of William Birch's *Preparation for War to Defend Commerce* (Figure 22), we have one of the few glimpses of ship construction as it was carried out in the preindustrial period.

House construction tradesmen, like shipbuilders, worked in groups with a premium placed on coordination and cooperation. In overall charge was the master carpenter, who was often the architect and general contractor as well. He subcontracted work to bricklayers, stonemasons, plasterers, painters, glaziers, joiners, and laborers. Edmund Woolley was such a master builder in Philadelphia, engaging and coordinating the labor of scores of artisans in the construction of the State House, later to be called Independence Hall. His supervision of the job was long—"a quagmire of contention, shortages of funds, and interminable construction."[12] Started in 1732, the interiors of the State House were not completed until 1748, and the brick tower, lodging the now iconic Liberty Bell, was finally finished in 1753. In an example of how the passing of time can alter public memory, Woolley for many years was credited as the master builder of the State House but not as its architect. Andrew Hamilton, speaker of the state assembly and famous for his defense of the New York printer John Peter Zenger, was for many years credited with designing the State House. But receipts found in the Penn Papers at the Historical Society in the early twentieth century suggest that Woolley prepared the drawings from which the State House was built.

Most of the products from the hands of Philadelphia's preindustrial artisans that have survived come from the luxury trades, whose craftsmen produced fine house furniture, silver, and other furnishings for the wealthy. For generations these have been the most sought after items from the early American past for two reasons. First, such artifacts symbolize a bygone era of careful craftsmanship and elegant taste, a time of the individually crafted rather than mass-produced articles. Second—perhaps more important—the exquisite desk, chair, or silver bowl, like a precious work of art, is an affirmation of the power and prestige of the elite and of the social system in which they governed.[13]

The Historical Society acquired the furniture, paintings, uniforms, and other possessions of the elite from the beginning, and the commitment to collecting the products of the luxury trades has not wavered down to the present day. Not until the end of the nineteenth century did interest arise in collecting and studying the artifactual history of non-elites. Swimming bravely against the tide, Henry Mercer, an antiquarian collector and amateur archaeologist, began gathering ordinary objects—apple parers, claw hammers, tin dinner horns, straw beehives, fireplace tongs, flax brakes—anything from what he called the "valueless masses of obsolete utensils or objects which were regarded as useless."[14] His fascination with discovering people from the distant past through their material remains began when Mercer, as a boy, unearthed arrowheads, fragments of pottery, and other objects from a Lenape camping ground on his father's property in Bucks County.

Much later, when associated with a group of archaeologists at the University of Pennsylvania Museum, Mercer went about creating an object-centered rather than book-and document-centered museum at the Bucks County Historical Society in Doylestown.

36
BAGDAD

Only by collecting and displaying the ordinary and commonplace, he reasoned, could the story of the American people be truly told. For Mercer, work was at the center of how a society and nation were built; therefore, through collecting and examining ordinary objects historians could tell the stories of the people who did most of the work. His first exhibition in Bucks County, in 1897, displayed 761 ordinary objects in a show titled "Tools of the Nation Maker." More than law books and politicians or field pieces and soldiers, Mercer argued, these simple tools and those who used them skillfully were the true makers of the nation. History was best written, he explained, "from the standpoint of objects rather than from laws, legislatures, and the proceedings of public assemblies." Trying to overthrow a document-based academic textual history of the elites, Mercer used tools and everyday objects to illuminate the lives of ordinary people (Figure 23). Sure of his method and his populist instincts, he spent decades scouring "penny lots" at country sales—the flea markets of an earlier era—and "rummaging the bake-ovens, wagon-houses, cellars, hay-lofts, smoke-houses, garrets, and chimney-corners" across the countryside.[15]

Deeply involved in collecting ordinary objects, Mercer explained in 1909 that he was sure that "the history of Pennsylvania was here profusely illustrated and from a new point of view."[16] In no other way could a more inclusive history be presented. Councillors of Philadelphia's cultural institutions paid little attention to Mercer's ideas that history resides with the common people and that people will flock to see what was part of their ancestors' daily life. So the fabulous collection he assembled of some 60,000 ordinary household objects filled up the fantastic six-story concrete castle he completed in 1916 in Doylestown for the Bucks County Historical Society, which he had helped found in 1880.

Visitors came in small numbers to Mercer's castle, but his ideas gained new currency during the Great Depression. Just seven years after Mercer died in 1930, the wealthy radio magnate Atwater Kent established a Museum of Philadelphia History that more or less adopted Mercer's mission: to collect material culture that would bring to light the social and cultural importance of daily urban life. Exhibiting for the first time in 1939, the museum has collected about eighty thousand artifacts, though only a small fraction of them tell stories of Philadelphia life before 1850.

The works of luxury craftsmen so prized by collectors cannot give the full picture of artisan life, but they tell a great deal. For example, the tall-case clocks of Peter Stretch, acquired by the Historical Society, Philadelphia Museum of Art, and Atwater Kent Museum, are examples of English artisanry transplanted to Philadelphia. Immigrating to the city in 1702, when he was thirty-two years old, Stretch produced dozens of tall-case hour-hand clocks that graced the city's finest houses. With two sons pursuing clock and

FIGURE 23. Interior of Mercer Museum, Bucks County Historical Society. This photograph of the central court of the Mercer Museum in Doylestown, Pennsylvania, shows how Henry Chapman Mercer wanted to create what one historian has called "carefully classified confusion." This "tight packing" of artifacts, reminiscent of an old-fashioned hardware store, gives a good sense of how objects were fashioned by craftsmen and used in daily work processes.

watch making, the Stretch family became Philadelphia's unofficial timekeepers. Peter produced the town clock in 1717; his eldest son made the clock for the State House in 1753. Stretch, like other American clockmakers, began copying European counterparts by putting minute hands on the clocks to make them easier to read—an example of the highly derivative nature of American craftsmanship. Reflecting Philadelphia's growth and commercial vigor, Stretch's restrained, flat-topped, plain-doored clocks of the early years became more ornate: rather than a molded base standing directly on the floor, a fancier clock stood on bun or bracket feet; rather than a simple flat top, the improved clock had carved moldings and cast iron or brass spandrels; mahogany sometimes replaced pine or poplar.

Philadelphia's rising wealth turned the city into North America's undisputed furniture capital by the third quarter of the eighteenth century. The well-heeled merchant owners of fine city houses and country seats required a massive amount of furniture, and increasingly they wanted it stylish enough to signal their authority and power. Orders for bespoke work poured into the shops of several hundred chair, chest, and table makers. One of the best-known and most prosperous was William Savery. He finished his apprenticeship about 1741 and soon became one of Philadelphia's leading chairmakers and a member of the Library Company. Engaged in producing top-of-the-line chairs, Savery also crafted handsome chests of drawers and tables. When the London cabinetmaker Thomas Affleck arrived in Philadelphia in 1763 bearing the third edition of Thomas Chippendale's *The Gentleman and Cabinet-Maker's Director*, which the Library Company shortly acquired, Savery began to produce rococo furniture in the Chippendale style. Like Stretch, Savery was a member of the Society of Friends, and both were patronized by Quakers throughout their careers.

Of all the trades for which Philadelphia's artisans became famous, none exceeded printing in establishing the city's reputation as a capital of culture. By the end of the colonial era, the city was a center of book, pamphlet, and newspaper publishing, and its most famous artisan, Benjamin Franklin, was a printer. By 1795, Philadelphia boasted forty-three printers, evidence of a print explosion in its early stages. Some printers also made printing presses and type, Franklin being the first of his trade in the English colonies to do the latter.

From its beginnings the Library Company, American Philosophical Society, and Historical Society were avid collectors of early Pennsylvania imprints that came from the hands of a host of German and English printers. William Bradford, the city's first printer, had established himself by 1685, and his *Kalendarium Pennsilvaniense, or America's Messinger, Being an Almanack for the Year of Grace 1686* is the earliest Philadelphia imprint in the Historical Society's collections. The society made its first large purchase of titles in 1879, received its first large gift of early books and pamphlets in 1882, and a year later received from a descendant of William Bradford a rich collection of works produced by successive generations of Bradfords. By that time, the Library Company's collections, after a century and a half of collecting, were unsurpassed, and the Philosophical Society had continued to develop its collection of Franklin imprints.

Eighteenth-century artisans are known primarily for what they produced: the beautiful and highly collectible objects created out of silver, pewter, wood, clay, leather, cloth, glass, steel, and iron. But behind the product lies a shrouded history of a person who was not only a craftsman but a head of family and a participant in the community's affairs. Not a single piece of furniture was joined, nor a boot cobbled, nor a weathervane smithied, nor a pot turned except by a man wielding his tools in a social and political context. The distance between the workbench and street was very small in towns such as Philadelphia, and the relationship between the craftsman and his clientele had political and social dimensions. As Philadelphia developed, craftsmen became more and more involved in life beyond their shop doors. Peter Stretch was not only a clockmaker but also a city councilman for thirty-eight unbroken years and unceasingly involved in the affairs of his Quaker monthly meeting—seeing that the youth were orderly, mentoring orphaned children, presenting incoming Quakers with their certificates of removal from their previous meeting. William Savery was not only a chair and cabinet maker but a member of the Fellowship Fire Company and by 1757 keeper of the keys for its engine; ward tax assessor at age thirty-four; a supporter of the Friendly Association, which tried to forge an enlightened Indian policy in the difficult mid-century era; and an active member of the Society of Friends.

Although history books teach us to think of the urban economy as male-driven and the artisan's world as masculine, Philadelphia's economy depended in no small way on women's paid and unpaid labor, and women by the hundreds were retailers, proprietoresses, and artisans. Most artisans lived and worked in the same structure; and in a world where home and shop were contiguous, the artisan's wife would often tend the shop when he was away and help in the ordering and processing of materials. Other women took over their husbands' or fathers' trades when they died. For example, in the early national era, three of Philadelphia's printers were women: Jane Aitken, who took over the business of her father, Robert Aitken, when he died in 1802; Lydia Bailey, who took over the business after the death of her husband, Robert Bailey; and Margaret Bache, widow of Benjamin Franklin Bache, who published the *Aurora* from November 1798 to March 1800.

Female trades also flourished in the preindustrial city. Anyone walking through the commercial district of the late colonial era would encounter tavernkeeper Rachel Draper, upholsterer Elizabeth Lawrence, tallow chandler Ann Wishart, optician shopkeeper Hannah Breintnall, dry goods shopkeeper Elizabeth Rawle, and dozens more. At least one third of all retailers were women, and perhaps one fifth of all inns, taverns, and boardinghouses were female managed. Though males dominated the craft shops, they included female bakers and braziers, distillers and winemakers; mantua makers, glovers and tailors; tinkers and sieve makers; soap boilers and spinners. Women served as well as healers, nurses, and midwives; teachers and preachers; keepers of inns, taverns, and boardinghouses. Much of women's work has been hidden from view because of the scarcity of records relating to both paid and unpaid labor. Yet account books of a few of these women found their way into the collections of the Historical Society and even into

FIGURE 24. Woman's pocket, c. 1745–55, PMA. Women's dresses were not made with pockets during this period. Instead, separate pockets, like this one, were tied around the waist or neck to hold small necessities. Like most other clothes signifying status, pockets came in many fabrics and styles. Female domestics probably wore plain cotton or muslin pockets, while the mistress of a well-to-do household expected to have one highly decorated and made of silk and linen as pictured here.

the holdings of Philadelphia's College of Physicians. Skillfully exploiting these scarce accounts and supplementing them with tax records, wills, and early census reports, women's historians in recent years have restored women to the urban economy.[17]

More familiar than women whose labor made them a conspicuous part of Philadelphia's street life was the labor of women in domestic settings. The chatelaine or "pocket" (Figure 24) was the badge of the mistress of the house and sometimes the shop—the manager who was responsible for conserving and distributing household stores. One historian has suggested that the pocket is a better symbol of eighteenth-century women than the spinning wheel because "this homely object symbolizes the obscurity, the versatility, and the personal nature of the housekeeping role. A woman sat at a wheel, but she carried her pocket with her from room to room, from house to yard, yard to street. . . .

Whether it contained cellar keys or a paper of pins, a packet of seeds or a baby's bib, a hand of yarn or a Testament, it characterized the social complexity as well as the demanding diversity of women's work."[18]

Symbols of Affluence, Signs of Distress

The absence of great wealth or dire poverty in Philadelphia's early decades, what some called "a pleasing mediocrity," was yielding to a new social order by the eve of the American Revolution. The range of social conditions had widened, and the distance between top and bottom had grown. Mixing together on the streets and wharves were merchant moguls, middling shopkeepers and artisans, and struggling—sometimes impecunious—mariners, laborers, and less successful artisans.

The collections of the city's cultural institutions have been repeatedly replenished with objects reflecting the comfort of the merchant-rentier class in the colonial city, so much so that it sometimes seems that everybody in the city prospered. But beneath the surface of genteel Philadelphia resided other layers of society that historians have disclosed only recently. Most of the physical evidence that would document the lives of ordinary Philadelphians has been used up, torn down, or thrown away. But historians are beginning to discover the lives of the laboring classes in tax lists, poor relief rolls, pay records, newspaper notices of runaway servants and slaves, vagrancy dockets, almshouse admission ledgers, and other records. Especially important are the inventories of household goods taken when a person died. But a full picture of life in the growing colonial city remains half-visible.

As today's builders of outsized mansions can appreciate, the house was the greatest symbol of wealth and social status in eighteenth-century America. Many of Philadelphia's successful merchants and gentlemen living on investments and inherited wealth built houses befitting their affluence during the building boom of the 1760s and 1770s, and the wealthiest of them retreated from the heat, dirt, and yellow fever epidemics of Philadelphia summers by building country houses along the Schuylkill and Delaware Rivers. Inside the urbane house, whether in or outside the city, fireplaces were an essential element for heating and a venue for the decorator's touch. House carpenters assembled mantels and then added ornaments according to their client's taste or their own.

If house size was a signifier of social status, so were the building materials of which the houses were made: brick and stone for the wealthier, wood for the humble. In the same way, inside the house the wood used in furniture signified a family's wealth and values. Softwood pine served ordinary people, more expensive cherry and maple for middling families. But for the affluent, hardwoods such as oak, walnut, and mahogany—the latter far more expensive because it had to be imported from British Honduras and other distant places—were the materials of choice (though some conservative Quakers shied away from the more ostentatious mahogany). Fine upholstered side chairs, a drop-leaf dinner table, crystal wine glasses, and Chinese porcelain plates (Figure 25) were far be-

FIGURE 25. Dining room setting, mid-eighteenth century, PMA. Wealthy Philadelphians enamored of Georgian-era furnishings created a local version of English upper-class life. The table shown here is set with a silver salver (the small footed tray at the center holding a serving dish), Chinese porcelain plates, silverware, and crystal glasses. These fine material possessions have been collected so passionately and displayed so frequently in museums and historical societies that the public's mental picture of colonial life in Philadelphia is based primarily on the household goods of the uppermost layer of urban society.

yond the means of common Philadelphians but comfortably within the budget of perhaps one hundred Philadelphia families.[19]

Samplers were a favorite form of female expression among the city's well-to-do families. Needlework efficiently combined lessons in writing and cultivated discipline, patience, and quietude—or so mothers and fathers hoped. Rebecca Jones was twelve in 1751 when she worked her sampler (Figure 26), probably under the watchful eye of her mother, a schoolmistress, or Ann Marsh, a Quaker woman skilled in needlepoint. Originally treasured for its age and beauty, the sampler has more recently become thought of as a valuable source of information on the education and socializing of eighteenth-century women.

The commercial wealth that propelled the city's economy forward created a much more self-conscious elite. The number of men identifying themselves to tax collectors as "gentleman" or "esquire" tripled between 1756 and 1772, and these rank-conscious urbanites strove to assert or reinforce their social status in a number of ways. One was to

FIGURE 26. Rebecca Jones sampler, 1751, Atwater Kent Museum. The young Rebecca worked birds, animals, and sprigs of flowers into her compartmented sampler, recorded the exact time of her birth, and stitched in a moral lesson. The Friends Historical Association donated it to the Atwater Kent Museum after World War II as part of a collection of eighteenth- and nineteenth-century Quaker clothes, decorated fabrics, and dolls.

commission oil-on-canvas portraits. Typically, the portrait showed the gentleman assuming erect posture—chin up, back straight, and shoulders back—in itself signaling high status. Likewise, the sitter's dress announced his social authority. No merchant, lawyer, or clergyman would have dreamed to appear on canvas coatless or in an unbuttoned vest or open-throated shirt, sure signs of a tradesman. The protocol of both posture and costume, clearly displayed in portraits, drew lines demarcating the urban gentleman from the ordinary city dweller. Although the public rarely laid eyes on the oil portrait, secure inside an urban mansion, its owner could view it daily as a reassurance of his class authority.

The leaders of Philadelphia's cultural institutions have attached great importance to acquiring portraits of such worthies as Thomas Lawrence, Thomas Mifflin and his wife, Robert Morris, and Charles Willing, Jr. because, like documents and artifacts, they forge links between the past and the present. But more particularly, the portraits of historically mighty figures reinforce the high social position of their institutional owners, many of them descended from the portrait sitters. The Historical Society's portrait collection of Philadelphia worthies reached sixty-seven by 1872. In the following decades the collection mounted rapidly, rising to several hundred by the mid-twentieth century.

Also important as emblems of cosmopolitanism and status were furniture designed for the upper classes. The comment of a New York merchant in 1757 applied as well to Philadelphia: "Our affluence, during the late war introduced a degree of luxury in tables, dress, and furniture with which we were before unacquainted."[20] Stylish furniture, arranged in carefully planned architectural spaces within the home, permitted social performances, such as tea drinking, and formal receptions governed by carefully cultivated rules of etiquette. Investment in more ornate and more aesthetically developed furniture became a hallmark of the middle third of the eighteenth century, adopted cautiously by Quakers and embraced wholeheartedly by others.

By the late nineteenth century, the Historical Society, the Athenaeum, and the Philosophical Society avidly collected furniture and house furnishings of the merchant and rentier elite because they attached a special value to the surviving artifacts of the colonial era that supported a romantic vision of a heroic American era. Indeed, as we will see in Chapter 8, a colonial revival was in full flood at this time. Today, historians see the rising desire for fashionable living, played out in acquisitiveness for material goods, as evidence of a "consumer revolution" that spread not only within the upper echelon but also among the middling ranks of American society. They also see the yen for display and the cultivation of refinement not only as a way for the affluent to separate themselves from the hoi polloi through conspicuous consumption but also as a commitment to living a more refined life according to what its participants thought was a superior moral code. "Brandishing possessions in the faces of the poor to demonstrate pecuniary superiority," writes one historian, "only signified a difference in wealth," but "creating parlors as a site for a refined life implied spiritual superiority."[21]

In fashionable Philadelphia, during its rise as a commercial center of great importance, one ate from as well as sat on crafted objects made of materials connoting class position. Wooden bowls and crude clay vessels sufficed for the poor and pewter and earthenware served the needs of the middle class, but the wealthy required silver and porcelain. As the American Revolution approached, silver tea- and coffee-ware, dining accessories, and personal articles became essential emblems of wealth and status. By the 1750s, about a dozen silversmiths worked in Philadelphia, producing increasingly specialized forms of silver tableware as well as ceremonial presentation pieces, silver peace medals, and gorgets produced for Indian chiefs to commemorate treaty signings and keep the Indian trade with Quaker merchants flowing.

Such a piece as a coffeepot (Figure 27) crafted by Joseph Richardson, Jr., one of the city's premier silversmiths before the Revolution, provides an example of how such an artifact can have multiple meanings. It can be viewed most directly as a handsome example of high-style eighteenth-century craftsmanship, as an intrinsically valuable work

FIGURE 27. Richardson coffeepot, PMA. Joseph Richardson's grandfather Francis Richardson, a mariner, immigrated to Philadelphia in 1681. His son, Francis Richardson, Jr., prospered in Philadelphia as a gold- and silversmith and consolidated the family's fortune by marrying Elizabeth Growden, daughter of a large landowner and provincial officer in nearby Bucks County. When Francis Richardson, Jr. died in 1729, he passed on to his sons, Francis and Joseph, his craftsman's skills, his clientele, and his enviable place among Philadelphia Quakers. Both sons practiced silver- and goldsmithing. The elegant pieces made by Joseph, one of Philadelphia's most notable silversmiths, found their way into almost every Philadelphia cultural institution and the homes of many private collectors.

of decorative art. Through a second lens, the coffeepot can be seen as a crucial piece of evidence in tracing the new meaning of gentility in the eighteenth century. Amid rising consumerism, in both England and its colonies, genteel people developed a new sense of refinement, acted out in elegant manners, witty conversation, and graceful movements on occasions that depended on the importation of new beverages from exotic ports of call—in this case coffee beans from South America. Through a third lens, the Richardson coffeepot can be considered, although not actually seen, with regard to the organization of rhythms of work of the artisan who crafted the object. Behind the coffeepot lay several work processes involving African cultivation of the coffee beans, the sailors who shipped them to Philadelphia, and the small silversmith workshop production that linked together the labor of apprentices, journeymen, and master craftsmen. Finally, behind the coffeepot, absent from the view of the lovely pot itself, resided the role of the crafts worker in the political and social life of a port town such as Philadelphia.

While creating domestic architectural spaces equipped with elegant furnishings, the colonial elite also developed new forms of gentility to display their status. It was not enough to dress well or live well; one had to walk with grace, appreciate music, dance and ride skillfully, and know classical literature and languages. One visitor to Philadelphia wrote that without refined manners "the best finished furniture or finest marble will lose half its luster, which, when added, decorates and greatly ornaments it."[22] The Library Company's Benjamin Franklin, immensely ambitious and intensely aware of appearances, edited from an English original America's first treatise on how to get on in business, including standards of decorum and propriety: *The American Instructor, or Young Man's Best Companion.*

Below the genteel resided the vast majority of urban dwellers. If they could not aspire to gentility, many Pennsylvanians believed that theirs was "the best poor man's country in the world," where ordinary people could get ahead and where the gap between kingly riches and grinding poverty, so common in Europe, had narrowed. Philadelphia did contain scores of examples of those who had started at the bottom and risen high. The city to which Franklin came as a journeyman printer in 1723 was filled with ambitious young men, and many of them rose to prominence, if not so spectacularly as "Poor Richard." No wonder, then, that Franklin became a hero of the city's leather-apron men and that his little book, variously entitled *Father Abraham's Speech* and *The Way to Wealth*, became a best-seller.

Yet while many artisans, like Franklin, watched their wives replace the pewter spoon and earthen porringer at the breakfast table with a silver spoon and china bowl, many others by the mid-eighteenth century were finding the road forward strewn with obstacles. Economic fluctuations, inclement weather, and personal injuries kept many artisans, mariners, and laborers on the knife edge of insecurity, and everyone knew of a bankrupt merchant. The Seven Years' War was particularly wrenching. It made many artisans flush with orders for boots, clothes, guns, and other military supplies, but it also left hundreds of war widows with children to support. Even at the beginning of that war the Quaker John Smith wrote in his diary, "It is remarkable what an increase of the number of Beggars there is about this town this winter." Then, at war's end, colonial cities experienced the greatest economic stagnation ever known.[23]

Compounding the economic suffering brought by the Seven Years' War and depression that set in when the fighting moved to the Caribbean theater in 1761 was the bitter winter of 1761-62, which left hundreds destitute. A wartime inflationary trend had driven up the price of firewood, always an item that, if needed in unusual amounts, could throw a poor laboring family into distress. "Many of the poor," reported the *Pennsylvania Gazette*, "are reduced to great Extremity and Distress" because of "the high Price of Firewood."[24] In this situation, Philadelphia leaders, with Quakers in the lead, formed a

	To whom Given	half cords of wood	Blankets	Stockings	by whom Recommended
1762	Brought forward	364	165	63 pair	
3mo 10	Robert Tomms	1			John mease
	Ann Tucket	1			Ditto
	Caesar Gisline	1			Ditto
	Thomas Gelpin	1			Joseph Richardson
	Rachel mullany	1			Jacob Lewes
	Rees Peters wife	1			Jno mease
	Thomas Stuart	1			Jams Pemberton
	Eleanor Allison	1			Ditto
	Rachel Sharel	1			James Stephens
	Deborah Waggoner	1			Ditto
	Cornt Duhavan	1			Ditto
	James Spears	1			James Pemberton
		376	165	63 pr	
	Wm Brown recd for Wm Peters Esqr in cash the value of ½ cord	1			
		377	165	63 pair	
					188½ whole Cords

FIGURE 28. Manuscript relief roll from Committee to Alleviate the Miseries of the Poor, HSP. Both Richardson and Ghiselin, whose names appear on this list, were grandsons of men who had immigrated to America in 1681, Francis Richardson from England and Cesar Ghiselin, a Huguenot, from France. Both families prospered at first, but while the Richardsons continued to rise, the Ghiselins remained on a plateau and then, in the third generation, declined sharply. Cesar Ghiselin, named after his grandfather, became a barber and by 1756 was rated on the tax list at one third the assessment of Joseph Richardson. In the next few years Ghiselin's world collapsed, leaving him indigent in the winter of 1761-62, when Richardson served as one of the leaders of the poor relief effort.

FIGURE 29. *A View of the House of Employment, Alms-house, Pensylvania Hospital, & part of the City of Philadelphia,* c.1767, LCP. The main part of the city, seen in the background to the right, emphasizes the bucolic setting of these buildings. Animals graze in the fields. Only the Bettering House and the first wing of the Pennsylvania Hospital, seen on the right, had been built by this time. As soon as its doors opened in October 1767 the Bettering House was filled with 284 persons. By the eve of the American Revolution it bulged with more than four hundred indigent men, women, and children. The name came from the growing feeling among the city's leaders that the poor were responsible for their poverty and could better themselves through a strict almshouse regimen designed to inculcate an abstemious work ethic.

special "Committee to Alleviate the Miseries of the Poor." The relief roll in Figure 28 is a partial list of the 329 "objects of Charity" who received blankets, stockings, and—that most precious commodity—firewood. One of the recipients of firewood, William Browne, lived across the street from Governor James Hamilton, poignant evidence of the class-mixed character of the city.

Philadelphia's construction artisans were glad for contracts in 1766-67 to build an extensive new almshouse, the largest building in the American colonies, but some of them probably wondered if they would become inmates themselves as the city's poor swelled in number. The new almshouse, or Bettering House as it was revealingly called, was built on Spruce Street, several blocks beyond the limits of residential development, on a site described by a visitor in 1774 as "a very bleak place" where "the North-Westers, which are very severe here, will have a full sweep at a body." It became an institution of last resort for poor Philadelphians, a place to obtain food and warmth during the winter when employment was scarce, a maternity hospital, and a place to die with a semblance of dignity. Standing near it was the Pennsylvania Hospital for the Sick Poor, built in 1755-56 (Figure 29). The first institution of its kind in North America, the hospital admitted mostly those too poor to pay a doctor who would treat them at home.

Recovering the lives of ordinary Philadelphians, such as those who went to the Hospital for the Sick Poor or to the almshouse, is hampered severely from the disappearance of most material evidence that would show how they conducted their lives, at home and at the workplace, and what they knew, thought, or cared about. Ironically, the impoverished and desolate in the social basement of urban society are more visible than the ordinary people above them—the countless, anonymous people who inhabited the lower middle class. Nobody noticed the plodders as much as the desperate. While institutions rarely collected materials from the middle, they often gathered evidence, if inadvertently, from the bottom.

This has happened in two ways. First, because the poor were the objects of reformers' zeal and the recipients of institutional assistance, their lives were recorded, very briefly to be sure, in the records of the criminal justice and poor relief systems. For example, the Pennsylvania Hospital's admission and financial records, along with rough minutes of its managers and medical staff, have been maintained nearly intact for more than two centuries. They provide historians with fascinating windows into the lives and travails of the laboring poor. So do the admission records of the Bettering House, supplemented by managers' records, which are housed at the Archives of the City of Philadelphia and are largely complete from the 1760s forward.

Second, because Philadelphia's wealthy merchants, lawyers, and land speculators were also the city's philanthropists, social reformers, and government officials, the traces of lower-class life are buried in what collecting societies assiduously acquired: double-entry ledgers, commercial correspondence, and, lodged in these commercial papers, records of charitable contributions, scraps of court proceedings, and material related to managing churches. In an era before modern record-keeping and before civil service, fragments of municipal records—even tax assessors' lists and quarter-session court records—surface in the private papers of civic leaders. For example, buried in the papers of Thomas Wharton, an important Philadelphia merchant in the late colonial era, is his proposal for building a new kind of poorhouse—the genesis of the so-called Bettering House. In this single document one finds evidence of changing attitudes toward the poor, as Quakers attempted to administer tough love to the down-and-out (an experiment that failed in a matter of years). Similarly, when the Historical Society leaders acquired the Wharton-Willing Papers by gift in 1973, adding to their hefty materials on two of the city's great eighteenth-century merchant families, they unexpectedly found buried in this rich collection the records of the Committee to Alleviate the Miseries of the Poor, an ad hoc group that distributed wood, blankets, and stockings in the bitter winter of 1761-62 and inscribed the name of each recipient—comprising, in effect, a group portrait of laboring families carried downward. Here, in capsule, was the story of the deranging effects of the Seven Years' War, the re-sorting of social classes in an era of commercial growth, and the evidence that in Franklin's Philadelphia not every leather-aproned artisan could cash in on Ben's penny aphorisms contained in "The Art of Making Money Plenty in Every Man's Pocket." One era's tastes and priorities in collecting have fortuitously provided materials for historians of another era with new questions to ask about the past. Much old wine has been decanted into new bottles.

If Pennsylvania was the "best poor man's country in the world," at least in good times and for many men, was it also the best poor woman's country in the world? The study of women's roles and contributions to the making of urban society is relatively new, but it is becoming a thriving subject of inquiry.[25] The founders and later directors of the Historical Society and other collecting institutions were little interested in this topic—and indeed historians, most of them males, were only occasionally drawn to the subject for generations after the Society's founding. Moreover, most of the Historical Society's holdings that bear on female lives tell us about women married to wealthy and publicly prominent men. The sources that would allow an investigation of how ordinary women helped shape church life, work life, and community life are much thinner. Still, the study of urban women that has been undertaken in the past several decades—drawing on constable's lists of householders, tax lists, probate records, newspaper advertisements, account books, diaries, correspondence, and ephemera—is now bringing Philadelphia's female world into view.

Over the years, the Historical Society, Library Company, and Philosophical Society did acquire the writings—letters, diaries, memoirs, accounts, and other materials—of a few eighteenth-century women, and now this has become a collecting priority everywhere. One of the most valuable is the diary of Elizabeth Sandwith Drinker (1734-1807). Married to Henry Drinker, a member of the Philadelphia Quaker elite, Elizabeth began her diary when she was twenty-four and kept it faithfully until she was near death, at age seventy-three. She was an astute observer of the world around her, and from the thirty-three manuscript volumes of the diary, acquired in 1955, can be garnered an abundance of information on family life, women's education and intellectual life, medical practices, household management and employer relations with servants, and the changing character of the city's neighborhoods.[26]

The Philadelphia Enlightenment

Few affluent Philadelphians doubted that hard work, sobriety, and moderation were the keys to social progress and personal advancement. To them, society was like a machine, the parts of which had to be improved and kept in good working order. As their city grew, many prosperous Philadelphians devoted some of their time and wealth to cultural activities and civic improvements. This benefited the city while fostering an identity among the wealthy as a distinct class with special claims to social authority. Most of the founders and early members of the Library Company, the Philosophical Society, and the Historical Society were descended from this group, which ushered in the American Enlightenment.

Philadelphia became an American center of the Enlightenment, a European intellectual movement based on the notion of human progress through rational thought and civic concern. From the city's merchants, lawyers, and prospering craftsmen came the Library Company (1731), which was America's first lending library, the College of Philadelphia (1751), the Pennsylvania Hospital for the Sick Poor (1752), the American Philosophical Society (1769), and numerous other organizations dedicated to promoting culture and perfecting the human condition.

Benjamin Franklin personified the Enlightenment's commitment to the acquisition of knowledge for bettering humankind. From helping to found America's first circulating library to designing a more efficient wood stove for heating rooms to installing the first streetlights in Philadelphia, Franklin was the civic improver par excellence.[27]

Franklin's fascination with electricity gained him international recognition. In 1746, already a successful printer and earnest civic organizer, he began his experiments. In that year, a Dutchman, Pieter van Musschenbroek, had learned how to condense electricity in a glass bottle (called a Leyden jar) and to produce electrical sparks by attaching a conductor to the two sides of the bottle. Throughout Europe, amateur scientists began to play with this device, but nobody really understood the source or the nature of the mysterious electrical "fluid."

By 1748, Franklin had constructed a number of experiments in his house on Market Street for producing brilliant sparks from Leyden jars. His *Experiments and Observations on Electricity Made at Philadelphia in America* was published in London three years later, putting his name on the lips of scientists all over Europe. Far more important than his household experiments, however, was his development of the technical means to test what many already believed—that lightning produced by thunderstorms was a form of electricity. His famous kite experiment constituted a breakthrough of one of the most formidable barriers of the unknown and opened up an entirely new field of controlled study and human advancement (Figure 30).

Franklin's Philadelphia experiments with electricity represented Enlightenment thinking at its practical best because it used ideas, or what we call scientific theory, to harness nature. Once he had learned the properties of electricity and had established that lightning was a form of it, he found it relatively easy to contrive a metal rod, coated to prevent rusting, that would "throw off" the electricity and render it harmless. By 1753, convinced that he had mastered the theory of electricity and lightning, Franklin published a practical essay, "How to Secure Houses &c. from Lightning," in his best-selling *Poor Richard's Almanack*. Here he explained a natural phenomenon that had always terrified people, providing the world with a relatively simple and inexpensive device to protect lives and property. Soon lightning rods appeared on houses and barns all over the American colonies, then before long in Europe and other parts of the world. Farmers, homeowners, mariners, and church wardens could rest easier, knowing that their dwellings, stables, houses, ships, and churches were safe. What had seemed to be the wrathful work of an angry God now became a force within the power of human beings to control. If the power of lightning could be harnessed by the son of a Boston candlemaker far from the centers of learning in Europe, what other forces of nature might be understood and brought under rein? "Franklin's reputation was more universal than that of Leibniz or Newton, Frederick or Voltaire," John Adams later wrote. "There was scarcely a peasant or a citizen . . . who did not consider him a friend to human kind."[28]

FIGURE 30. Benjamin West, *Benjamin Franklin Drawing Electricity from the Sky*, c.1805, PMA. Franklin's house was about to be demolished and Benjamin West was nearing the end of his life when he painted this heroic portrait. Of course, when Franklin conducted his famous kite experiment in 1752 he was not surrounded by cherubs (one in an Indian headdress); only his son William was at his side. However, the thunderstorm and the key tied to a metal kite string were real. West conveniently has cherubs playing with Franklin's electrical apparatus. Paintings of Philadelphia's most famous son were as migratory as the man himself. West's descendants in England kept this painting until 1898; then it was sold several times at auction in London, Paris, and New York before returning to the Philadelphia area in 1927.

In 1789, when Franklin was near death, the Philosophical Society commissioned Charles Willson Peale to paint a half-length portrait of the internationally recognized scientist. The ailing Franklin could pose for only fifteen minutes a day and died on April 17, 1790. Peale finished the work from memory, aided by his Franklin portrait of 1785. Peale depicted Franklin holding the manuscript for his famous book, *Experiments and Observations on Electricity*. The American Philosophical Society rejected the painting, perhaps because they did not consider it to be a life portrait. That act redounded to the Historical Society's good fortune, because more than half a century later James J. Barclay, a Philadelphia lawyer and an officer of the Historical Society, donated the portrait to the society.

Statesman as well as scientist, Franklin spent fifteen years in London between 1757 and 1775 as a colonial agent for the legislatures of Pennsylvania and several other colonies. These were the years when the American Enlightenment in Philadelphia began to influence the lives of several thousand Africans toiling in the city, all but a few of them as slaves. The origins of Philadelphia's reputation as an international capital of humanitarian reform now began with a tiny number who spoke out against slavery. The first whites to protest, four recently arrived German immigrants in Germantown, uttered their detestation of slavery in 1688. They were appalled that the Quaker colony, established for liberty of conscience, should deny men and women "liberty of the body," and they pointed to the inconsistency between professing pacifism and engaging in slavery, which was inherently violent. But for many years thereafter the only souls to decry slavery were regarded as misfits and disturbers of the peace. Such a man was Benjamin Lay. A former Barbadian slave owner, Lay joined the Society of Friends and moved to Philadelphia in 1731. He used personal example and dramatic acts to portray the evil of slavery. Lay made his own clothes to avoid materials grown with slave labor and publicly smashed his wife's teacups to discourage use of slave-produced sugar. His fiery condemnation of slavery, *All Slave-keepers, That Keep the Innocent in Bondage, Apostates* (1737) led to his repudiation by the Society of Friends. Not until he was near death in 1758, when the engraving in Figure 31 was done by Henry Dawkins, was his cause adopted officially by the Society of Friends.

Lay was followed by other antislavery spokesmen, though they were few in number before the American Revolution. The most committed and best known were John Woolman and Anthony Benezet. Both were ascetic and totally committed, caring little for the comforts of life or about the opinions of their contemporaries. These were the two humble men—one a tailor, the other a teacher of small children—who finally moved the Society of Friends to take a series of official positions against slavery between 1754 and 1774. In the latter year, the Society prohibited slave owning, and thereafter all Quakers had to release their slaves or face disownment by the Society of Friends. Decades of antislavery labor lay ahead, but a beginning had been made.[29]

Science and higher education were also part of Philadelphia's leadership in the American Enlightenment. In 1751, under Franklin's impetus, the Academy of Philadelphia, a nonsectarian school of higher education, held its first classes. It was granted college sta-

FIGURE 31. Henry Dawkins, *Benjamin Lay*, engraving, 1758, Haverford College. The engraving includes a basket of fruit—Lay was a vegetarian—and Lay is seen outside a cave he used as a retreat for meditation on his farm in Abington. Lay holds a book inscribed "TRION ON HAPPINESS"—a reference to the work of an early English Quaker, Thomas Tryon, whose *The Way to Health, Long Life and Happiness* (London, 1683) set forth a theory of temperance and moderation as the keys to a long and happy life. The painting from which the engraving was taken, by William Williams, who aroused Benjamin West's interest in painting, is at the National Gallery of Art in Washington.

FIGURE 32. Astronomical clock built by David Rittenhouse, APS. Instrument maker Rittenhouse built this clock for his observatory at Norriton and used it for his famous observation of the transit of Venus in 1769. Many prized Rittenhouse materials have found their way, by gift or purchase, to the Athenaeum, Historical Society, Library Company, Philosophical Society, and Atwater Kent Museum. Hundreds of pages of his meteorological observations in the 1780s and 1790s were presented to the Philosophical Society in 1898. The Society acquired the clock in about 1810 from Rittenhouse's executors. The centennial of Rittenhouse's birth went unnoticed in 1832, but Philadelphia celebrated the bicentenary in the middle of the Great Depression with modest fanfare.

tus four years later, but not until 1779 was it renamed the University of the State of Pennsylvania. The first board of trustees of the college included Anglicans and Presbyterians but only a few Quakers. The Society of Friends had traditionally rejected the more esoteric aspects of higher education in favor of practical learning. From its early period the college desultorily collected historical materials, but its connection with Franklin made it an important holder of Frankliniana.

Like his friend Benjamin Franklin, David Rittenhouse (1732-96) was a scientist, inventor, successful businessman, and Revolutionary leader. George Washington recognized his expertise as a mathematician and instrument maker by appointing him the first Superintendent of the United States Mint. Rittenhouse began his career as a clockmaker and gained fame in 1769 by observing the transit of Venus (Figure 32). His orrery, a moving mechanical model of the solar system based on precise mathematical calculations, also brought him fame. Both the Philosophical Society and the Library Company were venues of scientific experimentation, and Rittenhouse belonged to both, serving as the Philosophical Society's president after Franklin died in 1790.

Cosmopolitan from the beginning because of Penn's doctrine of religious tolerance and an open-door policy for immigrants, Philadelphia at the end of the colonial period stood on the threshold of receiving a new storm of strangers. As the largest North American town and situated midway between the two oldest areas of settlement and commercial development—New England and the Chesapeake—Penn's "greene country towne" was about to become the center of the revolutionary government that for ten years, from 1774 to 1783, coordinated the bloody fight to gain American independence. Into the city came delegates from all thirteen colonies to the First and Second Continental Congresses, along with those whom the Congress designated to go abroad as the nation's first emissaries. Through Philadelphia poured American and British armies. Into the city came French and Spanish diplomats, Indian chiefs, titled aristocrats eager to fight for the American cause, and streams of individuals displaced by the war. The commercial city was becoming the city of revolution.

Chapter 3

THE REVOLUTION'S MANY FACES

The American Revolution was the central event in the lives of most of those who lived through it. It engaged the passions and interests of nearly everyone and promised to usher in a new age. "We have it in our power to begin the world over again," wrote Philadelphia's famous pamphleteer, Thomas Paine. "A situation similar to the present has not happened since the days of Noah until now. The birthday of a new world is at hand."[1]

While the Revolution shaped the lives of most of its participants, it also became the touchstone of succeeding generations, especially those who were historically minded. In the fashioning of public memory in Philadelphia, the Revolution became a central event. However, this did not happen spontaneously or continually. The public had to be reminded and instructed again and again. But given the diverse and contrasting views its Philadelphia participants had held, stimulating, massaging, and managing public memory always ran into the problem of deciding just what the American Revolution meant. As later chapters will make clear, preserving a stable narrative of the Revolution was nearly as difficult as Washington's attempt to hold together a stable Continental army.

The difficulties in sustaining a unified view of the Revolution could hardly have been otherwise because the war was a continuously shifting and painfully ambiguous affair for the diverse people of the Philadelphia region (Figure 33). At bottom, of course, it was a bloody struggle to secure independence from what most colonists regarded as a corrupt and tyrannical English government. But it was also a prolonged negotiation among people of different points of view about what kind of society they wished to create should good fortune allow them to win the war. This debate divided families, neighbors, churches, and occupational groups, not only between "loyalists" and "patriots" but also among rebels who varied from conservative to radical on vexed internal questions: the breadth of the franchise, the powers of the governor, tax burdens, the criminal code, emancipating slaves, and much more. Casting themselves into a state of nature after renouncing the English charter and law under which they had lived, Pennsylvanians had to decide just what kind of laws, political structures, and constitutionally protected liberties they wished to live under and by what means they should create these new governmental arrangements.

This task proved difficult and divisive. United in their desire to begin anew as an in-

FIGURE 33. Edward Lamson Henry, *Cliveden During the Battle of Germantown*, Cliveden of the National Trust. On October 3, 1777, Washington's ragged Continentals attacked the British encamped at Cliveden, the mansion of Benjamin Chew, wealthy Philadelphia Loyalist landowner and officeholder who was exiled to New Jersey. Broken communications and fog contributed to the Americans' defeat in the battle shown in this nineteenth-century recreation. After the war Chew returned to Cliveden and won back his prominence in Philadelphia political and social circles. His descendants lived in the house until 1972, when they presented it to the National Trust for Historic Preservation.

dependent nation, Americans were at the same time frequently divided by region, class, religion, ethnicity, and gender. Nearly everyone carried into the fray an understanding of their own experiences in the colonial period, both in relation to the mother country and to each other. "Can America be happy?" asked Paine. "As happy as she wants, for she hath a clean slate to write upon." That was the rub. With many eager to step forward with chalk to inscribe their hopes for the future upon the blank slate, it took the entire course of the war to sort out competing ideas and to frame solutions. Even then, unresolved questions carried over into the postwar period. If citizens argued strenuously at the time, it is little wonder that their descendants would quarrel heatedly about the "true" nature of the Revolution.

Philadelphia played a central role in the dramatic events leading to war. As the meeting place of the First and Second Continental Congresses, it drew together insurgent leaders from all the colonies; in the prolonged debates over independence in early 1776, Pennsylvania became the "keystone" colony whose willingness to commit for independence proved decisive. During the war, the city was a strategic port and a military staging and production center as well as the center of state and national government.[2]

The founders of the Library Company, the Philosophical Society, and the Historical Society were all keenly interested in collecting material relating to the American Revolution. After all, the city was the nation's birthplace, where the Declaration of Independence was written and signed and where the Continental Congress sat while directing the war. Moreover, Philadelphia was the home of some of the most famous men of '76: Benjamin Franklin, John Dickinson, Thomas Paine, James Wilson, Benjamin Rush, and many others. This initial collecting interest never waned, and down to the present the city's collecting institutions have nourished a special interest in acquiring anything related to the nation's founding. Yet looking back on the Revolution was not a neutral activity, and hence for many years collecting institutions privileged some materials while downgrading others.

Quaker prominence in Philadelphia's cultural institutions has been the source of some confusion and tension in assembling, preserving, and presenting documents and artifacts of the revolutionary era. To put the matter bluntly, the American Revolution was nearly as painful in Quaker remembrance as was the revolutionary experience at the time. For Philadelphia Quakers, the Revolution was a frightful ordeal, the most traumatic chapter in their history. As principled pacifists, they refused to fight or even pay taxes for the war, and many of them were suspected of collaborating or at least sympathizing with the British because of close mercantile ties to overseas partners. On both counts they were reviled, ostracized, and in some cases exiled. All were disenfranchised, and only slowly in the postrevolutionary period did Pennsylvanians put aside their wartime disgust with the Quakers.[3]

The Quakers' patriot opponents were almost as interested as the Quakers themselves in allowing historical amnesia concerning this chapter of the Revolution to blot out remembrance. An internecine struggle hardly fit with the desire to show the revolutionary generation in untarnished, heroic terms, which, in the nineteenth century, was the dominant impulse among historians and historical societies. Nor has it been easy for non-Quaker historians to deal with Quaker pacifism and outright Toryism because of their general admiration of postrevolutionary Quaker efforts on behalf of woman's suffrage, abolition, Indian rights, world peace, and other liberal causes.

For all the pain associated with the Revolution, many of the Library Company's early Quaker councillors, librarians, and patrons knew that historical materials germane to the war for independence were of utmost value. And some had joined the Free Quakers, the splinter group that put aside pacifist principles and fully supported the American cause in word and deed. When the chance arose to acquire a bundle of revolutionary ephemeral materials, just one year after the war ended, the Library Company sprang into action. One of its members, the Swiss immigrant Pierre-Eugène Du Simitière, had assiduously gathered materials that few at the time thought to collect—newspapers, pamphlets, broadsides, cartoons, and prints— in order to write a history of the Revolution. But death claimed Du Simitière in 1784. The Library Company, positioning itself as a national library, promptly purchased his cache at auction, thus becoming a repository of special importance for materials bearing on the American Revolution. This set an unspoken precedent for collecting materials that, while distasteful to many of its leaders and members, could help establish the claim of being a civic public library as distinct from the sectarian libraries at the new nation's small number of colleges.

Nearly half a century later, the Historical Society's early Quaker leaders, remembering vividly the anguish of their parents and grandparents, probably recalled the Revolution as something more than simply "the glorious cause." But they also remembered that time had healed the wartime wounds and Quakers had been reincorporated into Philadelphia society. Materials connected to the Revolution, especially related to the war against England, became priceless items, for the American Revolution had become their heritage too, even if their fathers and grandfathers had opposed it at the time. If Quaker beliefs stressed pacifism, they did not prohibit the preservation of valuable documents from turbulent times.

It can be imagined that the American Philosophical Society's interest in the American Revolution must have been unequivocal, since Franklin, the society's founder, was a central revolutionary figure. Moreover, one year after Franklin's death in 1790, Thomas Jefferson became the institution's president. For many years, however, the Philosophical Society showed only casual interest in acquiring documents concerning the American Revolution. In 1803, when Benjamin Franklin's daughter put her father's library up for sale, the Philosophical Society purchased some books and manuscripts of its patron saint. But not until Du Ponceau proposed the acquisition of historical documents in 1811, a proposal that took another four years to implement when the society created a new historical and literary committee, was any priority given to revolutionary materials. The first fruit of this initiative came in 1815, when the Philosophical Society received a scrapbook of newspaper clippings accumulated by an Irish foot soldier who fought with the British during the Revolution and later became a steward in the household of one of Washington's leading generals—Nathanael Greene. Five years later came the papers of Greene himself, from Robert de Silver, a wealthy Philadelphia stationer and bookseller. In 1825, Richard Henry Lee, a Virginia delegate to and later president of the Continental Congress, presented some of his correspondence.

Not until 1840, when the Philosophical Society's interest in historical materials had waned, did its library acquire one of the crown jewels of revolutionary material—a voluminous collection of Benjamin Franklin's papers. This acquisition is an example of the circuitous disposition of what later generations would regard as priceless treasures. The Franklin papers, including his library of more than four thousand volumes, came indirectly from Benjamin's grandson, William Temple Franklin, who had little use for Philadelphia at all. The illegitimate son of William Franklin (himself an illegitimate offspring of Benjamin), Temple Franklin, as he was known, was raised by a London governess after his birth in 1760 and brought to Philadelphia by his famous grandfather in 1774. When Franklin became the Continental Congress's emissary to France in 1776, he took young Temple with him to Paris as his secretary. Temple returned to Philadelphia after the war but disliked the city. Shortly after his grandfather died in 1790, he returned to London, placing the immense trove of Franklin papers and books in the hands of George Fox, a Philadelphia doctor. Thirty-three years later, on his deathbed, Temple Franklin bequeathed them to Fox, along with his own papers. There they rested until Fox died, leaving the papers in 1840 to his son and daughter, who promptly presented them to the American Philosophical Society. Meanwhile, Franklin's collection had been broken up and sold at various times.[4]

Despite the Quaker leanings of its early councillors, the Historical Society began collecting materials on the violent Revolution just a year after its founding. John Fanning Watson was especially influential. In reply to a circular from the first president, William Rawle, for historical materials, Watson urged in 1825 that the Historical Society make a special effort "to rescue from oblivion, the facts of personal prowess, achievements, or sufferings by officers & soldiers of the Revolutionary War."[5] A pioneer of oral history, he argued that "the recitals of many brave men now going down to the tomb—of what they saw, or heard, or sustained, in that momentous struggle which set us free would form a fund of anecdotes and of individual history well deserving of our preservation." President Rawle's circular calling for materials had included a request for biographical notices of "eminent persons or of any persons in respect to whom remarkable events may have happened," and John Jay Smith, soon to become the librarian of the Library Company, circulated a list of questions regarding the Revolution. Watson added a populist twist, calling for attention to "many privates 'unknown to fame' peculiarly distinguished by their actions" and mentioned, by way of example, Zenas Macumber, a private in Washington's bodyguard who had served through the entire war and survived seventeen wounds.[6] However, the recollections and memorabilia of the Zenas Macumbers of the Revolution did not flow in, as Watson hoped. As close as the Historical Society came was the acquisition of the manuscript diaries of Christopher Marshall, a disowned Quaker druggist who figured importantly in Philadelphia's radical revolutionary circle. Covering the years from 1774 to 1785, the Marshall diaries were the one main source of information on the Revolution acquired in the early years of the Historical Society that told the story from the streets and coffeehouses rather than the counting houses and legislative chambers.

Breaking Ties

Contemplating independence was both exhilarating and frightening because the colonies were only loosely united and faced the world's greatest military power. No wonder, then, that in 1774 John Adams found the idea of independence "a Hobgoblin of so frightful Mien, that it would throw a delicate Person into Fits to look it in the Face."[7] Philadelphians, like other colonists, shuddered and argued for a decade before finally taking the plunge. As hosts of both Continental Congresses, they were first-hand observers of the debate about independence. Their publishing preeminence already established, the city's presses poured forth newspapers, broadsides, and pamphlets, thus assuring an airing of all sides of the question.

But Philadelphians had known political controversy since the early 1700s. The political campaigns of the mid-1760s were especially notable in mobilizing voters and using the press to raise the temperature of political debate. The election of 1764 brought forth

FIGURE 34. *Magna Britania her Colonies Reduc'd*, cartoon, 1765–66, LCP. Philadelphia's printers frequently but selectively copied cartoons from London sources. This cartoon was re-engraved in Philadelphia and distributed in a larger form after the news reached the city of the Townshend duties passed by Parliament in 1767. Du Simitière saved this copy of the card Franklin distributed in London. It is the only surviving copy.

a torrent of scurrilous pamphlets from both sides. "Stop your pamphleteers' mouths & shut up your presses," pleaded a shocked observer. "Such a torrent of low scurrility sure never came from any country as lately from Pennsylvania."[8] In mobilizing a record number of voters in Philadelphia, campaigns such as this helped prepare the ground for revolutionary involvement of ordinary people.

The role of the man in the streets became evident the very next year when boycotts of English goods were organized to force Parliament to repeal the detested Stamp Act of 1764. Philadelphia merchants joined those in other cities to vow they would import no further British goods. But many merchants opposed the nonimportation agreement and joined only "to appease [the people] and indeed for their own safety," as the revolutionary leader Charles Thomson observed.[9] Women, as the main purchasers of imported goods, and ordinary people involved in maintaining boycotts, were coming to the fore.

Political cartoons helped mobilize public opinion. Franklin believed they had greater effect than printed discourses. In Figure 34, a butchered America sits in a desolate scene representing Britain's "Colonies Reduced." An olive branch falls from the hand of the severed Pennsylvania. "The moral is," wrote Franklin to his sister, "that the Colonies may be ruined, but that Britain would thereby be maimed."[10] The motto, "Date Obolum Bellisario" (Give a Penny to Belisarius), asks members of Parliament, to whom Franklin had this cartoon-on-card delivered the day before the debate on repealing the Stamp Act, to remember that the Roman general Belisarius was blinded and left to beg for alms after accused of a conspiracy against Justinian. American protests forced the repeal of the hated Stamp Act, although Parliament continued to insist on its right to pass laws affecting the colonies without the assent of colonial representatives.

By the time Parliament passed the Tea Act in 1773, the artisans, mariners, and shopkeepers in Philadelphia had found their political voice and were nominating men from their own ranks for local and provincial offices. Conservatives within the merchant elite looked askance at this, one of them in Philadelphia sputtering that "the Mechanics . . . have no Right to *Speak* or *Think* for themselves."[11] But the artisans pushed on. They were prominent in the Committee for Tarring and Feathering, organized in October 1773. Six weeks later, the Committee published a strongly worded broadside (Figure 35) warning Delaware River pilots not to conduct British ships carrying tea into the port of Philadelphia. John Adams later told Benjamin Rush that these Philadelphians had inspired the Boston Tea Party. Similar broadsides encouraged women, who bought and served tea, to join the boycott.

Some artisans not only served as committeemen and street marshals during demonstrations but also became fervent propagandists for the patriot cause. Silversmith John Leacock used art as well as artisanry. Although associated with Philadelphia's Sons of Liberty, Leacock was never elected to one of the city's radical committees. But he made his contribution in an action-packed play published as the Second Continental Congress took the final steps toward independence. Widely advertised in the Philadelphia newspapers, Leacock's *Fall of British Tyranny: or, American Liberty Triumphant* had a diverse cast of characters who spoke sailor's bawdry, Roman oratory, and black dialect in a series of satiric vignettes lambasting the British and celebrating the Americans who resisted their tyrannical designs.

Like many well-to-do leaders, Philadelphia's John Dickinson feared the rising political consciousness of those beneath him. In 1768, Dickinson had published one of the most important protest pieces of the period, "The Patriotic American Farmer" or "Letters from a Farmer in Pennsylvania," which appeared serially in the *Pennsylvania Chronicle.* But by 1776, by which time Philadelphia's working people had become numerous on the committees that were assuming de facto powers of government, he had moderated his protests. A delegate to the second Continental Congress, he could not bring himself to sign the Declaration of Independence. At about the time the young Marylander Charles Willson Peale, who had recently arrived in Philadelphia, painted Dickinson's portrait in 1770. John Adams described Dickinson as "a Shadow—tall, but slender as a Reed—pale as ashes. One would think at first Sight that he would not live a Month."[12]

One of the men who frightened lawyers like John Dickinson was Thomas Paine, the tousled immigrant stay maker who emerged from obscurity only a year before the Revolution to play a major role in the final break with England. The hardhitting, pungent language of Paine's *Common Sense* contrasted sharply with the formal, legalistic rhetoric of

TO THE

Delaware Pilots.

WE took the Pleaſure, ſome Days ſince, of kindly admoniſhing you *to do your Duty*; if perchance you ſhould meet with the *(Tea,)* SHIP POLLY, CAPTAIN AYRES; a THREE DECKER which is hourly expected.

We have now to add, that Matters ripen faſt here; and that *much is expected from thoſe Lads who meet with the Tea Ship.*----There is ſome Talk of A HANDSOME REWARD FOR THE PILOT WHO GIVES THE FIRST GOOD ACCOUNT OF HER.----How that may be, we cannot *for certain* determine: But ALL agree, that TAR and FEATHERS will be his Portion, who pilots her into this Harbour. And we will anſwer for ourſelves, that, whoever is committed to us, as an Offender againſt the Rights of *America*, will experience the utmoſt Exertion of our Abilities; as

THE COMMITTEE FOR TARRING AND FEATHERING.

P. S. We expect you will furniſh yourſelves with Copies of the foregoing and following Letter; which are printed for this Purpoſe, that the Pilot who meets with Captain *Ayres* may favor him with a Sight of them.

Committee of Taring and Feathering.

TO

Capt. AYRES,

Of the SHIP *POLLY*, on a Voyage from *London* to *Philadelphia.*

SIR,

WE are informed that you have, imprudently, taken Charge of a Quantity of Tea; which has been ſent out by the *India* Company, *under the Auſpices of the Miniſtry*, as a Trial of *American* Virtue and Reſolution.

Now, as your Cargo, on your Arrival here, will moſt aſſuredly bring you into hot water; and as you are perhaps a Stranger *to theſe Parts*, we have concluded to adviſe you of the preſent Situation of Affairs in *Philadelphia*---that, taking Time by the Forelock, you may ſtop ſhort in your dangerous Errand----ſecure your Ship againſt the Rafts of combuſtible Matter which may be ſet on Fire, and turned looſe againſt her; and more than all this, that you may preſerve your own Perſon, from the Pitch and Feathers that are prepared for you.

In the firſt Place, we muſt tell you, that the *Pennſylvanians* are, *to a Man*, paſſionately fond of Freedom; the Birthright of *Americans*; and at all Events are determined to enjoy it.

That they ſincerely believe, no Power on the Face of the Earth has a Right to tax them without their Conſent.

That in their Opinion, the Tea in your Cuſtody is deſigned by the Miniſtry to enforce ſuch a Tax, which they will undoubtedly oppoſe; and in ſo doing, give you every poſſible Obſtruction.

We are nominated to a very diſagreeable, but neceſſary Service.---- To our Care are committed all Offenders againſt the Rights of *America*; and hapleſs is he, whoſe evil Deſtiny has doomed him to ſuffer at our Hands.

You are ſent out on a diabolical Service; and if you are ſo fooliſh and obſtinate as to compleat your Voyage; by bringing your Ship to Anchor in this Port; you may run ſuch a Gauntlet, as will induce you, in your laſt Moments, moſt heartily to curſe thoſe who have made you the Dupe of their Avarice and Ambition.

What think you Captain, of a Halter around your Neck----ten Gallons of liquid Tar decanted on your Pate----with the Feathers of a dozen wild Geeſe laid over that to enliven your Appearance?

Only think ſeriouſly of this----and fly to the Place from whence you came----fly without Heſitation----without the Formality of a Proteſt----and above all, Captain *Ayres* let us adviſe you to fly without the wild Geeſe Feathers.

Your Friends *to ſerve*

Philadelphia, Nov. 27, 1773 THE COMMITTEE *as before ſubſcribed*

FIGURE 35. *To the Delaware Pilots*, broadside, 1773, LCP. The wording in the broadside could hardly have been stronger: "*Pennsylvanians* are, *to a Man*, passionately fond of *Freedom*; the Birthright of *Americans*"; "no Power on the Face of the Earth has a Right to tax them without their Consent"; "What think you Captain, of a Halter around your Neck—ten Gallons of liquid Tar decanted on your Pate—with the Feathers of a dozen wild Geese laid over that to enliven your Appearance?" The Library Company purchased this broadside from Du Simitière's collection, along with other ephemera from Philadelphia's version of the more famous Boston Tea Party. The Historical Society acquired a copy 138 years later.

most protest pamphlets written by lawyers and clergymen. This helped make it the most widely read and influential tract in the protests against England.[13] But the Historical Society collected almost nothing related to Paine over the years—partly by happenstance, perhaps, but also indicative of the faint interest its councillors had in radicals such as Paine, who wanted not only independence but a thorough reformation of American society in the interest of greater equality. The Library Company had acquired *Common Sense* and also Paine's *American Crisis* as part of the Du Simitière purchase. But not until 1895, with eminent historians on its council, did the Historical Society purchase a copy of *Common Sense* owned by Paine's radical, warm-tempered compatriot, Timothy Matlack, a brewer who was disowned by the Quakers for chronic indebtedness and unruly behavior. The following year the society shelved "Eulogy of Thomas Paine," deposited by a Philadelphia physician in 1896, and not until 1921 did members hear a lecture on "The Real Thomas Paine, Patriot and Publicist; A Philosopher Misunderstood." Though the revolution's greatest propagandist was a member of the Philosophical Society, only in 1971 did the society receive by gift a rich assemblage of Paine materials—editions of his many books, letters, accounts and receipts, verses, and commentary on the author of *Common Sense*, *The American Crisis*, *Age of Reason*, and *Rights of Man*. The collection had been gathered lovingly over many years by Richard Gimbel, who fought Philadelphia officials for years to restore Paine to public memory by placing a bust of Paine in the Independence Hall Museum.

In June 1776, when the Pennsylvania members of the Continental Congress held back on the issue of independence, artisans and shopkeepers virtually took over the provincial government and demanded that their representatives support the break with England. This was history-making from the bottom up, though the full story was not told by historians until the 1960s. In 1891, the Historical Society acquired a fragment of John Dunlap's uncorrected printer's proof of the Declaration of Independence, representing perhaps the earliest version of the document to appear in print as a broadside. When Philadelphians heard the Declaration read aloud from the State House steps on July 8, they shouted "Huzzah!" Then they tore the royal coat of arms from above the State House door and tossed that symbol of colonial dependency into a roaring bonfire in what amounted to a king-killing ritual, the flames representing the transfer of sovereign power from George III to the American people at large.

One of the icons of American nationalism is the depiction of the signing of the Declaration of Independence. The best-known rendering of that event is John Trumbull's *Signing of the Declaration of Independence* (Figure 1). But the painting by Edward Savage (Figure 36) presents a truer picture than Trumbull's and provides a powerful example of how a single picture of the past can inform the contemporary restorationist movement. When the National Park Service became custodian of Independence Hall after World War II, its desire to restore the interior rooms of Independence Hall to their original condition led to research proving that the paneling portrayed in the Savage painting was much more accurate than in the Trumbull version. Included in this restoration of the 1960s were the replacement of upholstered leather armchairs, lovingly collected and in-

FIGURE 36. Edward Savage, *The Congress Voting Independence*, oil, HSP. Savage's painting is thought to have been partly based on an earlier unfinished portrayal of the Declaration's signing by Robert Edge Pine, an English immigrant who was attracted to the American Revolutionary cause and started a series of large historical paintings in the United States between 1784 and 1788. It may have been acquired by Savage, who completed his own painting about 1801. A definitive identification of all the figures in the painting is not possible. Some, like Franklin, are obvious, scholars disagree about others, and some are too indistinct to guess at. The identification of some figures, like that of Francis Hopkinson (leaning on the table near the center of the painting), are based on single portraits by Pine.

stalled during the refurbishing of Independence Hall for the 1876 Centennial Exposition. The Savage painting showed un-upholstered Windsor chairs in the famed Assembly Room, and National Park Service research also confirmed this detail. Windsor chairs were acquired to replace the unauthentic ones, leaving the descendants of the donors of the upholstered chairs crestfallen at the demoted status of prized heirlooms.[14]

When the Historical Society had an opportunity to purchase this painting in 1904, its leaders hastened to do so because such a painting fit perfectly into their view of the society as a temple for studying and contemplating the nation's origins and for inculcating national pride. Charles Henry Hart, one of the first historians of early American painting, had found the canvas languishing in a dark corner of the Boston Public Museum and sold it to the Historical Society for $600.

Of much less interest to the city's collecting institutions was an independence movement of a different kind—the breaking of ties between enslaved Philadelphians and their masters. Before and during the Revolution, the rhetoric of liberty and natural rights spilled over to areas not intended by the first protesters of British colonial policy in the 1760s. Enslaved Africans petitioned in other towns for their freedom. While no such petitions from Philadelphia slaves have surfaced, it can be imagined that they were moved toward action when, just five days before the minutemen took their stand at Concord and Lexington, ten white Philadelphians met to establish the first antislavery society in the world. Their immediate concern was the enslavement of an Indian woman, Dinah Nevill, and her three children, but the larger issue was the entrenched system of racial slavery that held one out of five inhabitants of the colonies in lifelong bondage. Almost a century after the founding of the Pennsylvania Abolition Society in 1775, the Historical Society began receiving its voluminous records, a source almost unexcelled for studying both abolitionism and African American life in the late eighteenth and early nineteenth centuries.

Loyal Subjects and Subjected Loyalists

Textbooks have usually taught us that the loyalists who remained faithful to the English crown were too selfish or timid to join the revolutionaries. In truth, the loyalists were a mixed group with widely varying motives. Some, like Benjamin Franklin's friend Joseph Galloway, had been early protesters against English policy but grew alarmed when ordinary Philadelphians began to take matters into their own hands and call for internal reforms as well as independence. Men like Galloway wanted independence but not a social revolution. Franklin's only son, William, remained loyal because he had served proudly as the royal governor of New Jersey and had acquired thoroughly English tastes when growing up with his father in London.

Anglican clergymen in America formed another group torn between loyalty to their English-directed church and their affection for their native ground. For example, the Reverend Jacob Duché, rector of the united parishes of Christ Church and St. Peter's, initially favored American independence. But many in his congregations were wealthy Philadelphians lukewarm or opposed to independence. Duché began to have misgivings after the Declaration of Independence, changed allegiances again when General Sir William Howe jailed him during the British occupation of 1777-78, and finally made a decision, in December 1777, to immigrate to London. A few months, later his wife and children followed him. There his son Thomas studied with Benjamin West, who, as the king's painter, was in no position to favor the American cause openly. As happened to many loyalists, Duché's American property was confiscated by order of the Pennsylvania Assembly, and he was not permitted to return until 1792.[15]

Philadelphia's collecting institutions therefore have little to show that would restore memory about the city's loyalists, except some materials relating to members of the Society of Friends. Many loyalists, such as William Franklin, Galloway, and Duché, voluntarily left for England or Nova Scotia or were driven out, taking their papers with them. The descendants of other loyalists who eventually returned had little reason in the nine-

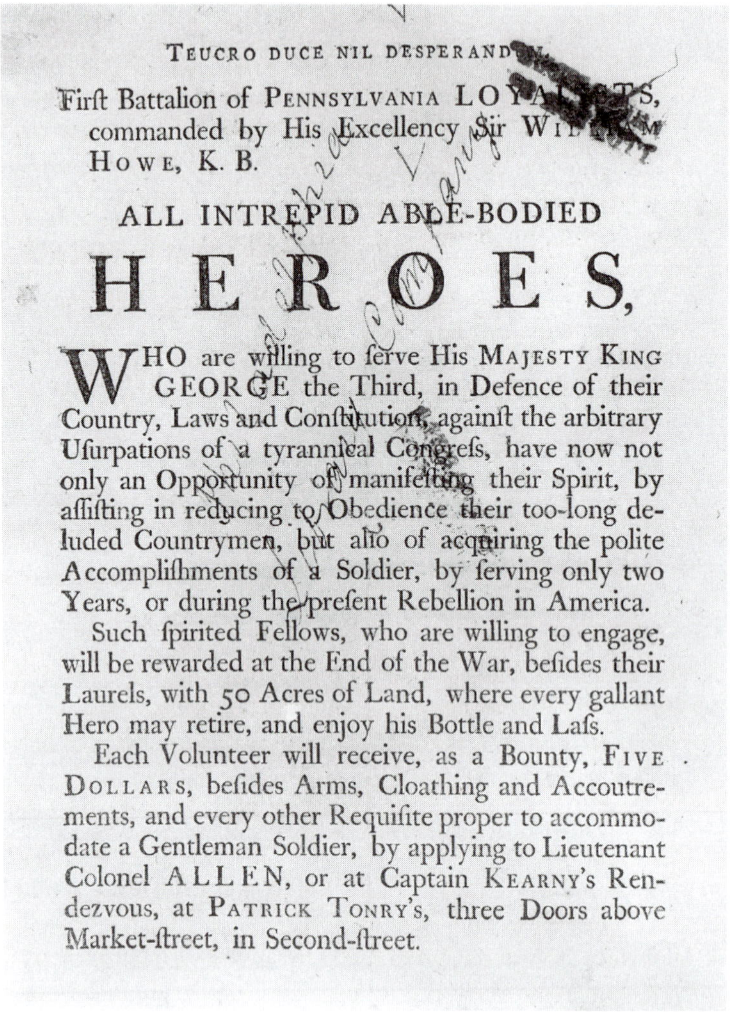

TEUCRO DUCE NIL DESPERANDUM.

Firſt Battalion of PENNSYLVANIA LOYALISTS, commanded by His Excellency Sir WILLIAM HOWE, K. B.

ALL INTREPID ABLE-BODIED

HEROES,

WHO are willing to ſerve His MAJESTY KING GEORGE the Third, in Defence of their Country, Laws and Conſtitution, againſt the arbitrary Uſurpations of a tyrannical Congreſs, have now not only an Opportunity of manifeſting their Spirit, by aſſiſting in reducing to Obedience their too-long deluded Countrymen, but alſo of acquiring the polite Accompliſhments of a Soldier, by ſerving only two Years, or during the preſent Rebellion in America.

Such ſpirited Fellows, who are willing to engage, will be rewarded at the End of the War, beſides their Laurels, with 50 Acres of Land, where every gallant Hero may retire, and enjoy his Bottle and Laſs.

Each Volunteer will receive, as a Bounty, FIVE DOLLARS, beſides Arms, Cloathing and Accoutrements, and every other Requiſite proper to accommodate a Gentleman Soldier, by applying to Lieutenant Colonel ALLEN, or at Captain KEARNY's Rendezvous, at PATRICK TONRY's, three Doors above Market-ſtreet, in Second-ſtreet.

FIGURE 37. First Battalion of Pennsylvania Loyalists recruitment broadside, LCP. How many "intrepid able-bodied HEROES" signed up for two years service and the promise to retire on fifty acres, in any county of his choice, to "enjoy his Bottle and Lass"? In New Jersey and southern New York, the British had no difficulty recruiting thousands of men. But the First Battalion of Pennsylvania Loyalists never formed, and only about forty-five men enlisted in a troop of Philadelphia Light Dragoons recruited in November and December 1777. Many wavering Philadelphians, presumably knowing that the promise of land in this broadside presupposed American defeat, saw the signing bonus as an empty promise.

teenth century to preserve the papers of parents and grandparents who refused to support the American cause. Nor were Philadelphia's collectors much interested in ferreting out archival materials or spending money on them to preserve a record documenting those who chose the losing side in the American Revolution. The collectors' passion was mainly directed at rekindling what they imagined were the spirit-stirring times of "the glorious cause." Diaries of Grace Growden Galloway, the wife of Philadelphia's most unpopular Tory, did survive because Mrs. Galloway was intent on saving the family's vast properties and was unwilling to follow her husband to England. Copies of letters and diaries of loyalist Rebecca Shoemaker and her daughters also made their way into the Historical Society's collections, but this was not until 1945, when the stigma of loyalism had passed after two world wars in which the Americans and the British were allies.

The appeal of loyalism operated among ordinary as well as wealthy Pennsylvanians. Some poor German immigrants, with particular grievances against Pennsylvania's government, were drawn to the Loyalist side. And many Americans were simply "sunshine patriots," as Paine called them. Looking to see where the wind blew, they changed sides when the revolutionary cause faltered. When the British captured Philadelphia in September 1777, they plastered the town with broadsides recruiting Philadelphians to the Queen's Rangers and First Battalion of Pennsylvania Loyalists (Figure 37).[16]

For hundreds of enslaved Philadelphians, the prospect of gaining freedom by fighting with the British was irresistible. Wherever the British army went, they fled their masters and joined up, inspired by Lord Dunmore's promise in 1775 of freedom to slaves and indentured servants. Many masters advertised for their runaway slaves in Philadelphia's newspapers, especially when the British were occupying Philadelphia between September 1777 and June 1778. Hundreds of former slaves from the southern colonies had their first look at the City of Brotherly Love when they arrived as part of the Black Guides and Pioneers, a regiment wholly composed of escaped slaves who fought throughout the war under Scottish officers.[17]

The British recruited not only African Americans but also thousands of Hessians, transported across the Atlantic as mercenaries to fight against the rebellious colonists. Thirty German regiments—with an estimated 35,000 soldiers—fought against the Americans. They sustained 12,000 casualties; another 5,000 were lost through desertion, most of whom took up life in the United States; and 18,000 returned home. On several occasions the Hessians fought against other Pennsylvanians who were natives of Germany or the sons of German immigrants, and what has been collected about this fratricidal story and how the Hessian deserters disappeared into New York and Pennsylvania German communities is remarkable for its thinness. One rare and intriguing artifact that has survived is a Hessian regimental flag captured by the Americans at the Battle of Trenton on December 26, 1776. The Historical Society received the flag, seized from 900 Hessian prisoners who were paraded through Philadelphia before being marched off to prison in Lancaster, as a gift in 1882.

Besides Hessians, the Americans had to face most of the eastern Indian tribes, who chose to join the redcoats; these tribes regarded the British as their protectors, whereas the Americans threatened their land and political sovereignty. Lieutenant Colonel Adam Hubley commanded the Eleventh Pennsylvania Regiment, composed of Pennsylvanian Germans, against the Mohawks in the Wyoming Valley of western Pennsylvania during General John Sullivan's grim campaign against the Iroquois tribes. In his journal, which the Historical Society acquired early in the twentieth century, Hubley sketched

FIGURE 38. Charles Willson Peale, *Joseph Brant*, oil, c. 1797, INHP. Peale did his part through his portrait of Brant to turn the greatly feared war chief fighting against the Americans into an admirable, bicultural figure—"a scientific curiosity," as Peale's main biographer puts it—who could fit well into Peale's new natural history museum. In this oil painting, we see not the fierce warrior of revolutionary days but a face "full of mildness and hope," signaling the harmony among Native Americans and whites that Peale and many of his generation hoped for. Brant's headdress includes a scalp lock decorated with a white feather, a tuft of grass, and red and white roses. The black headband has a double row of silver rings.

the plan of his encampment at Wyoming and copied the symbols the Indians painted on the forest trees. One of the Mohawk leaders that Hubley must have encountered was Thayendanegea, known to the Americans as Joseph Brant (Figure 38). Educated at what became Dartmouth College and a devoted Anglican, Thayendanegea had fought with the Americans during the Seven Years' War as a young man. But by 1776, after a trip to

England to parley with George III and his ministers, he was convinced that the Iroquois could maintain their independence only if the Americans did not gain theirs. Commissioned a captain in the British army, he led his people against the Americans in southern New York and northern Pennsylvania in some of the bloodiest fighting of the revolution. After the war, Thayendanegea pursued the Iroquois' interest in negotiations with Great Britain and the United States. Peale painted Joseph Brant, probably in 1797 when Brant made his last visit to Philadelphia, adding the painting to his public portrait gallery. By then, the bitterness about the Iroquois alliance with the British had dissipated, and the public's attention was focused on the diplomatic crisis with revolutionary France.[18]

The Spirit of '76

Later generations would recall how the "Spirit of '76" sustained the Americans in their uphill struggle against mighty England, and indeed the military aspects of the Revolution would come to dominate public memory, robbing it of much of its reformist zeal. But the initial *rage militaire*, so often celebrated later, seemed sadly lacking at the time. Like other Americans, Philadelphians became discouraged as England's might brought defeat after defeat and the colonists' major seaboard towns fell under British garrison rule until aid from France and Holland helped turn the tide in 1778.

Historians have had a difficult time learning what Americans truly felt during those dark months. Few "sunshine patriots" left records of their doubts, and few Americans in the following generations wanted to remember anything but the "Spirit of '76." After the war, remembering fallen soldiers and spilled blood became a way of imagining a common national community. Later, in a century of national expansion and rapid growth, the male warrior became an iconic figure, and his origins were to be found not only on the colonial Indian frontier but also at Saratoga, Valley Forge, Trenton, and Yorktown. Accordingly, the councillors, officers, and patrons of the city's cultural institutions avidly collected artifacts associated with the Revolution, especially with its military aspects. Motivated by a desire to inculcate *amor patriae* and to impart a unified understanding of the past, they unwaveringly pursued this goal from the 1880s through World War I—an era of the greatest influx of immigrants ever to enter the country, most of them at eastern port cities such as New York and Philadelphia. History became an important part of Americanizing new immigrants, and the history of the nation's beginnings, shown as a heroic sacrifice for "the glorious cause," became an especially vital history lesson. Hence, the kind of material deemed most collectible was that which inspired reverence and awe for the Founding Fathers and military heroes.

"I am determined, as the night is favorable, to cross the river." With these words George Washington, after five months of retreat, took the offensive on Christmas Day in 1776, and the words and the act have reverberated ever since in American history. The "glorious cause" was always most heroic on the battlefield, at least in retrospect. When 2,400 Americans crossed the ice-clogged Delaware River on a snowy Christmas night and took the British by surprise at Trenton, they gained their first and much-needed victory. Thus George Washington's letter to Colonel John Cadwalader, who commanded one of three columns of troops that were part of Washington's plans, became a treasured addition to the Historical Society's collection of Revolutionary materials after descendants of Cadwalader donated it in 1947.

Revolutionary weapons also became treasures. Most Americans have been fascinated with weapons, perhaps a legacy of the frontier experience or of something more deeply rooted in the human psyche. Weapons from earlier periods continually intrigue museumgoers, and the militaria of the Revolutionary period has proved no exception. The Historical Society never actively collected in this area, but the modest assemblage of material acquired through donation has been popular when displayed. Iron caltrops, scattered on the ground with sharpened points upward to puncture the horses' hooves; John Paul Jones's telescope, reputedly used on board the *Bonhomme Richard* during the moonlight battle with *Serapis* when he exclaimed, "I have not yet begun to fight"; *chevaux-de-frise*, systems of chains and spikes stretched invisibly underwater to tear holes in the hulls of enemy ships; canteens, powder horns, swords, flintlock muskets, pistols, regimental flags, and the red ensign belonging to the British general killed at the Battle of Germantown all came to the Historical Society. Donors have bestowed additional military paraphernalia on the Atwater Kent Museum, the Independence Seaport Museum, and even Philadelphia's Masonic Temple.

Rusty weapons and tattered uniforms kept memory of the Revolution alive in many private homes, but public art had greater reach. American painters, even before the war was over, launched a reverent iconographic history of the Revolution by taking the images of military, political, and diplomatic leaders. Enterprising Charles Willson Peale led them all. Cadging time from officering a Philadelphia militia company, he painted Washington at Valley Forge during the winter of 1777–78, for the second of seven life paintings Peale did of the Virginian. Lacking canvas, he painted on blue and white twilled bed ticking. Peale painted on and on through the Revolution and into the postwar years, capturing nearly anyone of even modest fame who would sit for him: Benjamin Franklin; Baron von Steuben; Daniel Morgan, one of Washington's brigadier generals; John Hazelwood, commodore of the Pennsylvania navy; David Rittenhouse; Jefferson; John Paul Jones; and dozens more. Peale also painted most of the important French officers, knowing full well that the Americans could not win the war without French aid, which came in the form of money and men. Among them were Conrad Alexandre Gerard, the French minister to the United States; Chevalier Du Portail, a French officer serving with the Marquis de Lafayette; and of course Lafayette, the most famous of the Frenchmen schooled to arms who joined the American cause. Virtually a surrogate son to the childless Washington, Lafayette named his first-born son George Washington Lafayette in 1779, and Peale promptly did a portrait of the living symbol of the Franco-American alliance. Philadelphians turned out en masse to welcome Lafayette fresh from the Yorktown victory in November 1781, just after Washington had taken up residence for four months in the city. By 1783, Peale wrote to a friend, "I have painted thirty or forty portraits of Principal Characters."[19] Peale's paintings found their way to the Historical Society, Philosophical Society, and Pennsylvania Academy of Fine Arts. But Peale kept most of the paintings for himself, for reasons that would soon become apparent.

Yet his selection of "principal characters" had certain boundaries. Though he had been a radical in the early stage of the Revolution, he moderated his views considerably by 1780. Philadelphians had elected him to the state assembly in 1779, and he was one of the "Furious Whigs" who orchestrated the public humiliation of the traitorous Benedict Arnold and had publicly attacked Robert Morris as a profiteer. But the next year, Peale lost his legislative seat, as did other Philadelphia radicals. After this, shaken by the battle at the house of James Wilson, where Philadelphia militiamen fought against merchants and lawyers resisting wartime price controls, he determined to give up politics and concentrate on painting, with which "he could not make any enemies and which most probably would be much more profitable."[20] Significantly, his brush did little to perpetuate the memory of his radical compatriots Thomas Young, George Bryan, James Cannon, Dr. James Hutchinson, Christopher Marshall, or Daniel Roberdeau. He did paint his close friend Paine, however, and he created a portrait of Timothy Matlack, though he never displayed it. In 1826, when he and Matlack were both very elderly, Peale took the image of his old friend again and displayed this portrait of the aged Revolutionary compatriot. Beyond this, for whatever reason, the Revolution's most prolific patriotic painter did little to memorialize those who shared the part of the political spectrum that he had occupied in the early years of the war.

Searing the images of the moderate and conservative war heroes into the public's consciousness became important even before the ink dried on the peace treaty drawn up in Paris in 1783. The Assembly Room of the State House, where the Declaration of Independence was signed, became an art gallery from 1783 to 1785. There the English artist Robert Edge Pine exhibited his portrait of General Washington and a historical tableau depicting the commander-in-chief handing his resignation to Congress. Then, in 1794, Peale got permission to move the museum he had created in his home into Philosophical Hall, where he displayed his growing collection of revolutionary heroes, along with the nation's finest display of natural history exhibits, for anyone with twenty-five cents to spend. In 1802, he moved his museum to the second floor of the State House, where it remained for twenty-six years.

The "spirit of '76" was remembered in painting almost entirely through the portraits of the new nation's leaders. Sea battle scenes became popular a few decades after the Revolution and an occasional painting evoked the heat of a battle. But not until the war-torn 1860s would Philadelphians be reminded of the pathos and human suffering of open conflict. In 1862, when the Pennsylvania Academy of Fine Arts exhibited Peter Rothermel's *State House on the Day of the Battle of Germantown* (Figure 39), museumgoers did not see a glorification of the Revolutionary War; instead, they contemplated women binding up the wounds and comforting the soldiers on the steps of the State House, which served as a hospital and prisoner-of-war jail for the maimed and bloodied Americans who had been brought there.

FIGURE 39. Peter Frederick Rothermel, *State House on the Day of the Battle of Germantown*, 1862, oil, PAFA. In featuring the prominent role women played in the Revolution, Rothermel may have been inspired by the Philadelphia women of the Civil War who launched the United States Sanitary Commission in 1861 to provide medical relief to wounded soldiers and sailors.

The War at Home

As in all wars, those who stayed behind, as well as those who fought, contributed and sacrificed for the effort. At home, women bore much of the burden. They organized "fast days" to pray for deliverance from the English; harassed merchants who monopolized goods or charged exorbitant prices; ran farms, shops, and businesses for husbands away at war; sewed bandages and uniforms; raised money for military supplies; coped with the galloping inflation of 1779 that wreaked havoc with household budgets; and wove homespun cloth to take the place of imported English textiles. By late 1776, 4,000 Philadelphia women, representing almost half the households in the city, were manufacturing their own cloth.

The pinnacle of women's wartime involvement in Philadelphia came in the summer of 1779, when Esther de Berdt Reed, wife of Joseph Reed, the president of Pennsylvania's Executive Council, and Sarah Franklin Bache, daughter of Benjamin Franklin (in Paris as the Continental Congress's emissary), organized a campaign to raise money for Washington's tattered army. Nailing up a broadside around the city titled *The Sentiments of an American Woman* (Figure 40), they announced that American women were "born for

THE SENTIMENTS of an AMERICAN WOMAN.

ON the commencement of actual war, the Women of America manifeſted a firm reſolution to contribute as much as could depend on them, to the deliverance of their country. Animated by the pureſt patriotiſm, they are ſenſible of ſorrow at this day, in not offering more than barren wiſhes for the ſucceſs of ſo glorious a Revolution. They aſpire to render themſelves more really uſeful; and this ſentiment is univerſal from the north to the ſouth of the Thirteen United States. Our ambition is kindled by the fame of thoſe heroines of antiquity, who have rendered their ſex illuſtrious, and have proved to the univerſe, that, if the weakneſs of our Conſtitution, if opinion and manners did not forbid us to march to glory by the ſame paths as the Men, we ſhould at leaſt equal, and ſometimes ſurpaſs them in our love for the public good. I glory in all that which my ſex has done great and commendable. I call to mind with enthuſiaſm and with admiration, all thoſe acts of courage, of conſtancy and patriotiſm, which hiſtory has tranſmitted to us: The people favoured by Heaven, preſerved from deſtruction by the virtues, the zeal and the reſolution of Deborah, of Judith, of Eſther! The fortitude of the mother of the Macchabees, in giving up her ſons to die before her eyes: Rome ſaved from the fury of a victorious enemy by the efforts of Volumnia, and other Roman Ladies: So many famous ſieges where the Women have been ſeen forgetting the weakneſs of their ſex, building new walls, digging trenches with their feeble hands, furniſhing arms to their defenders, they themſelves darting the miſſile weapons on the enemy, reſigning the ornaments of their apparel, and their fortune, to fill the public treaſury, and to haſten the deliverance of their country; burying themſelves under its ruins; throwing themſelves into the flames rather than ſubmit to the diſgrace of humiliation before a proud enemy.

Born for liberty, diſdaining to bear the irons of a tyrannic Government, we aſſociate ourſelves to the grandeur of thoſe Sovereigns, cheriſhed and revered, who have held with ſo much ſplendour the ſcepter of the greateſt States, The Batildas, the Elizabeths, the Maries, the Catharines, who have extended the empire of liberty, and contented to reign by ſweetneſs and juſtice, have broken the chains of ſlavery, forged by tyrants in the times of ignorance and barbarity. The Spaniſh Women, do they not make, at this moment, the moſt patriotic ſacrifices, to encreaſe the means of victory in the hands of their Sovereign. He is a friend to the French Nation. They are our allies. We call to mind, doubly intereſted, that it was a French Maid who kindled up amongſt her fellow-citizens, the flame of patriotiſm buried under long misfortunes: It was the Maid of Orleans who drove from the kingdom of France the anceſtors of thoſe ſame Britiſh, whoſe odious yoke we have juſt ſhaken off; and whom it is neceſſary that we drive from this Continent.

But I muſt limit myſelf to the recollection of this ſmall number of atchievements. Who knows if perſons diſpoſed to cenſure, and ſometimes too ſeverely with regard to us, may not diſapprove our appearing acquainted even with the actions of which our ſex boaſts? We are at leaſt certain, that he cannot be a good citizen who will not applaud our efforts for the relief of the armies which defend our lives, our poſſeſſions, our liberty? The ſituation of our ſoldiery has been repreſented to me; the evils inſeparable from war, and the firm and generous ſpirit which has enabled them to ſupport theſe. But it has been ſaid, that they may apprehend, that, in the courſe of a long war, the view of their diſtreſſes may be loſt, and their ſervices be forgotten. Forgotten! never; I can anſwer in the name of all my ſex. Brave Americans, your diſintereſtedneſs, your courage, and your conſtancy will always be dear to America, as long as ſhe ſhall preſerve her virtue.

We know that at a diſtance from the theatre of war, if we enjoy any tranquility, it is the fruit of your watchings, your labours, your dangers. If I live happy in the midſt of my family; if my huſband cultivates his field, and reaps his harveſt in peace; if, ſurrounded with my children, I myſelf nouriſh the youngeſt, and preſs it to my boſom, without being affraid of ſeeing myſelf ſeparated from it, by a ferocious enemy; if the houſe in which we dwell; if our barns, our orchards are ſafe at the preſent time from the hands of thoſe incendiaries, it is to you that we owe it. And ſhall we heſitate to evidence to you our gratitude? Shall we heſitate to wear a cloathing more ſimple; hair dreſſed leſs elegant, while at the price of this ſmall privation, we ſhall deſerve your benedictions. Who, amongſt us, will not renounce with the higheſt pleaſure, thoſe vain ornaments, when ſhe ſhall conſider that the valiant defenders of America will be able to draw ſome advantage from the money which ſhe may have laid out in theſe; that they will be better defended from the rigours of the ſeaſons, that after their painful toils, they will receive ſome extraordinary and unexpected relief; that theſe preſents will perhaps be valued by them at a greater price, when they will have it in their power to ſay: *This is the offering of the Ladies.* The time is arrived to diſplay the ſame ſentiments which animated us at the beginning of the Revolution, when we renounced the uſe of teas, however agreeable to our taſte, rather than receive them from our perſecutors; when we made it appear to them that we placed former neceſſaries in the rank of ſuperfluities, when our liberty was intereſted; when our republican and laborious hands ſpun the flax, prepared the linen intended for the uſe of our ſoldiers; when exiles and fugitives we ſupported with courage all the evils which are the concomitants of war. Let us not loſe a moment; let us be engaged to offer the homage of our gratitude at the altar of military valour, and you, our brave deliverers, while mercenary ſlaves combat to cauſe you to ſhare with them, the irons with which they are loaded, receive with a free hand our offering, the pureſt which can be preſented to your virtue,

BY AN AMERICAN WOMAN.

FIGURE 40. *The Sentiments of an American Woman*, broadside, June 10, 1779, LCP. One historian of American women has seen the broadside pictured here, which was posted around the city, as "an ideological justification for women's intrusion into politics that would become the standard model throughout the years of the early Republic." This key document for woman's history was acquired by the Library Company in 1784 as part of the Du Simitière collection.

liberty" and refused to "bear the irons of a tyrannic Government." They reminded Philadelphians that earlier societies had their politically active females: "Rome saved from the fury of a victorious enemy by the efforts of Volumnia . . . [and] famous sieges where the Women have been seen . . . building new walls, digging trenches with their feeble hands, furnishing arms to their defenders, they themselves darting the missile weapons on the enemy." Having prepared the public, the women of the Reed-Bache battalion took to the streets, going door to door rather than waiting for contributions to come in. "Of all absurdities the ladies going about for money exceeded everything," sputtered the loyalist Anna Rawle. But before they were done the women had collected about 300,000 paper dollars. Washington turned down their proposal to convert the money to specie and give each of his soldiers two dollars because he was afraid this gift would increase their discontent at getting only depreciated paper money for their regular pay. Instead, the women used the money to buy linen and made it into 2,200 shirts, which they hoped would "be worn with as much pleasure as they were made."[21]

Other women who lent money or held the loans as widows after their husbands died were not afraid to take their case to the public when they believed they received shabby treatment. Among those who tried to obtain repayment of money lent out during the war was Philadelphia's Letitia Cunningham. Abigail Adams believed that women should express their political views only in private, and Jefferson opined that American women would be "too wise to wrinkle their foreheads with politics."[22] But the widow Cunningham, furious that the government bonds she purchased might not bear interest, published a closely argued pamphlet, *The Case of the Whigs Who Loaned Their Money on the Public Faith Fairly Stated* (1783), to gain satisfaction.

While some Philadelphia women worked earnestly for the American cause, others showed more enthusiasm for serving the free-spending British soldiers who occupied their city from September 1777 to June 1778. The British occupation demonstrated just how divided the Americans were. Many Philadelphia shopkeepers, including many women, sold freely to the English, and wealthy families hosted the enemy at lavish dinner parties and balls. More than a few romances and marriages with local women occurred, leading Benjamin Franklin to quip that General Sir William Howe had not captured Philadelphia but Philadelphia had captured Howe. Such sympathy for the enemy in some quarters surfaced jubilantly at the Meschianza, the lavish fête staged by British officers to honor their commander, General Howe, as he left Philadelphia in May 1778. The estate of the wealthy loyalist merchant Joseph Wharton, located on the southern border of the city, provided the scene. Many of the most prominent Philadelphia families were on the guest list, including Bonds, Shippens, Chews, Redmans, and others who had collaborated and socialized with the British during their nine-month encampment in the city. British officers came costumed as medieval knights, and the Philadelphia ladies appeared dressed as Turkish maidens. Life-size, hand-painted dummy boards of British grenadiers decorated the regal Wharton gardens. A mock medieval chivalric tournament amused the guests before dinner. Then twenty-four slaves in Turkish outfits served courses almost beyond count. Fireworks and dancing followed, keeping some of the celebrants away from their beds until six the next morning. One of the wartime diaries that found its way to the Historical Society's collections, that of Sally Wister, describes how a six-foot painted grenadier was used to frighten an American officer. The descendants of one of the Meschianza celebrants gave memorabilia from the loyalist extravaganza to the Library Company in 1900, after more than a century had passed to diminish bitter feelings associated with the affair.

The Meschianza's knightly splendor, with slaves displayed conspicuously as symbols of subordination and aristocratic privilege, caused great resentment among ordinary Philadelphians and came to haunt Philadelphia's aristocratic families after the British left the city. On July 4, barely two weeks after the British evacuation, a raucous crowd paraded a local prostitute through the streets overdressed in high fashion headgear similar to that worn by Torified Philadelphia women during the British occupation. A half century later, when John Fanning Watson was writing his *Annals of Philadelphia*, he planned to include a disparaging poem written by Hannah Griffitts, who, as a young Quaker woman in Philadelphia during the occupation, had witnessed the Meschianza honoring the departing British officers. Griffitts had described the Meschianza as "A shameful scene of dissipation; The death of sense and reputation; A deep degeneracy of nature; A Frolick, for the lash of Satire; A feast of grandeur, fit for Kings; Formed of the following empty things; Ribbons and gewgaws, tints and tinsel; To glow beneath the Historic Pencil."[23] But even as his friend James McHenry was publishing a historical novel on the Meschianza—*Meredith; or the Mystery of the Meschianza, A Tale of the American Revolution* (1831)—Watson suppressed the poem to protect the reputations of "some of his respected friends" who had fraternized with the British troops attending the affair. One of those whose reputation Watson was protecting was the grandfather of Joseph Wharton, whose estate, Walnut Grove, had been the scene of the Meschianza. Joseph's grandson, Thomas I. Wharton, a noted lawyer, was one of the Historical Society's founders who worked closely with Watson and hosted the first meeting of the society.

Another family that suffered the disgust of ordinary Philadelphians for their loyalism was the Shippens. Edward Shippen's family, one of Philadelphia's wealthiest, was conspicuous at the Meschianza, and one of the belles of the ball was his youngest daughter, the beautiful eighteen-year-old Peggy Shippen. Ten months later, she succumbed to the courtship of Major General Benedict Arnold, the gallant hero of the American victories at Fort Ticonderoga in 1775 and Saratoga in 1777, but the unpopular military commander of Philadelphia after the British left. Within a month of their marriage, Arnold began negotiations with the British that soon led to his court-martial for using military forces for his own benefit and then, when in command of West Point, New York, treasonously arranging to surrender the fort to the British. At the beginning of the twentieth century, the Historical Society did its part to exonerate Peggy Shippen from any role in her husband's treachery by publishing a long defense of her in its journal, the *Pennsylvania Magazine of History and Biography*.[24] However, scholarship since then has documented her participation in her husband's intrigues, explained in part by her excessive spending. After the Americans discovered Arnold's plot with the British, Shippen fled from West

FIGURE 41. Charles Willson Peale, *A Representation of the figures Exhibited and Paraded Through the Streets of Philadelphia*, 1780, in Anthony Sharp's *Continental Almanac* (1781), HSP. The effigies of Arnold and the devil shown in this woodcut appeared in English- and German-language almanacs in 1780 (for the year 1781), thus keeping the anti-Arnold feeling alive. Conservative Quakers, such as the diarist Samuel Rowland Fisher, dismissed the noisy procession as "a frolick of the lowest sort of people." However, Peale's "Description of FIGURES" says the procession was led by "several gentlemen mounted on horseback, A line of Continental Officers, Sundry Gentlemen in a line, A guard of the City Infantry."

Point to her father's home in Philadelphia, but the state's wartime government banished her from Pennsylvania in 1780. She rejoined her husband in British-occupied New York, and in 1781 they sailed to England, where she lived out her life with her seven children and two stepchildren.

As the court-martialed Arnold and his Philadelphia wife became symbols of aristocratic self-indulgence and disloyalty, radicals employed art and street theater to carve their perfidy in public memory. On September 30, 1780, one day after learning of Arnold's treason, patriot Philadelphians paraded a papier-mâché figure of Arnold through the streets and then hung it from a gallows. Two days later, artist turned radical politician Charles Willson Peale, one of Philadelphia's elected assemblymen, orchestrated a more formal ritual humiliation. Peale created an elaborate life-size effigy of Arnold—dressed in a red coat for loyalism and with two faces to symbolize his duplicity—and fashioned another effigy of a huge black devil looking over his shoulder and shaking a purse of money at Arnold's ear (Figure 41). Cheering crowds accompanied the horse-drawn cart carrying the effigy of Arnold through the streets. Preceded by fifes and drums playing the "Rogue's March," the procession made its way to a huge bonfire where Arnold and the devil were unceremoniously burned. Shortly, a Philadelphia almanac included an image of the procession, describing how it "was attended with a numerous concourse of people, who after expressing their abhorrence of the Treason and the Traitor, committed him to the flames, and left both the effigy and the original to sink into ashes and oblivion."[25]

The Fractured Homefront

Revolutionary fervor spread from the battlefields to towns and cities. Ready to remake their society, radical revolutionaries raised weighty questions. How democratic should the state's constitution be? Should merchants be allowed to export wheat to distant markets while the poor went hungry at home? Should an opposition press be allowed to publish? Should slavery be allowed to continue in a nation being founded on the bedrock idea of natural rights and human equality? Should pacifist Quakers be fined to support the families of those who were fighting the war? On a multitude of issues, Philadelphians found that it was easier to declare independence than to erect a new social order that protected the "life, liberty, and pursuit of happiness" of *all* citizens.

Many of the issues involved in refurbishing society had to be confronted when Pennsylvanians wrote a constitution under which to live as an independent people. Drafted barely three months after the Declaration of Independence, it was the most democratic constitution in the new nation. It provided for a one-house legislature, almost eliminated the executive branch, yoked the judiciary to the will of the legislature, and extended the vote to white adult males without property. The most radical proposal of all, put forward by the militia companies of Philadelphia, proposed a redistribution of property within the state as a step essential to preserving republican liberty. "An enormous proportion of property vested in a few individuals," declared the petition, "is dangerous to the rights and destructive of the common happiness of mankind; and therefore every free state hath a right by its laws to discourage the possession of such property." Though not adopted, it reflected the bitterness of ordinary Philadelphians toward those who had amassed great wealth.[26]

Debate over the Constitution divided Pennsylvanians deeply. Opponents, led by men of wealth, condemned the document's supporters as "coffee-house demagogues" and "political upstarts" and accused them of wanting a "tyranny of the people." Benjamin Rush, who had earlier worked with the radicals who designed the Constitution, claimed it "substituted a mob government to one of the happiest governments in the world." The constitution's proponents, comprising artisans, farmers, and radical intellectuals such as the school teacher James Cannon, one of its main architects, shot back that their critics were "the rich and great men and the wise men, the lawyers and doctors," who thought they had no "common interest with the body of the people."[27]

Opponents of the Constitution could not defeat it, because it had been written by elected delegates who had no obligation to put it before the people for ratification and because it had been approved by the popular Benjamin Franklin, who presided over the Convention that wrote the document. But they could elect a new legislature hostile to the Constitution and hope that such an assembly would overturn it. Hundreds of disgruntled Philadelphians turned out on October 17, 1776 for a mass meeting at the State House to protest the new Constitution. Their objection that the Constitution did not treat the Christian religion "with proper respect" was a perfect illustration of the competing agendas of the revolutionaries, for some in Pennsylvania wanted to end the monopoly on officeholding that Protestants had enjoyed until this time. More oblique were the resolutions animated by the conferring of the vote on unpropertied white males and the emasculation of the executive branch—parts of the Constitution that its detractors would only call "strange *innovations*" and "unnecessary" deviations from "the former government of this State, to which the people have been accustomed." Their resolutions against the constitution were broadcast for all to consider in a broadside distributed throughout the city and, no doubt, sent into the countryside.

The fulminations against the Constitution of 1776 are far easier to unearth in the city's repositories than arguments in favor of it. The papers of the radicals were lost or never preserved, and most of the officers of collecting institutions were as suspicious of ordinary people elected to high places as were those who, at the time, deplored the 1776 Constitution. But the papers of such prominent opponents as Benjamin Rush, James Pemberton, John Dickinson, Thomas McKean, and James Wilson all found their way into the holdings of the Historical Society, Library Company, and Philosophical Society. The Historical Society enthusiastically purchased papers and manuscripts of Robert Proud, Pennsylvania's first historian and a staunchly conservative Quaker, in 1903. Among these documents was Proud's scathing attack on the 1776 Constitution—his rhymed reflection "On the Violation of Established and Lawful Order, Rule or Government":

> Of all the plagues, that scourge the human race,
> None can be worse, than *upstarts*, when in place;
> Their pow'r to shew, no action they forbear;
> They tyrannize o'er all, while all they fear;
> No savage rage, no rav'nous beast of prey,
> Exceeds the cruelty of Servile Sway!

Proud punctuated his point by adding a footnote on what he meant by the "cruelty of Servile Sway": that of "servants, slaves, or lower ranks of people, when by violence, they usurp the power over their former masters and rulers."[28]

One of the issues that the constitution of 1776 did not settle was the question of slavery. It was on everyone's mind. Even before the Declaration of Independence, the Society of Friends had already taken the momentous decision to ban slaveholding among its members, and many writers pointed out the hypocrisy of arguing for God-given natural liberties while domestic slavery flourished in the colonies. A young doctor in the city, Benjamin Rush, was one of the first white revolutionaries to inveigh against slavery. In *An Address . . . upon Slave-Keeping*, he urged the Pennsylvania Assembly, "ye ADVOCATES for American liberty"—to excise the cancer of slavery from the American body politic while they fought for their own freedom.

In August 1778, only two months after the British occupation of Philadelphia ended, the assembly took up the issue the Constitutional Convention had ignored two years before. Pennsylvania's Supreme Executive Council argued that by erasing this "opprobrium of America," Pennsylvanians would regain the respect of "all Europe, who are astonished to see a people eager for Liberty holding Negroes in Bondage."[29] After a year of debate and several revised drafts, the legislature passed the first abolition law in North America in October 1779. Although it freed no slaves outright, the law promised liberty to any child born of a slave mother after January 1, 1780, but not until that child reached the age of twenty-eight. Intense lobbying by representatives of slaveowners had secured this long period of servitude, but many still opposed any kind of abolition bill. When some representatives who voted for the bill in 1780 were swept out of office later that year, pressure mounted to repeal or amend the abolition act. In one of their first collective political acts, "divers Negroes" in Philadelphia petitioned the legislature to defeat the amendments being proposed. And a slave named Cato, who had gained his freedom because his master had not registered him as the 1780 law required, pleaded eloquently in a piece that appeared in *Freedom's Journal* in September 1781 that he not be re-enslaved through a rescinding of the abolition law. In a petition to the legislature two days after Cato's plea, free blacks declared: "We are fully sensible, that an address from persons of our rank is wholly unprecedented, and we are fearful of giving offence in the attempt." But "the great question of slavery or liberty is too important for us to be silent. It is the momentous question of our lives. If we are silent this day, we may be silent for ever."[30] These black authors may have been helped in forming their moving pleas, but it is equally likely that they had attended Anthony Benezet's school for black children.

Civil liberties took a beating in Philadelphia during the war in another sign of the divisions within Revolutionary American society. With the outcome of the war in doubt in 1777, the executive council suspended due process for the duration. Military authorities muzzled the Tory press in Philadelphia in that year, and the state banned from voting or holding office members of the Society of Friends, whose religious principles would not allow them to swear oaths of allegiance to the state. As soon as the British occupied the city in September 1777, they unmuzzled the Tory press while Whig publishers packed up printing presses, type, ink, and paper and fled the city. Depending on the lens one looked through, the Revolution appeared liberating or oppressive.

In August 1777, with the British army poised to strike Philadelphia, the state again showed how due process could fall victim to wartime exigencies. After arresting many Philadelphians "disaffected to the American cause," most of them Quakers suspected of collaborating with the British, the state's revolutionary government turned down the applications of the accused for writs of habeas corpus to force the authorities to provide evidence supporting the charges against them. Instead, the government quickly banished twenty Quakers to Virginia's desolate frontier, where many of them sickened and two of them died during the hard winter. They lived under what amounted to house arrest in the homes of local residents in Winchester. The following spring, Washington intervened on the exiles' behalf, granting them special permission to pass through American lines and return to their homes, although the British still occupied Philadelphia.[31] This story of martyrdom, from the Quaker point of view, is fully disclosed in the Historical

Society's holdings, including the diaries that Elizabeth Drinker kept for more than a half century and some fifty letters from her husband, Henry Drinker, the wealthy merchant and land baron who was a leader of the exiled Quakers.

The dislocations of the wartime economy—with shortages of essential commodities, profiteering, and hyperinflation caused by huge quantities of paper money issued to pay for the war—created further division in the American ranks. In general, the people with the least economic security, laborers and lower artisans, were hardest hit. In 1779, with bread in short supply, a crisis developed. Philadelphia artisans charged merchants with monopolizing the grain supply and selling flour out of the city so that poor families could hardly get their daily bread (Figure 42). Identified as the chief culprit was none other than Robert Morris, one of Philadelphia's wealthiest merchants and the treasurer of the Continental Congress, who was in overall charge of running the finances of the war. Fighting fire with fire, Morris issued a broadside, *To the Citizens of Pennsylvania*, to answer the complaints, but his arguments did not lessen the hatred of him among many of the city's craftsmen families.

Only a few weeks after Morris's broadside appeared, Philadelphia became the scene of bloodshed as the crisis over runaway prices and profiteering reached a climax. For several months radical militiamen had been calling on the city's ordinary people "in the name of our Bleeding Country, to rouse up as a Lyen out of his den, and make those Beasts of Prey . . . though puffed like a Toad," to stop their monopolizing and profiteering. Then, on October 4, 1779, the militiamen seized four Philadelphians whom they identified as Tories and marched them around the city "beating the Rogue's March," as Elizabeth Drinker noted in her diary. Lawyer James Wilson, convinced he was to be the next target of the crowd's wrath, rallied his friends and turned his house on Walnut Street into a fortress. When the militia marched to his house, shots rang out. In the next ten minutes, five militiamen were killed and fourteen wounded in what became known as the "Fort Wilson riot."[32]

Trying to restore order after the bloody confrontation, state assembly president Joseph Reed called for all participants to surrender to the sheriff and submit to prosecution. Twenty-seven militiamen were arrested, but in November 1780 Reed asked the assembly to pardon them, which was done five months later. Bitterness over the underlying causes of the incident did not subside, however. "Poor Pennsylvania has become the most miserable spot under the surface of the globe," cried Benjamin Rush. "Our streets have been stained already with fraternal blood—a sad prelude we fear of the future mischiefs our Constitution will bring upon us. They call it a democracy—a mobocracy in my opinion would be more proper."[33]

In April 1780, radicals plastered the city with a broadside, signed by "Slow and Sure," which urged the militia to meet to deliberate "matters of great importance" such as rising prices and unequal militia obligations—the old sources of discontent. "We are determined to be free," announced the broadside. Perhaps fearing another Fort Wilson riot, President Reed suppressed the right of the militiamen to assemble and speak. In his proclamation, he forbade the meeting and offered a £1,000 reward for the identity of

Committee-Room.

May 28. 1779.

R E S O L V E D,

THAT the Retail Prices of the underwritten Articles on the firſt Day of May were as follows----

Coffee, -	per pound,		£ 0 : 17 : 6
Bohea Tea,	ditto,		4 : 15 : 0
Loaf Sugar,	ditto,		2 : 15 : 0
Muſcovado Sugar,	ditto,	from	0 : 18 : 9 to £1 : 5 : 0 according to Quality.
Weſt India Rum,	by gallon or quart,		7 : 0 : 0
Country Rum,	by do. or do.		5 : 5 : 0
Whiſkey,	by do.		2 : 0 : 0
Rice,	per pound,		0 : 3 : 0

And as it is abſolutely neceſſary, that Dry Goods, and all other Commodities, whether imported or the Produce of the Country, ſhould fall in Price as well as thoſe Articles which are already Publiſhed; therefore,

Reſolved, That this Committee do earneſtly requeſt and expect, that no Perſon do ſell any Commodity whatever, at a Higher Price than the ſame was ſold for on the firſt Day of this Month.

By Order of the Committee,
WILLIAM HENRY, CHAIRMAN.

§*§ *The Committee meets at Nine o'Clock preciſely, on Monday Morning next, at the Court-Houſe.*

PHILADELPHIA: Printed by FRANCIS BAILEY, in *Market-Street.*

FIGURE 42. *Committee-Room,* broadside, May 28, 1779, LCP. This broadside issued by the committee to fix prices was intended to bring merchants and shopkeepers into compliance. Though they were printed in large numbers to rouse the citizenry, broadsides of this kind were ripped from lampposts and tavern doors by those offended by them and were saved by few of their supporters. A year later a radical broadside warned at the bottom: "If you mean to avoid the just resentment of an injur'd people don't tear this off." Meant to incite as well as inform, the broadsides are among the most valuable sources for studying plebeian thought and action. The Library Company's copy is probably unique.

the author or printer. Bitterness over these events in 1779-80 lasted for decades, though those who wished to unify Americans in the nineteenth century around the idea of a glorious national beginning wanted to let the memory of the bloody confrontation at Wilson's house molder.

Events such as the confrontation at Fort Wilson refueled the conservatives' determination to replace Pennsylvania's radical constitution. At the end of the war, they worked to repeal the test law that kept conservative Quakers from voting because of their refusal to swear allegiance to the state constitution of 1776. The assembly narrowly defeated the repeal of the test law in 1784. Two years later, when the radicals' power had diminished, the assembly revoked the law and Quakers reentered politics. In 1790, a new constitutional convention replaced the constitution of 1776 with a more conservative one that did away with the unicameral legislature and installed a governor with far more power than that exercised by the Supreme Executive Council. The radical phase of the American Revolution in Philadelphia was over.

But remembering the Revolution in Philadelphia was far from an agreed-upon story. While the new nation struggled to function under a weakened Continental Congress, the most publicly visible heroes of the Revolution, the officers of Washington's Continental army, found themselves tangled in disputes about how they wanted the public to remember the war. When some of Washington's trusted officers gathered to found the Society of Cincinnati in May 1783, they imagined that an honorary organization whose membership would pass from father to son would be well received, because its sole mission was "to perpetuate . . . the remembrance of this vast event [and] the mutual friendships which have been formed under the pressure of common danger, and in many instances cemented by the blood of the parties."[34] But almost instantly, the society came under attack as a proto-peerage with designs to control the memory of the Revolution for their own purposes. Only a small distance, charged critics, separated a hereditary order commemorating its martial triumphs from an aristocratic group poised to snatch hard-earned freedoms purchased with blood. Public gratitude for military heroes in a republic, they argued, must arise spontaneously from an uncudgeled people. Society members responded that the public was unlikely to preserve the memory of valiant revolutionary officers unless "their memories were not in some measure rescued from oblivion" by themselves.[35]

Many Philadelphians, and many soldiers of the Pennsylvania Line, had plenty of reasons for distrusting a hereditary society of officers. Throughout the war, staff officers in the Continental army had been widely reviled by enlisted men. Just five months before the founding of the Society of Cincinnati, 300 soldiers of the Pennsylvania Line had defied their officers and surrounded the State House with fixed bayonets to demand back pay. Duplicating an earlier mutiny of the Pennsylvania Line on New Year's Day in 1781, when enlisted men had killed one of their officers and wounded several others, the disaffected soldiers intimidated the Continental Congress. When Congress was unable to convince Pennsylvania's war government to use the state militia to suppress the soldiers, its delegates fled to Princeton, never to return. The soldiers melted away without their pay, returning to their homes and simply quitting the Pennsylvania Line. Their last memory of the American Revolution—short rations, back pay, ragged uniforms, and empty promises—was hardly one that the Society of Cincinnati wanted to celebrate; at the same time, the soldiers were not disposed to entrust their memories of the Revolution to a band of self-appointed officers.[36]

When the Society of Cincinnati held its first meeting in Philadelphia in May 1784, Philadelphians still had fresh in mind the chaos of the previous June. Given this situation, the public probably applauded the society's vote to end hereditary membership, in effect yielding to charges that it harbored aristocratic pretensions and was concocting an antirepublican plot. But the larger issue was whether any group would hold a monopoly on the memory of the American Revolution and how the Revolution would be etched in the public mind—as only a valorous war for independence or as a dual struggle for self-determination *and* the remaking of American society.

Chapter 4

A NEW CITY FOR A NEW NATION

Philadelphia expanded rapidly in the early national period, swelling from an overgrown provincial capital of 30,000 when the Revolution broke out, to a muscular commercial and industrializing city of nearly 110,000 in 1820. Just as it had played a critically important role in the American Revolution, Philadelphia became the center of constitution-making. And when Congress moved from New York City to Philadelphia in 1790, it became the seat of the newly strengthened national government for ten years—a short period but one filled with intense drama connected to the revolutions in France and Haiti, the Whiskey Rebellion and Jay's Treaty, and the turbulent, noisy birth of the two-party system of politics. Already, however, Philadelphia's future was uncertain. After the state capital moved to Lancaster in 1799 and Congress left the next year for the new national capital on the shores of the Potomac River, Philadelphia lost some of its cosmopolitan sheen. Baltimore challenged the city's flour trade and New York its financial dominance, but Philadelphia remained a center of law, medicine, science, and publishing; and, as in the past, its richly mixed population was its bone and sinew. People kept coming—immigrants from England and Ireland, migrants from the hinterland, and fleeing or emancipated slaves from the South.

Documenting the lives of the city's business and political leaders, its cultural institutions, and its important public buildings has been relatively easy for historians, but disclosing how Philadelphians in the middle and lower ranks conducted their lives—at the workplace, in their homes, at church, and in the streets—has required the sifting of sources that had limited interest for the leaders of the city's collecting institutions. Yet in the process of building magnificent collections of interest to their well-placed directors, the Historical Society, Library Company, Athenaeum, and Philosophical Society accumulated materials that contained hidden material on the lives of ordinary people.

The look, feel, smell, and sound of Philadelphia just after the Revolution is not easy to recapture because no artist saw fit—in the absence of patrons ready to subsidize such an effort—to render a series of "views" of the city and its buildings. But when the English immigrant William Russell Birch arrived in 1794, this changed sharply. Most of his views featured the city's finest buildings: banks, churches, public institutions, and the residences of the wealthy. However, some of his views give a feeling for Philadelphia's busy street life and waterfront character while emphasizing the new accumulation of wealth

FIGURE 43. William Russell Birch, *Second Street North from Market St. wth Christ Church*, LCP. Birch, who issued a series of mostly hand-colored engravings, "The City of Philadelphia," between 1798 and 1800, was the first to visually record the building boom and the popularity of classical architecture. Here he shows Christ Church and the Royal Arms Tavern in the center of the city's commercial district. Birch's views show a neat, orderly, nearly antiseptic city, but the reality was that Philadelphia, like all eighteenth-century cities, was strewn with garbage and manure and reeked with the smells from tanneries, potteries, and butcher shops. For example, the alley running behind the fashionable Walnut Street house of William White, first bishop of the Protestant Episcopal Church, was reportedly so full of garbage that a wagon could not pass through it. Like Currier & Ives engravings of a later period, Birch's views of Philadelphia pleased customers because this was how they wanted to imagine their city.

that underwrote the construction of substantial brick buildings in the Georgian or Classical style (Figure 43). Another immigrant, John James Barralet, of French and Irish parentage, provided designs for engravers and exhibited town views like *Market Street Bridge*, in which Philadelphia at its western edge appears distinctly bucolic around 1810.

Constitution-Making

"The same enthusiasm now pervades all classes in favor of *government* that actuated us in favor of *liberty* in the years 1774 and 1775 with this difference that we are more united in the former than we were in the latter pursuit." This is how Benjamin Rush, Philadelphia's famous doctor-politician-reformer, described the movement in 1787 to strengthen the national government while curbing the powers of the states.[1]

Rush's comment is an example of how any great historical event can be read differently, depending on the position of the observer. Not everyone, as Rush suggests, had been actuated in favor of liberty in 1774 and 1775; and in 1787, many emphatically opposed the movement to strengthen the hand of the national government. They feared that the Constitutional Convention's work would strip power from the state legislatures, which best represented the ordinary people. Patrick Henry called the work of the convention the "tyranny of Philadelphia" and feared it would equal "the tyranny of George III."

Almost all the delegates who assembled in the State House in the hot, muggy summer of 1787 were determined to strengthen the weak national government provided for in the Articles of Confederation. Many thought Pennsylvania's own government, with its one-house legislature, weak executive, and nearly universal manhood suffrage, offered a frightening example of "majority tyranny." Some, like Alexander Hamilton, had even decided that a limited monarchy was necessary to rein in the democratic impulses of the people. When western Massachusetts farmers rebelled in the summer of 1786, under the leadership of a little-known revolutionary soldier named Daniel Shays, conservative thinkers saw confirmation of their worst nightmares regarding the "people" taking matters into their own hands.[2]

One of Pennsylvania's eight delegates to the Constitutional Convention was James Wilson, the conservative revolutionary whose house had been the scene of a "mini-civil war" eight years before. Wilson had survived the hostility of Philadelphia's common people and emerged as one of the convention's most supple legal and constitutional minds. His first draft of the Constitution, given to the Historical Society in 1922 by Simon Gratz, son of an early Historical Society leader and wealthy merchant who built a fabulous collection of historical documents, is the earliest surviving version of the nation's most revered text. As a member of the Committee of Detail, which worked through many of the compromises effected at the Convention, Wilson probably wrote the August 1787 draft at the conclusion of the preliminary deliberations.

Philadelphians first saw the document their representatives would be asked to ratify on September 19, 1787, when it was published in the *Pennsylvania Packet and Daily Advertiser*. The newspaper's publishers, John Dunlap and David C. Claypoole, were able to scoop their competition because they were the official printers to the Convention and were setting the document in type as the delegates passed successive revisions. Fewer than twenty copies of this issue are known to exist, and each, to judge by the last one auctioned, is worth $70,000—a sign of the continuing appeal of foundational documents upon which national identity is constructed in an ethnically and culturally diverse society. Many Philadelphians looked to the new U.S. Constitution to undo some of the damage they believed had been caused by the democratic state constitution of 1776. "The new federal government," wrote Benjamin Rush, "like a new Continental waggon will overset our State dung cart, with all its dirty contents . . . and thereby restore order and happiness to Pennsylvania."[3]

Historians have fixed their gaze so intently on the Constitution of 1787 that they have not much noticed that constitution making of various kinds was taking place in Philadelphia in the same year. In April 1787, Philadelphia's growing free black community got a jump on the Constitutional Convention by writing articles of incorporation—a kind of constitution—for the Free African Society of Philadelphia, probably the first African American mutual aid organization in the nation (Figure 44). A few months later, led by Quakers, a group of Philadelphians wrote a constitution for the Philadelphia Society for Alleviating the Miseries of Public Prisons, an organization that would remain in the forefront of transatlantic debates over the treatment and reform of prison inmates. The Pennsylvania Abolition Society also wrote a new constitution in the spring of 1787 and adopted an aggressive strategy of litigation on behalf of free blacks. Anticipating the arrival of delegates to the Constitutional Convention in May, they attracted such influential new recruits as eighty-one-year-old Benjamin Franklin, who would shortly preside over the Abolition Society. They wasted little time in petitioning the convention, shortly after it convened, to prohibit the slave trade, "a Commerce that can only be conducted upon Rivers of Human tears and blood."[4]

Not everyone liked the national constitution that emerged from the convention in September 1787. In fact, the document met with fierce opposition, and the earliest printed attack on it appeared in the Philadelphia newspaper *Freeman's Journal*. In another Philadelphia newspaper, an opponent accused its supporters of being "either *downright Tories, lukewarm Whigs*, or disaffected to the cause of America and the Revolution." Among the leaders of what became known as the "antifederalists" was Philadelphia's Samuel Bryan, who wrote as "Centinel." Along with many others, he feared that the Constitution would establish centralized power and a "permanent aristocracy" of "the wealthy and ambitious, who in every community think they have a right to lord it over their fellow creatures." The outspoken Centinel essays were republished from Massachusetts to Georgia.[5]

Philadelphians debated the Constitution heatedly for more than six weeks as the public demonstrated in the streets and a barrage of articles, pro and con, appeared in the press—all meant to influence the election of delegates to the state's ratifying convention. Even after Pennsylvania's convention voted 46 to 23 to approve the Constitution in December 1787, twenty-one dissenting delegates—still convinced the new government would threaten the people's liberties—made their objections public in a widely circulated broadside.

Federalists were eager to stage an elaborate celebration of ratification to make a show of national unity. Among the many celebrations of ratification, Philadelphia's was one of the most colorful and elaborate. Seventeen thousand Philadelphians turned out for a parade that stretched through the streets for one-and-a-half miles with some 5,000 marching in the procession and then treated to barbecued beef and beer at a monstrous community picnic. Much of the city was represented: officeholders, judges, societies of various kinds, clergy, and farmers.

Especially impressive were the parading craftsmen. Forty-four crafts turned out in Philadelphia, each sporting banners and insignia (Figure 45) and marching beside hand-

FIGURE 44. Pavel Petrovich Svinin, *Night Life in Philadelphia: An Oyster Barrow in Front of the Chestnut Street Theater*, watercolor, 1814, Metropolitan Museum of Art. Svinin came to Philadelphia in 1811 as the secretary to the Russian consul general. During his short tenure in the city, he painted a series of remarkable watercolors, five of which show how much black Philadelphians were a part of street life. In this picture he portrayed black oystermen, in one of the occupations they controlled, selling their delicacies to theatergoers coming out of the Chestnut Street Theater. City directories, giving black occupations, confirm what Svinin pictured. But Svinin's watercolors never became part of the public memory of Philadelphia's vibrant black community because he returned to Russia with his artwork. An American Red Cross worker purchased a leather-bound folio containing the watercolors in 1925 and sold it to an Annapolis, Maryland collector. The Metropolitan Museum of Art in New York City purchased Svinin's work in 1942.

FIGURE 45. Banner of Philadelphia tobacconists for Federal Procession, 1788, LCP. Almost five feet square, this silk banner was carried by Thomas Leiper, a Scottish immigrant tobacconist, in the Grand Federal Procession. The banner is full of symbolism. The tobacco plant has thirteen leaves, three of them still not fully formed, to represent the three states that had not yet ratified the Constitution. Of the thirteen stars over the plant, ten shine brightly with silver while the other three remain dull. The tobacco plant is flanked by a hogshead of tobacco on the left and a bottle and a bladder of snuff on the right. The Library Company acquired Leiper's banner, along with an important collection of his business papers, in 1988 from one of his descendants.

or horse-drawn floats carrying symbolic displays of their handiwork. Upholsterers marched with a huge "Chair of State"; printers turned out broadsides, coopers hooped thirteen staves into a federal barrel; tailors sewed garments; potters turned pots at their kickwheels; and blacksmiths hammered old swords into plough irons. Pride of craft and pride of political participation was everywhere to be seen. With their banner proclaiming "Both buildings and rulers are the work of our hands," the bricklayers expressed a common artisan article of faith: that any government was contingent on the will of society's producers.

House-and shipbuilders presented the most magnificent tableaux. The shipbuilders' beautiful replica of the federal ship *Union*, manned with officers and seamen, was meant to remind spectators of the union of merchant capital with artisan skills under the new Constitution. Even more symbolic was the "Grand Federal Edifice" or "New Roof," mounted on a carriage drawn by ten white horses. The dome of the edifice was supported by thirteen Corinthian columns, with three left unfinished. Atop the dome stood the goddess Plenty, a subtle mocking of opponents of the Constitution who had wanted the nation to live under an old roof rather than a new one that the Federalists claimed would provide everyone a rosy future.

While turning the rolling floats into political lessons, Federalist organizers also meant to entertain. The stage of the printers, bookbinders, and stationers epitomized the marriage of instruction and entertainment. While printers turned off copies of Francis Hopkinson's *Song for Federal Mechanics*, which analogized the writing and ratifying of the Constitution with the raising of a new roof, a professional actor dressed as Mercury with wings on his head and feet and a garland of flowers around his temple glided back and forth on the float, releasing carrier pigeons from his helmet, each carrying a copy of the "Constitution Ode," to head off in various directions to the other states.

The procession's Federalist organizers worked hard to create unity and did not mind pretending that they were not rank-conscious. Eager to prove that they were not purse-proud aristocrats, as anti-Federalists had called them, they fixed the order of march by lot. But this demonstration of a democratic desire to avoid any appearance of a hierarchy of crafts, or even a superiority of officials and military officers over laboring men, could not entirely mask the rancor that still divided Philadelphians. Many had long memories of revolutionary disputes; all could remember the bruising battle over rechartering the Bank of North America, a pillar of conservative strength, a few years before; and everyone knew that the old opponents of the state's radical constitution of 1776 were presently preparing to rewrite it. But at least for a day, the federal procession gave the impression of harmony, and this appeared to be the case nine months later, on April 20, 1789, when Philadelphians turned out again to welcome Washington. The revolutionary hero was on his way from Mount Vernon through Philadelphia to New York, the nation's temporary capital, to assume the presidency (Figure 46). He would be back in Philadelphia a year later, when Congress decided to relocate to William Penn's city.

Pennsylvania's ratification of the Constitution in 1788 strengthened the desire of conservatives to dismantle the state's ultra-democratic constitution. They succeeded. In 1790, a new state constitution, closely modeled after the federal constitution, replaced the much-attacked constitution of 1776. Philadelphians now adjusted to a bicameral legislature and a governor with much enlarged executive powers; most also welcomed the restoration of Philadelphia's municipal powers, which in the constitution of 1776 had been reduced.

FIGURE 46. James Trenchard, *An East View of Gray's Ferry, near Philadelphia, with the Triumphal Arches, Columbian Magazine*, May 1789, LCP. Nine months after the procession celebrating ratification of the Constitution, Peale had another chance to enhance Washington's reputation as a Christian hero when the president came through Philadelphia on his way from Mount Vernon to New York for his inauguration. Peale turned the crude floating bridge spanning the Schuylkill River south of the city into an allegorical boulevard of triumph. Twenty-foot arches wreathed in laurel and flags of the eleven ratifying states decorated the railing. The twenty-five-foot liberty pole, with a beehive on top of it, flew a banner announcing DON'T TREAD ON ME. On the opposite shore, a banner displayed a sun with the motto BEHOLD THE RISING EMPIRE.

National Traditions

"'Tis done! We have become a nation," wrote Benjamin Rush on returning home from the federal procession of July 4, 1788. But making a nation required more than a parade. Having adopted the Constitution, Americans needed shared symbols to express their emerging sense of peoplehood. Such symbols, and national holidays to go with them, helped citizens extend their loyalties beyond the local community or home state to the nation at large. Cultural and political leaders eager to promote a national identity transformed George Washington from Virginia gentleman to larger-than-life national hero and began to celebrate their bold experiment in representative government in art and literature. Although local, state, and regional allegiances remained strong, Philadelphians gradually began to think of themselves as part of a broader national culture that was uniquely American. Thanksgiving was first celebrated as a national holiday in 1789; Congress established July 4 and Washington's birthday as national holidays in 1800, although Philadelphians had been celebrating these two holidays long before. John Adams predicted that Independence Day would be celebrated "as the great Anniversary festival . . . as the Day of Deliverance . . . solemnized with Pomp and Parade . . . with Shews, Games, Sports, Guns, Bells, Bonfires, and Illuminations from one end of this Continent

FIGURE 47. William Russell Birch, *High Street, from the Country Market-place Philadelphia: with the Procession in Commemoration of the Death of General George Washington, December 26th, 1799*, engraving, LCP. Birch's representation of Philadelphia's procession venerating Washington accords with the collective demonstration of grief and valorization that occurred in towns and cities across the nation. Birch was able to obtain subscriptions from more than two hundred patrons, who paid $28 for an uncolored set of twenty-eight Philadelphia views or $44.50 for a colored set. Four editions of these sets were published between 1800 and 1820, indelibly etching on the minds of those who saw in Birch's prints a very clean Philadelphia dominated by handsome buildings.

to the other." "Unruly rites of rebellion" in the 1760s and 1770s, writes one historian, were turning into "ruling rites of assent."[6]

We know something about what such holidays and commemorations involved in the era after the American Revolution from descriptions that have survived in letters, memoirs, and newspaper accounts. But the first known visual representation did not come until 1799, when William Birch executed an engraving of the city's procession commemorating the death of George Washington on December 26 of that year (Figure 47). If Birch recorded what he saw accurately, a riderless horse led a military guard escorting a black-draped catafalque. The streets are filled with mourners; others crowd windows and rooftops. A man turns away from the cortège and weeps into his handkerchief. Celebrations of Washington's birthday, and now his death, were useful to Federalism because they reached out to everyone in the name of national virtue.[7]

Birch created the first visual record of an American city, but not for another decade or so could Philadelphia find an artist interested in urban street scenes. Once again, the

FIGURE 48. John Lewis Krimmel, *Fourth of July in Centre Square*, oil, 1812, PAFA. In contrast to William Birch's prints, which featured buildings and usually included people as incidental, Krimmel focused on urban crowds, using buildings as a backdrop. Included in the crowd here are three black Philadelphians, a young boy and an adult couple. It is possible that Krimmel painted this picture just before the incident where white ruffians, driving black Philadelphians from Centre Square celebrations, initiated a "whites only" policy regulating freedom celebrations.

artist was a recently arrived immigrant—John Lewis Krimmel, from Württemberg. Krimmel was one of the nation's first artists to interest himself in urban street scenes that showed masses of people in all their variation, but his work showing scenes of daily life were so unpopular that he had to instruct young girls in drawing for a living. In portraying a colorful Fourth of July celebration (Figure 48), Krimmel shows people of all classes in the streets and much revelry, though not as much as probably occurred. Gamblers feasting off the meager earnings of apprentices and others had, in fact, made the holiday celebrations a profitable day of business. The revelry reached such a point that the city's mayor issued a proclamation in 1823 denouncing the "debauchery, gambling, and drunkenness" in Centre Square.[8]

National holidays, like historical societies, were invented to bind together a nation of diverse people, instilling them with beliefs and values that cut across religious, ethnic, racial, and class lines. But a nation that had buried the problem of slavery at the Constitutional Convention could never be fully united. Proof of this came when black Philadelphians adopted freedom holidays of their own, since July 4 held little meaning for them. The first was January 1, celebrated as a day of thanksgiving in 1808 to mark the ending of the American slave trade and commemorated annually. Absalom Jones, a founder of the first black church in Philadelphia and minister of St. Thomas's African Episcopal Church for many years, preached the sermon.

Notwithstanding the three black Philadelphians in Krimmel's watercolor of 1812, white Philadelphians began excluding black citizens from public celebrations—another reason for African Americans to create their own holidays. In 1813, the city's successful black sailmaker, James Forten, who maintained an integrated workforce in his riverfront sail loft, scourged his white neighbors for commemorating their commitment to liberty and equality with open displays of racial antipathy. On July 4, a few years before, whites had turned on the many free African Americans in the square facing Independence Hall and drove them off with a torrent of curses and stones. "Is it not wonderful," wrote Forten in his *Letters of a Gentleman of Colour* (1813), "that the day set apart for the festival of liberty, should be abused by the advocates of freedom, in endeavoring to sully what they profess to adore?"[9]

To exclude their black neighbors from public celebrations may have intensified white patriotism. "It is noteworthy," wrote visiting diplomatic official Pavel Svinin about 1812, "that every American considers it his sacred duty to have a likeness of Washington in his house, just as we have images of God's Saints."[10] Almost certainly, Svinin was referring to white Americans when he said "every American." After their Revolution, white Americans set about constructing a common memory of the struggle for independence and renewal. Writers and painters celebrated some Revolutionary participants as heroes and raised some heroes to the status of Founding Fathers. They glorified Washington above all. The Federalists were especially active in trying to create a national Washington cult. His picture graced parlor walls, water pitchers, seat cushions, and whiskey bottles. Rooms that he had slept in became hallowed spaces, and objects he had touched became treasured mementos (Figure 49).

After he died in 1799, Washington became even more celebrated and allowed Philadelphians, like other Americans, to turn anniversaries of his death into rituals of rejuvenation. Mythic narratives quickly followed. It took only a few months for Mason Locke Weems, America's first fabulist, to write his adulatory Washington biography, filled with prefabricated stories, as a morality tale for young Americans. Writing to Philadelphia publisher Mathew Carey shortly after the great man died, Weems explained: "Washington, you know, is gone! Millions are gaping to read something about him. I am very nearly prim'd and cock'd for 'em." Primed and cocked he was, for Weems's *Life of Washington* became a national bestseller, which the author embellished with further tales, such as the famous cherry tree story, in later editions. Nine years later, Carey purchased the copyright of *The Life and Memorable Actions of George Washington* and turned it into a printer's dream: nineteen editions, with print runs of several thousand each, between 1809 and 1825.[11]

Even before he became the *pater patriae*, or father of his country, Washington had been a subject for artists (Figure 50). His friend and comrade-in-arms, Charles Willson Peale, portrayed him in 1772 as colonel of the Virginia regiment in the French and Indian War. Given to the Historical Society in 1892, it is one of only two likenesses of Washington known to have been painted before the Revolution. The society had already received its first Washington portrait—that of Martha Washington by Peale's son, Rembrandt Peale, and it soon had Martha's cookbook as well. In 1898, the society received a bumper crop of Washingtoniana—1,092 engraved portraits and 1,146 medals, coins, and tokens, from William Spohn Baker, a Philadelphia conveyancer who had devoted twenty years to building his collection and writing about Washington prints, coins, and medals.

Once a historical society acquires a collection of the size and importance of the Baker collection on Washington, it cannot help but build on it. Anything associated with Washington, for example, a woman's slipper allegedly worn at a ball celebrating Washington's inauguration in New York in 1789, acquired great value. He was "first in war, first in peace, first in the hearts of his countrymen"—and first in the hearts of collectors. The Athenaeum portrait of Washington by Gilbert Stuart, probably the most widely reproduced image of the first president, did not come to Philadelphia, but Stuart made about seventy copies of this portrait, and one of them arrived at the Historical Society as a gift in 1903. Another portrait arrived in 1935, a likeness by Rembrandt Peale, and still another by James Peale, Rembrandt's uncle, found its way to the Historical Society. As late as 1972, the society was still receiving Washington portraits. Even the Library Company, which focused on books, not artifacts, acquired its share of Washingtoniana: a Washington life mask, a lock of his hair, slivers of wood from his coffin.

Less familiar than the deified image of Washington in attempts to bind the republic together was a female personification of the young American nation. She had started life as a representation of the American continent in European art in the 1500s. In this earliest incarnation she is an exotic Indian princess. In 1755, she adorned John Mitchell's huge map of the British colonies in North America, seated in front of tasseled maize and wearing a feather headdress and tobacco leaf skirt. In altered form, the Indian image continued to serve down through the revolutionary conflict with the mother country. A German artist, Carl Guttenberg, disregarded the entire dynamics of interracial relations in North America by showing the Indian Queen as Britannia's unruly daughter, a proponent for colonial liberty, while an African woman stood beside her looking sympathetically at a lantern show of American troops fighting the British army. In actuality, most Indian nations fought with the British and most African slaves understood that their chances of liberty lay primarily with reaching the British lines to gain the freedom promised in Lord Dunmore's proclamation of 1775.

Gradually, "Liberty" became more conservatively dressed, lost her Indian features, and after the French Revolution, began to carry a liberty cap on a pole (Figure 51). If a woman could not yet become a voting citizen, she was emerging as a symbol of the youthful United States. After the American Revolution, the female representation of America often reemerged in classical attire and sometimes kept her Indian plumes while assuming the name of "Columbia." One of Columbia's most triumphant appearances

FIGURE 49. Liverpool pitcher with image of Washington and American symbols, PMA. Cheap Liverpool creamware emblazoned with Washington's image put his face in front of huge numbers of children growing up in the years after the hero had passed on. If he was not already a household image, the first postage stamps issued in 1847 put Washington on the ten-cent stamp used for letter mail. (Franklin graced the five-cent stamp.) When the letter rate dropped to three cents four years later, Washington was again the choice.

FIGURE 50. Charles Willson Peale, *George Washington at Princeton*, oil, 1779, PAFA. This portrait of Washington, with his left hand on a cannon and his horse in the background, was commissioned by Pennsylvania's Supreme Executive Council in January 1779 to heap honor on the victor at Trenton and Princeton. At the lower right are Hessian flags and in the left background is the College of New Jersey's Nassau Hall with blue-coated Americans guarding the captured red-coated Hessians. Many copies were made, some carried by the American envoys to Holland and France, thus introducing Europe to Peale's work. The portrait was hung in the State House, where in 1781 vandals slashed it six times. Peale acquired the painting in some way, and it was sold by his descendants at the large 1854 Peale auction. The heirs of the private buyer presented it to the Pennsylvania Academy of Fine Arts in 1943.

FIGURE 51. Samuel Jennings, *Liberty Displaying the Arts and Sciences*, oil, 1792, LCP. Son of a sheriff in Northampton County, Jennings went to London to study painting and heard of the Library Company's plans to erect a new building. When he offered to present a painting, the Library Company's directors, many of whom were Quakers and members of the Pennsylvania Abolition Society, suggested the theme of Liberty displaying the arts and sciences while breaking the chains of grateful slaves.

was in an engraving commemorating the Peace of Ghent that ended the War of 1812. In a seven-by-eleven-foot painting by the French immigrant Julia Plantou, she rides through a triumphal arch in a Roman chariot waving a huge American flag at a gathering of classical deities. This was a major tourist attraction in Philadelphia in 1818.

The Federal Capital

In December 1790, the seat of the national government moved from New York City to Philadelphia; it remained there for ten years before migrating south to the Potomac River. As the nation's capital, Philadelphia attracted politicians, foreign dignitaries, delegations of Indian chiefs, refugees from revolutionary France and Haiti, and journalists. It also emerged as the nation's first financial center, a hub of newspaper and book publishing, and a center of artistic production. The growing nation needed banks to finance

FIGURE 52. *View of C_o_n_ss on the road to Philadelphia*, cartoon, 1790, HSP. Well schooled in cartoon propaganda from the 1760s and 1770s, urban artists had a heyday as controversies erupted under Washington's first administration. Here, Robert Morris clutches a money bag, announces he is Robert Coffer, and drags Congress down the road to Philadelphia while a bevy of aspiring politicians sit on the rungs of the "Ladder of Preferment."

development, journalists to report on the workings of a national government with greatly extended powers, and artists and architects to help Americans define their identity.[12]

Although Americans overwhelmingly supported the new government after ratification of the Constitution and the unanimous election of Washington as first president by presidential electors in the states, there was nothing about the operation of government that did not quickly become emotionally charged. The decision to move the federal capital south, with Philadelphia as a temporary capital, was one of the first controversies of the new government. One Massachusetts representative grumbled that the lobbying by Philadelphia and New York advocates was a "despicable grog-shop contest, whether the taverns of New York or Philadelphia shall get the custom of Congress." However, the decision was also part of the first struggle over Alexander Hamilton's program of assuming and funding the states' Revolutionary War debt. Philadelphia's Robert Morris was among those who stood to gain from such a plan and was at the center of the complicated negotiations to deliver Pennsylvania votes for Hamilton's economic plan in exchange for making Philadelphia the federal city. Many New Yorkers, dismayed at seeing their city lose the federal capital, saw Morris, the consummate deal maker, personally profiting from the removal of the capital to his hometown (Figure 52).

Banks became another subject of controversy. Before the Revolution, there had been no such thing as a bank. In 1780, the Bank of Pennsylvania was organized to raise funds for the Continental army. After the Revolution, debate raged on whether the federal government or the individual states should charter banks. Many feared the establishment of a truly national bank, which, as one Pennsylvanian argued, would necessarily "produce a degree of influence and power which cannot be entrusted in the hands of any set of men whatsoever without endangering the public safety."[13]

The fear of banks was rooted in the deep-seated suspicion of the Revolutionary generation of any concentration of power. But the day of banks could not be stopped because they were vital to pooling the capital needed to develop the country. Nor could bureaucracy be stopped, although many in the generation of '76 feared any government not directly answerable to the people. One of the Historical Society's prized possessions, George Washington's desk, was where the federal bureaucracy began. The Historical Society acquired it in 1867 from Charles Hare Hutchinson, president of the Athenaeum, director of the Academy of the Fine Arts, and later a vice president of the Historical Society.

While the city remained the federal capital, Philadelphians were accustomed to seeing Indian chiefs come to the city, as they had to the provincial capital for many years. Now, however, they were coming to parley with the national government because the Intercourse Act of 1790 gave responsibility for all treaty negotiations to the federal government. In 1792, President Washington summoned the Iroquois chiefs to Philadelphia, hoping the Iroquois would bring the western Indian tribes—Shawnees, Miamis, and others—to peace. Following the usual practice, the federal government presented engraved and die-struck silver medals to the forty-seven Iroquois chiefs who arrived in 1793 (Figure 53). As for many years past, Quaker silversmith Joseph Richardson, Jr. struck the medals. But silver medals would go just so far. "The President has assured us that he is not the cause of the hostilities," said Red Jacket (Segoyewatha), the chief orator for the Senecas. "Brother, we wish you to point out to us . . . what you think is the real cause."[14]

An older Philadelphia tradition endured alongside the glamor of the cosmopolitan capital as the city again became a refuge for those escaping violence and oppression. In the 1790s, French planters fleeing the slave rebellion in Saint Domingue, political refugees from the Irish Rebellion of 1798, and southern blacks fleeing slavery all streamed into the city. It has been relatively easy to document the fleeing French families because many of them became important in Philadelphia affairs and left papers and artifacts to the collecting institutions. But documents and artifacts that would allow historians to get beneath the surface of public events, to reconstruct the mingling of cultures when the Irish, black Saint Dominguans, and southern ex-slaves came to the federal city, have been more difficult to locate. After all, these groups had accumulated little to pass on, and any traces of their lives that did survive were not regarded at the time as valuable. No Pierre-Eugène Du Simitière of the revolutionary period—"a very curious man," as John Adams called him—emerged in the early republic to build a magpie's nest of ephemera. It is mostly from institutional records—church registers, almshouse admission books, deeds, wills, city directories (Figure 54), and marriage records—that the social life of the city, particularly for the lower classes, can be reconstructed.

FIGURE 53. William Birch, *Colonel Frederick Muhlenberg escorting the Indians*, watercolor, 1793, LCP. This was one of Birch's rare drawings that featured people rather than buildings. Here he captured part of the visiting delegation of forty-seven Senecas, Oneidas, Onondagas, Stockbridges, and Tuscaroras who performed war dances and were received at the State House by Governor Thomas Mifflin, awarded peace medals by President Washington, and shown around the city by Muhlenberg, speaker of the House of Representatives. Muhlenberg points to the German Zion Church, of which he was a member.

The slave rebellion in Saint Domingue, beginning in 1791 and climaxing with furious attacks that left Le Cap Français in smoking ashes by June 1793, drove French planters, dragging hundreds of slaves with them, to North American ports. Philadelphia became one of their favored places of refuge. They soon established French-language newspapers in the city, opened shops catering to their own kind, and began concocting schemes for French communities in western Pennsylvania. Federal Philadelphia was already sprinkled with French immigrants and French visitors, as well as with merchants such as Stephen Girard who had traded extensively with Saint Domingue; the new merchants and planters arriving from the French Caribbean added greatly to this group.

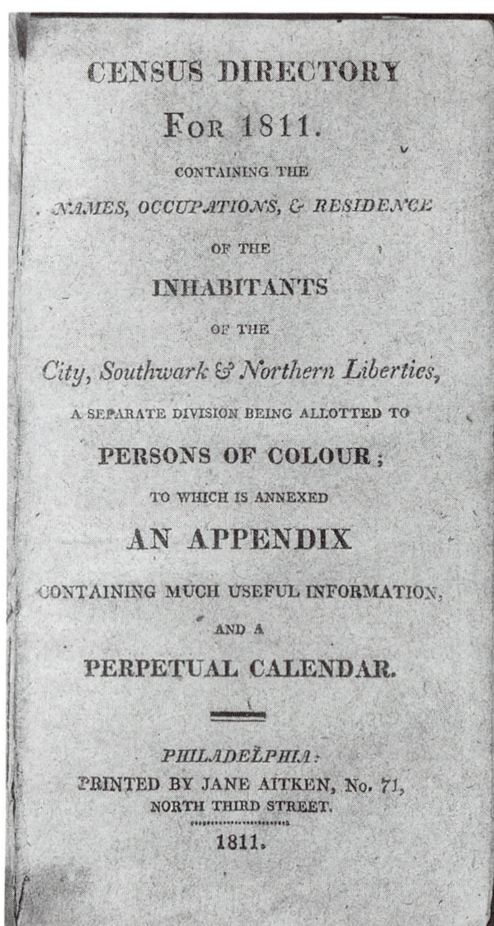

CENSUS DIRECTORY

FOR 1811.

CONTAINING THE

NAMES, OCCUPATIONS, & RESIDENCE

OF THE

INHABITANTS

OF THE

City, Southwark & Northern Liberties,

A SEPARATE DIVISION BEING ALLOTTED TO

PERSONS OF COLOUR;

TO WHICH IS ANNEXED

AN APPENDIX

CONTAINING MUCH USEFUL INFORMATION,

AND A

PERPETUAL CALENDAR.

PHILADELPHIA:

PRINTED BY JANE AITKEN, No. 71,

NORTH THIRD STREET.

1811.

372 FIG——GIB

Figero Joseph, labourer, back 153 Spruce
Finch Peter, carter, Mary
Fiss Edward, meadhouse, Eighth near Cedar
Fisher James, blacksmith, 24 Sugar alley
Fitch Dodd, waiter, 38 Carpenter
Fitzgerald Jacob, woodsawyer, back 219 Cherry
Fosses Arthur, labourer, 7 Pewterplatter alley
Francis Hannah, laundress, 78 George (S.)
Francis John, barber, 5 German
Francis John, barber, 167 Lombard
Francis William, mariner, 120 Lombard
Francis William, labourer, 36 Coates'
Freeman Cato, sweep master, 18 Charlotte
Freeman John, mariner, 55 Small
Freeman John, cook, Middle alley
Forrester Michael, labourer, back 70 Christian
Forten James, sailmaker, 92 Lombard
Fortunay ——, laundress, back 159 S. Sixth
Fortune John, barber, 17 Union

G.

GABRIEL Asa, mariner, 53 Passyunk
Gaiter Edward, labourer, 226 Lombard
Gale Joseph, mariner, Ninth near Spruce
Galloway Mary, seamstress, back 108 Cherry
Ganges Cæsar, sweep, 32 Union alley
Ganes James, capt. of salt carriers, Maria
Ganser William, labourer, 12th near Spruce
Gardner Charles, shoemaker, 134 Pine
Gardner Henrietta, laundress, 119 S. Sixth
Gardner Peter, waiter, 180 Shippen
Gardner William, mariner, 267 Catharine
Garrett Richard, labourer, near 72 Budd
German John, waiter, Middle alley
George William, labourer, 142 S. Eighth
Gibbs James, labourer, 36 Coates'
Gibbs Robert, labourer, Jones's alley
Gibson Benjamin, labourer, 156 Swanson
Gibson James, carter, back 459 S. Second

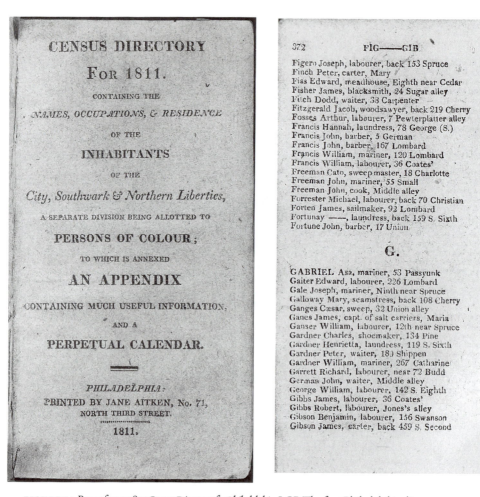

FIGURE 54. Pages from 1811 *Census Directory for Philadelphia*, LCP. The first Philadelphia directory appeared in 1785. Like today's telephone books, directories told people where they could find the shops of artisans and others. In 1811, Jane Aitken was the first printer to include a separate section on "persons of colour." Thereafter, printers began including black Philadelphians alphabetically with whites with an asterisk or dagger to the left of their name to indicate their race. The early directories have been an extraordinary source for historians in mapping urban social geography. As the page pictured here shows, black Philadelphians had many occupations. Many, such as Joseph Figero at "back 153 Spruce," lived in alleys or in small structures behind a house facing on a major street. Philadelphia's famous sailmaker James Forten appears here at 92 Lombard Street, near his sail loft. Arthur Fosses, variously spelled in directories as Fosset or Fausett, is the ancestor of Philadelphia's Harlem Renaissance figures Arthur and Jessie Fauset.

The Africans brought by these planters had escaped the hemisphere's most brutal slave regime. In Philadelphia, some 900 of them gained their freedom because the 1780 abolition act declared any slave brought into the state free after six months. But it was only a quasi-freedom because almost all were immediately indentured for long terms of service. Lundy, a twelve-year-old boy from Senegal, was only one of many who arrived in

Philadelphia with the name of their French master burned into their breasts (Figure 55). Names such as Alcindor, Felix, Felicitié, Zäire, Zéphir, Laviolet, and Figaro came to be commonly heard throughout the city, and soon the city's three Catholic churches became biracial congregations. The black Saint Dominguans also stiffened the antislavery resolve of Philadelphia's resident free blacks, for they came bearing firsthand reports of the most extensive black revolution in two centuries of slavery in the Western Hemisphere. After the Saint Domingue slaves completed their revolution in 1804, establishing the first black republic in the hemisphere, black Philadelphians for many years celebrated an epochal upheaval that had outlawed slavery entirely for the first time in the Americas. The arrival of black Saint Dominguans and their effect on the city's free black community was a chapter of Philadelphia history that would not be told until the 1980s.[15]

The chapter of Philadelphia's free black history in the Federal period that *did* enter the public consciousness pertained to the conjoint emergence of the city's first free black churches and the ghastly experience with yellow fever. The year 1793 was seared into Philadelphia's collective memory because the murderous yellow fever epidemic in the late summer, just after the peak of Saint Dominguan arrivals, drove the federal and state governments out of the city, convinced thousands to flee to the countryside, and turned Philadelphia into a morgue. In a city of 45,000, nearly 5,000 succumbed to the loathsome plague. In August, just as yellow fever struck down its first victims, black and white carpenters raised the roof on what would become Absalom Jones's St. Thomas's African Church of Philadelphia and then sat down to serve one another at a sumptuous dinner. Within a month, all construction stopped. Hundreds were perishing from the galloping yellow fever, the dead lay everywhere in the streets, and the city's social fabric collapsed. Into this calamitous breach stepped Philadelphia's free blacks, led by Absalom Jones and Richard Allen, who was preparing to erect a free black church of his own. Working with Benjamin Rush, one of the few doctors who remained in the city to fight the deadly fever, Allen, Jones, and their black followers nursed the sick, carted away the dead, dug graves, and transported the afflicted to an emergency lazaretto set up outside the city. Rush wrote movingly to his wife of "my African brethren" and quipped, in the midst of mass misery, that "we black folks have come into demand at last."[16] Mathew Carey, the Irish immigrant publisher in the city, gave scant credit to Jones's and Allen's legion in *A Short Account of the Malignant Fever* and claimed that some of the black nurses, death cart drivers, and grave diggers had charged exorbitant fees for their services. Jones and Allen responded vigorously with a pamphlet of their own, *A Narrative of the Proceedings of the Black People, During the Late Awful Calamity in Philadelphia.* It was the first published essay by African Americans in the city, and they proudly presented a copy to the Library Company. Perhaps at the urging of Library Company members, Carey revised his indictment in the fourth edition of his best-selling account.

Another refugee group, the Irish fleeing the failed rebellion against England in the 1790s, was small but enormously important in Philadelphia. From some 5,000 Irish-born Philadelphians in 1800 came much of the labor necessary to the binge of road and canal building that linked Philadelphia more securely to the hinterland. Both Protestant

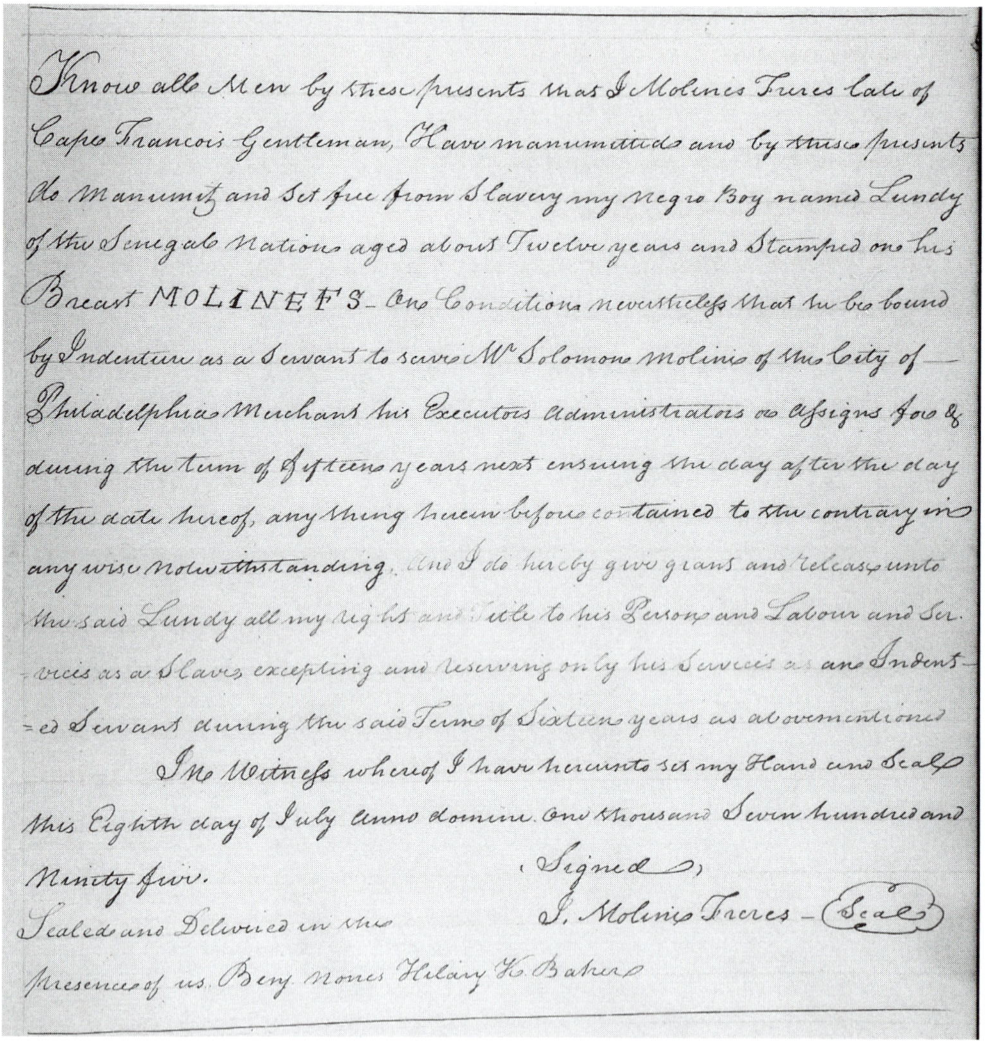

Know all Men by these presents that I Molines Treres late of
Cape Francois Gentleman, Have manumitted and by these presents
do Manumit and Set free from Slavery my Negro Boy named Lundy
of the Senegal Nation aged about Twelve years and Stamped on his
Breast MOLINEFS – On Condition nevertheless that he be bound
by Indenture as a Servant to serve Mr Solomon Molinis of the City of —
Philadelphia Merchant his Executors Administrators or Assigns for &
during the term of fifteen years next ensuing the day after the day
of the date hereof, any thing herein before contained to the contrary in
any wise notwithstanding. And I do hereby give grant and release unto
the said Lundy all my right and Title to his Person and Labour and Services as a Slave, excepting and reserving only his Services as an Indent-
ed Servant during the said Term of Sixteen years as abovementioned
In Witness whereof I have hereunto set my Hand and Seal
this Eighth day of July Anno domini One thousand Seven hundred and
Ninety five. (Signed)
Sealed and Delivered in the I. Molines Treres – (Seal)
Presence of us. Benj. Nones Hilary H. Baker

FIGURE 55. Indenture of Lundy, black Saint Domingue refugee, 1793, Pennsylvania Abolition Society Indenture Book D, HSP. Note the identifying brand of the young Senegalese boy's master in this indenture recorded by the Abolition Society. The voluminous papers of the Pennsylvania Abolition Society are the single most important source for studying the formation of Philadelphia's free black community in the early Republic. Over a period of several decades the society recorded the manumission and indenture papers of several thousand slaves who reached Philadelphia from nearly every point on the compass. The society also kept careful minutes of committee meetings, preserved legal papers relating to attempts to gain freedom for illegally held slaves, saved correspondence covering the entire Atlantic world, and collected abolitionist pamphlets. In the late nineteenth century, the society devoted itself to the relief and education of African Americans, a function it still pursues today. It began entrusting its papers to the Historical Society in the 1920s and completed this assignment in 1976.

and Catholic, they also could be found on most construction sites, whether house- or shipbuilding. Philadelphians with English roots or English ties looked down on them as "wild Irishmen," a slur cultivated for more than two centuries of English conquest and exploitation of Ireland. Hugh Henry Brackenridge regaled proper Philadelphians with his *Modern Chivalry* (1792) in which Teague O'Regan, an illiterate indentured servant dedicated to his whiskey bottle, eventually outshone his master; not only was O'Regan nominated to public office but he was also invited by the American Philosophical Society to become a member. Laughing at the Irish or, instead, tagging them as what one Federalist senator called "the most God-provoking democrats this side of hell" might satisfy urbane Anglophiles, but Philadelphia construction employers and mill owners knew nonetheless that the cheap labor of the Irish, like that of African Americans, was essential in a rapidly expanding city.[17]

Alongside the mass of impoverished Irish immigrants arrived a group of Irishmen who soon loomed large in Philadelphia's intellectual and artistic life. They carried their hatred of England with them to Philadelphia and became stalwarts of the emerging Democratic-Republican party of Jefferson. Their ranks included Mathew Carey, who founded one of the city's premier publishing houses and became a distinguished political economist; William Duane, the longtime editor of the *Aurora*, the newspaper established by Benjamin Franklin's grandson; John Binns, editor of the *Democratic Press*, which played to the laboring people of the city for many years; Joseph Gales, another promoter of urban Jeffersonianism; Doctor James Reynolds, an ardent Philadelphia Jeffersonian; John Dougherty, a pioneer in canal-boat transportation across the Alleghenies; and Denis Driscol, an ex-Roman Catholic priest who launched a deist magazine, *The Temple of Reason*, in Philadelphia. All would become embroiled in the controversy surrounding the emergence of the nation's two-party system, in which Philadelphia, as the nation's capital, figured crucially. But none of the group, except for Duane and Carey, would leave substantial records of their involvement.[18]

Party Politics

"We must drive far away the demon of party spirit," counseled Washington in 1790. Yet the policies of his own government sowed the seeds for an opposition party to take root. Soon, Federalists and Democratic-Republicans were organizing, first at the local and state level, then as national parties, each with their own newspapers, pamphleteers, and leaders in Congress. "Mad dogs!" howled the Federalist *Gazette of the United States* against the critics of Washington's new government. Jefferson's Republicans, in turn, called a Federalist editor a "white-livered, black hearted thing . . . a public pest and bane of decency." The level of participation in politics was higher in the 1790s than ever before in Philadelphia and probably higher than it would be for the next century.[19]

Revolution in France further divided the city and country. Some saw the French revolutionists fulfilling the promise of the unfinished American Revolution. Others saw

FIGURE 56. *A Peep into the Antifederal Club*, cartoon, 1793, LCP. David Rittenhouse, president of the Democratic Society, peers through a telescope with a devil on his left. The big-bellied Dr. James Hutchinson, fellow of the College of Physicians and co-founder of the Democratic Society, drinks a toast: "Damnation to the Federal Government." Also shown are Tom Paine, Thomas Jefferson, a Frenchman, and a black Philadelphian—all identified with the vocal political opposition that had arisen by this time. The alleged creed of the Democratic Society includes such slogans as "Liberty is the Power of doing anything we like," "All Power in one body and that Body Ourselves," and "Governments but another name for Aristocracy." How widely these often scurrilous cartoons were circulated is an open question.

only anarchy, atheism, and an excess of democracy. Both Federalists and Democratic-Republicans became adept at mobilizing demonstrations of popular politics, which often had an edge of violence. John Adams later recalled that "ten thousand People in the Streets of Philadelphia, day after day, threatened to drag Washington out of his house, and effect a Revolution in Government."[20] In May 1798, a Federalist crowd stormed the house of Benjamin Franklin Bache while another band of youths played the "Rogue's March" beneath the windows of Vice President Jefferson.

Philadelphia's Democratic-Republican Society, founded in 1793, was part of the budding Jeffersonian opposition to the financial policies of Washington's first administration. The Society also fervently supported the French Revolution and democratic institutions in the United States. *A Peep into the Antifederal Club* (Figure 56), a Federalist cartoon designed to ridicule the Democratic Society, was an early contribution to what became a torrent of political cartoons in the turbulent 1790s.

Political controversy waxed in 1794-95. Hamilton's excise tax on whiskey touched off a rebellion in western Pennsylvania in 1794; and in the same year Jay's Treaty with England, which settled several disputes with the British but not all, proved detestable to many Philadelphians. Philadelphian Blair McClenachan, a Jeffersonian leader, urged an angry crowd to "kick this damned treaty to hell."[21] If they could not kick the treaty to hell, a plebeian crowd could at least drag a carted effigy of Jay through the streets and attack the mansion of William Bingham, a Federalist merchant, U.S. senator, close associate of Robert Morris, and leading defender of Jay's Treaty. Bingham's mansion was an appropriate target for democratic-minded protestors because it was a perfect symbol of what Democratic-Republicans saw as a resurgence of Tory-like, aristocracy-minded conservatism. The most pretentious residence built in this era, the lavishly furnished mansion had become the scene of glittering dances and banquets, regally presided over by Anne Willing Bingham. Abigail Adams called her "the dazzling Mrs. Bingham" and clucked at the latter's entertaining such royalty as the émigré duc d'Orléans (later King Louis-Philippe) and the duc de la Rochefoucauld-Liancourt.

In 1798, the first crisis in civil liberties struck Philadelphia. When a Federalist-dominated Congress passed the Alien and Sedition acts, attempting to muzzle the Jeffersonian press and undercut the participation in politics of Irish immigrants, the first victim of the attacks on a free press was Benjamin Franklin Bache, grandson of Benjamin and Deborah Franklin. Bache owned and edited the *Aurora*, the city's leading Democratic-Republican newspaper, and published hard-hitting pamphlets against the Federalists. Even when jailed for seditious libel of the president (for what today would be nothing more than ordinary criticism of the chief executive), he refused to be silenced. Rather, it was yellow fever that silenced him. He died before the case reached court.[22]

If the Federalists were as aristocratic as critics such as Bache charged, they were anything but aristocratic in returning the journalistic volleys of the Democratic-Republicans. Their chief cannoneer was William Cobbett, who wrote for hire as "Peter Porcupine" and scribbled prolifically to support his large family (Figure 57). Mathew Carey, who hated the English, emerged as the most able Jeffersonian propagandist; he was fully capable of matching Cobbett's venom and provided an effective contact with Irish voters in the city. Carey sent his *A Plumb Pudding for . . . Peter Porcupine* (1799) to his network of booksellers far and wide and flooded the seaboard with 6,000 broadsides quoting pungent selections from this anti-Federalist diatribe. Cobbett finally fled the city to escape punishment for libeling Benjamin Rush.

The rhetorical political violence of the 1790s makes it seem unlikely that women would enter this overheated political milieu, but they did as never before. Building on their involvement in the American Revolution, Philadelphia's women became actively engaged, though they lacked any official political status. The arrival in 1792 of Mary Wollstonecraft's *Vindication of the Rights of Women* and two quickly run off Philadelphia reprints of several thousand copies heightened the discussion of gender roles and broadened the opinion that women's political and economic rights ought to be widened. Even conservative Quaker Elizabeth Drinker, a devoted Federalist, thought Wollstonecraft "speaks my mind." How fast this sentiment spread was evident in the salutatorian ad-

FIGURE 57. *Porcupine, in Colours Just Portrayed*, cartoon, c. 1799, HSP. The verbal violence of the late 1790s proved a big boon for artists adept at caricature, because both political parties saw the advantage of pillorying their opponents in cheaply produced sheets. This Jeffersonian cartoon by an unknown artist shows a grotesque devil, a Federalist advisor with his bag of gold (a common portrayal for this era), and the British lion encouraging Cobbett the porcupine, while the Goddess Liberty, with her phrygian cap on a pike, weeps over the bust of Benjamin Franklin with his coonskin cap. Cobbett says, "I hate this country and will sow the seeds of discord in it," while the devil promises to "destroy this Idol liberty."

dress of the young Priscilla Mason at the Philadelphia Young Ladies' Academy, founded in 1787, the first chartered female academy in the United States. Mason struck out at "our high and mighty lords (thanks to their arbitrary constitutions) [who] have denied us the means of knowledge, and then reproached us for the want of it." The Female Academy was proof that "a more liberal way of thinking begins to prevail," she allowed, but what outlets would educated women find for their talent? "The Church, the Bar, and the Senate are shut against us. Who shut them? *Man*; despotic man, first made us incapable of the duty, and then forbid us the exercise."[23]

Adding to the galvanizing effect of Wollstonecraft's *Vindication* was the role of women in the French Revolution, then widely noticed in the press and in pamphlets reaching Philadelphia. The men who served in the state and national governments were both meeting in the city, and their wives frequently organized political salons and contributed to the airing of weighty issues. Numerous young girls sporting tricolored ribbons took part in the festive public rituals celebrating French victories, and theater-going Philadelphians watched Mrs. Violence and Mrs. Turbulence arguing heatedly over Jay's Treaty—all a reflection of how women were becoming caught up in the escalating tension as the French Revolution entered its most violent stage and war spread across Europe, as Napoleon's armies crushed counterrevolutionaries. Among the most caught up was Deborah Norris Logan, descended from one of the city's oldest Quaker families and married to the descendant of another. When her husband, Doctor George Logan, embarked on a peace mission to Paris to defuse the crisis with France that Democratic-Republicans believed was the work of pro-English Federalists, Deborah Logan put herself in the middle of the pitched battle between the two parties. The Federalist press, led by William Cobbett, heaped abuse on her as she made Stenton, the Logan residence outside the city, a center of political gatherings. Logan considered herself "as much interested in the welfare of the state as anybody, and fit to be intrusted with its secrets."[24]

The officers and patrons of Philadelphia's collecting institutions of this era—the Philosophical Society and Library Company—were strongly Federalist; aghast at the violence of the French Revolution, they wanted to remain aloof from the bruising political battles, local and national, that swirled around them. In any event, their interests were scientific, literary, and mildly religious. Nonetheless, true to its tradition of collecting whatever was of interest to its patrons, the Library Company's catalogue of books in 1807 showed about 250 political pamphlets published in the tumultuous 1790s. Much later, the first organizers of the Historical Society had the same distaste for the rise of popular politics, then flourishing in Jackson's era of the common man. Yet fascinating materials entered their collections, mostly in the second half of the twentieth century, when descendants of early republic leaders began recognizing the Historical Society as a premier repository of archival materials. Historians in recent decades have used the political correspondence and business records of dozens of important Federalist and Jeffersonian merchants, lawyers, publishers, and bankers—individuals such as Mathew Carey, Thomas McKean, George and Deborah Logan, Tench Coxe, Francis Hopkinson, and Henry and Elizabeth Drinker—to reveal the seamiest aspects of politics and social turmoil in the new republic.

Peale's Museum and Historical Memory

If Philadelphia's collecting institutions had limited interest in Paine and his radical associates, as we have seen in Chapter 3, they were absolutely in love with one of the early compatriots of the author of *Common Sense*—and have been so ever since. Charles Willson Peale had been a brother-in-arms with Paine in the first year of the Revolutionary War, was deeply implicated with Paine in Philadelphia's radical politics of 1778-80, and regarded Paine as a close friend and ally. Both were romantic idealists. Both believed in reason rather than religion as the way forward. Both were propagandists, Paine using his pen, Peale his brush. But the careers of the two men veered sharply by the mid-1780s.

Paine left Philadelphia for France in 1787, not to return until 1803, while Peale made the city his permanent home. Peale worked with a singular determination to shape the city's remembrance of the American Revolution, as a way of helping his community to discover "the American genius." He became a cultural hero in his own right as he turned to instruct and entertain a mass audience. Meanwhile, the memory of Paine began to fade, and his attitude toward Washington, whom he reviled just before the general's death, made him an antihero.[25]

Peale's mission to shape public memory of the Revolution began even before the war was over. His experiences as a militia captain at the second battle of Trenton and at Princeton and his bonding with Washington at Valley Forge proved only the beginning of his efforts to emblazon the commander-in-chief in the consciousness of the citizenry. Fresh from the victory at Yorktown in late October 1781, Washington found himself welcomed in Philadelphia by a display of allegorical transparencies, backlit paintings on varnished paper, at Peale's house at Third and Lombard Streets. In one window the public could gaze on large pictures of Washington and Rochambeau, with rays of glory springing from their heads; another window glowed with an illuminated *Genius of America*, a woman wearing flowing white with a purple girdle. Marked VIRTUE, she was depicted trampling a figure of Discord with snakes in place of hair. Still other illuminated windows displayed *The Temple of Independence*, with thirteen columns for the states supported by a base inscribed THE VOICE OF THE PEOPLE, and another architectural element inscribed with the names of great battles. Peale was learning how to use public art to memorialize the Revolution even before anyone knew whether Cornwallis's surrender at Yorktown would actually bring an end to the war with a satisfactory peace treaty.

Eager that Americans be "animated with a sacred love for their country," Peale opened a portrait gallery in a new sixty-six-foot addition to his house where, for a modest fee, Philadelphians could see about thirty of his bust portraits of such personages as Franklin, many of Washington's generals, presidents of the Continental Congress, and a number of foreign emissaries, all presided over by a full-length portrait of Washington.[26] Opening in November 1782, this was the first Philadelphia installation that invited reflection on the American Revolution and veneration of its heroes, even as the drama continued to unfold. The situation remained highly volatile, as suggested by the mutiny of unpaid soldiers that drove Congress from Philadelphia to Princeton in September 1783.

Then, in December 1783, Congress offered Peale the chance to show Philadelphians how to celebrate properly the ratification of the peace treaty with England—and in the bargain bolster his faltering finances. With a £600 subsidy, Peale unleashed all his artist-inventor ingenuity. After building a set of Roman arches fifty-six feet wide to stretch across Market Street and dressing them with Ionic pillars and balustrades, he painted revolutionary scenes and mottoes on transparent paper. These were stretched across the arches and backlit by 1,150 lamps controlled by various mechanical devices. One of the transparencies showed Indians erecting churches in the wilderness; others showed war heroes thrashing the redcoats; another portrayed laurel-crowned Washington as Cincinnatus going back to his plow. The central arch was emblazoned with a Latin motto, which those in the know could read as "By divine favor, a great and new order of the ages commences."

Peale was denied his triumph—and almost lost his life—in the effort to bring patriotism to a proper pitch on the evening of January 22, 1784. He had built a monumental figure of Peace with her attendant deities atop the house of Pennsylvania's executive council president, close to the triumphal arches, and had contrived for the figure of Peace to descend along a rope from which she would ignite a fuse that would touch off the 1,150 lamps. With all the transparencies of Washington and conquering heroes illuminated, 700 rockets were to erupt from the top of the arch to open the celebration. The pyrotechnics backfired, however, raining down on the crowd and nearly igniting Peale, who was standing atop the main arch. Built of varnished paper and cloth over scaffolding, the gigantic arch broke into flames. Peale leaped from the top of the arch to a lower platform and then hurled himself away from a mass of exploding rockets. Falling twenty feet to the ground, he broke several ribs and was burned badly.

Bedridden for three weeks, Peale suffered through his painful injuries, but he wore his wounds like battle scars. His spirits dampened only slightly, he was soon at work on putting Washington's image in everyone's home. Peale had painted Washington at the request of the Continental Congress in 1776, and versions of this portrait were used for engravings that were reaching many parts of Europe. But now, with commissions from Virginia and Maryland to do full-length portraits of the commander-in-chief, Peale began painting Washington in earnest, thus beginning a family industry that, over the next several decades, produced several hundred paintings and miniatures of the general—and, what was more profitable, prints struck off from the oil paintings. His paintings of Washington at Princeton and elsewhere gave Americans a Washington with an "affable mien and stout physique," a man of "mildness combined with strength, a quality of benevolent power."[27]

With many portraits of Washington under his belt, Peale began painting other revolutionary figures to supplement the thirty already on display in his home. Included were political titans such as John Jay and Franklin, Washington generals such as Anthony Wayne and Henry Knox, signers of the Declaration of Independence such as John Witherspoon and Henry Laurens, and foreign emissaries such as Diego de Gardoqui and Chevalier de Cambray-Digny. But now, when he opened a new portrait gallery and museum on July 7, 1786, in his Lombard Street house, about fifty revolutionary heroes looked down on stuffed quadrupeds and birds displayed in painted habitats along with Indian figures dressed in ceremonial garb. Lectures and laboratory demonstrations supplemented the ever-changing exhibits. Peale had seized on the idea of a natural history museum that might even be more interesting and instructive than the portraits. His paintings would engrave on citizens' minds the great figures of the Revolution, but the natural history displays would provide "rational entertainment" and improve "the morals of the people." For Peale, like many of his generation, only a "virtuous education" would maintain "the liberties of the people."[28]

The arrival of the Constitutional Convention in the summer of 1787 provided Peale with new opportunities to shape public memory of the recent past. Knowing there could never be too many Washingtons, he importuned the general, now emerging from a year of retirement at Mount Vernon, to sit for a new portrait. Washington posed for three mornings before attending the sessions of the convention in the State House, and Peale turned the painting into a mezzotint that went on sale ten days after the convention adjourned. When it sold only modestly at one dollar, he dropped the price to two-thirds of a dollar.

Peale soon had a fresh chance to establish common values while creating greater rapport with the public and solidifying his relations with his old political enemies of a decade before. The Federalist managers of the federal procession in 1788—Federalist Francis Hopkinson was the chairman of the organizing committee—meant to celebrate the ratification of the Constitution and lay the groundwork for its acceptance by submerging the anti-Federalist malcontents in a show of unity. Much of the sense of spontaneous cohesion that the procession created can be credited to Peale's ingenuity and mastery of public art. Peale helped plot the procession's route, painted many of the floats, engineered simulated water for the "Federal Ship" to glide on, and helped design the Grand Federal Edifice—a thirty-six-foot-high domed building with thirteen Corinthian columns and a Peale-constructed Goddess dispensing blessings. Public art was on display to venerate, as a herald in the procession proclaimed, "a new aera" aborning.

Peale soon returned to the business of creating his Philadelphia Museum, familiarly known as "Peale's Museum" (Figure 58). In 1794, when his omnivorous natural history collecting and production of new portraits cramped the space in his Lombard Street house, Peale moved his stuffed quadrupeds, birds, fish, scientific demonstrations, insects, and shells to the newly built Philosophical Hall, across the street from the State House. Later that summer, Peale helped found the Columbianum to promote and exhibit the work of American artists; it failed but led to the creation of the Pennsylvania Academy of Fine Arts eleven years later, where many paintings of the Peale family found a permanent home.

No Philadelphia institution summed up so well as Peale's Museum the notion that there was something special about America. Like many other Philadelphians, Peale believed that collecting, cataloguing, and studying the works of man and nature would fulfill the promise of the American "national genius." The admission ticket to his museum proclaimed: "NATURE. The Birds and Beasts will teach thee." Part of the reason why this became the first popular museum of natural history is that Peale kept the admission price to twenty-five cents, gave complete access to his growing store of paintings and natural history exhibits, and carefully cultivated broad patronage. To be sure, even twenty-five cents was more than many Philadelphians could afford, and recent scholarship confirms what is true today even at free museums—that museumgoers who went to see Peale's assemblage of artifacts and portraits were drawn overwhelmingly from the middle and upper classes.

Peale regarded his museum as "a world in miniature," its objects to be arranged according to the accepted Linnaean system wherein everything was part of an ordered and

FIGURE 58. Charles Willson Peale, *The Artist in His Museum*, oil, 1779, PAFA. Commissioned by the trustees of his museum "to paint a full length likeness of himself for the Museum," Peale went to work at age eighty-one. His brushes and palette lie on the table at the right. Giant mastodon bones and the lower part of the huge skeleton that attracted thousands of visitors each year appear to the right. But Peale himself dominates the scene as he lifts the curtain, inviting the visitor to enter a room filled with natural history cases, all surmounted by the rows of portraits. At his feet are taxidermy tools beside a wild turkey ready for mounting. In the background, a lady in a Quaker bonnet raises her arms in astonishment while looking at the giant mastodon skeleton.

unified world. In fact, as he announced, the museum gave Philadelphians a closer look at "the wonderful works of nature" than had ever before been possible. They could see golden pheasants from Mount Vernon, enormous rattlesnakes, an anteater measuring more than seven feet from snout to tail, a jackal, swordfish, East Indian insects, birds by the hundreds, a Damascus sword, skulls of the royal tiger, an African bow brought to South Carolina by a slave, and wax models of humans from afar, including a Chinese laborer, a "sooty African," a Sandwich Islander, and several American Indians. An odd grouping of stuffed animals in the corner of a home-based portrait gallery was turning into one of the new nation's premier cultural and scientific institutions.

After 1801, when Peale purchased the bones of a mastodon excavated in Ulster County, New York, and dug for five months with the assistance of his son Rembrandt and his slave Moses Williams to find other bones of the extinct mammoth, the public soon marveled at an assembled skeleton standing eleven feet high and fifteen feet long, with eleven-foot tusks. By 1814, the museum, advertised as "little inferior to the imperial Museums of Europe," had 212 animals in the quadruped room, including a Madagascar bat measuring three feet two inches, tip to tip; an elephant seal from the South Seas; 1,240 birds, 148 snakes, and 112 lizards; shells of great Indian Ocean oysters weighing 350 pounds; some 800 dresses from distant parts of the world; and instruments of war, tools, scientific instruments—in all, more than one hundred thousand artifacts. In displaying material from distant cultures and Native Americans, Peale hoped to "promote the peaceful coexistence of diverse peoples."[29] Yet he was thoroughly a man of his time in portraying a hierarchy of races, from primitive to civilized, as designed by nature. His attempt to synthesize hierarchy and harmony may have seemed fanciful if not blind to the Shawnee leaders who toured the museum while in Philadelphia in 1796 for treaty negotiations, for they knew they had recently been defeated at Fallen Timbers while attempting to protect their ancient homelands in the Ohio River valley.

If the natural history exhibits in Peale's museum were a "world in miniature" replete with messages about the laws of nature, his portrait gallery showed visitors what Peale wanted his fellow citizens to remember vividly about the American Revolution and the new nation. Peale increased the gallery from 43 portraits in 1784 to 70 in 1804, 136 in 1814, and 180 by 1818, adding many men of religion and science, some of the latter from abroad, as well as portraits of nonagenarians and centenarians whom Peale venerated for their extreme age (Figure 59). Many were painted by his brother and son to become part of a national pantheon. Though he had formally retired from portrait painting on commission by the early 1790s, when his museum absorbed his interests almost entirely and provided the income that had eluded him for so long, Peale painted those he wanted in his portrait gallery. But he added few that would broaden the spectrum of remembrance among the thousands of visitors who paid their twenty-five cents and trooped through his museum. By the time Peale moved his museum and portrait gallery to the State House in 1802, where he leased the entire second floor and the east room of the first floor, visitors received a visual lesson on the revolutionary heroes fit for public veneration.

But only the rare painting would remind people of the "furious Whigs" from the

FIGURE 59. Charles Willson Peale, *Yarrow Mamout*, oil, 1817, HSP. After the Revolution, Peale painted few figures who had shared his own radical political inclinations. Perhaps this was because they did not commission him, but he painted ordinary people without fee who excited his interest. One was Yarrow Mamout, a Muslim slave who bought his freedom, acquired property, and settled in Georgetown, District of Columbia. Peale painted this portrait after seeking out Mamout, who at the time was reputed to be 134 years old. Longevity was a phenomenon of great interest to Peale and provided his reason for including this painting in his Museum. In an interesting case of lost historical memory, the Pennsylvania Academy of Fine Arts, when exhibiting an astounding 317 portraits of the Peale family, identified Yarrow Mamout as Billy Lee, George Washington's servant who ran away in Philadelphia, one of at least forty-seven slaves who fled Washington over his many years as a slaveholder. Not until 1947, almost a century later, was this mistaken identity remedied—remarkable considering that William Lee, who looked very little like Yarrow Mamout, appeared in several widely exhibited paintings of Washington.

1770s, of which Peale was one, or of any prominent Pennsylvania anti-Federalists of the 1780s, or of any of Philadelphia's Jeffersonian leaders in the 1790s (though national leaders such as Madison, Gallatin, and Jefferson himself were included). Visitors would see a dozen of Washington's generals; a dozen French noblemen who came to fight with the Americans; plenty of conservative Philadelphia Whigs of the revolutionary era, such as John Dickinson, Robert Morris, Benjamin Rush, Thomas Mifflin, Thomas McKean, Charles Thomson, and Joseph Reed; and national Federalist figures such as John Adams, Alexander Hamilton, and James Madison. But visitors would never see the faces of James Cannon, principal author of the radical constitution of 1776 and leader of the Committee of Privates; Jonathan Dickinson Sergeant, a fervid Whig; George Bryan, leader of the radicals and author of the 1780 abolition act; or John Swanwick, Alexander Dallas, or Michel Leib, Jeffersonian leaders in Philadelphia. Peale did include his old friend Paine, but he was the only "furious Whig" from the days of radical republicanism during the Revolution who gazed down on the public. And it would be half a century before visitors glimpsed Timothy Matlack. Peale had painted him twice and finally put a third portrait in the gallery in 1826, when Matlack was in his nineties.

Peale's carefully adjusted national pantheon can be explained by the fact that the success of his museum depended in part on the prestige he could gain by attracting rich and famous supporters. Scorched in 1779-80 for his radical politics, he seems to have seen the wisdom of not offending conservative political and cultural leaders, who had succeeded in overturning the radical state constitution of 1776 and replacing it with a much more conservative one in 1790. After all, Peale had a large family to house and feed and the best of the patrons of art, as his chief biographer tells us, "were cool to a Furious Whig who had publicly investigated Robert Morris as a profiteer." This was no time, as the present editor of the Peale Papers puts it, for Peale "to be caught isolated on the left."[30] Hence, Peale's portrait gallery, meant to define the values derived from the past, recalled the American revolutionary era selectively. For good reasons in terms of promoting his museum, Peale manipulated history by erasing parts of the revolutionary past in which he himself had been passionately involved. Ironically, wooing a broad patronage involved bowing to conservative patrons.

Athens of the Western World

Prophecies of America's greatness in the arts and sciences began to appear in the mid-eighteenth century. "'Tis the Art's delight," Franklin pronounced, "to travel Westward." Many Americans expected the Revolution to usher in a new age of culture, as the people cast off the restraining bonds of Britain's empire and the national genius was given full rein. Indeed, the emergence of a uniquely American culture seemed essential to molding a nation out of loosely confederated states.

"The days of Greece may be revived in the woods of America, and Philadelphia become the Athens of the Western world," wrote architect Benjamin Henry Latrobe in

1811. The city fulfilled Latrobe's hopes when the elite's reading of history demanded a break from Georgian architecture associated with a corrupt line of kings, in favor of an architectural style reminding people of a classical epoch of public virtue and untarnished heroes. His Bank of Pennsylvania (1801) began the Greek Revival in American architecture, linking classical ideas with the political principles of the new republic. Latrobe trained William Strickland, who by the 1820s was at the center of the Greek Revival boom in city architecture. Of Strickland it has been said that, like Caesar Augustus in Rome, he found Philadelphia a city of brick and left it a city of marble. Also in the midst of the Greek Revival, as it gained momentum in the antebellum period, were the English immigrants John Haviland and Thomas U. Walter. The latter, later the architect of the U.S. Capitol, left his stamp on the Philadelphia area through his government buildings in surrounding county seats.[31]

The establishment of the Pennsylvania Academy of the Fine Arts in 1805 was an indispensable element in the flourishing of high culture in Philadelphia. Ten years before, Philadelphia artists organized the first major art exhibition ever mounted in the United States, which they called the Columbianum. This led to the academy's annual exhibition, which made possible the notion of professionalism for American artists and encouraged their search for more sophisticated patrons. The academy's teachers trained generations of artists, who in turn taught all over the United States. But their efforts at nation-making proved to have a very limited effect on public memory. This was because the academy's exhibitions, like those that soon began in other cities, emulated those of London's Royal Academy, where a clear hierarchy of artistic subject matter, or genres, prevailed. Judged most worthy were paintings of literary subjects, Biblical narratives, and historical events. People as they lived from day to day were deemed less desirable subjects. The academy was a site for genteel contemplation rather than public engagement with the past.

The War of 1812 did allow artists to engage the public in historic events. Capturing naval battle scenes became a specialty for Thomas Birch, son of William Birch whose city scenes were widely admired. Thomas Birch's rendering of the U.S.S. *Constitution* (built in Philadelphia) and the *Guerrière* was one of a number of heralded paintings related to the war. Later in the nineteenth century and into the twentieth, the Historical Society, like most of the nation, celebrated the War of 1812 as an early chapter in manifest destiny. Hampton Carson, writing in the 1920s, praised the artists who captured naval battle scenes in the war that "revealed us as a nation triumphant on the sea and the lakes over the navy of Great Britain." Behind the naval victories, "so glorious in themselves, lay the growing consciousness of the strength of the young but potentially giant nation, a Hercules in his cradle."[32]

Publishing became part of the cultural efflorescence. In the early nineteenth century, advances in technology and expanding markets greatly encouraged the publication of prints, books, newspapers, and periodicals. In 1786, Philadelphia's printers had issued only 174 imprints, but by 1810 some 425 streamed off the presses of a flourishing publishing industry. Such a book boom necessarily augmented the demand for engravers.

FIGURE 60. William Charles, *A Boxing Match, or Another Bloody Nose for John Bull*, LCP. The clever title for this cartoon alludes to the victory of the American frigate *Enterprise* in September 1813 over the British warship *Boxer*. King George III, with bleeding nose and blackened eye, cries for mercy. James Madison on the right retorts: "Ha-Ah Johnny! You thought yourself a *Boxer* did you—I'll let you know we are an *Enterprize*ing Nation and ready to meet you with equal force any day." Shortly after this cartoon appeared, British naval and land forces burned the American capitol in Washington, D.C.

From a scant three working in the city during the American Revolution, their number grew to sixty by 1810. Established firms like Mathew Carey's (later Carey and Son and then Carey and Lea) soon faced stiff competition from a host of publishers like Thomas Dobson, who took great risk when he issued the first American edition of the *Encyclopaedia Britannica*, in twenty-two quarto volumes and 542 copper plates, between 1790 and 1802. Projects of this size and sumptuousness would have been unthinkable only a few years before, but once they proved feasible, many others followed. Perhaps the most breathtaking was Alexander Wilson's nine-volume *American Ornithology* (1807–14), advertised as the most beautiful book ever published in the country. Appealing to American pride, the publisher Samuel F. Bradford trumpeted its all-American character: American paper, American type, American ink, American colors (including a spectacular yellow "from the laboratory of Messrs. Peale and Son, of the Museum of this city"), and American-built presses. On its heels came an American edition of Rees's *Cyclopedia; or, Universal Dictionary of Arts, Sciences, and Literature* (1810–27), in a spectacular forty-one volumes with more than 1,400 engravings.

The War of 1812 also revived another artistic form, though it involved vernacular rather than polite art. This was political cartooning, in which Philadelphia had no monopoly but nevertheless seemed to lead the nation. Needing controversy or subjects to ridicule, the cartoonists had languished after Jefferson's election in 1800, ending the bruising political controversies of the 1790s. But the second war with England brought forth a rush of topical cartoons, most of them lampooning the British. William Charles, who had arrived from England about 1806, showed his allegiance to his adopted country with a series of stinging attacks on John Bull (Figure 60).

For the Historical Society's early leaders, this foundation period of the American political system was certainly hallowed; but their emphasis before the Civil War was on collecting materials related to the founding of Pennsylvania and to the Revolutionary War. It was in the post-Civil War era, when the reunion of the states demanded a vision of the past that stressed unity and shared loyalties, that greater interest arose in collecting materials from what was becoming known as the "early national" period.

Though Philadelphia became a center for setting the standards of early nineteenth-century American culture, expressed in natural history, art and architecture, theater, political oratory, and science, "official culture" neither represented nor appealed to many urban people. Immigrants, laboring people, African Americans, and others established alternative cultures that paralleled and sometimes challenged what leading citizens defined as the culture of America. By the early 1820s, this trend was apparent, indeed painfully obvious, to some of the city's leading figures, who bestirred themselves to remedy what they feared was the fragmentation of a society only beginning to construct its unique American identity.

Chapter 5

A CITY IN FLUX

Between 1815 and 1860, Philadelphians experienced dizzying growth and a tangled set of changes that were both exhilarating and wrenching (Figure 61). Their commercial seaport and center of government became a major manufacturing center in the "Age of Iron." Though stripped of its federal and state capital status, the relatively contained city of just under one hundred thousand grew into a sprawling metropolis of more than half a million. With growth and manufacturing in the nation's second-largest city came unheard of opportunities for some, a higher standard of living for many, terrible deprivation for others, and many knotty problems. Historians now believe this was the most violent era of the city's history. Philadelphians had to face that reality collectively.

The new manufacturing city demanded workers. From the hinterland came young rural men and women seeking new opportunities in the city. From the South came thousands of African Americans, free or fleeing slavery. And from abroad came the English, the Scots, the Germans, and especially the Irish. Rapid industrial expansion and heavy immigration proved an explosive mix, so filling the city with political, religious, racial, and economic strife that the old concept of brotherly love seemed a lost and distant memory.

New Immigrants

Except when the embargo of 1807-9 and war with England in 1812-15 stopped shipping, a year never passed during the antebellum era without dozens of immigrant ships arriving at Philadelphia. In the vanguard of the nation's economic development, Philadelphia became the destination of thousands of Europeans from small farms and tiny villages who became part of a long-term, rural-to-urban phenomenon developing in the Atlantic economy. Famine in Ireland and revolution in Germany brought especially heavy immigration from the late 1840s to the eve of the Civil War. By 1850, when the city and county of Philadelphia had 409,000 residents, nearly 30 percent were foreign-born, whereas census takers twenty years before had found that only ten of every hundred Philadelphians who were born abroad. Almost 60 percent of all the new immigrants were from Ireland, with Germans (19 percent) and English and Scottish (17 percent) contributing smaller numbers to the ethnic mélange.

As in other seaboard urban centers, the immigrants found much that was heartening

FIGURE 61. J. C. Wild, *Panorama of Philadelphia, from the State House Steeple,* lithograph, 1838, LCP. Like so many of Philadelphia's lithographers, Wild was an immigrant, arriving from Switzerland in 1831. Seven years later, he did four panoramic views of Philadelphia from the steeple of the State House. In this view, looking east to the Delaware River, Market Street can be seen to the left and the American Philosophical Society in the foreground. The steeple of Christ Church is at the upper left.

and much that was heartbreaking. Those arriving with skills—more English and German than Irish—readily found good jobs, yet steady employment was elusive in the half century before the Civil War, when the nation's economy suffered three major depressions. For those without personal resources or urban skills, including almost all the Irish, keeping body and soul together was a continual struggle. When Mathew Carey, friend of the immigrant Irish, calculated the annual wages of a laborer in 1829 at about $58, he discovered that two thirds of this amount was eaten up by house rent and fuel.[1]

Much like other American cities, Philadelphia in the middle third of the nineteenth century grew prodigiously into a city with fine new mansions, luxury shops, and a flourishing genteel culture. Simultaneously, it spread west to the Schuylkill River and north and south out of the old commercial core into neighborhoods of shanty-filled back alleys and teeming courtyards, whose inhabitants suffered from frightening infant mortality rates, cholera, and malnutrition. But between these extremes emerged a city of solid, sober, middling urban dwellers who proudly called Philadelphia "a city of homes." Advantaged by a gridiron pattern of streets that allowed the orderly plotting of home lots and doubly advantaged by the colonial phenomenon of "ground rent" whereby a lot could be rented cheaply for a long period rather than purchased, Philadelphians on the

FIGURE 62. Peter Augustus Kollner, *The Draymen*, in *Common Sights in Town & Country*, FLP. Kollner was deeply involved in Philadelphia's growing German American community from which he derived much business in lithographing *taufscheins* (birth certificates). Noted for his technical expertise in drawing horses, Kollner used them in city and country scenes wherever possible. *The Draymen* shows two roustabouts racing through the street. The morally uplifting point in the text is to treat animals kindly and avoid endangering pedestrians. "How much mischief comes from inconsideration," concludes the text. The Historical Society, Library Company, and Free Library acquired copies of several editions of *Common Sights in Town & Country*.

rise could buy or build a two-story brick row house with water and gas service for $1,000-$2,500 in 1850. Statistics-minded observers boasted that half the laboring families owned their own house by 1860, and Philadelphia's density of 6.7 persons per house shamed tenement-infested New York where density was 13.7 per house. Life for the Irish, near the bottom of the ladder in the impoverished neighborhoods of the Schuylkill and Port Richmond districts, was difficult but better than in the grim Boston districts of Fort Hill and South Boston.[2]

Only scattered remnants of the immigrants' culture have found their way into the collections of the Historical Society and other collecting institutions except for the papers of immigrants who rose high in urban society, such as printer-publisher Mathew Carey and textile manufacturer J. J. Borie. Carey was one of the few immigrants who took up his pen on behalf of the impoverished. Just eight years after arriving in Philadelphia in 1784, he organized the Hibernian Society for the Relief of Emigrants from Ireland, and from that point on he concerned himself with their struggles. Particularly, he cudgeled

Philadelphians for keeping their purses shut while charging that the poor were starving because of their idleness and fondness for drink. To this day, his essays on the desperate struggles of working women—*The Wages of Female Labour* (1829), *The Case of the Seamstresses* (1833), *Letters on the Condition of the Poor... Containing Instances of Intense Suffering in Philadelphia, Not Exceeded in London or Paris* (1835), and *A Plea for the Poor* (1837)—are a vital source of information on immigrant life at the bottom. That his funeral procession in 1839 was the second-largest known in the city testified to the gratitude of the shanty Irish and all the other poor Philadelphians who benefited from his support.

Seldom did drawings capture the world of the immigrants, though in the decades before the Civil War, artists ushered in an exciting new era of lithography that pictured the city more vigorously and variously than ever before. For example, David J. Kennedy, an immigrant from Scotland who took up residence in Philadelphia in 1839, drew circuses, ice-skating scenes on the river, coal and lumber yards, taverns, cigar stores, and factories as well as bridges, churches, public buildings, and notable mansions. But with the exception of a watercolor portraying immigrants landing at the Walnut Street wharf in 1851, Kennedy's drawings seldom included people of any sort, let alone immigrants, except as faceless generic figures. Cephas Grier Childs was another engraver of Philadelphia views, which he produced between 1827 and 1830 and dedicated to the Historical Society of Pennsylvania "as a token of zeal for its objects and of esteem for its valuable labours," but these views were architecture-centered, with people included only incidentally. Why would any lithographer care to document the shantytown Schuylkill or Moyamensing districts where the Irish and African Americans huddled?

An exception was Peter Augustus Kollner, an immigrant from Germany who arrived in 1839 and became a prolific producer of cityscapes alive with people pursuing ordinary trades available to immigrants—the iceman making his rounds, the oysterman at his barrow, draymen urging their horses over the city's cobblestones. When the American Sunday-School Union began flooding the city with illustrated books bearing large legible morals, it chose Kollner as its illustrator. Though *Common Sights in Town & Country Delineated & Described for Young Children* made no specific reference to immigrants, children at least for the first time saw ordinary people at work (Figure 62).

While immigrants by tens of thousands disembarked from oceangoing ships at Philadelphia's wharves, African Americans freed from slavery in other states or fleeing from it arrived by foot, wagon, or coastal boat. As the southernmost northern city, Philadelphia became an important terminus of the Underground Railroad flourishing in the 1850s. By the time the Historical Society was founded in 1824, Philadelphia was the most important urban center of free blacks in the country. Its black churches, schools, and mutual aid associations were more numerous than in any other American city, and the city's black community produced many state and national leaders. On the eve of the Civil War, Philadelphia was home to more than 22,000 African Americans, the largest urban concentration outside the South. A report in 1847 showed that nearly half of Philadelphia's African Americans were born outside the state.[3]

It seems paradoxical that, of all the newcomers to Philadelphia in the decades before

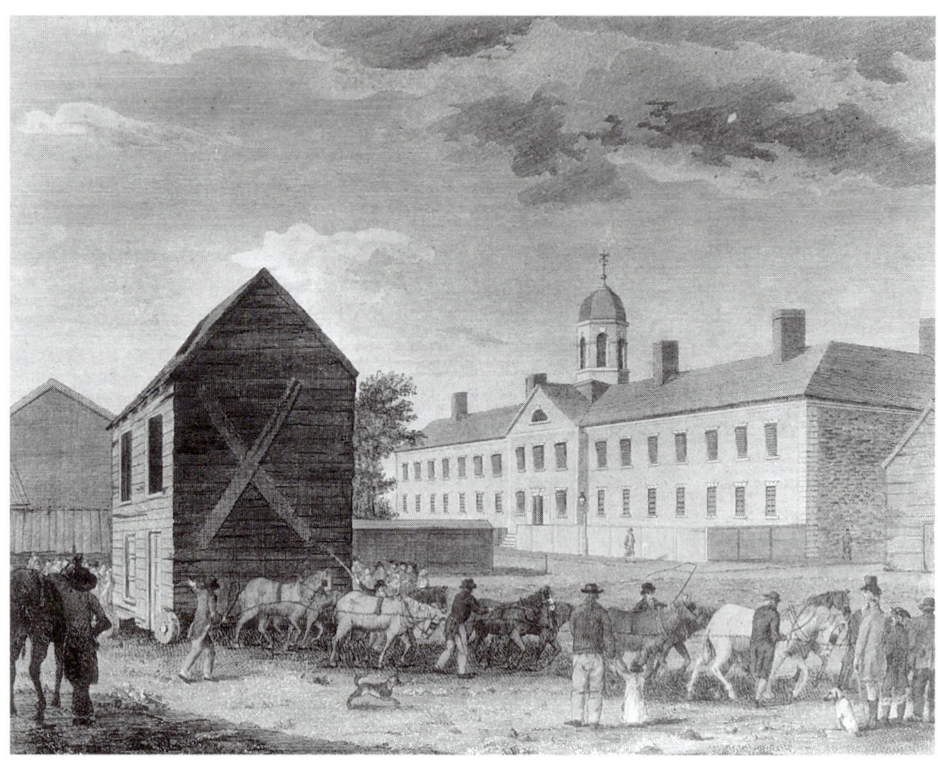

FIGURE 63. William Birch, *Gaol in Walnut Street, Philadelphia*, engraving, 1799, LCP. In one of his liveliest Philadelphia views, Birch portrayed the Walnut Street jail between Fourth and Fifth Streets, facing the back of the State House. Two centuries later, the print is treasured for its portrayal of a framed two-story blacksmith's shop being hauled on wheels through the streets by a team of horses. Purchased by Richard Allen and hauled to Sixth and Lombard Streets in May 1794, the building was renovated, named Bethel, and opened for services by Allen seven weeks later. It is not known why Birch dropped this engraving from the second, third, and fourth editions of his Philadelphia views, but it is probable that a jail and blacksmith's shop did not gain the same favor as views of the Bank of the United States, Christ Church, the State House, and other more elegant buildings.

the Civil War, African Americans are the *least* difficult to trace in the city's historical collections. Though on the bottom rung of the city's ladder of economic opportunity, black Philadelphians' lives were documented far better than those of the Irish, English, or German immigrants. The explanation is that slavery and the plight of free blacks came to preoccupy the Quakers and some others who stood high in the city's social register and who played important roles in the city's cultural institutions. For example, the Historical Society's first president, William Rawle, was also president of the Pennsylvania Abolition Society and sometime director of the Library Company and Philosophical Society. Roberts Vaux was another consummate organization man, a Historical Society founder, Philosophical Society member, and Abolition Society stalwart.

How preservation of Philadelphia's past sometimes came from the most intense discrimination and suffering is illustrated in the quarter century before the Civil War. This was when black Philadelphians faced growing hostility and collapsing opportunities. But from those dismal circumstances came probably the most stunning accumulation of data of a dispossessed people ever assembled in a pre-Civil War American city. Concerned about the plan to amend the Pennsylvania constitution specifically to disfranchise free blacks, the Quaker-filled Pennsylvania Abolition Society employed agents, coordinated by the black Presbyterian minister Charles W. Gardner, "to visit every colored family in the city and suburbs" in 1838 in order to undermine the charges that black Philadelphians were "unworthy of any favor" and simply "nuisances in the community fit only to fill alms houses and jails."[4] Though unsuccessful in fending off the disfranchisement move, the private census produced an extraordinary portrait of the black population with far richer data than the federal decennial censuses provided: birthplace of the adult householders, religious affiliation, schooling of their children, occupation, real and personal wealth, and beneficial society membership. Additional private censuses conducted by Quakers in 1847 and 1856, each time resulting in printed pamphlets summarizing the data on the condition of black Philadelphians, mounted up statistical evidence for historians to use that is unavailable even for middle class whites. All three data banks remained in the voluminous records of the Abolition Society that were deposited at the Historical Society almost a century later.

Philadelphia's pre-Civil War black community also gained greater historical visibility than the immigrant Irish or even the immigrant Germans, because the city's black clergymen and a handful of others were unusually conscious of history's importance. The funeral sermons for departed leaders such as Richard Allen, who died in 1831, and James Forten, who died eleven years later, were in effect heroic biographies that established them in African American memory as black founding fathers. Black literary societies and a black library company in the 1830s furthered the collecting of historical materials. By midcentury, William Still, an energetic and able black leader, began building a huge compendium of oral histories of escaped slaves. Soon, history-minded black Philadelphians, often in humble positions, began keeping black church and school records and the minutes and membership lists of mutual aid societies and literary organizations that, in time, would be gathered together by the city's American Negro Historical Society, founded in 1897.

Also important in preserving a record of the accomplishments of the city's early free blacks were histories of the first independent black churches (Figure 63). That these accounts were published at all, written as they were by educationally disadvantaged men and published with meager resources, testifies to the conviction of the importance of memorializing pioneering free blacks. In 1857, William T. Catto, a black Presbyterian minister, published a semi-centenary history of the First African Presbyterian church, one of the first church histories published in Philadelphia. Five years later, the black Episcopalian minister William Douglass gathered together early membership lists, birth and baptism records, minutes of church committees, and recollections of aged parishioners and wove them into a documentary history of the church that Absalom Jones had

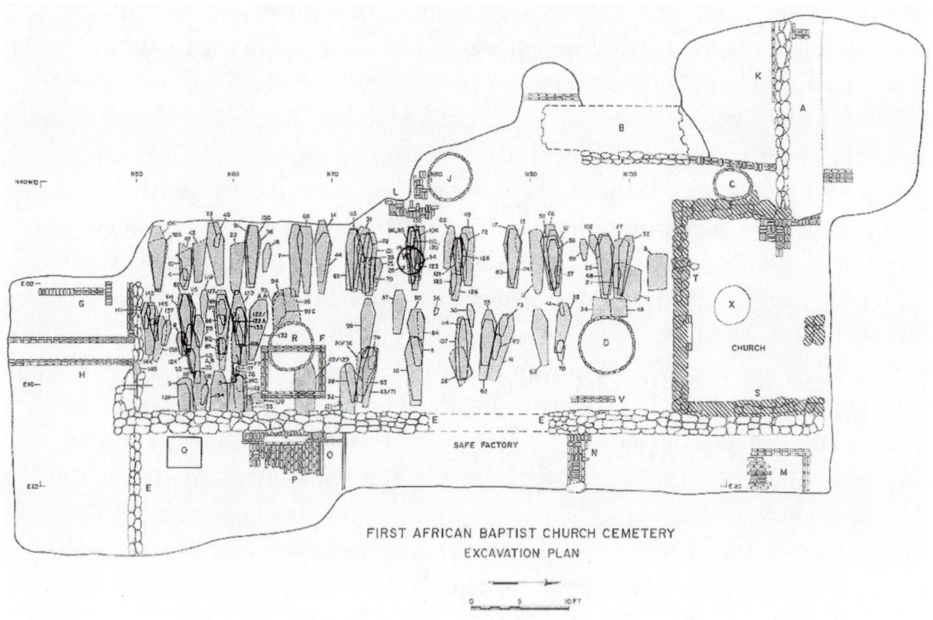

FIGURE 64. First African Baptist Church Cemetery, Excavation Plan, Redevelopment Authority of the City of Philadelphia. The skeletal remains of the 140 bodies buried in the cemetery of the First African Baptist Church were reinterred in Eden Cemetery in Delaware County in 1986. The child's coffin was given by the Redevelopment Authority to the Historical Society.

founded. A memorial to Jones, as well as to the early members of the city's first independent black worshipers, Douglass's *Annals of the First African Church in the United States of America, Now Styled the African Church of St. Thomas* would not enter the libraries of the Historical Society or Library Company for many years, but in poorer parts of town it was prized nonetheless as the collective memory of the first generation of free black Philadelphians.

Richard Allen and James Forten were held in special reverence as the black founding fathers of Philadelphia. Forten was of enormous importance to the hopes of the city's black citizens, not only because of his business success but also because he had nearly obliterated the color line. This was clear at his funeral procession, which included thousands of whites paying their respects. Nearly everyone knew of Forten's background—how his great-grandfather had arrived as a slave even before Penn and the Quakers, probably as a slave of the Dutch West India Company; how his grandfather had purchased his freedom and raised a son; how his father became a sailmaker along the Delaware wharves, dying when his son was a boy; and how James attended Anthony Benezet's school for black children, where he learned to read and write and imbibed many of the kindly Quaker's principles about the universality of humankind. Nearly two-thirds of a century after the event, Forten's memorialists—Stephen Gloucester, a Presbyterian minister, and Robert Purvis, businessman and Forten's son-in-law—reminded the city in moving funeral discourses how the young Forten, at age fifteen, signed on Stephen Decatur's *Royal Louis* as a powder boy, was captured by the British, refused to go to England as the companion of the British captain's son, walked back to Philadelphia barefoot from New York after escaping the prison ship on which he was placed, and launched a notable career. After the war, Forten worked in the Front Street sail-loft of Robert Bridges, and when Forten bought the business upon Bridge's retirement in 1798, he turned it into one of Philadelphia's premier maritime enterprises. By 1807, Forten had amassed a fortune exceeding $100,000. His racially mixed crew of thirty workmen produced the precisely fabricated sails for many of the city's largest merchant ships. A tireless abolitionist, who provided William Lloyd Garrison with the money to buy paper for the first issue of his *Liberator*, Forten was a living legend whose demise in 1842 would not be forgotten.[5]

Unearthing the history of Philadelphia's free blacks in the nineteenth century has been much more important to white-dominated repositories of culture since World War II, and sometimes this has happened literally and unexpectedly. When the Reading and Pennsylvania railroad terminals in center city were being linked by tunnel in the mid-1980s, the operator of an earthmoving machine began to uncover coffins. Archaeologists were brought in to find, to their amazement, the long-forgotten cemetery of Philadelphia's First African Baptist Church, established in 1809. Cemeteries are generally regarded as sacred places, but in this case the church property had been owned by Henry Simmons, the church's minister. Born a slave in Virginia, Simmons gained his freedom near the beginning of the nineteenth century, came north to Philadelphia where he worked as a ragman, and formed the church with twelve other free blacks. When he died in 1848, the property fell into the hands of a now forgotten developer who built row houses. Sometime in the 1850s an enterprising Philadelphian erected a factory for building safes on the site of the cemetery.[6]

With federal and foundation support, archaeologists excavated an almost intact infant coffin and the skeletal remains of 140 black Philadelphians (Figure 64). The gabled lid and tapering shape of the child's coffin attest to the attention given to the construction of this final resting place. Of equal significance is the high percentage of infant coffins found in the cemetery; nearly half of these children, osteological analysis showed, had suffered severe dietary deficiencies. Mathew Carey in his *Letters on the Condition of the Poor* gave many instances of the appalling infant mortality among poor whites, but the cemetery excavations of a black church nearly 150 years later fill in the story of an even grimmer black impoverishment.

The partial recovery of a black congregation's history from time's mists was possible because the late twentieth-century interest in African American history brought forth considerable amounts of money to delay the commuter rail tunnel project and send all skeletal remains to the Smithsonian Institution for osteopathic analysis. No records have been found that would disclose the names or life stories of the congregants of the African Baptist Church, which lasted only from 1809 until 1848. But the graves themselves tell stories. In two cases, archaeologists found Chinese porcelain plates placed on the stomach of the deceased, and in eight cases, a coin was left near the head of the body. In six other cases leather shoes had been placed atop the coffin. Such funerary practices, different from Christian burial traditions, show that a portion of the black Baptists still followed African burial customs: to assure the journey of the dead to an afterlife in the African homeland, material possessions were placed in or on the coffin to ease the way. Coins represented the fee to guarantee the spirit's return to the homeland, while the shoes assisted, at least symbolically, on the long trip. Ceramic plates were prized possessions to be used in the afterlife. The African Baptist Church of Philadelphia was indeed still part African in spirit.

Age of Iron and Steam

The period between 1815 and 1860 marked America's first great phase of converting craft workshops to large-scale, factory-based water- and steam-driven processing and production. In this transition, the Delaware River valley became a center of the new American industrial productivity that brought cheaper goods to a growing population spread over a vastly expanded territory. If Philadelphia was the Athens of America in the early nineteenth century, by midcentury it also became the Manchester of America, the transatlantic cousin of England's smoky industrial center. By the 1840s, Philadelphia was the most highly industrialized city in the nation.

The rush toward manufacturing revolved around the production of textiles and the fabrication of machines, especially precision tools, locomotives, fire engines, and stationary steam engines. Lacking a major waterfall, Philadelphia could not build complexes of large mechanized factories. This disadvantage was overcome by an early reliance on steam power, which utilized the readily available coal from nearby anthracite fields.

Collectively, the hundreds of textile manufacturers, who operated small, specialized, family-owned companies, were the city's largest employers. Very different from the native-born New England textile magnates who drew upon rural Yankee farm girls and established corporate giants, the mostly immigrant textile entrepreneurs of Philadelphia "followed a different path to profit, prominence, and accumulation."[7] Proprietary rather than corporate, these businesses were privately owned by men who managed shop floor processes besides raising capital, making business decisions, and experimenting with new technology. Their labor forces were mostly immigrant and heavily reliant on female and child labor. By 1850, three partly interlinked sites of textile production—Kensington, Germantown, and Manayunk—teemed with hundreds of textile enterprises. In densely inhabited Kensington, immigrant handloom weavers, mostly Irish, resisted the new steam-driven machinery as they produced carpets and other fabrics. In Germantown, mostly British immigrant hosiers turned out stockings on handframes but began to shift to powered spinning in small mills. In Manayunk, the city's mill town, factory machine tenders were poor and subordinate—"the young to their elders, the machine tenders to their overseers, the skilled to their bosses."[8]

In metal fabrication, Philadelphia stood first among American cities by the 1830s and

FIGURE 65. Thomas Sinclair, *Morris Iron Works*, lithograph, 1840, HSP. This lithograph is one of the few in this era to show work routines on the shop floor. As in the case of textile mills, the lithographic depictions of metal fabrication, produced as advertisements, seldom give clues to the noise, dirt, clutter, and draining work of these operations. In highly antiseptic views, the buildings and the machinery claimed the artist's attention, and the human workers are sticklike figures when they appear at all. That is how most owners who commissioned lithographs wanted it. Even in this unusual image the top-hatted owner occupies the foreground.

1840s. One fourth of the nation's iron- and steel-based production took place in Philadelphia plants such as the Alfred Jenks plant in Bridesburg, the Samuel V. Merrick and Sons facility in Southwark, and the Morris Iron Works (Figure 65), where machinists built steam engines, pumps, lathes, hydraulic presses, and other apparatus for the new industrial age. Especially, the city became a center of steam engine construction, with more than forty manufacturers competing in the trade by the 1840s.

Oliver Evans was one of a new generation of brilliant men who designed the machines that harnessed water and steam power. In 1795, he revolutionized the milling industry by automating most mill processes, from unloading grain to sacking flour. Nine years later, he designed the "Orukter Amphibolus," an amphibious steam-powered dredge for the Delaware River that was the talk of the town. Evans led the way in establishing a great tradition of machine builders in Philadelphia. George E. Sellers, Isaiah Lukens, Matthias Baldwin, and Samuel Vaughan Merrick strode in his footsteps. Among them, they introduced important innovations in fire engine, marine, printing, and textile technology; designed the city's first gasworks in 1836; took out patents on thousands of technological innovations; and, adding organizational skills to this ingenuity, established some of the largest production and transportation companies on the eastern seaboard.

Propelling Philadelphia's industrial development forward was the establishment in 1824 of the Franklin Institute. Conceived by Merrick as a society for the diffusion of science and the mechanic arts, the Franklin Institute for the Promotion of the Mechanic Arts took form at an American Philosophical Society meeting, where Merrick's uncle, John Vaughan, was a central figure. Its first goals were modest: to present lectures, form a library and a museum of mechanical models, and award prizes to ingenious inventors. In this blending of science with practical skill, the institute soon became more ambitious. Within a few years, it provided a laboratory for perfecting new inventions; launched a mechanical drawing school, the "first concerted effort . . . to provide technical training for a large class of the citizenry"; held annual industrial exhibits, which soon drew thousands of visitors; dictated the character of technological development by establishing premium prizes in areas that its directors saw as crucial to exploiting coal and iron, Pennsylvania's two most important natural resources; and took the lead in challenging the nation's technological backwardness by setting new standards for mechanical ingenuity.[9] By the early 1830s, the institute was on its way toward inspiring several generations of men through its marrying of theory and practice—mind and hand—in support of industrial development. At the same time, the institute became a collecting and publishing institution. While gathering scientific and technical journals for the use of its members, it launched the *Franklin Journal and American Mechanics' Magazine* (later to become the *Journal of the Franklin Institute*).

Philadelphia's rise to industrial eminence was not possible without a transportation revolution and an expansion of the banking sector, both of which proceeded hand-in-hand with the Industrial Revolution. The new ability to manufacture goods more efficiently depended on getting raw materials to the manufacturing centers and finished goods into the hands of consumers in distant places. During the Jefferson presidency, the United States was still a nation with a primitive transportation system. Few bridges crossed its rivers, only a handful of canals meandered through the countryside, and railroads were unknown. In Philadelphia, only ferries and floating bridges spanned the Schuylkill River before the completion of the Market Street Bridge in 1804. Eight years later, a company principally owned by Jacob Ridgway, some of whose wealth came to the Library Company in 1869 through his daughter, employed the German-born engineer Lewis Wernwag to build the largest single-span bridge in the world, across the Schuylkill River about a mile west of the city center.

Steamboats were in the vanguard of the transportation revolution, although they proved the least successful part of it. John Fitch—goldsmith, clockmaker, and surveyor—built and operated the first American steamboat in Philadelphia in 1786. Fitch's boat chugged up the Delaware River in 1787 at seven miles per hour while delegates to the Constitutional Convention looked on. However, Fitch was never able to make his venture a commercial success as Robert Fulton later did.

Canals were indispensable to industrial expansion in the pre-railroad era. Canal boats could carry much heavier loads than horse-drawn wagons, and the canals allowed boats to avoid rapids, falls, swift currents, low summertime water levels, and other impediments that frustrated river traffic. Relying heavily on immigrant labor, especially Irish, canal companies such as the Schuylkill Navigation Company undertook the most massive labor-intensive projects in the city's history. On the Schuylkill Canal, paralleling the river and completed in 1825, canal boats brought lumber, wheat, whiskey, and other farm products to market; above all, they carried coal to drive the steam engines that were coming to rule factory production. After Irish coalheavers unloaded the canal boats on the Schuylkill docks, they reloaded the boats with factory-made goods for return trips to the farms and towns of Pennsylvania's interior. The shipment of coal to Philadelphia by canal jumped from 6,500 tons in 1825 to an astounding total of 227,000 tons nine years later.

By the 1830s, railroads began to overtake canals as the most vital elements of the nation's transportation system. The Philadelphia, Germantown, and Norristown Railroad, built in 1832, marked Philadelphia's entry into the railroad age. From modest beginnings such as this, Philadelphia became a railroad giant, both as a railroad hub with seven major railroads feeding into the city and as a center of locomotive manufacturing. The 1840s witnessed the indisputable triumph of the railroads. Railroads could move coal much more cheaply than the canals, and gaining this advantage provided railroads with a powerful new impetus for growth. From hauling coal and farm products, they turned to hauling human beings. The opening of the Philadelphia and Reading Railroad, extending from Pottsville to Philadelphia, in 1842 initiated passenger service to the Schuylkill valley while simultaneously ending the profitable monopoly of the Schuylkill Navigation Company on the coal-hauling business. On the initial run of the Philadelphia and Reading's passenger service, on New Year's Day in 1842, a single engine pulled seventy-five passenger cars with 2,150 passengers and three bands (Figure 66). Later, the Pennsylvania Railroad easily surpassed the Philadelphia and Reading, for its tracks ran all the way west to Pittsburgh and eventually to Chicago, making it the most important corporate enterprise in America for many decades.

Locomotive building for the nation's fast-growing railroads was virtually a Philadelphia monopoly. The plants of Richard Norris & Son, Baldwin Locomotive Works, the American Steam Carriage Company, and Garrett and Eastwick turned out hundreds of coal-burning steam locomotives each year (Figure 67). Norris's locomotives, known around the world, were shipped to England, Austria, Cuba, Australia, and South America. By 1838, only eight years after the first locomotive was built in the United States, Matthias W. Baldwin could boast that 45 percent of all American-built engines in use in the United States bore his name. By the 1880s, Baldwin was producing six hundred locomotives annually.[10]

Shipbuilding complemented locomotive production in Philadelphia's pivotal role in the transportation revolution. In a string of shipyards and engineering works strung along the Delaware River from League Island to Kensington, marine artisans had to be flexible and ingenious because they were part of the transition from wooden-hulled sail-

FIGURE 66. David Kennedy, *Sketch of the First Passenger train to Reading*, watercolor, 1858, HSP. Kennedy, who sketched the first passenger train to Reading, worked for the railroad, but his avocation was methodically drawing hundreds of old buildings in Philadelphia, thereby creating one of the most important visual records of the city in the antebellum era. Kennedy's watercolor is dated 1858 but he sketched the scene in 1842, when the train made its first run. Hundreds of his drawings, which constitute a virtual artistic survey of the city, were purchased by the Historical Society and added to by subsequent purchases and gifts.

ing ships to iron-hulled, steam-driven vessels. Leading the way was the shipyard of William Cramp. Descended from eighteenth-century German immigrants, Cramp was a paragon of unincorporated capitalist production. For two decades after establishing his shipyard in 1828, he designed hulls and supervised a small army of wooden ship carpenters, joiners, and mast makers who carried their own broadaxes, saws, rules, chisels, mallets, caulking irons, and bevels to work. By the 1850s, when the sun was setting on wooden shipbuilding, Cramp and his sons led the way toward a new era of iron, steel, and steam. By the eve of Civil War, he was poised to assume a central role in the building of the nation's merchant and naval fleets.[11]

Industrialization delighted most Philadelphians because it brought wealth and new cosmopolitanism to their city, underpinned a host of new cultural institutions, and made possible new municipal conveniences such as gas lighting and water piped into homes. The latter began in 1801, when the Centre Square Waterworks, the first water system in a large American city, began operating. Designed by the immigrant architect and engineer Benjamin Latrobe in the classical style, it used a steam engine to pump water from the Schuylkill River through an underground culvert to Centre Square. There a second steam engine pumped the water into a tank atop the building, from which it flowed by gravity to various parts of the city through a series of wooden pipes. Philadelphians hoped that abundant water to wash the streets would help prevent a dreaded repeat of the yellow fever epidemic, which had devastated the city in the 1790s, and would aid in

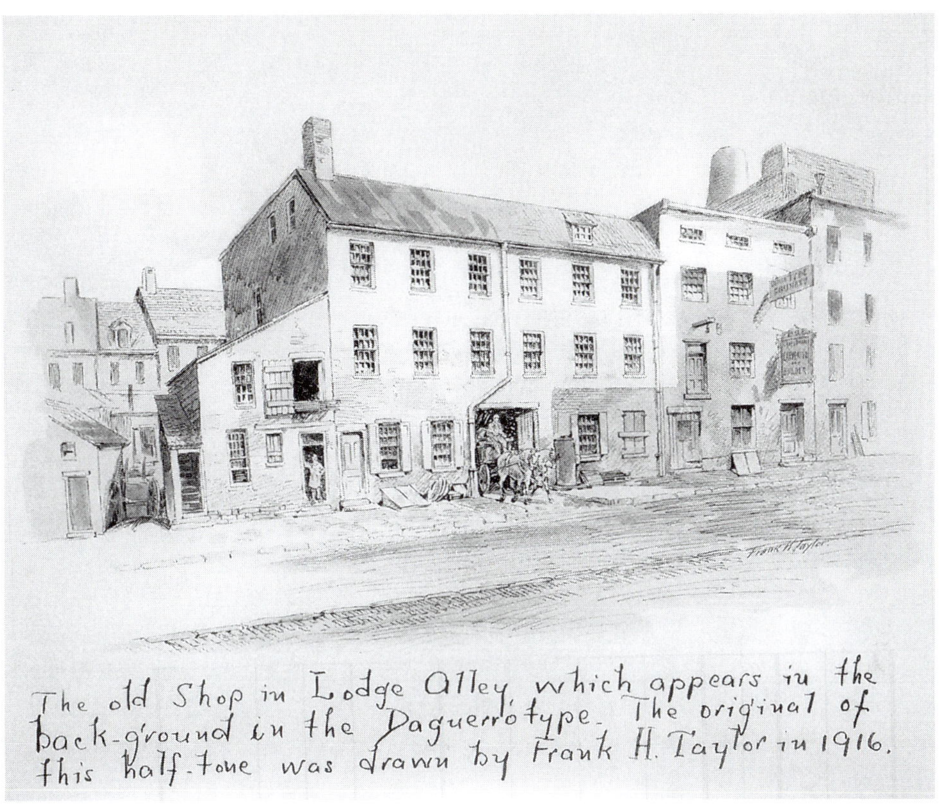

The old Shop in Lodge Alley, which appears in the
back-ground in the Daguerrotype. The original of
this half-tone was drawn by Frank H. Taylor in 1916.

FIGURE 67. Baldwin's Lodge Alley shop, c.1831, Smithsonian Institution. A talented mechanic, Matthias Baldwin constructed his first locomotive in this three-story shop in 1831 after Charles Willson Peale's son Franklin commissioned it for the Peale Museum. Five years later, Baldwin turned out forty locomotives at a much larger plant at Hamilton and Broad Streets.

fighting fires. Businesses and city residents had to pay a fee to get piped water. At first, most families, unable to afford the fee, relied on the wells and cisterns that had always been their source or took city water from street hydrants. But gradually, the price of water fell. In its first year of operation, the waterworks delivered water to just 63 houses, four breweries, and a sugar refinery. By 1811, 2,127 houses were paying for piped water; in 1837, nearly 20,000.[12]

In just the period when Philadelphia was becoming an industrial center, the founders and early leaders of the Historical Society were launching their memory-making enterprise. Deeply ambivalent about the way economic development was proceeding, their uneasiness affected their collecting interests and their entire approach to history. Most of them came from families whose fortunes had been built on overseas trade in the era when the bustling wharves on the Delaware River connected the city and its agricultural hinterland with most of the world. But by the 1820s, Philadelphia's commercial supremacy was slipping badly, as New York City, Boston, and Baltimore surpassed the city in imports and in the export of wheat, flour, and other farm products. They were men who preferred the past to the Philadelphia of their own time and hence were reluctant heralds of the city's future.

Given the nostalgia for an earlier era, it is not surprising that members of the Historical Society, throughout its first half century or so, gave scant priority to collecting materials chronicling the new industrial city taking shape around them. They were fascinated with the colonial and revolutionary past and how it might shape the attitudes of those in the present. The accession books of the society show that even later in the nineteenth century and into the early twentieth century, very little was acquired by or donated to the society that would preserve the record of the first era of industrialization that occurred before the Civil War. Most of the society's holdings that pertain to the period from 1820 to 1860 have been gathered in the past half century, and the antebellum period is still the most thinly documented in Philadelphia's history.

Complicating the interpretation of the first era of industrialization is the fact that few artists were interested in painting work or neighborhood scenes that portrayed industrialization and its effects on the social geography of the city. For example, by analyzing city directories and manuscript census reports, historians know that as handicraft production gave way to factory production, owners of businesses, who once lived within walking distance of their workplace in class-integrated neighborhoods, now moved away from noisy, crowded sites of production. But this was not a topic for artists, because it was a rare Philadelphian who would pay a painter for recording such a phenomenon.

It was left to lithographers to capture the industrial transformation of Philadelphia, and every early lithographer knew that the market for his visual work was Philadelphians who wanted to see their city in a favorable light, with views of what was most forward-looking and notable about the city, such as new bridges and the waterworks, banks and institutions built in the classical style, and thriving commercial establishments. With urban lithography and boosterism married in the early nineteenth century, a more realistic view of urban places would have to await the advent of photography. Augustus Kollner, the artist most interested in ordinary workplaces and the throbbing quality of urban industrial life, found almost no market for his outpouring of genre illustrations (Figure 68). In 1906, his daughter, trying to clear the house of a mountain of pictures after Kollner's death, sold them to a junkman for wastepaper for two dollars.[13]

Lithographs portraying the water-driven textile mills are a good example of how those who depicted Philadelphia's early industrialization calibrated their angle of vision to reflect the optimism of early textile capitalists and their confidence that industrialization would bring better wages to working people while enlarging profits that would allow entrepreneurs to invest further in the city's economic future. For example, tinted lithographs portraying the three- and four-story factories of Manayunk from a distance gave little hint of the work processes inside the buildings or of the relations between capital and labor. John Caspar Wild's view of Joseph Ripka's mills (Figure 69) depicts a bucolic scene with workers' houses nestled in the hills rising steeply from the Schuylkill River where the factory is picturesquely sited. However, Manayunk was a scene of bitter

FIGURE 68. Augustus Kollner trade card for John Krider, Atwater Kent Museum. This trade card for the noted Philadelphia gun maker and later sporting goods retailer is one reminder that the old labor-intensive craft shop tradition was far from dead in the city. Kollner produced scores of such trade cards for craftsmen, retailers, and small manufacturers. With hundreds of others, Krider exhibited his guns at annual industrial exhibits of the Franklin Institute.

FIGURE 69. J. C. Wild, *Manyunk, Near Philadelphia,* from *Views of Philadelphia and its Vicinity*, lithograph, 1838, LCP. This lithograph of Joseph Ripka's mills is one of many portraying the Manayunk textile factories. One hundred years later the mills were shutting down; since the 1960s, they have been recycled into condominiums, artists' lofts, and commercial complexes—all of which has sharply boosted the price of pre-Civil War romantic lithographs of Manayunk.

labor conflict in the 1820s and 1830s, where Ripka was known for his severe labor practices. His employees endured fourteen-hour work days, six days a week in lung-infesting, dust-ridden air; their pay was heavily docked if they were more than fifteen minutes late for work; and their wages were held back if they left without notice. A series of strikes, in which women workers were among the organizers, rocked Ripka's mills just before Wild drew this lithograph in 1838.

Like most Americans, the city's cultural elite were fascinated with the first era of canal, railroad, and iron hull shipbuilding. This is understandable especially in Philadelphia because old family mercantile wealth was diverted not into textiles or other forms of manufacturing but into banking, canal and railroad construction, and mining. But as collectors they were much more interested in the end product and the entrepreneurial aspects of transport and extractive capitalism than in the labor side of the equation. Lithographs and paintings of early railroads and canals were of interest, and, later, so were the organizational aspects of canal and railroad building, as evidenced by the Historical Society's acquisition of records and reports of several canal companies and its purchase in 1915 of the papers of Jay Cooke, a central figure in building the Northern

Pacific Railroad after the Civil War. But for the most part, the nineteenth-century collecting yen focused on the founding and revolutionary period. Documenting the sooty, sweaty side of the transportation revolution, filled with Irish brogues and industrial strife, was far from the minds of those who were trying to build historical societies and museums that would present a heroic view of the past, one in which the "great men" of earlier ages occupied center stage. The kind of records that would place the faceless immigrant laborers in the story—hiring accounts, payroll ledgers, and injury reports, for example—were never sought and, indeed, were probably not regarded as worth preserving. Hence, the city's repositories are relatively rich in bucolic lithographs and paintings that show canals threading their way lazily through pastoral farmland but poor in the materials that labor and social historians in later generations coveted to explain the human side of the transportation revolution. More plentiful, and becoming available only in recent decades, are records such as those of the Cramp shipyards, given to the Independence Seaport Museum founded in 1961, the Pennsylvania Railroad Collection assembled at the Urban Archives of Temple University, and the Philadelphia and Reading Railroad Company Collection acquired by the Hagley Museum and Library in Wilmington.

In collecting documentary material on early industrialization, the two institutions that did follow the far-seeing advice of William Rawle, the Historical Society's first president (1825-36), were the Library Company and the Franklin Institute. In his inaugural address, Rawle urged that the society collect "whatever may be of interest in relation to time that is present" as well as times past. In following its mission going back more than a century, the Library Company tried to satisfy the demands of its casual users as well as its shareholding members. On the assumption that printed books, newspapers, and pamphlets were vital whereas manuscripts were peripheral, the library acquired many of the printed materials—annual reports, promotional pamphlets, and investigative findings—emanating from railroad and canal companies, banks, insurance companies, and other entities deeply involved in Philadelphia's industrial development. When these were not acquired at the time, they came to the Library Company's shelves through the compulsive collecting of a series of ephemera gatherers who passed on their yields at death or in old age. For quite a different reason, the Franklin Institute gathered similar materials, because anything related to machinery, scientific inquiry, or industrial innovation was regarded as their lifeblood and therefore assiduously added to their library resources. However, the institute was much less interested in the mass of workers who lived mostly by their sweat rather than by mechanical ingenuity.

Labor's Travails

Who built Philadelphia? The traditional credit goes mostly to the capitalist moguls, shrewd bankers, ingenious inventors, and clever corporate managers. These are the figures who appeared in nineteenth-century histories of "eminent Philadelphians," in

FIGURE 70. L. Hugg after John Lewis Krimmel, *White's Great Cattle Show, and Grand Procession of the Victuallers*, lithograph, 1861, PMA. The two-mile long procession of victuallers on March 15, 1821, captured by the genre painter John Krimmel as they turned the corner at Fourth and Chestnut Streets in front of Mathew Carey's bookstore, was a brilliant display of tradesmen's pride. The procession of butchers with their carts carrying meat from a cattle market show was organized to encourage the breeding of cattle and attracted 300,000 people if the *Philadelphia Gazette* is to be believed. It took one hundred carts to carry 86,731 pounds of meat, including bear and deer meat. The butchers and victualers proudly flew their banner "We Feed the Hungry." Krimmel dressed up the crowd, showing women with Grecian hair styles wearing Empire style gowns and neck ruffs. The painting showed laboring men in the best light since patrician Philadelphians liked to think about workers as orderly and patriotic. Two lithographers produced copies, indicating that it became a popular work.

the newspapers, in the history books that formed the minds of young people, and in monuments and museum portraits. In historical memory, the workers occupy a marginal niche, akin to secondary figures in a play who wait in the wings, where the lighting is very dim. The task of labor historians in recent years has been to bring workers from the wings to center stage and then turn up the lights on them. Given the collecting priorities of the city's cultural agencies in the nineteenth century, this has been a formidable task.[14]

Looking backward, we can see that industrialization meant one thing for factory owners, investors, and inventors and something else for workers. For many of Philadelphia's old mercantile families, investments in the canal-building Schuylkill Navigation Company or Pennsylvania Railroad brought a vast augmentation of wealth. For the immigrant Irish, these companies meant recruitment into gangs who lived in makeshift barracks or shanties while clearing, digging, and grading the canals and railbeds. In the city, the opportunity to amass wealth through large-scale production lifted many families to an entirely unprecedented level of affluence. But beneath them, accustomed to living on the edge, working men and women adjusted only gradually, and often painfully, to the wage labor and work regimens of the new factory system. At first, factory work seemed to promise steady wages. Workers hoped this would make up for their loss of artisan skills and control at the workplace while opening the door, if only a crack, to eventually operating their own businesses (Figure 70). But three severe economic depressions—the first from 1816 to 1822, a second beginning in 1837 and continuing with flurries of recovery for nearly fifteen years, and a third in 1857—brought home the lesson that capitalist development was a roller-coaster ride. Unemployment always resided just outside the door of the working family's cramped quarters. It skyrocketed in the depression that followed the War of 1812, when soup kitchens made their first appearance in Philadelphia; and rose above 25 percent, sometimes approaching 40 percent, in the even more severe depression that followed the panic of 1837. Even after Philadelphia rebounded from this, the *Evening Bulletin* reported that as many as five thousand Philadelphians survived primarily by begging or stealing. "There are thousands, absolutely *thousands*, who rise in the morning without knowledge where they are to obtain a mouthful of food, or where their wretched heads are to rest at night," wrote one reformer in 1853.[15]

While Philadelphia's craftsmen struggled to preserve their small shops—and many of them did—thousands of factory workers, especially new immigrants, learned that their labor might earn them $4.33 for a fourteen-hour day, six days a week. That was if they were lucky enough not to be laid off. A match factory owner in 1846 offered women $2.50-3.00 per week. Paid vacations were unknown, and the Fourth of July was their only holiday. In 1853, a reporter for the *Evening Bulletin* found slum shops selling meals for one cent from food procured by begging at the back doors of the wealthy. The clergy supported the capitalist class, counseling the jobless and poor that the economic order was subject only to God's guiding hand. No wonder the dispossessed took small comfort from the words of Reverend James W. Alexander, who regarded the "happy yeomanry" as misled by foreign trade unionists and told workers in 1847, quoting Bunyan, that "He that is down needs fear no fall."[16] Instead, they began to heed the words of militant labor groups.

Attempts at labor organization had begun before the American Revolution but increased in the early nineteenth century. Capitalist owners fought back with the odds much in their favor. This was apparent in the landmark trial of journeymen boot and shoemakers in 1806. When workingmen struck for what they regarded as the minimum wage that would allow them to support their families, they were charged and convicted of a conspiracy to restrain trade. *The Trial of the Boot and Shoemakers of Philadelphia for . . . Conspiracy* (1806) was hardly the kind of book that the Philosophical Society or Historical Society panted to acquire, but logically it found its place on the shelves of the Franklin Institute, founded by men who were latter-day versions of their heroic namesake, and of the Library Company, which acquired it from one of its ephemera-collecting friends.

By the 1820s, Philadelphia became a center of the workingmen's movement that fought for a ten-hour day, dismantlement of militia training with its system of fines, free public schools, abolition of imprisonment for debt, and a mechanic's lien law (to give workers the advantage in collecting debts from bankrupt customers). In pushing for the ten-hour day, laboring Philadelphians based their demand on their rights and responsibilities as active citizens in a democratic republic. Such a status necessarily required workingmen to find time to read, think, and discuss community, state, and national affairs. Striking journeymen carpenters in 1827 pointed to the "grievous and slavelike system of labor" that precluded the fulfillment of their role as responsible parents and citizens. Other groups followed. Out of this movement emerged the nation's first city-wide, all-trade union, the Philadelphia Mechanics' Union of Trade Associations. Also from this strike arose the first Working Men's Party, which nominated its own candidates and created the first labor newspaper—William Heighton's *Mechanics Free Press*, established in 1828.[17]

By the mid-1830s, the labor movement in Philadelphia took another momentous turn as skilled workers joined with the unskilled for the first time. In 1835, after Irish coal heavers had walked off their jobs on the grimy Schuylkill River docks, their march through the city on June 3 ignited the first general strike in American history. Seeing the marchers, shoemakers threw down their awls and joined in the march shouting, "We are all day laborers!" House painters denounced "the present system of labor as oppressive and unjust and destructive of social happiness." Many other groups—sailors, hod carriers, wood sawyers, and others—joined the strike. Seamstresses and tailoresses also organized—the first salvo by female needleworkers in a long campaign that continued for many generations.[18]

The depression of 1837-42 knocked the props out from under a unified labor movement, and the heavy immigration of Irish and Germans in the late 1840s created a surplus labor pool that continued to hamper union organizing. But labor militancy did not disappear. Hand-loom weavers became the vanguard of the labor movement by the early 1840s. Owners of their own looms and working in their own houses, they resisted the mechanization of the textile industry. When employers drove their wages further down in 1842, which left them with sixty cents for a fourteen-hour day at the loom, they were faced with what the *Public Ledger* called "the awful doctrine of 'blood or bread.'"[19] In this desperate situation they struck and rioted. For six months, weavers in Kensington quit their looms, attacking weavers who would not join them and repulsing the sheriff's posse in the 1842 battle at the Nanny Goat Market.

Even when continued immigration undercut labor organizing and labor militancy, a few friends of labor kept its cause in the public eye. Newspapers by and large were not the workingman's friend because they were firmly aligned with business interests, fervid boosters of the city, and skittish about offending their largely middle-class clientele. But even an obscure or radical person could place something before the public—in pamphlets, niche newspapers, or short books—if the author used direct language and could pay a small amount of money to get into print. Then, all depended upon the power of the pen. It was in just this way that by the late 1840s, a raw crusading journalist and budding novelist, George Lippard, took up labor's cause. Flaying rich capitalists, he became the city's most widely read author (Figure 71).

FIGURE 71. Daguerreotype of George Lippard, c.1850, Library of Congress. This only known photographic image of George Lippard, by an unidentified photographer, was part of the John McAllister Collection that Marian S. Carson acquired from a McAllister descendant. She gave the collection to the Library of Congress in 1996 as part of her huge collection of Americana. By this gift, from the daughter-in-law of Hampton L. Carson, the Historical Society's president from 1921 to 1929, and the granddaughter of Julius Sachse, a much-involved Historical Society member, the city lost one of the most important collections of early Philadelphia material assembled in the twentieth century.

Coming to the city at age fifteen in 1837, Lippard saw first hand the great depression of 1837-44 and was shocked at the widespread starvation and squalid lives of the laboring poor. By age twenty, he had become "a writer for the masses." Sharpening his skills as a writer for the penny newspapers *Spirit of the Times*, whose motto was "Democratic and Fearless," and *Citizen Soldier*, Lippard turned into a "literary volcano constantly erupting with hot rage against America's ruling class."[20] In 1848, he launched his own newspaper, the *Quaker City* weekly, which by the next year achieved a circulation of 20,000—no surprise because Lippard's gothic novel *The Quaker City; or, the Monks of Monk Hall* (1844) had already sold several hundred thousand copies and had made him the most widely read author in the nation. In the midst of a reading revolution, promoted by the beginnings of public education, Lippard's work reached deeply into the social strata.

Lippard never put things nicely. In fact, he flaunted polite discourse. In the newspaper *Quaker City*, he described Philadelphia as a grotesque subversion of American democracy, with its venerated leaders displaying a "callow indifference to the poor . . . equaled only by their private venality and licentiousness." In 1848, writing about the "wretchedness of working women," he asked, "Do you not hear those voices . . . from the heart of the city, from dark courts where disease rankles and festers and kills? Do you not hear those awful voices, asking not for wealth—not even for comfort—but—O, God of Mercy! Can this be true, in enlightened, Protestant Philadelphia?—asking for a rag to cover their nakedness—asking for bread."[21] The next year, after lamenting that hardly anyone would speak on behalf of the desperate poor since Mathew Carey had gone to his grave, Lippard established the Brotherhood of the Union, a socialist labor organization, to "espouse the cause of the Masses, and battle against the tyrants of the Social System—against corrupt Bankers, against Land Monopolists and against all Monied Oppressors."[22] Lippard proposed free distribution of public lands under a homestead law and worker-based buyer cooperatives. But most of all he yearned to reorganize radically a factory system that distributed wealth grotesquely while grinding up the lives of factory operatives. If peaceful reform failed, wrote Lippard, "We would advise Labor to go to War, in any and all forms—War with the Rifle, Sword, and Knife! . . . War in the name of that God who has declared his Judgement against the Robbers of Labor. The War of Labor—waged with pen or sword—is a Holy War."[23]

Lippard's Brotherhood of the Union continued for several generations after his death but lost its radical edge by World War II. Renamed the Brotherhood of America, it turned into a social and mutual aid society. Dissolving in 1995, it sold its records—including Lippard's diary for 1852-54, fourteen autograph letters, manuscripts on Brotherhood rituals, Brotherhood printed reports, and the Lippard family bible—to the Library Company.

Lippard's "Gospel of the Rifle" never brought Philadelphia's working classes to the barricades, and his Brotherhood of the Union was never able to rebuild the cross-trade union of the 1820s and early 1830s. Always hamstrung by the surplus of labor ensuing from continued immigration, laboring Philadelphians reverted to trade unionism in the 1850s, with the many skilled groups all pursuing their own interests and in general leaving the unskilled to their own miseries. Yet Lippard was read and listened to as he poured out a million words a year, and he lectured widely before dying of tuberculosis in 1854 at age thirty-two. Even *Godey's Lady's Book*, the fashion magazine Lippard hated, admitted that he "has struck out on an entirely new path, . . . is unquestionably the most popular writer of the day, and his books are sold, edition after edition, thousand after thousand, while those of others accumulate, like useless lumber, on the shelves of the publishers."[24]

The early leaders of the Historical Society and other cultural institutions were troubled by the new and abrasive labor relations spawned by the emerging industrial order. They deplored union organizing and labor militancy, and certainly their collecting tastes did not extend to acquiring materials documenting the organization of labor. To this day, material on the early labor movement in Philadelphia, which led the nation in the creation of labor unions in the antebellum period, is uncommonly scarce. Some material found its way into the library of the Franklin Institute, but even there the pivotal figures were upwardly mobile men, like its founder Samuel V. Merrick, who began as a foundryman, rose to establish his own foundry for producing heavy machinery and boilers, and became the first president of the Pennsylvania Railroad. Lippard's flame-throwing, sensationalist writings were shunned even by the usually tolerant Library Company. However, the Library Company was a haunt of Philadelphia antiquarians who collected ephemeral materials, including many of the pamphlets connected to union organizing and labor strife that later would enter the Library Company's collections. For example, Charles Poulson, son of Zachariah Poulson, the company's librarian from 1785 to 1806, collected ephemera passionately and bequeathed his scrapbooks, along with books and works of art, in 1866. Another of the company's benefactors was John A. McAllister, who made a fortune in his optical supply business and turned into "an incorrigible magpie." He donated his "comprehensive pickings of a lifetime," mounted in folio scrapbooks of "prints, photographs, broadsides, playbills, song sheets, letters and memorabilia of all sorts," in 1885.[25] Similarly, in the same year Lloyd Pearsall Smith, librarian from 1851 to 1886, gave 400 volumes of pamphlets he had gathered on eighteenth- and nineteenth-century social, economic, political, cultural, religious, and philanthropic life. After his death in 1886, his widow sold several hundred more volumes of pamphlets to the Library Company for $300. The Library Company did not actively acquire the kinds of material that would reveal life among laboring Philadelphians, but rather, as in the case of other ephemera, "it waited for others to do so and give the material to them."[26]

Fissures

Labor's struggle for shorter working hours, decent wages, some control over the workplace, and public education often pitted worker against worker. The city's African American population, growing from 12,000 in 1820 to 22,000 in 1850 but now vastly outnumbered by Irish immigrants, was driven out of most of the trades and suffered grievous attacks on churches, meeting halls, and residences. Philadelphia's first serious racial attack broke out in November 1829; it was caused, according to white accounts, by a loud and emotional black church service. For white newspapers the "furious battle" was the fault of black worshipers, who "on Sundays, especially . . . seem to think themselves above all restraint and their insolence is intolerable."[27] But two months earlier, white Philadelphians had rioted to protest lectures by Fanny Wright on racial equality.

Race hostility grew in the 1830s. It emanated from the bottom tier of society, where

FIGURE 72. J. C. Wild (presumed), *Destruction by Fire of Pennsylvania Hall, On the night of the 17th May, 1838,* lithograph, 1838, LCP. This lithograph was the first showing the burning of Pennsylvania Hall to issue from the shop of J. T. Bowen, an English immigrant who had just arrived in Philadelphia. The Pennsylvania Hall Association did not have the money to rebuild the abolitionist gathering place, nor did they believe the city could protect a new building. However, they quickly published a *History of Pennsylvania Hall, which was Destroyed by a Mob, on the 17th of May, 1838,* using as a frontispiece a different lithograph of the conflagration from the one shown here, and distributed the pamphlet to convince Americans of the baseness of the pro-slavery legions.

African Americans and Irish vied for menial work, but it was also fueled by Negrophobia preached from the middle and top. In the summer of 1834, a violent attack on black Philadelphians began with an ugly confrontation in South Street, where blacks and whites assembled to ride the Flying Horses, an early carousel. By the next evening organized mayhem broke out. A white assault severely damaged black houses, including one owned by a son of James Forten. White marauders smashed windows and doors, destroyed furniture, dragged black residents into the streets to be beaten, leveled a frame black Methodist church on Wharton Street, severely damaged the Second African Presbyterian Church (targeted as a center of strident abolitionism), and threatened the African Grand Lodge of Masons. The next summer, a white mob attempted to invoke history by its actions. Claiming to follow in the tradition of the Boston Tea Party of 1773, an angry white crowd hurled boxes of abolitionist literature into the Delaware River with the city's mayor standing by.[28]

By 1838, white abolitionists became as much the targets of white hostility as black churches and meeting places. In May of that year, a taunting white crowd of several thousand attacked the newly opened Pennsylvania Hall, built by abolitionist supporters at Sixth Street near Franklin Square as a rallying place and symbol of the new abolitionist determination. Sarah Grimké, her sister Angelina (who had just married Theodore Weld), Abby Kelly, Lucretia Mott, William Lloyd Garrison, Benjamin Lundy, and other national leaders who were attending the meeting of the Anti-Slavery Convention of American Women and the Pennsylvania Anti-Slavery Society watched helplessly as the crowd stormed the building, threw abolitionist literature into the streets, and torched the new hall (Figure 72). Many decades later, in 1911, the Historical Society received the diary of thirty-year-old Augustus Pleasonton, an officer in the Pennsylvania militia who organized the defense of Philadelphia during the Civil War. The diarist described how bricks flew through the windows, how the mob pummeled African Americans fleeing the scene, and how the fire companies refused to fight the blaze. The next night, undeterred by city officials, the crowd stormed the Society of Friends Shelter for Colored Orphans and a black church in the northern part of the city. Both were burned to the ground. The City Council investigating the arson blamed the victims for "openly promulgating and advocating doctrines repulsive to the moral sense of a large majority of our community."[29]

The 1840s brought more racial violence. In 1842, white resentment erupted when black Philadelphians celebrated August 1 as their own independence day to commemorate slave emancipation in the British West Indies in 1834. When the Negro Young Men's Vigilant Association trooped through the streets in a procession organized by the Moyamensing Temperance Society, whites attacked the paraders (Figure 73). They rioted through the night and into the next day, looting black residences; beating men, women, and children; and razing the Second African Presbyterian Church and the still unfinished Smith Beneficial Hall, the latter having been built for educational, literary, moral, and religious improvement but regarded by whites as a "second Pennsylvania Hall."[30] The beleaguered black Philadelphians hoped for justice and compensation for their destroyed buildings. But a grand jury investigation blamed the marchers for inciting whites by presuming to use public space. Adding salt to the wounds, Moyamensing officials immediately ordered the New Temperance Hall of the district's African Americans torn down because they could not protect it from white arsonists whose fires might spread to white-owned buildings. Shaking his head at this, Robert Purvis, so light-skinned that he could have passed for white, wrote to an abolitionist friend: "I know not where to begin, nor where nor how to end, in a detail of the wantonness, brutality and murderous spirit of the actors in the late riots; nor of the apathy and inhumanity of the whole community, in regard to the matter. Press, church, magistrates, clergymen and evils are against us . . . I am convinced of our utter and complete nothingness in public estimation. . . . I am sick, miserably sick."[31] Four years later, the incident still rankling, Frederick Douglass despaired that "the colored population cannot move through the streets of Philadelphia if they have virtue and liberty on their banners. . . . Let them go through the streets, however, poor, mean pitiful drunkards, and then the pro-slavery

FIGURE 73. Henry R. Robinson, A *View of the City of Brotherly Love*, lithograph, c.1842, HSP. Robinson was a New York caricaturist and lithographer; the main scene of this sardonic print of unbrotherly love is the white attack in 1842 on black celebrants commemorating the emancipation of slaves in England's West Indies colonies on August 1, 1834. The *Public Ledger* claimed that the banner leading the parade depicted a slave with manacles still around his limbs under the words "Liberty or Death." Actually, the black figure had broken his chains and pointed to the word "Liberty" above his head. This lithographic record of the 1842 mayhem also depicts the burning of Pennsylvania Hall, an event that occurred four years earlier on the other side of the city. On the left, the Goodwill Fire Company douses the rioters; however, the volunteer fire companies in this era rarely intervened to protect black Philadelphians. At the bottom right, the musical instruments of the parading African Americans lie shattered. A chagrined William Penn looks down on the scene with the motto "Wise Laws and a prompt and just administration of them."

people will smile and say, 'Look at that poor fellow, it is very evident there is an impassible barrier between us and thou.'"[32]

If fissures scarred Philadelphia by race, divisions also bloodied the city along religious lines. The growing tide of Irish Catholic immigrants encountered intense hostility in the Jacksonian period. Protestant militancy peaked in the 1840s, when the city abandoned its tradition of ethnic and religious tolerance and became a center of rabid anti-Catholicism. Native-born Protestants and even Irish Protestants saw the Irish Catholics as diseased, crime-prone, uneducable, intemperate, superstitious papists. Worst of all, Protestants regarded the pride and fierce fighting qualities of the Irish as evidence that they were hopeless candidates for citizenship in a Protestant white man's country. In 1842, when the Catholic bishop, Francis P. Kendrick, asked the Philadelphia School Controllers to allow Catholic children to use their own Bible in the public schools and be excused from Protestant instruction, Protestants organized with a militancy bordering on fanaticism. Egged on by the demagogic and xenophobic press, Protestants rushed to the Native American (or anti-Catholic) Party, which won numerous local and state elections by 1844 on a platform that proposed to deny citizenship to any immigrant for twenty-one years after touching American soil. Party banners, emblazoned with unsubtle slogans, helped recruit followers. Protestant Philadelphia women did their part. Though involved in a movement for their own rights, they had little sympathy for the rights of Irish Catholic Philadelphians. *The American Woman*, a short-lived woman's newspaper that began publishing just after the bloody riots of the summer of 1844, helped roil the waters of religious hostility.

In 1844, Protestant anger over the flood of cheap immigrant labor produced the worst violence in Philadelphia's history. Since 1842, the Protestant Institute, led by Presbyterians, had been flooding the city with anti-Catholic literature, and this flammable situation now exploded. Conflict began in Kensington when shots from the Irish Hibernia Hose Company firehouse, aimed at a nearby political rally of the blustering nativist American Republican Association, killed eighteen-year-old George Shiffler (Figure 74). In the annals of Protestant martyrology, Shiffler died defending an American flag from the anti-American Irish mob. Native American Party leaders canonized him immediately. An Irish Catholic witness testified later that the flag was torn and muddy because Protestant nativists had dragged the flag through the streets, in the middle of a cloudburst, in their flight to the Nanny Goat Market. This testimony had little effect. The propaganda mismatch was signaled five weeks after the riots, when the grand jury's presentment blamed the affray on Bishop Kendrick's request that Catholic children be allowed to read their own Bibles, turning this request into an attempt of Catholics to exclude the Bible from the schools.[33]

Manipulating memory about the unlikely Protestant hero took several forms. Educated Philadelphia Protestants deployed their pens. "Six Months Later," an anonymous epic poem, commemorated the half-year anniversary of Shiffler's death. A decade later, John Hancock Lee, descended from old-stock Protestants and named for a founding father, tried to make official the Native American history of the Kensington riots in his *Origin and Progress of the American Party in Politics: Embracing a Complete History of the Philadelphia Riots in May and July 1844* (1855). Meanwhile, laboring Protestants helped solidify Shiffler's martyrdom as the accepted story by naming a hose company, a Southwark street gang, and several branches of the "Young Native" clubs after him.

Catholics had another version of the riots, which they told at least partially in *The Truth Unveiled; or, A Calm and Impartial Exposition of the Origin and Immediate Cause of the Terrible Riots in Philadelphia* (1844). But in a city where 121 of the 128 churches were Protestant and Catholics represented only 10 percent of the population, the Catholic understanding of the riots had little claim on the public memory. Bishop Kendrick was probably right in saying that "hardly anyone dares to say anything in the papers for fear that the printing houses may be destroyed."[34]

Anti-Catholic oratory in the Independence Hall yard the day after Shiffler's death propelled Philadelphia Protestants forward to defend American values. "The bloody

FIGURE 74. J. L. Magee, *Death of George Shiffer, in Kensington*, lithograph, c. 1845, LCP. Protestants controlled lithography and other forms of art production in Philadelphia, so the visual record of labor and religious strife had a pronounced Protestant cast. A Catholic lithograph of Shiffler's death would have told a different tale, probably casting Shiffler as a brawling, intemperate anti-Catholic teenager.

FIGURE 75. H. Buchholtzer for J. Baillie and J. Soule, *Riot in Philadelphia, July 7th, 1844*, lithograph, 1844, FLP. The scene of the July 7, 1844 anti-Catholic riot was captured hardly with strict accuracy. The lithograph, tinted in color, put a Protestant spin on the bloody event. The battling Protestants were surely not gentlemen in the top hats and cutaway coats pictured here but mainly laboring men who competed with immigrant Catholics in the work place. Philadelphia militiamen are shown bravely repulsing the rioters, but the brawling Protestants were able to batter down the front door and set a fire in St. Philip de Neri Catholic Church, built only four years before. Included among the extensive and important papers of the Cadwalader family, given to the Historical Society in 1947, was an account of the "awful riots of 1844" by General George Cadwalader, who was the commanding officer of the Philadelphia Troop.

hand of the Pope has stretched forth to our destruction. Now we call on our fellow-citizens, who regard free institutions . . . to arm," cried the Native American newspaper. The mob that sallied forth to Kensington held aloft a soiled, torn American flag, which they claimed was the one Shiffler tried to defend. A banner pronounced that "This is the FLAG that was trampled UNDERFOOT by the IRISH PAPISTS."[35] Intoxicated with this version of yesterday's history, the Protestant crowd burned the Hibernia Hose Company's firehouse to the ground and then turned its fury on the recently built St. Michael's Church and St. Augustine Church, along with the houses of at least thirty Catholic families and the Female Seminary of the Sisters of Charity. All these structures went up in flames, along with the 5,000 books in the library of St. Augustine Church. A pitched battle took place near the Nanny Goat Market, where handloom weavers had battled the Philadelphia militia just fifteen months before. The Protestant-Catholic battling went on for three days before the Philadelphia First Brigade restored order.

Two months later, in July 1844, Catholic-Protestant violence erupted again in the midst of July 4 celebrations (Figure 75). Nervous Catholics in Southwark, mindful that

Protestants had razed the two Catholic churches in Kensington two months before, prepared to defend St. Philip de Neri Catholic church, even holding drills in the church's aisles on the night of July Fourth. Protestants regarded this act as an invitation to disarm the Catholics, even though Pennsylvania's governor had authorized the Catholic leaders to arm the church as a defensive measure. When Protestants set blazes in the church, street skirmishing erupted. "We are in the midst of a civil war!" cried one newspaper, "Riot and anarchy are around us! Death and destruction stare us in the face."[36] A three-day street battle ensued before Generals George Cadwalader and Robert Patterson's 5,000 volunteer militia troops restored order. For the first time, Philadelphia troops had stood between the mobbing Protestants and their immigrant Catholic enemies—at the cost of a dozen civilian and two militia fatalities. Protestant bitterness was intense at what they regarded as their defense of American liberties, but the rioting in the wake of the Native American July Fourth procession convinced most Philadelphians that it was time to halt rampant violence in the city.

With Protestants controlling the press, jury system, lithographers and artists, and cultural institutions, Philadelphia's fast-growing Catholic community had little opportunity to tell their version of history. Not until 1885 would Philadelphia Catholics establish the American Catholic Historical Society for "the investigation of Catholic American history, especially that of Philadelphia, and the development of interest in Catholic historical research."[37] Even then, its priority was collecting and preserving Catholic church records, leaving to another generation the historical reconstruction of Philadelphia's Catholics in an era when their neighborhoods and churches were beleaguered by Protestant militants. When a Philadelphia priest published the first full account of early Catholic Philadelphia in 1909, he minced no words in attributing the 1844 riots "to the religious revival begun by a concerted action of the Presbyterians of the United States, in the second quarter of the century."[38]

If Philadelphia Catholics were outnumbered, outspent, and assigned blame for the vicious bloodletting in 1844, they were nonetheless intent on bringing Philadelphia history to their rescue. The *Catholic Herald*, the city's only non-Protestant newspaper, printed the counsel of Bishop Kendrick after the May riots in Kensington: that Catholics keep their peace and leave revenge to God. But the diocesan newspaper also indicted the Protestants as "church burners" and asked readers to imagine the visitor to Philadelphia peering at "the smoldering ruins of St. Augustine's and St. Michael's" after walking from Independence Hall, where he could view the Liberty Bell bearing the inscription of how "liberty was proclaimed throughout the land" and where "justice and liberty seem to have chosen a dwelling place that was said to be eternal."[39] Making another claim on the memories of Protestant Philadelphians, the *Catholic Herald* publicized the rioters' overturning of headstones in St. Augustine's churchyard and their threats to destroy St. Mary's Church, where the remains of the "father of the American Navy," the revolutionary blue-water hero James Barry, were buried.

From a great distance, it seems remarkable that the three-decade period of brawling, arson, and intergroup violence in Philadelphia came to a close in the late 1840s, just as the immigration of Irish Catholics and Protestant Germans reached new heights. Historians have yet to explain why the arrival of new waves of Irish Catholics did not lead to further violence. The reduction of mayhem can be explained in part by the vigorous action of shocked Philadelphians in positions of power who took the first steps toward building an effective police force that could quell urban disturbances. In April 1845, they got legislative approval for establishing a police force of one officer for every 150 taxable families in Philadelphia and the contiguous districts. This led in a few years to a more permanent remedy for the collapse of public order: the consolidation of Philadelphia County's twenty-nine separate districts into a single municipal corporation where police power could be exerted from the center. Partly, the shaky truce among warring groups may owe something to the declaration of war against Mexico in 1847. This may have refocused the attention of many violence-prone Philadelphians while drawing several thousand aggressive young men into thirty companies of volunteers to do battle far to the south. Though only a fraction of the volunteers were called into action to save another part of the world from Catholicism, men of different religions and ethnicities now had a common cause that helped transcend local hostilities. Some Philadelphians opposed what they regarded as "a wicked & disgraceful war," "an unjust and aggressive war," as clothes retailer Joseph Sill put it.[40] But even Philadelphia Catholics supported the Mexican War, because it offered an opportunity to show their colors as one-hundred-percent Americans. Finally, the return of a healthier economy by the late 1840s seems to have lessened the misery of many at the bottom and hence leached away some of the group antagonism that plagued the city in previous decades.

Chapter 6

REFORMING PHILADELPHIA

In trying to cope with the problems arising from rapid growth, unprecedented immigration of non-Protestants, and industrialization in all its bewildering facets, Philadelphians—like other Americans—struck off reform societies in the antebellum era like so many new coins (Figure 76). Public education, the Sunday School movement, temperance, a charter of rights for working people, reclamation projects for fallen women, and the penitentiary movement were all part of the "moral industry" that formulated solutions to what seemed the grand paradox of the era: as America grew in size and strength, social cohesion declined and social problems increased. Three other movements—antislavery, women's rights, and recolonization to Africa—also had specific goals but raised more fundamental questions about the American democratic experiment.

Founding a historical society and staging elaborate celebrations of events in the past were also responses to what seemed a disordered and disorderly new world. John Fanning Watson and his patrician friends believed that a historical society might also restore the imagined stability of an earlier era. By privately preserving the artifacts of olden times, by publishing the first histories of the city, and by publicly invoking the heroes of the founding and revolutionary periods through carefully staged commemorative pageantry, they would convey their understanding of American history—and Philadelphia's role in it—to unruly newcomers. Yet the city's cultural leaders could not make the managing of memory their exclusive right. The very plebeian and insubordinate elements of urban society that frightened them had memories of their own, and some of them were as eager as their social superiors to inscribe alternative versions of the past on the city's collective memory.

Bringing Order to the City

"Whoever shall write a history of Philadelphia from the Thirties to the end of the Fifties will record a popular period of turbulence and outrages so extensive as to now appear almost incredible." These were the words of Charles Godfrey Leland, one of Philadelphia's most talented journalists and poets, who was reflecting in the 1890s on a life of covering the city.[1] Certainly he was right, for nothing unsettled Philadelphians more in the antebellum decades than crime and violence. Street gangs such as the Moyamensing Killers,

FIGURE 76. P. S. Duval, *Bird's Eye View of Philadelphia*, lithograph, 1857, HSP. Duval, a French immigrant, published this panoramic view of the city in 1857, by which time the city had reached the half-million mark in population. In Europe, only Paris and London were larger.

Gumballs, Bloodtubs, Scroungers, Hyenas, Bedbugs, Swampoodle Terriers, Nighthawks, Flayers, and Deathfetchers represented a frightening new aspect of urban life. By 1854, fifty-one street gangs were known, composed of teenagers and young men who battled for turf rights, terrorized pedestrians, and covered fences and walls with graffiti.

But more ominous than gang life and gang predation was organized violence, which flourished partly because it had been sanctioned by the rhetoric of those who stood in positions of political and cultural authority and partly because Philadelphia, like other American cities, had law enforcement agencies so small that they were nearly useless in the face of determined rioters. The militia system was supposed to bulwark the small force of constables, but militia units, heavily composed of white workingmen, were rife with resentment against their officers and the system itself. In the riots of the 1840s, militia units were often unable, sometimes unwilling, to contain the antiblack and anti-Catholic rioters whose views they usually shared. After the second anti-Catholic riot in the summer of 1844, the city council bolstered its capacity to defend churches and houses by authorizing a battalion of artillery, a regiment of infantry, and a full troop of horse—1,350 men in all. In 1850, the state stepped in to create a beefed-up Philadelphia police district with authority over Northern Liberties, Spring Garden, Kensington, Moyamensing, Southwark, and other outlying districts—working-class areas where most of the rioting and mayhem against Catholics and African Americans occurred. The militia's poor performance and the shocking violence of the 1830s and 1840s convinced almost everyone that a much enlarged and professionally trained police was necessary.[2]

Gaining control of the uproarious masses meant putting restraints on the volunteer fire companies. These companies went back to Franklin's early years in the city, when leading citizens belonged to them, but by the 1820s they had evolved into fiercely competitive brotherhoods. Privately organized, they not only protected property from the greatest urban menace but also served as fraternal organizations, often with political overtones, that elicited the fiercest attachment among the urban middle and lower classes. Volunteer firemen saw themselves as urban versions of the frontier folk hero Davy Crockett—manly, proud, self-reliant, in short, the republic's ideal citizen, rough and ready but risking all for the community's weal. Firemen also took pride in terrifying the police and judges, and their masculine culture involved them in fighting each other as often as they fought fires. An investigating committee in 1853, alarmed at sixty-nine riots the previous year, was sure that "there is scarcely a single case of riot brought before the court that has not its origins in the fire companies, their members, or adherents."[3] This led to the prompt disbandment of twenty-five hose companies.

Also to curb violence, urban reformers consolidated twenty-nine separate municipalities into an enlarged city of Philadelphia. This allowed police to cross the boundaries of previously autonomous districts in pursuit of criminals; to turn a small band of weaponless constables into a 1,000-man armed police force; and to professionalize the volunteer fire companies, a gradual process completed in 1871. By shifting power from local to central authority, the Consolidation Act of 1854, which enlarged the city from 2 to 129 square miles, lessened violence but did not eliminate it. Many of the volunteer fire companies survived as social clubs and nodes of ward-level political activity. But gradually a centralized bureaucracy with unprecedented police power took hold.

Bringing order to the city could contain violent and antisocial impulses but could not treat its causes. That was the work of a generation of reformers in the antebellum era. The reformers did not share common views about what needed correction, nor did they have a single strategy for remaking society. Some Philadelphians saw a connection between heavy immigration and the rise of poverty, violence, and disease. Their solution was simple: "Americanize" the newcomers through public education, temperance societies, and evangelical Protestantism. If the poor, unruly, and diseased were black Philadelphians, the solution was even simpler: induce them to go to Africa.

Other Philadelphians, equally dismayed at the chaos accompanying industrialization and uncontrolled growth, searched for institutional remedies for society's ills. Planned factory communities might end industrial strife; better water and sewer service might limit disease; carefully controlled prisons, almshouses, orphanages, and hospitals might remold wayward individuals and return them to society as disciplined workers and citizens.[4]

The uses of history also figured in the minds of many reformers. As sectional conflict grew, the need for national unity based on founding principles became all the more apparent. As sectarian schisms erupted and tore churches apart, the evocation of legendary religious leaders became crucially important. As old sobriquets for the city—Penn's "greene country towne" or the "City of Brotherly Love"—became wildly inappropriate, civic worship of past heroes, presented as unblemished paragons, assumed new importance. If a carefully abridged past could help shape an intractable present and an uncertain future, then now was the time to make it matter.

Evangelicalism and Reform

When the Frenchman Alexis de Tocqueville visited the United States in 1831-32, he could find "no country in the whole world in which the Christian religion retains a greater influence over the souls of men than in America."[5] What Tocqueville was describing was a powerful new wave of spiritual commitment sweeping over the nation that was tightly interwoven with reform activities. Philadelphia became a major center for this "Protestant crusade." Stressing the perfection of the individual and the society at large, it reached its peak in the 1840s, with echoes continuing through the remainder of the century. Presbyterian, Baptist, and Methodist churches were at the heart of evangelicalism, though other religious groups—Unitarians, Catholics, Jews, and Episcopalians—were by no means uninvolved.

Among the fiery and eloquent gospel preachers in Philadelphia were a number of women who only in this period began to gain the right to speak publicly that Quaker women had exercised for more than a century. One of the most spiritually gifted was an impoverished young African American woman, Jarena Lee. In 1807, at age twenty-four, she felt the call to preach. She was the first outside the Society of Friends to break the gender barrier in Philadelphia. Initially an itinerant minister, speaking at outdoor gatherings, in 1817 she preached for the first time at a church, Richard Allen's Mother Bethel.[6] The voices of Quaker women, such as Lucretia Mott, also began to move people outside denominational circles. Even in more staid Presbyterian churches, itinerant women were given the pulpit, though this led to censure from the Presbytery of Philadelphia. If such women were still uncommon, it was not unusual for women to form charitable associations within their congregations and play key roles in rescuing desperate women from prostitution, taking the bottle out of the hand of abusive husbands and fathers, ministering to the poor, and continuing the fight against slavery.

In a disordered and disorderly city, nothing was more fundamental to the reform impulse than religious education. This led to a spectacular proliferation of Sunday schools and Bible tract societies. But secular public education was not far behind. Only a literate male citizenry could make informed choices. Likewise, only educated girls would become civic-minded mothers capable of preparing their sons and daughters to be responsible citizens, as Benjamin Rush, the city's generalissimo of reform, argued as early as 1787.

The idea of public education proved more acceptable than the financing of it through public funds raised from taxes. Families of means sent their children to private schools,

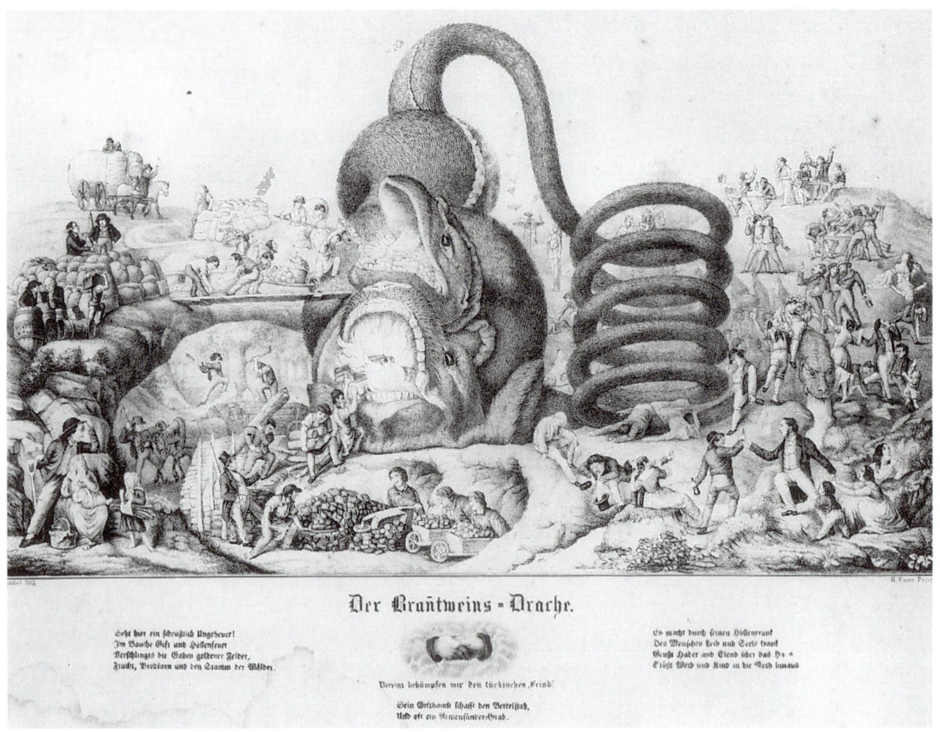

FIGURE 77. Morris H. Traubel, *Der Brantweins-Drache*, lithograph, c. 1853, LCP. In the temperance movement, cartoons were an important weapon of propaganda, partly because of their supposed appeal to the illiterate lower classes, who paid little heed to printed sermons. In *Der Brantweins Drache* (the distillery dragon), the immigrant lithographer portrays a two-headed monster in the shape of a still stoked with grain and charcoal that provides profits for the corpulent merchant in the left foreground. A gallows scene and pleading wives and children remind the viewer of the fate awaiting those who imbibe. Beneath the clasped hands appears the slogan "Together we battle the treacherous fiend."

as they had done for generations. A generation of arguing the necessity of public schools passed before Philadelphia initiated tax-supported public schools in 1818—but only for white children, until the Pennsylvania Abolition Society embarrassed white school administrators into opening schoolrooms in 1822 for black children. Twenty years later came Philadelphia's Central High School for Boys, the first public high school outside New England. Known as "the Poor Man's College," it received sanction from the state legislature in 1849 to confer the bachelor of arts degree.

Reflecting Philadelphia's race relations in general, public schools were entirely segregated, and the black schools were much inferior to white schools in physical condition and quality of teachers. The city's white school controllers provided no black high school. By the 1840s, frustrated by the controllers' neglect of the segregated black schools, black Philadelphians "turned to their own institutions and schools for help."[7] By the 1850s, about half the African American schoolchildren attending school went to nine "colored" public schools, while the other half went to private schools organized by black churches or founded by benevolent whites. One school stood above all others—the Institute for Colored Youth. Founded in 1832 with a bequest from a West Indies Quaker, it limped along for years. But it gained momentum in the 1850s, becoming the first black school in the nation with a real academic program and the first with a "firm mission: to train, under Quaker auspices, black teachers through other black teachers."[8]

Just as education was closely connected with evangelical religion, so was the temperance movement, one of the pillars of the house of reform but one of the least successful. By 1841, the city and county of Philadelphia boasted nineteen temperance societies, which advocated moderation in the consumption of alcohol, and seven total abstinence societies. Many others formed later. Like most other social reform movements, temperance had two faces: one as the reformers saw it; another as seen by the objects of the reformers' zeal. Temperance and abstinence advocates saw demon rum as the main cause of poverty; the poor saw it an opiate from misery (Figure 77). Whether a cause or an effect of poverty, the use of liquor complicated industrial labor. From the employer's point of view, the laborer's age-old use of spirits during work breaks had no place in a new industrial world; it could only lead to drunkenness on the job and habitual absenteeism. But most workingmen saw it differently. To them it was clear that the evangelical Presbyterians who led the temperance movement also spoke for the capitalist mill owners, who drove down wages and forced workers to strike for a living wage. "My company all drank a little," observed Benjamin Sewell, a Philadelphia tanner and local labor leader, "but 'nothing to hurt,' we used to say."[9] Some temperance societies originated among the working classes themselves. But most were directed from above, and most were resented for the stiff moralism of their Protestant clergymen leaders, who rarely stood with labor on issues of wages, hours, workplace safety, and public education. Membership in the temperance societies probably never exceeded twenty thousand in a city whose population rose above half a million by 1860.

Among black Philadelphians temperance *was* widely embraced—far more than among whites. Leaders such as William Whipper, a stalwart of the American Moral Reform Society, saw intemperance as worse than slavery, as binding men in chains that were even stronger than slavery's shackles. By the 1840s, temperance and abolitionism had become almost synonymous in black households. Visiting Philadelphia, Frederick Douglass found that almost all the black mutual aid societies subscribed to temperance, and several other visitors remarked that "it is a much more rare occurrence to see a drunken colored man than a drunken white man."[10] The widespread involvement of black women, organized into the Daughters of Temperance, explains much of the success.

If not the national leader in temperance reform, Philadelphia was indisputably the leader in penal reform. Under Quaker influence, colonial Pennsylvania had abolished the death penalty except for the most heinous crimes and in 1794 limited capital punishment to first-degree murder. Public whipping was abandoned in 1786. Four years later, public labor—convicts were chained to wheelbarrows as they performed street repairs—was replaced with imprisonment. Convinced that reflection and contemplation were the keys

FIGURE 78. P. S. Duval, *The State Penitentiary For the Eastern District of Pennsylvania,* lithograph of Samuel Cowperthwaite drawing, 1855, LCP. Convict #2954 drew his place of confinement in 1855. The thin walls depicted here were actually twelve feet thick and thirty feet high. It took thirteen years to complete the prison, known as Cherry Hill because it was constructed on the site of an old cherry orchard. Prints of the penitentiary came from many Philadelphia lithographers; they spread around the world to influence the building of similar spoke-like rows of cells in Asia, Latin America, and Europe. The prison has survived numerous demolition plans since closing in 1945 and remains today as a popular state historical site with guided tours.

to reforming criminals, reformers laid the cornerstone for the massive Eastern State Penitentiary in the northern district of the city in 1823 (Figure 78). Constructed to contain every prisoner in strict solitary confinement, the granite fortress represented a half century of thinking about how to rehabilitate criminals. Reformers believed that when the state inflicted bodily punishment, ferocious criminals became even more violent.[11] Instead, freed from prison brawling and violent treatment by guards, convicts would learn to be penitent in solitude and then eventually reclaim themselves as useful members of society.

The attempt to modify criminal behavior at Cherry Hill drew national and international attention. Nearly every out-of-town visitor, including Alexis de Tocqueville, Gustave de Beaumont, and Charles Dickens, toured Cherry Hill. Most were horrified at what they found. Dickens, who was allowed to go from cell to cell to talk with the prisoners, called it "a most dreadful fearful place." He wrote in his *American Notes* that the "benevolent gentlemen" who constructed the system of solitary confinement "do not know what it is that they are doing," and he judged "daily tampering with the mysteries of the brain, to be immeasurably worse than any torture of the body." Called "a crucible of good intentions" by a recent historian, Cherry Hill failed to meet its creators' hopes—the "means of restoring our fellow-creatures to virtue and happiness."[12]

The Historical Society and Library Company quickly became repositories for materials connected to the antebellum reform impulse in Philadelphia because many of their leaders were passionately involved in these reforms. Roberts Vaux is a prime example. Called by his memorialist the embodiment of "energetic benevolence," Vaux, a charter member of the Historical Society, was also a leader of the Pennsylvania Temperance Society and the Pennsylvania Abolition Society, the first president of the board of controllers of the Philadelphia public schools, the founder of an apprentices' library, the driving force behind the Philadelphia Society for Alleviating the Miseries of Public Prisons, and the motor force in building Eastern State Penitentiary. Through the nature of interlocking directorships, the Historical Society, Library Company, and Philosophical Society received the records of reform organizations, sometimes many decades after the reform era had ended. For example, the papers of the Society for Alleviating the Miseries of Public Prisons, later renamed the Pennsylvania Prison Society, reached the Historical Society in 1968. The Historical Society was a logical repository, since many of the Prison Society's founders had been so closely linked with that organization.

Women's Roles, Women's Rights

Activist women, invariably connecting religion and social remedies, were important in almost every reform movement of the antebellum era. Their emergence in the public arena led naturally to calls for woman's suffrage and to the widening of opportunities for women in the professions. Philadelphia became an important center of the woman's rights movement, in part because it was the cradle of American Quakerism. Quaker women had a long tradition of involvement both within and outside their meetings, and they became increasingly active in nineteenth-century women's causes. Not all women favored civic rights for women; in fact, most were tepid if not hostile to the idea of women voting and holding office. But even these women were part of a generation busily carving out new roles for females.

A prime example of female urban reform was engagement with the endemic problem of prostitution, rooted in desperate poverty in the minds of some, caused by moral frailty in the view of others. By the 1830s, the old male-led Magdalen Society of Philadelphia began to rely on genteel women to carry out its work of rehabilitating fallen women, though maintaining its patriarchal organizational structure. Thus, middle-class women began home visits to prostitutes to convince them to enter the asylum that the Magdalen Society had built in 1808. In 1837, the Female Moral Reform Society shifted attention from the prostitutes to the men who engaged in illicit sex. But by exposing "licentious men" and attempting to ostracize them, they put at risk the reputations of many high-placed Philadelphians. Threatening the sexual liberties and good name of males, the Moral Reform Society got no support from other moral reform groups and, moreover, encountered "a coldness and indifference, and, in some instances, hostility."[13] Ten years later, the Rosine Association, dominated by women, tried to help prostitutes with a new approach. Whereas the Magdalen Society saw prostitution as the result of individual degeneracy (though males might have set the woman on the course to moral corruption), the Rosine Association understood that prostitution was tied to the wage economy and that a young lower-class woman's resort to prostitution was mainly a matter of economic survival. Pressured by the Rosine Association's position, the Magdalen Society in 1849 initiated efforts to educate girls and young women for decent jobs.

Of much wider influence than the prostitution reformers were two New England women, Lucretia Coffin Mott and Sarah Josepha Hale, who burst on the Philadelphia scene in the antebellum period. They could hardly have been more different in the way they imagined how the American woman might reshape the democracy and preside as guardian of virtue over the American home. During a long career in Philadelphia, Hale attracted by far the larger following as a magazine editor, but Mott had much greater historical effect as a political activist.

"I grew up so thoroughly imbued with women's rights," wrote Lucretia Mott, "that it was the most important question of my life from a very early day."[14] Daughter of a Quaker sea captain from Nantucket Island, Massachusetts, Mott came to Philadelphia in 1809 at age sixteen. Deeply religious, she began preaching at age twenty-five, and three years later the Society of Friends recorded her as a minister. The transition from the ministers' gallery to the public platform came easily to this eloquent, principled woman. A follower of Elias Hicks, an adamant abolitionist who urged Quakers to boycott anything produced with slave labor, she became an antislavery activist by the early 1830s and played a major role in organizing the Philadelphia Female Anti-Slavery Society. A forceful speaker for the national American Anti-Slavery Society, she helped blaze the way in memorializing Congress to abolish slavery in the District of Columbia and the U.S. territories.

Associating the plight of the dominated slave with that of the dominated white woman, Mott joined Elizabeth Cady Stanton in 1848 in launching a national convention in Seneca Falls, New York, to promulgate the famous manifesto titled "Declaration of Sentiments." It began with the ringing words, "We hold these truths to be self-evident that all men and women are created equal." In the form of the Declaration of Independence, where a weighty list of grievances had been used to justify a call to arms, the "Declaration of Sentiments" scorched the "absolute tyranny" of men and cited "repeated injuries and usurpations": exclusion of women from higher education, the pulpit, the professions, profitable trades and commerce, the vote, and the right to hold public office; denial of property rights after marriage and guardianship of their children after divorce; and an assault on woman's "confidence in her own power, to lessen her self-respect, and to make her willing to lead a dependent and abject life."[15]

To her death in 1880, Mott remained dedicated to emancipation—of African Americans from slavery, of women from the narrow confines constructed historically to limit their possibilities, of the human mind from religious narrowness and bigotry. She attended nearly every annual convention of women's rights until her eighty-seventh year, pressed for black suffrage after the Civil War, threw herself into the work of Quaker schools for freedmen and freedwomen in the South during Reconstruction, served as vice-president of the Pennsylvania Peace Society, and was named president at the first meeting of the American Equal Rights Association in 1866. If reviled for her strenuous abolitionist and feminist stances, Mott gained wide admiration as a courageous woman with unshakable beliefs.

Sarah Josepha Hale was nearly as devout as Mott, but her Episcopalian faith took her in a different direction. Although involved in philanthropic and moral reform societies, she had little use for abolitionism and took a position on woman's suffrage that she maintained her entire life—that "to induce women to think they have a just right to participate in the public duties of government [is] injurious to their best interests and derogatory to their character."[16] Love of the nation for Mott meant ridding America of the cancer of slavery; patriotism for Hale was organizing a fund-raising campaign in 1830 to complete the Bunker Hill monument in Boston and another, two decades later, to restore Washington's Mount Vernon.

Hale came to Philadelphia in 1841 after the city's Louis Godey bought the *Ladies' Magazine* that Hale had edited in Boston and hired her as the editor of his new *Godey's Lady's Book*. Its pages filled with a mixture of music and poetry; patterns for needlework; illustrated "model cottages" with appropriate furniture, draperies, and other furnishings; "moral and instructive" literature; advice on child rearing, domestic tranquility, and husband management; and especially fashion, the magazine became the most widely circulated women's journal in the nation. "We are true to the creed that the civilization of the world is to be the work of woman," she wrote, "and so we keep the chronicle of her progress as the index of the world's advancement." But civilizing the world did not extend to politics, religious disputes, or anything outside the domestic realm because, as Hale explained to her readers, "other subjects are more important for our sex and more proper for our sphere." Far outdistancing rivals, Philadelphia's *Godey's Lady's Book* reached a circulation of 160,000 by 1860. Louis Godey, wrote an envious New York magazine, "keeps almost as many ladies in his employ as the Grand Turk."[17]

As tireless as she was in commending "meekness" as "woman's highest ornament," Hale also recognized that intellectual respect from men required accomplishment beyond the home. In this belief she became an impassioned promoter of woman's education in state normal schools. She also publicized the Female Medical College of Pennsylvania, the first medical school for women in the nation, formed in 1850. Hale tried to raise respect for women with a compendium of twenty-five hundred thumbnail sketches of distinguished women from the creation to the present. In *Woman's Record* (1853), she omitted most feminist and abolitionist women of her own generation, though she included Lucretia Mott, whose "fallacies of reasoning" she criticized.

Over the past generation, collecting material related to women's history has become a priority at almost every museum and historical society in the United States, but this took a long time. The Historical Society unofficially admitted its first female member—Deborah Norris Logan—in its early years but no others for many decades to follow. The Library Company was an exception. It had a female member as early as 1769 and in-

FIGURE 79. Women's Room at the Library Company, photograph in Abbott, *Short History of the Library Company*, LCP. When the Library Company erected a new building at Juniper and Locust Streets in 1880, architect Frank Furness included a women's room, pictured here in an undated photograph.

cluded a women's reading room in its new building completed in 1880 (Figure 79). Material relevant to women's studies came to the Library Company by gift: works by women writers and artists, biographies of famous women, publications of women's reform societies, and books and pamphlets addressed to women on a range of family, health, and domestic issues. But like many other nineteenth-century libraries, the Library Company had contempt for popular American fiction written by women (and men as well) and kept its shelves generally free of the work of prolific authors such as Ann S. Stephens, Caroline Lee Hentz, and Mrs. E.D.E.N. Southworth.

The ability of the city's institutions to acquire women's history and literature materials was limited by the fact that Quaker women, in the forefront of social reform causes and especially woman's suffrage and abolitionism, left their materials (with some notable exceptions) to Quaker institutions such as Haverford and Swarthmore Colleges rather than to the Historical Society and Library Company. Collection development followed the different character of the two colleges. Hicksite from the beginning, Swarthmore has gathered materials from abolitionist and radical Quakers; Orthodox from the beginning, Haverford has acquired materials from more conservative Quaker families.

Race and Reform

Closely linked to the women's rights movement was the crusade to abolish slavery. Philadelphia was the home of the nation's first abolitionist society, founded in 1775, and the city's Quakers had been in the vanguard of abolitionism from the beginning. But in the early years of the nineteenth century, the antislavery impulse waned as cotton cultivation spread prodigiously in the lower South and Philadelphia entrepreneurs made the city and its outlying regions a center of cotton textile production. The city's connections to the South deepened in the second quarter of the nineteenth century. When New York and Boston eclipsed Philadelphia as centers of overseas commerce, domestic trade with the South became critically important to the city's economy.

The rise of the American Colonization Society also sapped the antislavery impulse in the city, draining off money and oratorical talent. Henry Clay had promoted colonization as a noble design to "rid our country of a useless and pernicious, if not dangerous, portion of its population." Characterizing the increasingly complex free black communities as monolithic masses of degraded and unreconstructable people, he argued that "Contaminating themselves, they extend their vices to all around them."[18] That was exactly how most Philadelphia's leaders viewed the growing free black population. Horace Binney, leader of the Philadelphia bar; Robert Ralston, director of the United States Bank; William Meredith, Federalist leader; William White, bishop of the Episcopal Church; and Jacob Janeway, leader of the city's Presbyterian churches, all endorsed the Colonization Society.

When the society's expatriation programs lagged in the 1820s—only a few hundred African Americans had returned to Africa—its leaders tried to breathe new life into the organization by creating state and local auxiliaries. In the midst of bitter Quaker debates over the democratic doctrines of Elias Hicks and control of local meetings, conservative Quakers began to embrace colonization while almost all Hicksite Quakers opposed it. The Pennsylvania auxiliary of the Colonization Society was founded in late 1826, by which time the leader of the parent organization reported from Philadelphia that "The sentiments of the Quakers have, I believe, changed much in our favour."[19] By the following year, William Meredith, John Sargeant, Joseph Ingersoll, and Roberts Vaux, charter members of the newly formed Historical Society, enlisted, as did several directors of the Library Company. So did Mathew Carey, the city's eminent publisher. Earlier, Carey had declared that he regarded colonization as being "almost as Utopian as it would be to attempt to drain Lake Erie with a ladle," but now he declared it promised "a harvest of blessings."[20]

Support for colonization became the safety valve of those suffering a failure of nerve in the antislavery cause. Horrified by the militant antislavery agitation initiated in Boston by David Walker and William Lloyd Garrison, most white Philadelphians supported the repatriation of free African Americans. Most were convinced by the Colonization Society's propaganda that abolitionism had embittered the minds of southern

Share A.

Names	Age	value	rate	Remarks. 8
Nero	51	300	3/4	
Nanny	51	200	1/2	
John	17	1.100	3/4	Foot Cut.—
Jeane	15	950	1/4	
Nero	13	700	1/4	
Cudjo	10	550		
Billy	29	1.100	Full	
Fanny	23	700	3/4	delicate.
Nanny	3	150		
Betsey	2	150		
Amos.	32	1.000	Full	
Sue	27	900	do	
Munn	8	450		
{ Marshall	3.	200		
{ Frank	3	200		
Cooper Jeffrey	51	550	3/4	Cooper
Melinda	47	400	3/4	
Sam	54	400	3/4	
Betty	51	200	1/2	
Carter	22	1.000	Full	Small
Willoughby	20	900	Full	do
Caddy	16	750	1/4	do
Violet	53	350	3/4	Midwife
Abraham	22	1.100	Full	
Pinkey	21	950	Full	
Primus	19	1.100	Full	
	26.	$16350		

slave owners with the result that "the cords have been tightened, the chains riveted."[21] In 1832, the Pennsylvania legislature endorsed the American Colonization Society, and by this time, most Presbyterian churches—and many others—made annual contributions. Two years later, in the attacks on the black community, the houses of leaders such as James Forten were targeted for destruction, because their refusal to go to Liberia "prevented others from leaving the country."[22] Forten countered: "Here I have dwelt until I am nearly sixty years of age, and have brought up and educated a family. . . . Yet some ingenious gentlemen have recently discovered that I am still an African; that a continent three thousand miles, and more, from the place where I was born, is my native country. And I am advised to go home. Well, it may be so. Perhaps if I should only be set on the shore of that distant land," the old sailmaker concluded sardonically, "I should recognize all I might see there, and run at once to the old hut where my forefathers lived a hundred years ago."[23]

After about 1830, only rare clergymen, notably the Unitarian pastor William Henry Furness, preached against slavery from Philadelphia pulpits. Other ministers adopted the position of Albert Barnes, the weighty pastor at First Presbyterian Church, that "slavery, though a great evil is not the *only* evil in the land" and that preachers "should assail in preaching . . . [evils] which are near and not those which are remote."[24] Well they might, because most ministers looked down from the pulpit on Sunday to see plenty of southern-born parishioners, others in the pews who manufactured cotton textiles based on slave labor, still others who supplied southerners with Philadelphia-produced machines and manufactured goods, and even pillars of the church who owned hundreds of slaves on their southern plantations while maintaining residence in Philadelphia. Pierce Butler was a prominent example. A vestryman of the Episcopal Church of the Epiphany, Butler owned more than nine hundred slaves on St. Simon's and Butler islands in Georgia (Figure 80). When his minister spoke out against slavery in 1856, Butler led the parishioners in driving Reverend Dudley Tyng from the pulpit.[25]

The retreat from abolitionism was a contributing cause of the Hicksite schism that sharply divided the Society of Friends in 1827. Philadelphia followers of Elias Hicks, an ardent abolitionist, attracted such uncompromising abolitionists as James and Lucretia

FIGURE 80. Partial list of slaves sold at auction from Pierce Butler estate, Savannah, 1859, Wister Family Papers, HSP. This page from the sale of 436 slaves owned by Pierce Butler of Philadelphia and Georgia received extensive newspaper coverage. The *New York Tribune* called it the "largest sale of human chattels . . . in star-spangled America for several years" and made much of the fact that Butler was a fixture of Philadelphia society. Butler sold about half his slaves for $300,000 to satisfy his gambling debts and financial losses in the crash of 1857–58. His brother-in-law, George Cadwalader of Philadelphia, represented the creditors. The glamorous English actress Fanny Kemble was married to Butler for fourteen years before divorcing him in 1849, largely because of her hatred of slavery as she saw it practiced on Butler's Island in Georgia. Butler was the son of Doctor James Mease, a curator and councillor of the Philosophical Society and a founder of the Athenaeum. His two sons, Pierce and John, had their surnames changed to Butler, their mother's maiden name, in order to inherit a huge fortune in slaves and cotton lands from their maternal grandfather.

Mott as well as perhaps one third of Philadelphia's Quakers and a majority of those outside the city. Hicksite women, among them Lydia White, backed the Free Produce movement—an old idea, endorsed by Hicks since 1811—premised on the belief that slavery could be made into an economic liability if enough people refused to purchase anything produced by slave labor. Changing the name of her store to "Lydia White's Requited Labor Grocery and Dry-Goods Store," White sold candles inscribed with such slogans as "If slavery comes by color, which God gave; Fashion may change, and you become the slave."[26]

Opposing the Hicksite Quakers were Orthodox Quakers who had made their accommodation with the emerging industrial world and had softened their stance on slavery. Hicksites pictured Orthodox Quakers as men of wealth with "a thirst for popularity and worldly aggrandizement," as one reformer put it, with "a love of the world and a reluctance to bear the cross."[27] The Hicksites accused the Quaker elders of trying to squelch the views of the humbler Friends, reformers who wanted to return Quakerism to its early spirituality exemplified by George Fox, their founder, and William Penn. From the view of the prosperous and self-assured Orthodox Quakers, the Hicksites were a destabilizing force ready to deny the authority of elders who controlled the quarterly and yearly meetings.

In 1833, Philadelphia Hicksites were prominent among those joining Garrison's new American Anti-Slavery Society. In 1837, they launched a local branch, the Pennsylvania Anti-Slavery Society (Figure 81). They followed Garrison's call for the immediate and complete abolition of slavery and endorsed his denunciation of the Constitution as a proslavery document. Unlike the old Pennsylvania Abolition Society, the Anti-Slavery Society was a biracial organization, with four black Philadelphians serving on the first board of managers. But since it did not admit women, Hicksite Friends established a female auxiliary, the Philadelphia Female Anti-Slavery Society. It too was a biracial group; four black women, including three members of James Forten's family, were among the founding members. Lucretia Mott was always near the center of the society's activities, which made her a logical choice as one of the organizers of the Anti-Slavery Convention of American Women in 1837. She was the center of controversy in 1840, when she was refused a seat on the platform as an American delegate to the World Anti-Slavery Convention in London.

After abolitionism entered its radical phase in 1830, the leaders of the Historical Society, Philosophical Society, Athenaeum, and Franklin Institute lost stomach for the antislavery crusade. When the Historical Society published its first volume of addresses to assembled members in 1826, it included the essay "Notices of Negro Slavery as Connected with Pennsylvania," which was an exploration not of slavery so much as of Quaker protests against it going back to the Germantown protest of 1688. But seven years later, Roberts Vaux, who previously had published memoirs of the early Quaker abolitionists Anthony Benezet and Benjamin Lay, refused to serve as president of the American Anti-Slavery Society. In 1837, when Peter S. Du Ponceau took office as the Historical Society's second president, his inaugural address signaled how the cultural leadership of the city

FIGURE 81. Frederick Gutekunst, *Board of Managers, Pennsylvania Anti-Slavery Society*, photograph, 1851, Friends Historical Library, Swarthmore College. The Pennsylvania Anti-Slavery Society had by this time changed its all-male policy. Gutekunst was an important photographer who backed radical causes. Quaker minister Lucretia Coffin Mott, second from the right in the front row, provided an important link between the abolition and woman's rights movements. Robert Purvis, at Mott's right, was one of the city's most important black leaders, serving at various times as vice-president and president of the Society. When the Anti-Slavery Society disbanded after the Civil War, it gave its newspaper, *Pennsylvania Freeman*, along with other abolitionist papers, to the Library Company.

had turned away from abolitionism. Seventy-seven years old, Du Ponceau had served as president of the American Philosophical Society, where he had been one of its pillars and a devoted philologist; he also served as an Athenaeum councillor. Now, while agreeing that the history of African Americans in Pennsylvania and their emancipation was a fruitful topic for study, he disavowed abolitionism. "Pennsylvania has done her duty to herself," he counseled, and should "abstain from meddling with the policy of her sister states," which, "if left to themselves" would "pursue the most proper course." Reflecting the views of the society's membership, he warned that the abolitionists' interference with slavery would lead to "storms and tempests on the horizon that will shake our union to its centre."[28] The Historical Society had many Quaker members, but few of them joined the fervid abolitionists who formed the new Hicksite branch of the Society of Friends and bolstered the Pennsylvania Anti-Slavery Society.

Most Philadelphians shared Du Ponceau's cautiousness regarding slavery, and detachment was especially evident among personages associated with the Historical Society, Philosophical Society, Athenaeum, and Franklin Institute. John Vaughan, the Philosophical Society's librarian from 1803 to 1845, and director of the Athenaeum from 1816 to 1842, said he "could not bear to hear a word on the subject [of slavery]," when his minister at the Unitarian Church, William Henry Furness, began preaching abolitionism in 1839, after the burning of Pennsylvania Hall awakened him from "the sleep of the soul."[29] The Athenaeum's reading room at the Philosophical Society's building became a haunt of visiting southerners because Vaughan took many of them there as his guest. Two years later, Samuel Vaughan Merrick, founder of the Franklin Institute and its president from 1841 to 1845, resigned from the Unitarian Church in protest over the minister's antislavery sermons. In the same year, a visiting English Quaker concluded that "there is probably no city in the known world where dislike, amounting to hatred of the coloured population, prevails more than in the city of brotherly love!"[30] In 1850, at a huge "Great Union Meeting" to condemn the abolitionists and support the white South, John Sergeant, a charter member of the Historical Society, brother of its president at the time and a national figure, chaired the meeting, while another early member and committeeman of the Historical Society, George M. Dallas, denounced the "imported fanaticism" of the abolitionists.

Battered by assaults on their churches and residences, relegated to inferior segregated public schools, and excluded from industrial employment, black Philadelphians struggled on during the discouraging antebellum decades. If not fully welcomed to white abolition societies, they could establish their own, as they did in 1836—the Philadelphia Young Men's Anti-Slavery Society. If not welcome at the Library Company, they could form their own, as they did in 1837—the Philadelphia Library Company of Colored People. If they could find few white allies when they were confronted with a proposal to alter the state's constitution to specify that only certain "white freemen" had the right to vote, they could make their own case, as they did in Robert Purvis's *Appeal of Forty Thousand Citizens Threatened with Disenfranchisement, to the People of Pennsylvania.* "When you have taken from an individual his right to vote," wrote Purvis, "you have made the government, in respect to him a mere despotism." Though this appeal to bedrock principles of revolutionary republicanism had no effect, black Philadelphians gathered in their churches, about twenty of them by 1850, to find strategies for fighting slavery in the South and racial discrimination in the North. Whether militant or moderate, whether depending on moral suasion or outright demands for political rights as the best way forward, many black Philadelphians were involved in the struggle for racial equality and color-blind justice.[31]

Of great importance to black abolitionists—and thrilling to the black masses—was the dramatic mutiny on the high seas in 1839, when a group of enslaved Africans revolted against their Spanish captors. Led by Cinqué, later named Joseph Cinqué, the mutineers killed the captain of the slave ship *Amistad* off the coast of Cuba and demanded that the Spanish crew take them back to their homeland. But the wily *Amistad* mariners tacked back and forth and finally shipwrecked on Long Island, where the Africans tumbled ashore and then were taken into custody and transported to New Haven. In the course

FIGURE 82. John Sartain after Nathaniel Jocelyn, *Joseph Cinqué*, c.1841, LCP. Nathaniel Jocelyn, of New Haven, Connecticut, was the brother of Simeon S. Jocelyn, a Congregationalist minister who cofounded the Amistad Committee to raise money for the defense of the African mutineers aboard the *Amistad*. The original Jocelyn portrait hangs in the New Haven Historical Society. Lithographic replicas by Sartain were sold for one dollar apiece to contribute to this fund. Purvis believed that the Jocelyn and Sartain images of Cinqué inspired another successful mutiny by two hundred captive Africans.

of the year-long trials of the African mutineers, which ended with acquittal after a spirited defense before the Supreme Court by retired president John Quincy Adams, many whites were converted to abolitionism.[32]

Though broad coverage of the *Amistad* mutineers won some Philadelphians over to the abolitionists' cause, anti-abolitionism still ruled the city so decisively that a line was sharply drawn showing the connection between politics and public art. This became clear when Robert Purvis commissioned a painting of Cinqué from artist Nathaniel Jocelyn (Figure 82). After receiving the portrait, Purvis submitted it to the Artists' Fund Society for exhibition, at the request of one of its members. Full of admiration for the painting itself, the society made Jocelyn an honorary member. But the "hanging committee" of the society, chaired by John Neagle, refused to exhibit the portrait. Why, asked the *National Anti-Slavery Standard*, was the painting banned? Certainly not because of the character of Cinqué. The Supreme Court had ruled him guiltless for the mutiny, and he had "stirred every heart and been the theme of every tongue." Could he not take his place among the military heroes whose portraits were exhibited by the Artists' Fund? The hanging committee rejected the portrait, it claimed, because of "the excitement of the times" and because it was "contrary to usage to display works of that character." Keenly aware that a mob had burned Pennsylvania Hall to the ground three years before, the committee bowed before the anti-abolitionist sentiment. But the *Anti-Slavery Standard* went to the heart of the matter: the picture could not be displayed publicly because "This is a Negro-*hating* and a negro-*stealing* nation. A slaveholding people. The negro-*haters* of the north, and the negro-*stealers* of the south will not tolerate a portrait of a negro in a picture gallery."[33]

Abolitionists pressed home the point: using art to stimulate public reverence for guardians of liberty was a hypocritical exercise if white heroes were the only appropriate subjects for veneration while black heroes pursuing equivalent rights were inappropriate. Would Philadelphia, by default, put public art only in the service of the slaveocracy? Exhibiting the portrait of Cinqué "would be a standing anti-slavery lecture to slaveholders and their apologists," the *Anti-Slavery Standard* insisted. "To have it in the gallery would lead to discussions about slavery and the 'inalienable' rights of man. . . . So 'the hanging committee' bowed their necks to the yoke and bared their backs to the scourge, installed slavery as doorkeeper to the gallery, carefully to exclude every thing that can speak of freedom and inalienable rights." The *Anti-Slavery Standard* vowed that "posterity will talk about [John Neagle] when slavery is abolished, as it surely will be; and then all his fame, as an artist, will not save him from merited condemnation."[34]

While Neagle and other white artists flinched before proslavery white mobs, black leaders confronted this animus daily and hardly had the luxury of flinching. Successful coal merchant William Still was one of the many who continued the fight. Still joined the Vigilant Committee of Philadelphia, founded in the same year as Cinqué's mutiny, to help runaway slaves reach safe places and fend off the kidnappers who seized blacks and hustled them back south into slavery. In 1850, Still discovered that a fugitive slave who had just arrived in the city was his long-lost brother. Now convinced that the fugitives' escape stories and family connections were politically useful and enormously valuable as a vital part of the political and historical record, Still began interviewing southern blacks fleeing north to Philadelphia (Figure 83). His interviews and notes concerning many of some 1,100 fugitives who reached Philadelphia gradually grew into a huge oral history manuscript, which he published in 1862 as *The Underground Railroad*. Contributors of essays to the Historical Society's *Memoirs* in this era were highly educated lawyers, doctors, and businessmen, but none exceeded the historical contribution of the self-taught Still, the eighteenth child of former slaves. Fifty-nine years later, in 1931, his daughter Frances E. Still gave the Historical Society her father's manuscript, along with his letter books, an account book, and other papers.

FIGURE 83. *The Rescue of Jane Johnson and Her Children [at the Camden and Amboy R.R. Wharf in Philadelphia]*, engraving in William Still, *The Underground Railroad* (1872), LCP. One of the oral histories Still recorded involved Jane Johnson and her children. In this engraving, Passmore Williamson, a Quaker lawyer working for the Vigilant Committee, restrains Colonel John H. Wheeler, U.S. minister to Nicaragua, who intended to take his slaves from New York to Central America. William Still, in top hat and cutaway coat, after explaining that Pennsylvania's 1847 personal liberty law forbade slave owners the right of transit through the state, leads Wheeler's slaves down the gangway from the New York-bound ship. A U.S. marshal arrested Williamson and five black dockside porters who helped him assist Jane Johnson and her children ashore. All were charged with riot, assault, and battery. They were cleared, but Williamson was sentenced to one hundred days in Moyamensing Prison for contempt of court.

Antislavery continued to be a burning issue in Philadelphia down to the advent of the Civil War. The Fugitive Slave Act of 1850 caused great suffering among black Philadelphians, who bore the brunt of fighting off kidnappers coming north to reclaim slave refugees. Denying a seized African American the right to testify or receive a jury trial, the law turned the federal district court that met in Independence Hall into an uproar. The Unitarian church's William Furness pledged from the pulpit that he would oppose the law and called on all Christians to join him. He was much in the minority, as was evident when 5,000 Philadelphians packed the grand salon of the Chinese Museum to hear eminent leaders, including many Historical Society councillors, support the Fugitive Slave Act. However, in 1851, the treason trial of black and white Pennsylvanians who had fought off a posse of slave-catchers from Maryland and killed its leader at Christiana, south of the city, galvanized antislavery stalwarts. With the trials being conducted in Independence Hall, the entire city was abuzz at this harbinger of armed conflict between the North and South over slavery.[35]

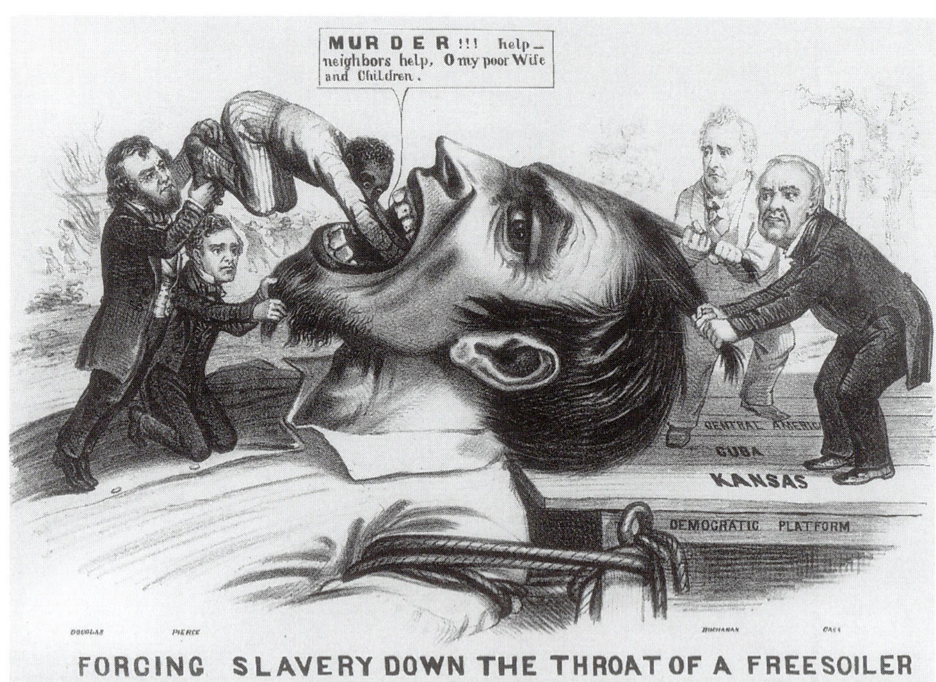

FIGURE 84. John L. Magee, *Forcing Slavery Down the Throat of a Freesoiler*, lithograph, 1856, Library of Congress. Philadelphia lithographer Magee specialized in disaster scenes and crude political cartoons. Here Democrats are blamed for violence against antislavery settlers in Kansas. Franklin Pierce, Democratic president, and Stephen A. Douglas, Democratic senator, force a black man into the mouth of a Kansas freesoiler who is tied to the Democratic platform. Restraining the freesoiler by the hair are Pennsylvania's James Buchanan, the Democratic presidential candidate, and Democratic senator Lewis Cass. Kansas, Cuba, and Central America are inscribed on the Democratic platform in reference to the party's hopes to extend slavery.

Three years later, the Kansas-Nebraska Act of 1854, which allowed citizens in new territories to decide whether to allow slavery (in effect, denying Congress power over territorial slavery), led to fierce conflict among freesoiler and proslavery settlers in "Bloody Kansas" and further roiled the political scene in Philadelphia. In the presidential election of 1856, both parties played the race card, bringing deep discouragement to Philadelphia's African American neighborhoods (Figure 84). John Frémont, the Republican candidate, received only 11 percent of Philadelphia's vote, a not surprising outcome in a city where only one of the many newspapers supported the abolition of slavery and the Democratic Party was rabidly antiblack and pro-southern. Most of the city's whites were unwilling to risk war with the southern states over the question of slavery, while confidence in the moral suasion and passive resistance tactics of the Garrisonians ebbed among black Philadelphians.

Philadelphia's general hostility toward the antislavery movement surfaced again in regard to the crusade of John Brown, the freebooting, biblically inspired guerrilla who

FIGURE 85. David Bustill Bowser, *John Brown*, oil, 1860, HSP. African American artist Bowser executed this sympathetic portrait of Brown the year after Brown was executed. Bowser's portrait was used by many other painters who showed Brown, alternately, as a crazed agitator bent on ruining the country or as a sainted martyr defending the nation's most fundamental principles. The Historical Society acquired by gift, at an unknown time, two muskets and a pike carried by Brown, his sons, and their compatriots into the battle at Harpers Ferry. Apparently, these items have never been shown in Philadelphia and are now stored in a warehouse, along with the Historical Society's entire artifact collection.

saw the slaveholding South, like a venomous snake, wrapping the republic in its lethal coils. Most Philadelphians, like most white southerners, regarded the fiery abolitionist as the country's most dangerous radical and a man who was pushing the nation to the brink of civil war. They had lived through the turbulent Christiana trial in 1851, the largest treason trial in American history, and even the Republicans who would later found the pro-Lincoln Union League condemned Brown's 1859 raid on the federal arsenal at Harpers Ferry as a similar crime of treason. So great was the hatred of Brown that after his execution on December 2, 1859, when the body was brought to Philadelphia by train for undertakers to prepare it for burial, the corpse had to be secreted away to prevent a proslavery riot at the railroad station. Meanwhile, Brown's widow took refuge in the home of William Still. But Brown's crusade for the freedom of enslaved African Americans and his willingness to die for black Americans made him a hero to Philadelphia's small circle of white antislavery reformers and to most black Philadelphians (Figure 85).

One way of preserving the memory of fallen heroes was to memorialize them at their death, thus carving a niche for them in the national pantheon with words and leaving for future generations scripts of veneration. With this in mind, four hundred black Philadelphians, along with about twenty whites, gathered at the Shiloh Baptist Church to pay respects to Brown and think about history's course. Reverend Jonathan C. Gibbs prayed for John Brown and also mourned that part of the Gibbs family was still enslaved. From the pews cries went up, "So is mine."[36] Other black ministers rose to condemn the ill treatment of black Philadelphians and to urge African Americans to stop truckling to white oppressors. Stiffen their sinew, the ministers told them, and write a new page of history as Brown had done, following in the steps of other martyrs—Touissant L'Ouverture, Gabriel Prosser, Denmark Vesey, and Nat Turner.

Meanwhile, white abolitionists called a meeting at National Hall, at Market near Twelfth Street. James Mott chaired the meeting and among the speakers were his wife, Lucretia Mott, Robert Purvis, and William H. Furness, the Unitarian minister. Mott and Purvis were interrupted and jeered by southern medical students studying in Philadelphia as they spoke to immortalize Brown as an upholder of what the Founding Fathers had promised. Then Furness, reminding the "immense crowd" that the anniversary of Washington's death was twelve days ahead, compared John Brown with George Washington, whom he pictured as another insurrectionist prepared to die for freedom's cause. December 2, exclaimed Furness, should be remembered "as a great historical day," when Brown led seventeen "heroes" at Harpers Ferry "against the mightiest and most inhuman oppression the sun ever shone upon." This history lesson led to an eruption of angry, anti-abolitionist listeners who hissed and shouted. The avenging angel for some was the anti-hero for others.[37]

In the Theater, Theater in the Streets

Shakespeare with Edwin Forrest at the luxurious Walnut Street Theater or a concert at the elegant new Academy of Music: this is what the newspapers, magazines, and playbills recognized as Philadelphia's culture in the antebellum era. And some patrician Philadelphians turned to science to redefine the American republic. But large numbers of urban dwellers could not afford the price of admission to the theater or Academy of Music. They made the streets and squares of the city their outdoor theaters—places to revel in holiday parades, festivals, folk dramas, political burlesques, popular music, and dancing.

Within polite culture, the Philadelphia-born Edwin Forrest was esteemed as a lion of the stage. Although a hostile critic once described him as "striding, screeching, howling, tearing passions to tatters, disregarding the sacred bounds of propriety," this was exactly what made him so popular. Quaker influence had kept the theater restricted to the fringes of the city before the American Revolution. But the stage overwhelmed Quaker opposition after the war, and by the mid-nineteenth century, theater was one of the chief forms of entertainment for all but the bottom quarter or third of society. Forrest's brawny interpretations of Shakespeare stood in pointed contrast to the more mannered versions of such English actors as William McCreedy.[38]

Rivaling the Philadelphia theater was classical music, especially after local business leaders organized the American Academy of Music in 1852 and began raising money for the opera house, now the oldest in continuous use in the United States. The managers made special efforts to make the public areas attractive to respectable women and to exclude prostitutes, who often loitered in theater lobbies. Black Philadelphians, in a day when nearly all public facilities were segregated, could buy seats in the amphitheater but had to use a separate entrance.

Art fared poorly in Philadelphia in the antebellum period. But if the center of American art had migrated to New York, Philadelphia remained the home of some important painters, such as Henry Inman, John Neagle, Thomas Sully, and Jacob Eicholtz. While art slipped from favor, lithography and photography flourished. The panoramic city views of lithographers were popular because they played to white pride in the city's extraordinary growth in the first half of the nineteenth century while depicting a spic-and-span city innocent of turmoil and violence.

Challenging the lithograph was the new enterprise of photography in which German immigrant brothers, Frederick and William Langenheim, took the lead. By the 1840s, they were producing a series of photographic views of the city and, by the next decade, were carrying off medals for their daguerreotypes, stereographs, and magic lantern slides awarded at the Franklin Institute's annual exhibitions. Others followed, making Philadelphia a center of the fascinating magic of photography. For several decades, photographers remained as boosterish as the lithographers, which was logical because most of their trade came from photographic portraits of the well positioned, who were also interested in carefully framed shots of churches and public buildings, bridges and ships, mayors, lawyers, and bank presidents. But, in time, photographers began to capture factories and slums, street urchins and prostitutes, riots and crime victims—to visualize the city more ambivalently. The Library Company and the Historical Society acquired important collections of photography that recorded Philadelphia's history as it unfolded day by day. Particularly important was the interest of John McAllister, the city's premier grinder of optical lenses. Having befriended the Langenheims from the days of their early arrival, he went on to become a photographer in his own right and a collector of daguerreotypes and photographs; he and his son bequeathed hundreds of photographs to the Library Company and the Historical Society. Much later, the Free Library, the City Archives, and the Urban Archives at Temple University became important repositories of photographic images of the city.

African Americans could never break into the immigrant-dominated lithographers' circle that busily recorded the city's growth, but they contributed several painters and at least one photographer of note in this period. Included were Robert Douglass, Jr. and David Bustill Bowser. It was Douglass whose gigantic illuminated transparencies of George Washington crossing the Delaware hung in front of Independence Hall in 1832 for the hundredth anniversary of Washington's birth, arousing cheers from thousands of

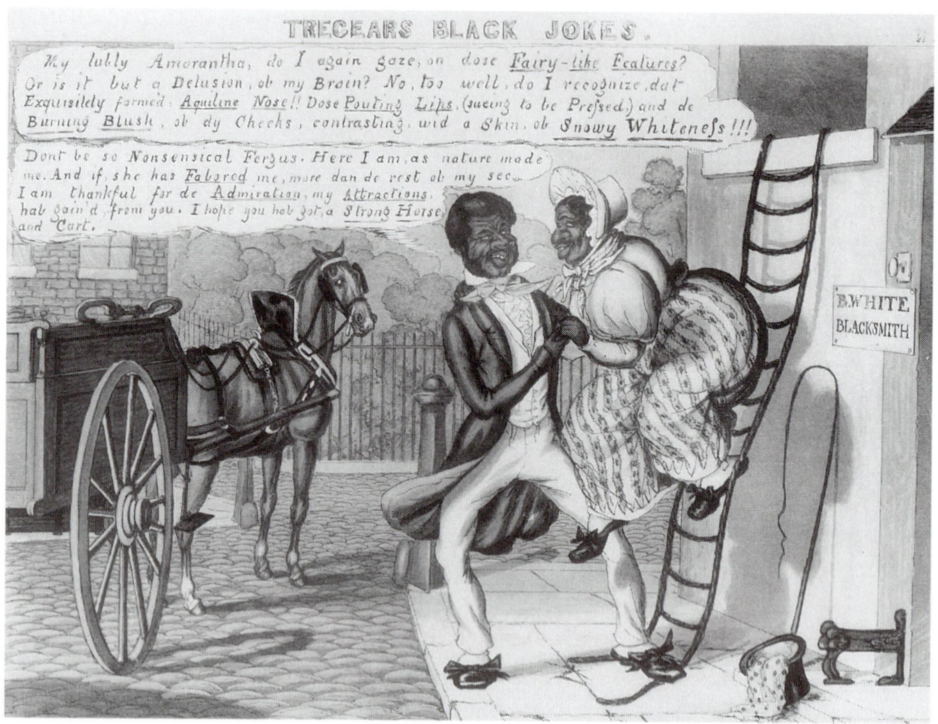

FIGURE 86. Edward Clay, *The Elopement*, as embellished in *Tregear's Black Jokes*, LCP. Clay's *Life in Philadelphia* series resurfaced in London in 1834 in embellished form as *Tregear's Black Jokes: Being a Series of Laughable Caricatures on the March of Manners Amongst the Blacks*. Seventy years later, Alfred Rosenthal, unofficial curator of Independence Hall's historical collection, lent his series of ten Clay prints, which were displayed there for almost twenty years. When Edward Raymond Turner, the first African American historian of black Pennsylvanians, saw the *Life in Philadelphia* series as part of the exhibits meant to cultivate historical memory at the nation's shrine, he took offense in his *The Negro in Pennsylvania*, published in 1912.

celebrators. Douglass was the first and apparently only photographer to capture images of Frank Johnson, the city's celebrated black musician. Bowser's landscapes were not commercially successful among white Philadelphians, for prejudice among the upper classes against black artists was as deep as working-class prejudice against black craftsmen. However, Bowser was highly regarded among Philadelphia's black bourgeoisie, and his commercial work—elaborately decorated fire engine panels, fire company parade hats, and commercial signs—was in demand.

Cheaply produced prints, often with watercolor added by hand, also found a market while leaving behind iconographic evidence of growing racial and ethnic antagonism in the city. Edward Clay and David Claypool Johnston were the most prolific of the printmakers, and both found it profitable to make black and Irish Philadelphians the butt of their mordant humor. During the 1820s, Clay was especially successful with a lithographic series titled *Life in Philadelphia* in which he mocked the aspirations and vanities of middle-class black citizens. "Printed rotten eggs" thrown at the black community, as one historian has called them, his lithographs became so popular that the *Saturday Evening Post* republished them in the 1830s (Figure 86).[39]

Clay's biting caricatures played to the fears of white Philadelphians, who, alarmed at the growing population of free blacks, hoped for their colonization—in Sierra Leone, Liberia, Haiti, Canada, or anywhere else. But if black Philadelphians would not leave, they could be belittled and derided. By picturing black Philadelphians as laughably pretentious and sorely incapable of learning proper English, artists like Clay fed the feeling that people of color were inherently ineligible for the role of virtuous citizen. By creating an imaginary black urbanite, the consummate dandy, Clay made it easier to typecast the city's African Americans as counterfeit citizens. His comical black Philadelphians with twisted language were already surfacing in minstrelsy, the most popular form of entertainment in the northern cities for the rest of the nineteenth century.

While minstrelsy had political overtones, theater in the streets often became explicitly political. In 1825, for example, smoldering discontent with the militia laws escalated into ribald opposition. For years, workingmen had resented the unequal burden of militia service, which took them from work, without compensation, and obliged them to equip and uniform themselves at their own expense. Moreover, militia troops were often reluctant to confront fellow townsmen, sometimes their neighbors or co-workers. Many were fined for noncompliance, and few had shoulder weapons or uniforms of any kind. Volunteer militia units, usually led by high-placed Philadelphians such as George Cadwalader, were generally better trained and better equipped. Now, in 1825, during the elections for militia officers, the men of the Eighty-Fourth Foot Regiment voted for John Pluck, a poor, bow-legged, hunchbacked, illiterate man who cleaned stables for a living (Figure 87). Outraged division officers invalidated the election and ordered a new one. This time Pluck received 447 votes to 79, divided between two respectable candidates. In full cry against the militia system, Pluck ordered a parade through the city. Thousands turned out to see "the Grand Military farce," as the *Saturday Evening Post* described it. Mocking the uniforms of militia officers, Pluck rode astride a spavined white nag and was dressed in an oversized woman's bonnet draping down to his shoulders, a huge buckle holding up his baggy burlap pants, and a rusty sword at his side. His men followed in tattered clothes, shouldering cornstalks and brooms. The next spring, Colonel Pluck repeated the performance.[40]

The irreverence for military authority and the inversion of the social order appealed to "the depraved part of the crowd," according to one newspaper. But others applauded these demonstrations of "republican simplicity" and the exposure of corruption spreading throughout local and state offices. "Since the militia laws are clearly a farce," opined the *Pennsylvania Gazette*, "none should complain about this [burlesque parading]; therefore, let [the militia system] be ridiculed until those in authority either amend it or abolish it altogether."[41] Even the press, usually beholden to "respectable" Philadelphians, had endorsed the use of the streets by the irreverent lower classes.

Election Day was another occasion for people from multitudinous backgrounds to mingle in front of Independence Hall. Diaries, autobiographies, and newspaper reports

FIGURE 87. Edward Clay, *The Nation's Bulwark: A Well-Disciplined Militia*, lithograph,1829, LCP. Clay's mocking depiction of the Philadelphia militia was apparently inspired by Colonel Pluck's tatterdemalion burlesque parade in 1825. The print did little to restore respect for the militia system, which the United States *Gazette* said had been dealt "a death blow." This was not far from the mark because militia units continued to demonstrate against the system. In 1833, the Eighty-Fourth Regiment paraded with two banners inscribed "Hollow Guards, the Terror of the World" and "The Nation's Bulwark—the Bloody 84th."

chronicled the pageantry and friction of the elections, though mostly when an election turned violent. An aspiring immigrant painter, John Lewis Krimmel, captured a peaceful Philadelphia election scene in 1815. Krimmel was the first to do genre painting, as scenes of everyday life were called. His *Election Scene* (Figure 88) was not particularly popular at first, but if Americans wanted a democratically conceived art freed from European standards of painting, they got it in Krimmel's genre work. In time, prints made from his paintings and the exhibition of his watercolors and oils in Philadelphia and other cities encouraged other artists to adopt everyday subjects. This helped to dissolve the common prejudice against art, which prevailed because it so often displayed "certain indications of the concentration of wealth and power in the hands of the few," as Benjamin Latrobe expressed it to the Pennsylvania Academy of Fine Arts in his address in 1811.[42]

In the jostling of cultures in Philadelphia before the Civil War, a figure occasionally appeared who bridged the gap between the "rowdy" and the "respectable." Such a man was the black West Indian immigrant Francis (Frank) Johnson (Figure 89). A brilliant

FIGURE 88. John Lewis Krimmel, *Election Day in Philadelphia*, oil, 1815, Winterthur Museum. Krimmel learned his trade in Württemberg, where he encountered the work of European genre artists. In 1809, at age twenty-three, he immigrated to Philadelphia. By 1815, he was aware that to succeed in America an artist needed to reflect optimistic faith in republican values and American progress. The buoyant spirit reflected in *Election Scene* is somewhat compromised by the seemingly drunken workingmen, all too ready to be bribed, at the center of the picture. A year after this painting was completed, Krimmel did a watercolor of the scene, which the Historical Society acquired by donation in 1872. Krimmel's death by drowning in 1821 at age thirty-five deprived Philadelphia of untold numbers of street scenes.

composer, conductor, and instrumentalist, Johnson became Philadelphia's music man for whites and blacks alike. His band played Johnson's own compositions at the Grand Ball and reception for Lafayette in 1824 and also played at many of the Saturday salons hosted by Phoebe Ann Ridgway Rush, the wife of the Library Company's post-Civil War benefactor. For the cotillions and silk-stocking military processions of wealthy white city dwellers, his band was in great demand. After a European tour in 1837, culminating with a command performance before Queen Victoria, Johnson returned to introduce white Philadelphians to "concerts à la musard," light classical music accompanied by a promenade, which became all the rage in the city.

Johnson was as much in demand among black Philadelphians and abolitionists as among white anti-abolitionists. He played frequently at the social gatherings of the city's black residents, wrote a cotillion celebrating Haiti's President Boyer, played his composition *Grave of the Slave* with lyrics by Sarah Forten, and performed at the annual fairs of the Female Anti-Slavery Society. He also introduced black music lovers to Handel's *Oratorio*, which he performed in a black church.

FIGURE 89. Albert Hoffy, *Frank Johnson*, lithograph, 1846, HSP. Hoffy, a lithographer who came to Philadelphia to draw Indians for J. T. Bowen, engraved Frank Johnson's image on stone from a Robert Douglass, Jr. daguerreotype. Hoffy was known for correct likenesses. Johnson presented a manuscript album of his musical compositions to Phoebe Ann Ridgway Rush, and it was willed to the Library Company by her husband, James Rush, when he died in 1869. The Free Library acquired other Johnson material from the Philadelphia Mercantile Library when the latter disbanded in 1944 after 123 years of existence. A private collector, Harry Dichter, sold and willed additional Johnson material to the Free Library in the late 1970s.

In an era when musical talent was one of the few attributes that allowed African Americans to cross the color line, another cultural go-between was Elizabeth Taylor Greenfield, a gifted soprano. Born of enslaved Indian and African American parents in Mississippi and later known as the "Black Swan," she came to Philadelphia at a young age with her mistress, who freed her after joining the Society of Friends. Largely self-educated in piano, harp, guitar, and voice, Greenfield thrilled a Buffalo, New York audience in 1851 and soon became a popular concert artist in eastern cities. On a concert tour in England in 1854, she sang before Queen Victoria, eighteen years after the monarch heard Frank Johnson play. Through the 1850s and 1860s, Greenfield taught voice lessons and gave concerts in Philadelphia.

The History Project

In the forty years preceding the Civil War, a battle for public memory occurred in Philadelphia. The contest was initiated from the top among a small group of cultural leaders who imagined that remembering the past through civic pageants, monuments, publicly displayed paintings, and published biographies and memoirs relating to the heroes of the colonial and revolutionary generations might provide a restorative to their fast-growing, industrializing, uproarious, and splintering city. What they did not foresee was that Philadelphians, in all their variety and all their antagonisms, might find the history project of the white Protestant upper class another manifestation of class power. For this reason, the self-appointed official arbiters of the past were by no means the clear-cut winners in the competition for manipulating the past.

Events in 1821 can be seen as marking the initial volley in the antebellum contest for history. This was the year when John Fanning Watson launched an oral history project in order to write a history of Philadelphia's colonial and revolutionary eras, and also when seventeen Philadelphians commissioned John Krimmel to paint a huge six-by-nine-foot canvas, *The Landing of William Penn at Newcastle in October 1682*, apparently to be given to the city for hanging in Independence Hall. The names of only three benefactors are known: Peter Du Ponceau, Roberts Vaux, and Joseph Parker Norris, the president of the Bank of Pennsylvania and a direct descendant of Isaac Norris, one of Penn's closest friends and a political and mercantile titan of the colonial era. Krimmel's untimely death left the painting unfinished, but the group soon formed the Society for the Commemoration of the Landing of William Penn, popularly known as the Penn Society. If New Englanders had celebrated the Pilgrim landing at Plymouth Rock since 1798, why did Philadelphians neglect public commemorations of the arrival of Penn? This oversight, thought the group, should now be remedied for what they deemed the common good of the city.

Lafayette's visit to Philadelphia in 1824 gave the Penn promoters an indirect boost. The return of the French hero of the American Revolution provided a unique occasion for sharing patriotic sentiment and national memory as well as nurturing reverence of Washington, by now well advanced in the nation's literature, art, and popular culture. Philadelphia's civic procession for Washington's comrade-in-arms wound through thirteen triumphal arches before reaching Independence Hall. To prepare for Lafayette's visit, the city funded a major restoration of the decayed Independence Hall, an important step in the conversion of the old State House relic into a national shrine. With this

much accomplished, the Penn Society was in a position to promote Pennsylvania's founder: as Christian colony builder, lawgiver, statesman, promoter of interracial harmony, and dispenser of justice.

Meeting at the Laetitia Penn House to celebrate the 142nd anniversary of William Penn's landing, the Penn Society ate possum to honor the legend that the humble rodent was served at Penn's first dinner in Philadelphia. Then the gentlemen concocted their plan for a historical society. "Our Penn Dinner has made a great stir, and is very popular," wrote Roberts Vaux to John F. Watson. "The Historical Society will go on, and in short a new current of feeling seems to have set in, highly creditable to Pennsylvania past, present and to come." Three months elapsed before a constitution and bylaws could be agreed upon, partly because some of the first charter members would not agree that Historical Society membership must require birth in Pennsylvania. In fact, William Rawle would not accept the presidency of the infant society until this rule was changed to qualify any *resident* of Pennsylvania for membership. By this time, Watson was busily gathering materials for his *Annals of Philadelphia*, aided by his good friend John Jay Smith, soon to become librarian of the Library Company.[43]

In 1825, Penn Society members, now almost undistinguishable from the founders of the Historical Society, renewed their attempt to emblazon Penn's memory in the public's mind. They commissioned Henry Inman, a struggling artist from New York, to paint a heroic William Penn. Inman's work, to be seen by innumerable visitors trooping through Independence Hall over the next century, portrayed Penn at the fabled treaty meeting at Shackamaxon (Figure 90). It owed much to Benjamin West's *William Penn's Treaty with the Indians*, regarded now as an allegorical lesson about idealized interaction between Quakers and Indians but challenged as historically inaccurate only in 1836. Inman had captured the legend, and Quaker members of the Penn Society and Historical Society were glad to embrace it. A mythic Penn had the potential to bind Quakers' wounds over the Hicksite separation in 1827, when Orthodox and radical Quakers had both claimed Penn as the embodiment of their position on religious conviction and the authority of individual Quaker congregations. The eminent Roberts Vaux, who had been shouted down in 1827 by Hicks's followers at a Quaker quarterly meeting, must have taken some satisfaction that Orthodox Quakers commissioned Inman to execute his painting.[44]

FIGURE 90. Henry Inman, *William Penn*, oil, c. 1832, INHP. Here Penn holds his charter from Charles II, and dominates the picture, with Indians standing inconspicuously in the background by the fabled elm tree. A comparison with West's *Penn's Treaty with the Indians* (Figure 8) shows that Inman was far less explicit about the comity between Lenape and English, but it is likely that the Penn Society founders applauded the picture as a worshipful memorial to the state's founder. A New York journalist transplanted to Philadelphia a decade later described Inman's work as "a sweet, dreamy portrait of WILLIAM PENN, who must have been one of the most romantic, poetical souls ever created, whatever History may say to the contrary. . . . It is a face to fall in love with and to have forever haunting one's memory like a benignant and friendly vision." The Penn Society presented it to city authorities at Independence Hall in December 1832, where it would hang alongside the only other two paintings the city displayed at the hallowed site—one of George Washington, the other of Lafayette.

FIGURE 91. W. L. Breton, *The Slate House of PENN in Second Street*, watercolor, c.1826, Athenaeum. Watson's preservationist and antiquarian interests led him in the 1820s to commission the newly arrived immigrant Breton to do watercolors of prerevolutionary buildings, including some about to be demolished. Breton lived in Penn's Slate House during his brief sojourns in Philadelphia. Breton did twenty-six half-page lithographs for the 1830 publication of Watson's *Annals of Philadelphia*. Copies of the watercolors, which at the time sold at twenty-five cents each, were given many decades later to the Athenaeum and Historical Society.

Even before Inman completed his painting, John F. Watson was hard at work to preserve history in bricks and mortar (Figure 91). Believing that ancient glory and virtue oozed almost mystically from the physical past, he proposed purchasing the Laetitia Penn House, then occupied as the Rising Sun Inn, "for the sake of its perpetual preservation, as a memorable City Relic, worthy to be held in perpetual remembrance, as the actual contrast, *at all times*, between the beginning and the progress of our city." The house had briefly been the home of Penn's flamboyant daughter, and Watson, consumed with antiquarian zeal, claimed he would be "deeply mortified if the apathy of Philadelphia should allow the house to be pulled down." The house, if saved, could "revive the picture of olden time." Philadelphia's first preservationist, Watson drummed up support for what could be "a perfect museum, where many of our citizens could be brought to deposit their old relics," items such as "old high-backed chairs, settles and Settees, pictures and looking glasses . . . old fashioned dresses, house ornaments, &c."[45]

Watson could not find enough kindred spirits or well-heeled funders to turn the Laetitia Penn House into the nation's first historic home (though it would survive to be rescued a half century later). But according to admirers, he continued to act "in spirit with those who lived on earth some fifty or a hundred years ago," as he went about putting the finishing touches on his *Annals of Philadelphia*. In the process, he ran head-on into the perils of writing about the past while trying to preserve it. Watson had a great regard for the authenticity of historical materials and collected them avidly. He borrowed liberally from materials that his friend John Jay Smith provided from papers still in the extensive Logan family collection. Deborah Norris Logan, Smith's cousin, also provided Watson with artifacts and papers relating to William Penn and James Logan. But when Watson showed Deborah Logan a manuscript of his *Annals*, she and her female cousins leaned on the annalist to suppress material unflattering to their family. In particular, Watson's use of a letter he had uncovered in the privately held Charles Thomson papers threw a dark light on the political stance of the colonial leader John Dickinson, who had lost courage on declaring independence. Dickinson happened to be Deborah Logan's uncle and the father of her female cousins. When Deborah implored Watson to suppress the letter and, indeed, to bury a separate paper he showed her entitled "The Revolution," he yielded. In no position to challenge the Logan family, Watson gave in to social pressure, not only suppressing his use of a key letter questioning Dickinson's anti-British warmth but also having "surrendered," as Logan wrote in her diary, "the objectionable document . . . to do as I pleased with, without keeping any copy of it for himself." Having drawn blood, Deborah Logan asked for more. "Once family honor became the criterion for judgment of historical fact," writes Watson's biographer, he "had difficulty in pleasing the Logans."[46] Deborah Logan, who later edited the vast Logan-Penn correspondence, published by the Historical Society, and made massive deletions of material she thought might cast a shadow on her husband's great-grandfather, became an unofficial censor of the *Annals of Philadelphia*. Watson's essay on the Revolution disappeared forever.

In trying to immortalize colonial and revolutionary heroes, Watson merely reflected a historical consciousness from his social vantage point and from his bone-deep antiquarianism. He could justify bending to what his patroness Deborah Logan called the "traditionary recollections" of her family because of his fondness for collecting oral histories. But when oral history could not be sustained by the documentary evidence, Watson's justification for purging his stories lost credibility. A review of the *Annals of Philadelphia* in the *National Gazette* noted that Watson "has imbibed a strong affection for ancient modes and customs, and seems to think the former state of society preferable to the present."[47]

Although self-censorship compromised Watson's *Annals*, his energetic efforts to cultivate historical memory paid off. In 1832, two years after Watson's *Annals* reached Philadelphia's bookstores, the city staged an elaborate procession to commemorate the centennial of Washington's birth, while also promoting the skills of its manufacturers and artisans. Philadelphians got started only three weeks before the birthday of February 22, 1832, but feverish float-building produced a procession that involved some eleven thousand men, including two thousand in military uniform. The marchers fell in behind

FIGURE 92. M. E. D. Brown, *The Gold and Silver Artificers of Phila. in Civic Procession*, lithograph, 1832, LCP. The gold- and silversmiths in the procession shown in front of the Second Bank struck off medals with Washington's image. One hundred years later, on the bicentennial of Washington's birth, the Historical Society received a parade apron worn by one of Philadelphia's hatters for the 1832 celebration.

eighteen axe-wielding pioneers dressed in white frocks and leather caps, in what was perhaps the first ritual costuming of the colonial period. The parade included gold-and silversmiths (Figure 92), tailors, cordwainers, hatters, and dozens of other craftsmen groups. Printers peeled off copies of Washington's "Farewell Address" from a horse-drawn press, bakers distributed hot bread fresh from a mobile oven, tobacconists handed out fresh-rolled cigars, and stonecutters displayed the cornerstone for a proposed Washington monument. That the procession organizers wanted the public to see how the past was joined to the present was apparent in many of the floats and banners. With the nullification crisis on everyone's mind—the South's hatred of Congressional protective tariffs on manufactured goods that favored the North had led to talk of refusing to obey federal law—spectators watched paraders march by with standards proclaiming, "The Territories Yet Remain" and "Behold the Union as it Stands." Coopers displayed a hoop and staves with a banner reading "United Thus."

Though this was Washington's parade and the organizers did their best to keep attention focused on him, one group of artisans had a history lesson of their own to purvey. Two hundred blacksmiths marched along displaying an outsized copy of John Neagle's *Pat Lyon at the Forge* (Figure 93). This was a pointed political statement, for Lyon was a brawny and prosperous blacksmith, locksmith, and builder of fire engines whom Neagle painted in 1826 to etch in memory Lyon's successful battle for justice against prosecution for a crime he did not commit. In 1798, amid fierce partisan politicking, the

FIGURE 93. John Neagle, *Pat Lyon at the Forge*, oil, 1829, PAFA. In Neagle's second oil painting of locksmith Lyon, the cupola, weather vane, and roof of the Walnut Street Prison show in the left background. Lyon's apprentice is behind him. Lyon's fame as falsely accused was long-lasting. Memory of his struggle for justice was resuscitated through a play staged in the 1840s, and the story was adapted in 1854 for a children's book, *The Locksmith of Philadelphia*.

Jeffersonian Lyon had been imprisoned under a charge of robbing the Bank of Pennsylvania. Incarcerated for three months in Walnut Street Prison during a yellow fever epidemic that killed his wife and child, he barely survived and was convinced he was victimized by Federalist leaders, who knew him as a political radical. Lyon fought the charges for seven years before gaining acquittal and became something of a Jeffersonian hero. Although by 1826 Lyon was wealthy, he told Neagle, "I do not desire to be represented in the picture as a gentleman—to which character I have no pretension. I want you to paint me at work at my anvil, with my sleeves rolled up and a leather apron on." This was the image the blacksmiths held aloft as they marched in the Washington procession.[48]

Philadelphia's leaders hoped that parades and civic gatherings on Washington's birthday and July Fourth would unify the city, but by the 1840s, noted the diarist Joseph Sill, the birthday parades were "but a shadow of what they used to be."[49] Nor was it possible for city leaders, for all the care they took in trying to manage July Fourth celebrations, to stop them from erupting into spasms of religious or racial intolerance when white nativist feelings ran high. A dramatic example of the latter was the enormous parade of July 4, 1844, a procession produced by the so-called Native American Party that led directly to violent rioting against the Catholic Irish two days later.

As with virtually all civic parades, the directors of the July Fourth procession had an explicit purpose: to mobilize Protestant nativism and demonstrate the growing strength of anti-Catholic sentiment in Philadelphia. But parade directors don't get everything they want, and sometimes not even what they have in mind. Catholics would willingly have marched in the procession to demonstrate their allegiance to the nation, as their newspaper, the *Catholic Herald*, insisted repeatedly. That the Native American Party was able to obtain city approval to monopolize public space for an explicitly anti-Irish Catholic celebration signifies the sway Protestants had at city hall.

Some 4,500 people, mostly from fifty ward and township branches of the Native American Party, entered the march with floats, bands, many images of Washington, and slogans distorting famous phrases of the first president, such as "Beware of Foreign Influence," into anti-immigrant mottos (Figure 94). One float featured Miss Liberty, above her an American eagle clutching a liberty pole in one claw and an image of Washington in the other. At Miss Liberty's feet lay a dead serpent, symbolizing Rome. Another banner featured a snake coiled around the American flag, hissing at it furiously.

Yet Catholics could respond with unofficial power. In a dawn attack on July 5, Catholic boys and workingmen descended on an encampment of Protestant revelers in Fisher's Woods at the edge of the city and avenged the patriotic Protestants' use of historical imagery to condemn "Irish papists" as aliens beholden only to the Pope. Unable to organize or march in a Protestant July Fourth procession, most Catholics stayed home to express their resentment privately. But some, for at least a moment, had their say by demolishing the tents and paraphernalia of the hungover Protestant patriots.[50]

By the time the smoke had cleared from the anti-Catholic riots in the summer of

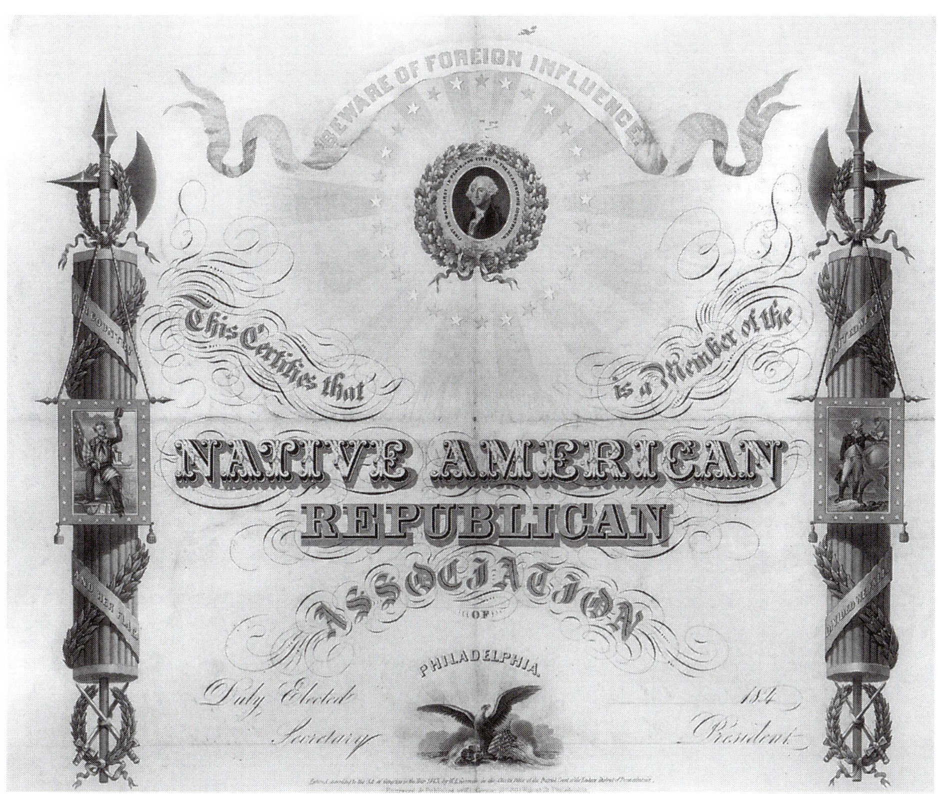

FIGURE 94. Native American Republican Association membership certificate, Library of Congress. Certificates such as this were distributed by some fifty branches of the Native American Republican Association of Philadelphia in 1844–45. Washington is featured in a replica of Gilbert Stuart's portrait surmounted by a banner with a motto frequently used by the party: "Beware of Foreign Influence." Washington with his horse also appears on the right in a Revolutionary War battle portrait, while on the left an American seaman holds a flag and waves his hat. At the bottom, an American bald eagle on a rock lifts its wings above a stormy sea. The engraver and publisher of the certificate was Washington L. Germon.

1844, leaders of the history project initiated by founders of the Penn Society and the Historical Society were understandably discouraged. They could look back on some small advances, even a modest William Penn revival. They held annual dinners, select to be sure, to commemorate the landing of Penn in 1682. A fetching linen handkerchief with an approximation of Benjamin West's famous painting of Penn's treaty with the Indians at Shackamaxon kept the Penn Treaty legend alive (Figure 95). More public was the gala opening in 1829 of the Chesapeake and Delaware Canal, linking two important bays, where the steamer *William Penn*, with Frank Johnson's African American band providing the music, became the main venue of the celebration. At triennial fire company parades, beginning in 1833, the public was treated to the colorful dramaturgy of the William Penn Hose Company. Parading firemen dressed as Quakers and Indians, and

FIGURE 95. Printed linen handkerchief from Germantown Print Works, c. 1824, Swarthmore College Peace Collection. The linen handkerchief, printed commercially about 1824, shows the Friends Meeting House at Fourth and Arch Streets. But the featured image is that of William Penn and fellow Quakers treating with Indian chiefs below the Treaty Elm in Shackamaxon. The articles of trade that Penn offered in exchange for land are enumerated, though the rum almost always included in land exchanges was omitted.

the company leader dressed as Penn himself, in a black broad-brimmed hat, and posed beneath a papier mâché treaty elm. Watson had followed his *Annals of Philadelphia* with a children's version, *Historic Tales of Philadelphia*, in 1833. He came out with a revised and extended version of his *Annals* in 1844, while from 1828 to 1836, Samuel Hazard had published annual volumes of *The Register of Pennsylvania Devoted to the Preservation of Facts . . . Respecting the State of Pennsylvania.*

But all these evocations of the idealized past could not prevent the bitter religious divisions that tore apart Quakers, Presbyterians, and Baptists in the antebellum era or quell the church burnings and lethal riots of the 1830s and 1840s. In 1826, in the midst of the Hicksite furor, one of the Historical Society founders had written that everyone felt the "necessity . . . for the preservation of records"; but even among the most respectable Philadelphians "impressions remaining from military and political struggles, and existing differences of religious opinions and feelings, were hard to reconcile in a common labor."[51] In 1838, a year after the great schism of Philadelphia's Presbyterians, the Historical Society nearly dissolved, to be saved only by the efforts of the Philosophical Society's John Vaughan and several others. In 1846, just two years after the "awful riots of 1844," a charter member of the Historical Society regretted that the society was "known to, or at least deeply appreciated by . . . only a small portion of our community" and suffered "from penury, both in members and in purse."[52]

Watson the preservationist was also grieved by the failed attempt of the Historical Society to purchase and preserve one of Philadelphia's most venerable and history-soaked buildings, the Slate Roof House. Built on Second Street below Chestnut in 1683–85 by Samuel Carpenter, a friend, confidant, and business partner of William Penn, the house had lodged Penn during his second trip to Philadelphia and was the birthplace of his son John Penn. Passing through various hands, it was owned in 1846 by Mary Norris Dickinson, the elderly unmarried daughter of John Dickinson, author of the famous *Letters of a Farmer in Pennsylvania*. When Mary Dickinson bypassed the Historical Society and accepted a better offer, the Slate Roof House passed into other private hands and did not fare well. Despairing of its survival in 1856, Watson proposed historic site markers that would bear sculptural images of the venerable buildings after they were torn down. A year later he pleaded again that "such a house should be rescued from its present forlorn neglect, . . . bought and consecrated to some lasting memorial of its former character."[53] When the Slate Roof House was offered for sale in 1864, four years after Watson died, the Historical Society was again unable to buy it and save it from the wreckers who leveled the house in 1867.

How little regard Philadelphians were paying to their city's most venerable buildings was apparent again in the abuse of Carpenters' Company Hall, where the First Continental Congress had met in 1774. In 1830, Watson lamented the neglect and current uses of the building, reprinting a scorching indictment from a visiting Virginian. In this structure "that will ever be deemed *sacred* while rational liberty is cherished on earth," wrote the Virginian, in "these sublime apartments, which first resounded with the indignant murmur of our immortal ancestors," now "ring with the din of urchins conning over their tasks" in the upper chambers while on the ground floor an auctioneer "stuns my ears and distracts my brain" in a hall "lumbered up with beds, looking glasses, chairs, tables, pictures, ready made clothes, and all the trash and trumpery which usually grace the premises of a knight of the hammer."[54]

But Watson could do little to rescue Carpenters' Hall. In 1848, the historian Benson J. Lossing tried. Coming to see a building "consecrated by the holiest associations which cluster around the birthtime of our republic," he found a shabby auction house. "What a desecration! Covering the facade of the very Temple of Freedom with placards of groveling mammon! If sensibility is shocked with this outward pollution, it is overwhelmed with indignant shame on entering the hall where . . . the godfathers of our republic convened to stand as sponsors at the baptism of infant American Liberty, to find it filled with every species of merchandise." Lossing tried to shame Philadelphians: "Is there not patriotism strong enough and bold enough in Philadelphia to enter this temple and 'cast out all them that buy and sell and overthrow the table of the money-changers?'"[55] In 1856, the Carpenters' Company decided to evict their tenants and restore the house to "its original finish." Watson may have been the one who finally rallied the members, who at last rediscovering the "sacred trust committed to us by our predecessors."

Watson and his friend John Jay Smith, the Library Company's librarian, had anticipated what is commonly thought to be the first house museum preservation project—the Hasbrouck House in Newburgh, New York, which served as one of Washington's Revolutionary War headquarters. But their reverence for remainders of bygone days stood little chance in the face of the frantic rebuilding of industrializing Philadelphia. However, for a pittance or even a profit, Smith and Watson could raise to iconic status artifacts and documents of the colonial and revolutionary eras. "*Our* early and romantic past," they wrote in 1849, in the introduction to a volume of facsimiles, "has the merit of being known and truly related." Some of the "most rare Historical and Literary Curiosities," they explained, were hidden away in private collections; many, in fact, were in the hands of Watson, Smith, and their friends. Now "the present and future generations" can learn from these documents "*what* things were done, but . . . also learn *how* things were done."[56] Drawing on the talents of artists suffering for lack of work in one of the city's periodic recessions, Smith and Watson published a series of thirty four facsimiles, including broadsides of plays in British-occupied Philadelphia, a sketch of the ancient meeting-house at Chester where Penn had worshiped, Penn's first letter to the Indians, a color lithograph of Washington's coach, a silver plate presented by Charles II to the Queen of Pamunkey "to conciliate the tribes," and much more. Smith and Watson surely were pleased that to satisfy public demand they were obliged to commission six imprints of their facsimile volume between 1849 and 1860. Just after Watson's death in the latter year, Smith added thirty additional facsimiles for a new edition of *American Historical and Literary Curiosities*.

While attempting to cure public amnesia about what they regarded as Philadelphia's golden age, Watson and Smith had qualms about another Philadelphian, a human volcano intent on using the past to legitimize a different set of priorities. This was not a president of the Historical Society or a director of the Philosophical Society, Athenaeum, or Library Company but the founder of the socialist Brotherhood of the Union, arrayed against the very interests aligned with the city's cultural institutions. George Lippard was born in 1822, only two years before the founding of the Historical Society, but by the time of the 1844 riots he had a mass following in Philadelphia and was reorienting public memory in ways diametrically opposed to what the Historical Society leaders intended. For the city's cultural arbiters, Lippard gave polite history a bad name. But the public loved him; he turned out to be *their* cultural arbiter and provided *their* understanding of the past.

Restless and melodramatic, Lippard by 1846 was churning out legends of the American Revolution that freshened the public memory of local battles at Germantown and Brandywine and, at a deeper level, urged readers to rethink the meaning of "hero" and "heroism." John F. Watson had provided Lippard with many hoary stories about the Battle of Germantown, but Watson and his colleagues were soon appalled at the radical friend of labor in their midst. Mixing hair-raising descriptions of the terrors of war with florid portraits of American battlefield heroism, Lippard presented the Revolution as a poor man's war and a model of the mid-nineteenth-century labor reform that Lippard was promoting. His stories in *Washington and His Generals; or Legends of the American Revolution* (1847) and *Washington and His Men* (1849) gave Washington his due, but it was the common man on the battlefield who was the true hero. "Let me make a frank confession," Lippard told the City Institute in 1852. "I have been led astray. I have looked upon effigies and . . . bowed down to uniforms and done reverence to epaulettes. . . . Gilt and paint and spangles have for ages commanded reverence, while men made in the image of God have died in the ditch." Lippard got more particular: "The General who receives all the glory of the battles said to have been fought under his eye; who is worshiped in poetry and in history; received in every city which he may enter by hundreds of thousands, who makes the heavens ring with his name; this General then is not *the* hero. No; the hero is the private soldier, who stands upon the battle field; . . . the poor soldier . . . whose skull bleaches in the sands, while the general whose glory the volunteer helped to win is warm and comfortable upon his mimic throne." Lippard cautioned his audience to "worship the hero . . . [and] reverence the heroic; but have a care that you are not swindled by a bastard heroism; be very careful of the sham hero."[57]

In a separate book, *Thomas Paine, Author-Soldier* (1852), Lippard also helped restore Paine's reputation, which had gone into deep eclipse after Paine's attacks on Christianity in *The Age of Reason* left him an unattractive figure in an era of evangelical fervor. New editions of Paine's writings appeared in the 1850s, at least in part because Lippard rescued him as the bold revolutionary herald of democracy who had more to say to the struggling urban masses than all the revolutionary generals and statesmen. A year after Lippard's death in 1854, "the Friends of Universal Liberty & Freedom, Emancipation & General Ruction" celebrated "St. Thomas" Paine's birthday in Philadelphia.[58]

That Lippard had more power to manipulate memories of the Revolution than those placed far higher in Philadelphia society must have been obvious when he became the most popular lecturer in Philadelphia on revolutionary tales. Many of them dissolved the line between fiction and history. Having Paine convert to Christianity on his deathbed or having a dying Benedict Arnold recant and don his old Continental uniform were good examples of the liberties he took. The *Saturday Evening Post* charged that he had "taken the liberty to palter with and corrupt the pages of history." Lippard countered that in the hands of genteel historians, "The thing which generally passes for History, is the most impudent, swaggering bully, the most graceless braggart, the most reckless equivocator that ever staggered forth on the great stage of the world."[59] Perhaps he embellished. But a legend from his hand, he explained, was "one of those heart-warm stories, which, quivering in rude, earnest language from the lips of a spectator of a battle, or the survivor of some event of olden time, fill up the cold outlines of history, and clothe the skeleton with flesh and blood, give it eyes and tongue, force it at once to look into our eyes and talk with us!"[60]

The power of Lippard as master manipulator is clear in the effect of his Liberty Bell story. In "The Fourth of July, 1776," one of his legends of the American Revolution written for Philadelphia's *Saturday Courier*, Lippard has fifty-six Founding Fathers signing the Declaration of Independence on July 4, 1776, after hearing an oration from Patrick Henry. During the signing ceremony, an old man climbs the stairs of the State House bell tower and waits for a little blue-eyed boy to shout "Ring" as soon as he hears below that the signing of the Declaration had been completed. When John Hancock comes out of the State House, the boy, "swelling his little chest," shouts "Ring!" "The old man is young again; his veins are filled with new life. . . . With sturdy strokes, he swings the Tongue. The bell speaks out! The crowd in the street hear it, and burst forth in one long shout! Old Delaware hears it, and gives it back in the hurrah of her thousand sailors. The city hears it, and starts up from the desk and workbench, as though an earthquake had spoken. . . . The Bell speaks to the city and the world."[61] In fact, Patrick Henry was not present, the signing of the parchment did not begin until August 2, the last signer did not ink his name until January 18, 1777, and the Declaration was first read by the Philadelphia sheriff on July 8. But Lippard's legend lived on, repeated in guidebooks and taken as fact in the *Dictionary of United States History* (1894) by John Franklin Jameson, president of the American Historical Association, and repeated again in John H. Hazelton's scholarly *The Declaration of Independence* (1906).

Lippard's revolutionary legends fired American chauvinistic pride and served well in kindling the enthusiasm of soldiers dispatched in 1847 to fight in the Mexican-American War. But his retelling of revolutionary tales, with the common soldier becoming the true hero, was meant to put history in the service of desperately poor urban laborers. In his address on Thomas Paine, in which he redefined the meaning of "hero" and "heroism," he moved immediately from a discussion of the general and the foot soldier to the urban situation: "You may depend upon it, John Smith, the rentpayer, is a greater man, a truer hero, than Bloodhound the general, or Pumfrog the politician. True, when John is dead there is only another grave added to the graves of the forgotten poor, while your general and your politician have piles of white marble over their fleshen skulls. But judging a hero by the rule that he who suffers most endures most, works most, is the true hero. . . . When you read the praises of Great Statesmen, in the papers, don't be fooled from the truth by these sugar-tits of panegyric. These statesmen are not heroes."[62]

Philadelphia's elite tried to ignore Lippard, and most claimed it was beneath them to read his trashy *Quaker City; or The Monks of Monk Hall* (1845). They cringed at Lippard's lurid exposés of sex, violence, terror, lust, and exploitation and his blunt indictments that the city "William Penn had built in hope and honor,—whose root was planted deep in the soil of truth and peace," had now become "poison and rottenness, Riot, Arson, Murder and Wrong."[63] But *Quaker City* sold 60,000 copies in the first year, more than all the copies sold between 1800 and 1830 of Parson Weem's fanciful biography of Washington, which nearly beatified the founding father. *Quaker City* went through twenty-seven editions, and at Lippard's premature death in 1854 it was still selling 30,000 copies a year. This made Lippard the most widely read author in the United States; only *Uncle Tom's Cabin* (1852) eclipsed *Quaker City*. But this popularity did not earn him a place in the Library Company's holdings. The newspapers he wrote for or edited never reached the Library Company's reading rooms. His revolutionary tales were of some interest but were acquired only in the 1870s as the centennial of the Revolution approached. His novels were particularly offensive, especially to Lloyd Pearson Smith, the librarian from 1851 to 1886. A founder of the American Library Association in 1876, Smith led a campaign to keep sensational fiction out of public libraries. It is probable that only after his death in 1886 did the Library Company acquire reprints of *Quaker City* and other novels by Lippard.

Did Lippard's popularity extend to the African American community? If black Philadelphians read Lippard's legend of the battle of Brandywine, they must have been pleased. One of the heroes of the "Oath-Bound Five" was the muscular Black Sampson, who avenged the murder of his white mistress by plunging into battle against the British with "Debbil," his murderous dog. However, they would also have found plenty of racist caricaturing of northern free blacks in Lippard's *Quaker City*.

Regardless, by the 1840s, African Americans were appropriating history for their own purposes. The patriotic Robert Douglass, Jr. who made the gigantic transparencies for the Washington celebration in 1832 had become the black antislavery Douglass by 1846. Entering the building used by the Female Anti-Slavery Society for their annual fundraiser, Philadelphians saw a large painting of the Liberty Bell emblazoned with the venerable slogan "Proclaim liberty throughout the land" but also inscribed with "Duty is Ours; Consequences are God's. Are we not verily guilty concerning our brother?" Four years later, the Society's annual fair featured Douglass's *Liberty Pronouncing Judgment Against Slavery*, with the North Star above the allegorical figure of Liberty and inscribed, "Right is of no sex; Truth is of no color, God is the father of us all, and all we are brethren." His *Slave Market at Constantinople* was also displayed conspicuously.[64] So far as is known, the Pennsylvania Academy of Fine Arts—eager to avoid controversy over abolitionism—never exhibited Douglass's work, so his paintings were shown primarily to those already converted to the abolitionist cause.

Though disfranchised and increasingly excluded from the trades, black Philadelphians by mid-century were intent on establishing their entitlement to public spaces. Hearing of a public demonstration in Independence Square in April 1848, where immigrants were celebrating the republican movements in Germany, Italy, and France, black orators rushed to join the demonstration on behalf of liberty. Many followers gathered around them. Philadelphia constables tried to eject the black Philadelphians, but European immigrants—despised by devotees of the Native American Party—insisted on the right of the African Americans to share the public forum.

The determination of African Americans to insist on their civil rights surfaced again in 1859, at the Fourth of July public festivities. Reclaiming Independence Hall yard, from which they had been ejected half a century before, they rallied around William Henry Johnson, a black doctor and community leader. "We have assembled here to-day to pay a tribute of respect to the noble men who gave us the declaration," Johnson proclaimed. But while honoring the Declaration, "[We] hold up to the scorn of the wide world those narrow-minded, small-fisted, and bullet-headed politicians who have for a number of years traduced and subverted its truths." Independence Hall had given birth to a document in 1776 proclaiming unalienable rights, Johnson continued; it had also given birth to a document in 1787 that compromised these rights. And referring to the Fugitive Slave Act of 1850, which granted a hunting license to southern agents pursuing runaway slaves in the North, Johnson reminded the audience that "There are tories to-day, and their business is to hunt down the poor fugitive Negro, and to handcuff and drag him hundreds of miles from his home to be tried as a slave, and to be remanded . . . under the sound of the old State House bell, and within sight of the hall where independence was declared." Black Philadelphians capped their gathering with a deft revision of the Declaration's resounding words: "We do hold it to be a self-evident truth . . . that all men, irrespective of colour or condition, by virtue of their constitution, have a natural indefeasible right to life, liberty, and the possession of property." [65]

The contest for public memory in the late antebellum era was encapsulated by two decisions at the end of Lippard's life about honoring past heroes. In 1853, one year before his death, Lippard protested a proposal to erect a monument to Benjamin Franklin, arguing that Philadelphia's "First Citizen" had received enough attention and it was time to give homage to lesser-known figures. This followed from his view that "there are many kinds of heroes in this world but neither the general who is made glorious by the accident of his position, nor the statesman who makes a trade of special legislation are heroes in my way of thinking."[66] In part as a result of Lippard's protest, the Benjamin Franklin monument was never built. The memory of Franklin was by no means erased, but a new monumental reminder had been blocked.

The next year, when the portrait collection of Charles Willson Peale was put up for auction, another partial erasure occurred, this time of Tom Paine. Peale had died many years before, in 1827, and P. T. Barnum had snapped up the best of his natural history exhibits at rock bottom rates. But his portrait collection had survived largely intact, remaining in the possession of two of the old painter's grandsons. When the auction began, the city—then under an administration tied to the Native American Party—tried to buy all the Peale family paintings in order to install a portrait gallery of Revolutionary War and early republic worthies in Independence Hall. When the city's bid of $7,000 was refused, the auction proceeded painting by painting. "Mr. Erben," the city's silent buyer, purchased 84 of the 271 portraits, most of them likenesses of signers of the Declaration of Independence and the Constitution, revolutionary officers, and distinguished statesmen, scientists, lawyers, doctors, explorers, and men of letters. For a total of $175, the librarian of the Historical Society won bids for nine paintings, later to be sold at cost to the city. But the city did not bid on the painting of Tom Paine. A private collector car-

FIGURE 96. Max Rosenthal, *Interior View of Independence Hall*, lithograph, 1855, LCP. This view of Independence Hall's interior was taken shortly after the city installed its new collection of portraits. The life-size statue of George Washington, occupying a prominent place in the Independence Hall museum, was an essential part of the Native American Party's effort to sacralize the founding fathers. William Rush, Philadelphia's preeminent wood carver, created the statute in 1814 from pine and painted it white. It was placed in Independence Hall for the first time in 1824, at the time of Lafayette's arrival. It was installed at the Second Bank of the United States in 1970, where it stands today amid scores of Charles Willson Peale's portraits of revolutionary worthies.

ried it off for $6.50. It disappeared and has not been found to the present day; a story circulates that it was burned up with the house of its owner.

Within a year, the city hung its new collection of "the enshrined images of the founders of the American republic" (Figure 96).[67] Paine had not only disappeared from the national pantheon, he was also nearly the only revolutionary figure of note whose likeness the city chose not to purchase. Lippard had done his part to rescue Paine from the historical dustbin where he had been consigned because of his attacks on Washington at the general's death and for his indictments of Christianity. More recently, Paine's name had been associated with the abolitionist Hicksites, all the more reason why Native American Party stalwarts in City Hall found his portrait objectionable. Five years later, when the Native American Party had lost much of its clout in the city, a group of ordinary Philadelphians, including Frederick Gutekunst, the talented Philadelphia photographer, donated a copy of a Bass Otis portrait of Paine to the city. It is not clear whether the Paine portrait was ever put on display, but if so, it was soon taken down and stored away. The catalogs of the portrait gallery published in 1869 and 1872 do not list the man whose pen was one of the most powerful weapons in the arsenal of the revolutionary generation.

Philadelphia's cultural leaders had hoped that as the rightful custodians of tradition they could transform William Penn and revolutionary heroes into worshiped icons in order to bring back the stability and harmony that they imagined were part of an earlier age. But as dark clouds of secession loomed over the nation in the late 1850s, they had little reason for optimism. Concerned about debates in the present, they also fretted over related controversies regarding the past. And many worried that upstart and unsanctioned notions of history had crowded out what they believed were the true uses of the past. By the time Lincoln entered the White House in January 1861, Philadelphia's historical consciousness had been raised as never before. But this varied population had no unified version of the past. Philadelphians were as divided as they had been nearly a century before, when the American Revolution split the Delaware River capital apart, and historical memory had proven nearly useless in reconciling the passionately held positions on which they differed. To the city's fathers, if history could be made to rescue Philadelphians from themselves, it would have to await another day. For others, variant histories were performing their proper role—to reveal differences and help explain them.

Chapter 7

IN CIVIL WAR AND RECONSTRUCTION

Five days after John Brown's execution on December 2, 1859, a "Great Union Meeting" organized by anti-abolitionist Philadelphians convened in Jayne's Hall, two blocks from Independence Hall, to rebuke those who had sympathized with Brown and to assure white Southerners that Philadelphia stood with them. Streamers flew from ships, factories, public buildings, and hotels; cannons boomed; banners proclaimed "Union Forever! Pennsylvania Greets her Sister State, Virginia" (Figure 97).[1] The song composed for the pro-Southern rally set the tone:

> The South shall have her rights—O'er her
> Our eagle spreads its wings—
> The treason plotters, *brown* or white,
> Shall on the gallows swing.[2]

An overflow crowd of fifteen to twenty thousand cheered when Colonel James Page called for hanging or shooting all "abolitionists of the John Brown stamp." Charles Ingersoll, son of a charter member of the Historical Society, called abolitionists "animals [who] . . . come among us to splash with . . . venom all that is sacred." Chairing the meeting was his brother, Joseph Ingersoll, who would assume the presidency of the Historical Society the next year. Former Democratic mayor Richard Vaux, son of a Historical Society and Philosophical Society leader, vowed that abolitionists would never again be allowed to gather in Philadelphia to spread their treasonous doctrines. In the climactic speech, Henry M. Fuller took all human agency out of the slavery question: "Slavery is a fact. We are not responsible for it; the people of the South are not responsible for it. It was brought here before the Union was born. A mysterious Providence has cast upon this continent two races, distinct in origin, character, and color."[3]

Brown's attack on the U.S. arsenal at Harpers Ferry—a martyr's blow against slavery that heightened the sectional tension—increased Democratic votes in Philadelphia but did not deter committed abolitionists such as William H. Furness and Lucretia Mott from continuing to insist that the nation could never survive the perpetuation of racial bondage. Nor did African Americans relent in their work to provide refuge for fleeing slaves. Whig Republicans gradually began to drift away from their support of the South

FIGURE 97. *Chestnut Street*, photograph, c. 1865, FLP. This photograph looking west from Fifth Street was probably taken in 1865 with the many American flags waving in celebration of the end of the Civil War. The *Public Ledger* building shows through the trees on the left. The visual record of the changing urban landscape left by Philadelphia's many photographers has provided historians with a much richer sense of the post-Civil War city than did lithographers.

when they saw free assembly and free speech sacrificed in the service of upholding slavery. Deepened by Brown's raid and his execution, the sectional crisis reached its climax one year later. The confusion that reigned in Philadelphia in 1859-60, with both the Democratic and Whig Republican Parties internally divided, finally began to end as Philadelphians, in spite of the deep pockets of secession supporters, rallied around Lincoln's administration. "The long agony is over!" were the words a Unitarian minister chose to open his sermon two weeks after South Carolinians fired on Fort Sumter. But in reality the agony would continue for a long time. Swords and uniforms, banners, and heroic paintings—all evoke visions of the Civil War as the great patriotic struggle to preserve the Union. The fighting, however, was anything but heroic for most of its participants, whose casualty rate was far higher than in World War II. The war's meaning varied widely among those involved in it, and unity in the North was as difficult to achieve as during the American Revolution. In Philadelphia, by now almost as much a southern as a northern city, this was especially true.

White Americans' fascination with Civil War battles has been so great that the other war—the war at home—is scarcely remembered. Yet by looking through different lenses, we can see how the world's first experience with total war expanded the roles of women in the workplace and in public life, how through military sacrifice it socialized recent immigrants to American life, and how it spurred technological innovation and some sectors of industrial growth. Mostly forgotten is the central paradox of the Civil War: while it abolished slavery, the devastating conflict did little to alter white racial attitudes in either the North or the South. In Pennsylvania, most white citizens and soldiers worked and fought to preserve the Union, not to free the slaves or bring about racial equality.

For the Historical Society of Pennsylvania, the Civil War produced an extraordinary new vigor—but not at first. The quarter century before the outbreak of war had not been good for the society, or for the American Philosophical Society. In the late 1830s and early 1840s, the Historical Society was on the verge of collapse: membership lagged and attendance at meetings was often insufficient to obtain a quorum. Energy began to flow back into the institution in the mid-1850s, so that the institution was no longer, as the society's historian later wrote, "but a small club of young enthusiasts, encouraged by the presence of a few grey heads, but a growing body carrying on its rolls the names of those eminent as business men, merchants, lawyers, judges, physicians, bankers, manufacturers, druggists, publishers, book-sellers, and writers."[4] Acquisitions during the period 1845-60 flowed in at a higher rate than before, and the society made notable additions to its manuscripts, paintings, and artifacts relating to the founding and revolutionary periods.

The outbreak of war, however, wreaked havoc with the society's finances and with executive council attendance. The society's historian judged that the affairs of the society were in a state of "imminent collapse" in 1861, partly because its old-family aristocrats were deeply divided between Republican unionists and Peace Democrats supporting southern secession. But the decision in 1862 to open the membership to women and to those not of American birth attracted a wave of new members. John McAllister, an avid collector of Philadelphia ephemera, nominated 126 new members, including devotees of Thomas Paine such as the photographer Frederick F. Gutekunst, and staunch abolitionists such as Passmore Williamson, William Furness, and John Price Wetherill.[5] Of the 113 "resident" members, 28 were clergymen in what seems to have been McAllister's attempt to connect mainstream Philadelphia churches to the Historical Society. The infusion of so many members instantly diversified the membership while diluting the old-family, pro-southern aristocracy.

When the titanic Battle of Gettysburg in July 1863 led to calls for a battle monument, the Historical Society was poised to adopt an activist, pro-Union stance. For the first time in its history, galvanized by the momentous events occurring daily, the society enlarged "its designs and labors" by going beyond rescuing "from dumb forgetfulness the records of earlier days." The time had come, urged John W. Wallace, its vice president, to collect and preserve materials of the present; when "this present shall have become the past," what the Historical Society collected will "stand forth genuine, undenied and honorable."[6] Soon the society made its first such purchase—a lottery drum used to draft soldiers. At the same time, society members heard addresses from officers on leaves of absence describing epic battles and heroic deeds. For many years, the organization was receptive to Civil War remembrances and, over time, received a large number of wartime diaries.

Preserving the Union

After the Confederate capture of the federal Fort Sumter in South Carolina on April 13, 1861, Philadelphians stood, in one brief rush of emotion, with the rest of Pennsylvania behind Lincoln's Republican administration. As soon as the city received news of the surrender of Fort Sumter, patriotism deluged the city. "Chestnut Street is a sight," wrote Sarah Butler Wister, daughter of Pierce Butler. "Flags large & small flaunt from every building, the dry-goods shops have red white & blue materials draped together in their windows, in the ribbon stores the national colors hang in long steamers, and even the book sellers place the red, white and blue bindings together."[7] Black Philadelphians had been meeting at the Banneker Institute, where they were advised to be prepared to take up arms so that "our footprints [will] mark the hardened soil of oppression." At home, they were reading the *Weekly Anglo-African*, which demanded, "We want Nat Turner—not speeches; Denmark Vesey—not resolutions; John Brown—not meetings."[8]

In the initial outburst of patriotism, the city's large pro-southern population found itself on the defensive. A crowd coursed through the streets to be sure that people were flying the Stars and Stripes in support of the Union. When it reached the offices of the *Palmetto Flag*, a pro-secession newspaper, the crowd threatened to destroy the paper's offices if the editor did not pull down the palmetto flag, South Carolina's symbol of secession, and replace it with the Stars and Stripes. Several thousand Philadelphians descended on the Walnut Street mansions of Generals Robert Patterson and George Cadwalader, both owners of large slave plantations in the South, and smashed windows before being driven off by the police. The direct intercession of the mayor and the police saved the house of pro-secessionist William B. Reed, a longtime councillor of the Historical Society. For several months, pro-southern Philadelphians had to lie low.

Federal recruiters and local regimental commanders called the North to arms with posters, parades, and banners (Figure 98). Eager volunteers flooded into Pennsylvania's recruiting centers in Philadelphia and Harrisburg at a faster rate than the War Department could provide them with uniforms, weapons, food, housing, and training. However, the initial enthusiasm for the war soon cooled as trainloads of maimed and

FIGURE 98. *Rally for the Defence of the City*, 1863, LCP. One of many recruitment posters published in Philadelphia, this one cudgeled men to join up after the city learned on June 15, 1863 that Lee was advancing through Maryland for an attack on Pennsylvania. Note the poster's invocation of the famous inscription on the Liberty Bell. Printed on cheap paper, the posters were not meant to be saved. But John A. McAllister, Jr. and several other collectors of Civil War ephemera tucked away nearly every "paper bullet" that issued from Philadelphia's print shops. The Library Company acquired a fabulous collection of more than three hundred of these posters from McAllister's gift two decades after the war ended.

wounded soldiers streamed back into the city. By the summer of 1863, the federal government resorted to drafting men between the ages of eighteen and forty-five. Draft authorities in Philadelphia used the lottery drum to select names at random, although during most of the war the offer of liberal bounties to induce enlistments—as high as $1,000 per man by 1864—made the resort to the draft an occasional rather than a usual device for meeting the city's manpower quotas.[9]

In some parts of the North, laboring people fiercely resisted conscription. They rioted in Pennsylvania's central mountains and coal regions as well as in New York City, where the most famous and bloody draft riot of the war took place. Just as southerners and southern sympathizers sought to defend their constitutional liberties as they saw them, many northerners regarded conscription as a violation of the constitutional liberties that the Union forces were fighting to defend. But Philadelphia was spared such riots because plenty of recruits stood ready to fill the ranks if the bounty was high enough, and a disciplined police force had become proficient in crowd management. Moreover, conscription laws allowed commutation from the draft by paying a fee for a substitute. Thousands of Philadelphians followed this route to avoid the war. George Wolff Fahnestock, a drug merchant and book collector, detailed in his diary how he paid $900 for a draft broker to secure "a good countenanced Irishman" to serve in his place. However, Fahnestock felt "indignant and sick at the rascality of the brokers and their pimps," who he believed would rob his substitute "of every dollar before a week."[10] From a population of about 600,000 at the beginning of the war, some 90,000-100,000 Philadelphians served in the Union army—more than half of the males of military age.

As in the case of so many northern units, Philadelphia soldiers' main problem was rapid preparation for war. The raw regiments, filled with men of no military experience and often newly arrived in the country, had little time to become battle-ready. Most of their training at first consisted of imitating the impressive parade moves and esprit de corps of existing militia groups and marching societies, especially the colorfully garbed Zouave units, who patterned their uniforms after the world-famous French Algerian troops. The 114th Regiment of Pennsylvania Volunteers, known as the Philadelphia Zouave Corps, took great pride in their fancy bayonet drills, but soon abandoned these, as well as their inappropriate uniforms, having quickly learned what it took to survive in one of the first "modern" wars.

After the issuing of the Emancipation Proclamation on January 1, 1863, federal authorities called for African American military volunteers. But only when General Lee invaded Pennsylvania, in June, did panicking white Philadelphians drop their opposition to the use of black troops. Most free African Americans and escaped slaves welcomed the opportunity to fight as a way of asserting their equal interest in the guarantees of the Constitution. Black Philadelphians had offered their services previously in the spring of 1861, only to be refused by Pennsylvania's governor. Determined to fight and aroused by a visit from Frederick Douglass in March 1863, some three hundred of the city's black citizens enlisted in Massachusetts regiments. One company of the famous Massachusetts Fifty-Fourth Regiment was entirely composed of black Philadelphians (Figure 99).

FIGURE 99. P. S. Duval, *United States Soldiers at Camp "William Penn" Philadelphia PA*, lithograph, 1863, LCP. Philadelphia's African American recruits trained at Camp William Penn, eight miles from the city near the farm of Lucretia Mott and her husband. Naming the military camp after Pennsylvania's pacifist founder offended many Quakers. The city's black newspaper, the *Christian Recorder*, ran editorials urging black enlistment. White Philadelphians were especially enthusiastic about this when the War Department decided that black recruits would be credited against the state's quota. "I only wish we had two hundred thousand [blacks] in our army," wrote one diarist, "to save the valuable lives of our white men."

Many black Philadelphians who had lived through murderous attacks on their community in the 1830s and 1840s wondered why they should help defend a white man's government. But younger leaders counseled full engagement. "We have been denounced as cowards," explained one black schoolteacher organizing black recruits in Philadelphia. "Rise up and cast off the foul stigma. Shame on him who would hold back at the call of his country. Go with the view that you will return free men. And if you should never return, you will die with the satisfaction of knowing that you have struck a blow for freedom and assisted in giving liberty to our race in the land of our birth."[11]

Some of this ambivalence about fighting surfaced on July 6, 1863, when Frederick Douglass spoke at a recruitment rally at the Franklin Institute and later at Mother Bethel Church (Figure 100). Stephen Smith, a black businessman, and Anna E. Dickinson, a Quaker abolitionist and suffragist lecturer, warmed up the crowd of an estimated five thousand black and white Philadelphians before Frederick Douglass rose to thunderous applause. "I say at once, in peace, and war," Douglass told the crowd, "I am content with

FIGURE 100. Thomas Nast, *Philadelphia Recruitment Rally*, *Harper's Weekly*, July 18, 1863, LCP. Nast, *Harper's Weekly* illustrator, pictured a recruitment rally in front of Independence Hall in Philadelphia in July 1863. Below the main picture is Mother Bethel Church, where many of the city's black ministers spoke. In a series of resolutions, the assemblage pledged to those in slavery "the protection of our home and firesides, a part of our personal property, and a share of our daily bread, even to a portion of our last crumb." Three weeks later, Philadelphia's mayor would not allow the Third U.S. Colored Regiment, composed mainly of Philadelphians, to hold a dress parade with shoulder arms for fear of an attack by whites. But the Sixth Colored Regiment did march through the streets in October, fully uniformed and bayonets flashing. Thereafter, dress parades of the U.S. Colored Troops were uncontested.

nothing for the black man short of equal and exact justice."[12] With the audience shouting and calling out answers to his questions, he argued for swallowing bitterness at white America's ill-treatment of African Americans. The crowd followed Douglass in proclaiming their patriotism. But they tempered their commitment with a reflection on their historical experiences in the city: "We, the colored people of Philadelphia, throwing aside the unpleasant memories of the past, looking only to the future, and asking merely the same guarantees, the same open field and fair play that are given our white fellow-countrymen, desire here and now to express our willingness and readiness to come forward to the defence of our imperilled country." They also reminded white citizens that the first to leave Philadelphia to defend the state capital at Harrisburg the previous month had been "the colored company of ninety men, raised in six hours" and that three full companies of eighty men each had volunteered over the following twenty-four hours. "Though despised, hated, scourged, calumniated by the people of these States, [we] may show them and the world how unjust has been the estimate of our character, and that we are not wanting in any element of a vigorous manhood, least of all in a pure and lofty patriotism."[13]

By 1865, even though they were paid less than white volunteers and had to agree to serve for three years rather than for customary shorter terms, Pennsylvania's African Americans had fielded eleven black regiments of about one thousand men each, and at least eight of these units came from Philadelphia. A house in Chestnut Street became a military school for white officers preparing to command African American troops. These troops trained at Camp William Penn, just north of the city, and many fought in the Wilderness battles, at New Market Heights, at Fort Fisher in North Carolina, and in the ghastly Florida campaign of 1864, where black Philadelphians suffered heavy casualties at the Battle of Olustee.

Divided Sentiments

Philadelphia's ties to the South, both economic and emotional, were so strong that the city remained deeply divided throughout the Civil War. A visitor remarked on the eve of war that "everything Southern was exalted and worshiped" in Philadelphia. On a single block of fashionable Walnut Street, according to one newspaper, lived seven Virginia families, five from South Carolina and Mississippi, and ten more from other slave states. The city's upper class, lawyers as well as merchants and manufacturers, identified closely with the Peace Democrats, called Copperheads by the Republicans, after the poisonous snake. Among the Peace Democrats were many of the councillors from the Historical Society and Athenaeum, including Charles J. Biddle, Peter McCall, William B. Reed, Charles and Edward Ingersoll, Richard Vaux, and J. Francis Fisher. Weeks after the Confederacy adopted its constitution, a southern woman sent the printed edition to the librarian of the Historical Society. Even the Historical Society's Republican members had social connections to the southern aristocracy, and many were engaged in business with the South.

Pro-southern sentiment in Philadelphia was inseparable from the issue of race and slavery. Most white Philadelphians had little love for abolitionists or for African Americans. William Wells Brown, a black leader, believed that "colorphobia" was "more rampant" in Philadelphia "than in the pro-slavery, negro-hating city of New York."[14] Though emancipation was not a goal of President Lincoln or the Republican Party in 1861, it was widely understood that northern abolitionism and southern secession were closely connected.

The surface unanimity that appeared after the outbreak of war faded quickly. Democrats mistrusted Lincoln's administration, inveighed against its assumption of extraordinary wartime powers, and—most of all—feared that the northern public was tilting toward the belief that slavery must be destroyed. For most Philadelphia Democrats, slavery was a curse but not a cancer. Curses could be tolerated, they reasoned, and the North had its own. Moreover, the South could never be rejoined to the Union if the North confiscated its human property. With much of its following in the bitterly Negrophobic Irish laboring class, the Democratic leaders counseled that, given "how deeply the Providence of God has rooted the institution of slavery in this land, . . . it can be safely eradicated only by a gradual process, in which neither the civil nor the military power of the Federal government can intervene with profit." Charles Ingersoll called for "Conciliation and Compromise"—the only way the North could make amends as "the party who plotted to dissolve the Union long before South Carolina did."[15]

Favoring negotiation and compromise, Pennsylvania Democrats unfurled the banners of white supremacy at its 1862 convention. Resolving that "abolitionism is the parent of secessionism" and trumpeting that "this is a government of white men, and was established exclusively for the white race," the convention warned that Lincoln's party would "turn the slaves of Southern States loose to overrun the North and enter into competition with the white laboring masses, thus degrading and insulting their manhood by placing them on an equality with Negroes."[16]

Lincoln's Emancipation Proclamation further infuriated the Philadelphia Democrats. Seven days later, Historical Society members, including William B. Reed, Charles Ingersoll, Charles J. Biddle, and George W. Biddle, were instrumental in forming the Central Democratic Club, whose constitution began, "That in the State of Pennsylvania all power is inherent in the WHITE PEOPLE and that our Government is founded on THEIR authority . . . and that the FREE INSTITUTIONS established by our Revolutionary Fathers were committed to the charge of the white race; and that all attempts, directly and indirectly, on the part of the Federal Government to frustrate this intention, or change the relative status of the superior white, and inferior black races, . . . are subversive of the original design."[17] Ingersoll became president and George W. Biddle a vice president. The club applauded Ingersoll's inaugural address, in which he professed his belief that slave property was as "sacred as any other property" and expressed his sympathy for "the South in their desire to preserve it." As his brother-in-law Sidney George Fisher had earlier confided to his diary, Ingersoll was "wholly insensible to argument, and incapable of any but the most petty views of the situation of the country."[18]

Though Peace Democrats controlled Philadelphia for the first two years of the war, they began to lose their hold in the October 1863 elections. At a mass meeting at Independence Square the previous month, Democratic leaders swore allegiance to the Union cause but still insisted that Lincoln's policy of emancipating the slaves "is alike unconstitutional and impolitic."[19] The Democrats upheld their peace policy with a guarantee of preserving slavery for the remainder of the war. But their losses in the 1863 elections were followed by a drubbing at the polls in 1864. Philadelphians had gradually come to suspect Democratic disloyalty to the Union and to regard the repeated defense of slavery as objectionable when African Americans from the North were providing more than their share of the manpower needed to win the war. Yet even as late as spring 1865, Edward Ingersoll was attacking the emancipation of slaves and asserting the right of the South to secession. One day before Lincoln's assassination he repudiated the national debt accumulating through what he called an "unconstitutional war" and declared that he stood with southerners—"a gallant people struggling nobly for their liberty against as sordid and vile a tyranny as ever proposed the degradation of our race."[20] A few days later, with the city still numbed by Lincoln's assassination, a Philadelphia crowd mobbed Ingersoll and his brother, who came to his defense.

One major factor in the Democrats' eclipse was the founding of the Union League of Philadelphia in 1862, to counter the Peace Democrats or, as its early leader said, "take treason by the throat." Studded with lawyers, businessmen, and doctors, most of them not from Philadelphia's old wealthy families, the Union League launched an extensive campaign to support Lincoln's administration and shore up the city's wavering commitment to the war cause. League members helped raise new regiments when volunteers were scarce. They also promoted the first black regiments raised in Pennsylvania.[21]

But publishing broadsides and pamphlets supporting Lincoln and the war was the league's main activity. One of their sponsored pamphlets was especially poignant. In *The Views of Judge Woodward and Bishop Hopkins on Negro Slavery in the South*, Fanny Kemble, the famous English actress who had been married to the slaveowning Philadelphian and Georgian Pierce Butler, attempted to discredit the 1863 Peace Democratic candidate for governor, George W. Woodward, by equating his proslavery position with support for the South's right to secede. Most effective of all was the pamphlet of Charles Janeway Stillé, *How a Free People Conduct a Long War*. A Philadelphia lawyer and president of the Historical Society at the end of the nineteenth century, Stillé picked up the spirits of a discouraged North, wearied by military failures for the first eighteen months of the war. He used England's two-decade struggle against Napoleon and the English peninsular campaign in Spain as an example of the dissension that always accompanied a free people's fight to protect founding principles. His pamphlet was published in a modest edition of 75 copies in 1862. But the essay caught on, going through thirteen editions, with at least 250,000 copies distributed, and was reprinted in numerous northern newspapers. It was read in the field, passed from officers to enlisted men, much like Paine's *Crisis Papers* during the Revolution. One historian regarded it as worth a "half dozen brigades" to the Union cause.[22]

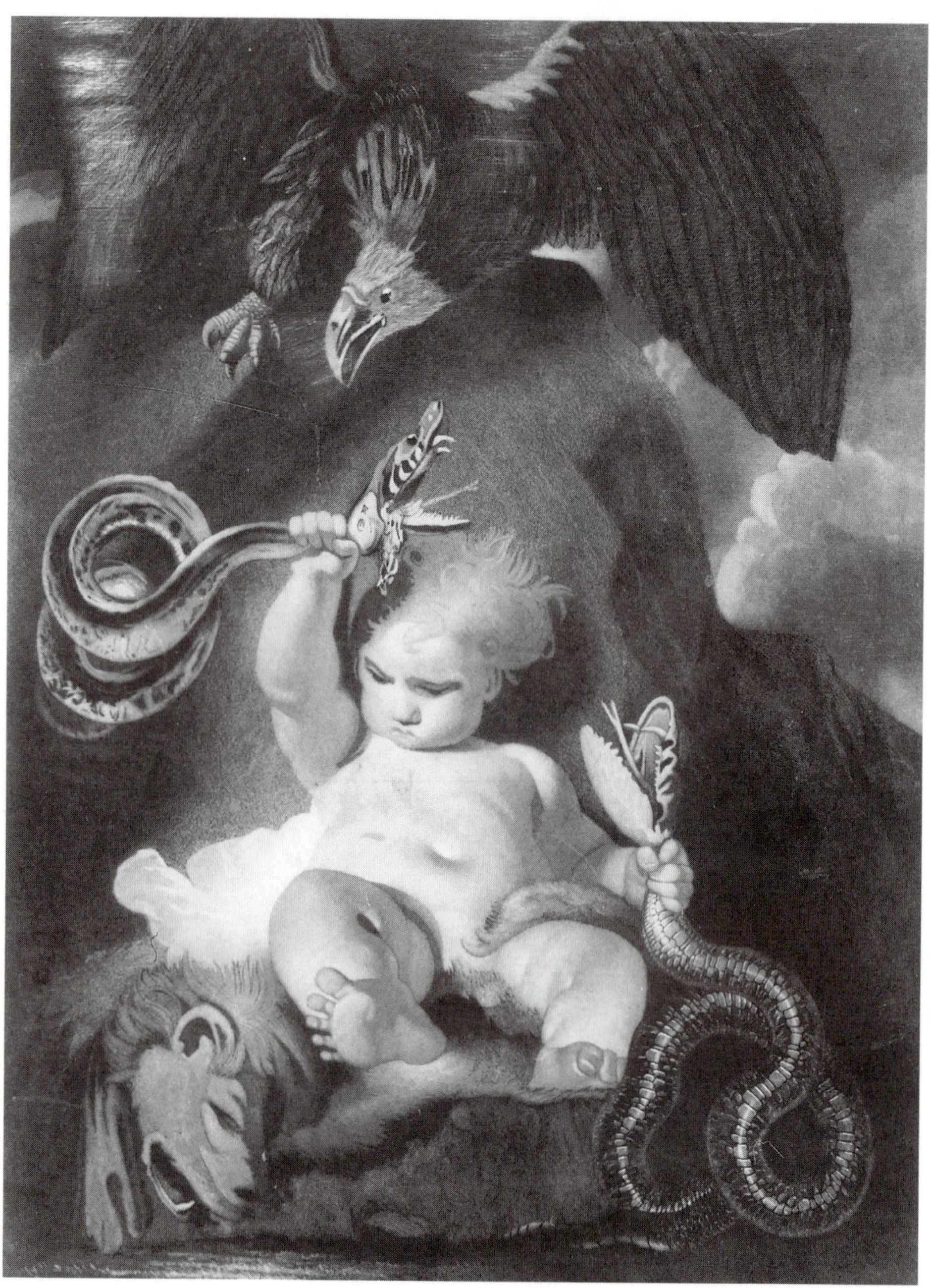

FIGURE 101. William Sartain, *Young America Crushing Rebellion and Sedition*, engraving, 1863, HSP. William Sartain engraved this pudgy Young America grasping venomous snakes, which symbolize sedition and rebellion, as a screeching eagle is poised for the kill. Sartain was the son of John Sartain, the city's premier portrait engraver. Almost every Philadelphia collecting institution has Sartain lithographs. The Free Library received scores of his engraved images in 1931 as part of the John Frederick Lewis Portrait Collection.

FIGURE 102. Frederic F. Cavada, *Battle of Fredericksburg*, oil, c. 1868, HSP. Cavada's journal and sketches from his six-month imprisonment were published in Philadelphia in 1864 as *Libby Life*. Cavada returned to Cuba to fight in an insurgency against Spain, where he was captured and executed in 1871. Fernando F. Cavada, the artist's grand-nephew, gave the painting to the Historical Society in 1930.

Blurred Portraits of War

Philadelphians were led by the popular press to view the war in romantic terms, at least in its early stages. John W. Forney's *Press*, which started out as a Democratic organ but later supported Lincoln's war policies, distributed a romantic print (Figure 101) as a free gift to subscribers, who were encouraged to see the war as a noble defense of the American experiment in democracy. Hundreds of recruiting posters fed a glorified version of what war might entail, for what purpose could have been served by showing other than strong, handsome men in dashing uniforms?

Only rarely did participants in the war paint battle scenes, but when they did they were likely to be more realistic than the poster art of regimental recruiters. Lt. Colonel Frederic F. Cavada, born in Cuba but raised in Philadelphia, served with the Twenty-Third Regiment of Pennsylvania Volunteers and fought in many of the bloodiest battles of the war. He was at the battle of Fredericksburg in December 1862, where the superior Union forces were shattered in a series of desperate assaults against the Confederate positions. Cavada's painting of the battle (Figure 102) faithfully conveys the atmosphere—the noise, smoke, and confusion of the doomed Union assault on Marye's Heights. Early

FIGURE 103. Andrew J. Russell, *Stone Wall at Fredericksburg*, photograph, HSP. U.S. Army Captain Andrew J. Russell took this grisly photograph in 1862 after the battle of Fredricksburg. The Library of Congress has other war photographs taken by Russell. This one was given to the Historical Society in 1949.

in the war such contests of resolve, in which brave officers inspired their men to hold their ground or advance into the hail of bullets, were common. Later, seasoned veterans learned to dig trenches and advance slowly, crawling on their bellies. Six months after the battle of Fredericksburg, Cavada was captured at the battle of Gettysburg and interned at Libby Prison in Richmond. There he kept a journal and sketchbook, which exposed the inhuman conditions in southern military prisons. He also wrote a bitter satirical poem, *Idyll of an Ass*, expressing his disenchantment with the Union cause and his resentment toward African Americans, who had gained freedom while northern soldiers were left rotting in prison.

More realistic views of the war eventually came from the press, which flourished during the war years, when people hungered for battle news. Most Philadelphia newspapers, like those in other cities, paid little attention to African American contributions to the war effort, even though some 180,000 black troops were under arms by 1864. But when the *Press* sent T. Morris Chester south in 1864 to cover the fighting, white Philadelphians got their first coverage of black troop activity in northern Virginia. Thirty-year-old Chester was one of the nation's first African American journalists and the only one with such a wartime assignment. He wrote one of his last dispatches while seated in the Speaker's chair of the Confederate Congress. From there, he described the Union army's victorious entry into Richmond. Chester later served as the American ambassador to

Liberia and then as brigadier general of the Louisiana state militia during Reconstruction. In 1882, he became the first black lawyer admitted to practice before the Pennsylvania Supreme Court.[23]

Black Philadelphians were much better informed about the activities of their sons, brothers, and fathers serving in Union forces because two African American weeklies, the *Weekly Anglo-American*, published in New York, and the *Christian Recorder*, published in Philadelphia, gave extensive coverage. George E. Stephens, a black Philadelphia cabinetmaker and mariner, wrote long letters to the *Anglo-American* throughout the war, while for several years serving as a cook and servant for Benjamin C. Tilghman, an officer of the Twenty-Sixth Pennsylvania Regiment. Many of his letters gave graphic evidence of the intractability of white racism among Union soldiers, even after military necessity convinced northern leaders that they could not win the war without black men under arms. If there was any romance left about the war among whites, none existed among African Americans in the North who read Stephens's dispatches.

While journalists covered the war, often with graphic realism, a new breed of photographers provided even more chilling images, though their work was rarely displayed in the war's aftermath. U.S. Army Captain Andrew J. Russell, whose works have often been misattributed to Mathew Brady, was one of several photographers who advanced the medium of photography by capturing history as it was happening. Although photographs could not show much actual fighting because the long exposure time made it impossible to freeze motion, they graphically portrayed the wholesale slaughter (Figure 103).

Once the war ended, artists and printmakers, North and South, glorified the ghastly struggle with heroic art. Deeply scarred by the war, the nation tried to bind wounds with an idealization of male warriors. The Historical Society and other Philadelphia institutions enthusiastically collected military scenes because Republican members saw themselves as standing at a crossroads of history. For them the war had been a patriotic struggle to preserve the Union that their fathers and grandfathers had fought to create during the Revolution. Seven years after the bloodletting stopped, the Pennsylvania legislature commissioned Peter F. Rothermel, a well-known Philadelphia painter who specialized in historical scenes, to commemorate the battle of Gettysburg. In a theatrical rendition of the climactic third day of the battle, Rothermel used a huge canvas in 1875 to portray the individual courage of Union soldiers valiantly overcoming the charge of Pickett's Confederate forces (Figure 104).

Monuments to Martial Glory

Americans continued to glorify military accomplishments after the war, collecting flags, uniforms, and battlefield relics as symbols of victory and national pride. Not martial glory but mass casualties, primitive medical care, camp fever, constant hardship, mud, dust, poor rations, and sheer boredom were most often the realities of the Civil War. The

FIGURE 104. John Sartain, *Battle of Gettysburg*, engraving, 1863, LCP. Peter Rothermel's painting of the battle of Gettysburg featured the commanding Union general, George Meade, on the crest of Cemetery Ridge at the height of the assault on the stone wall in the "Bloody Angle," as it came to be known. General Winfield S. Hancock, commander of the Second Corps, is also seen. John Sartain introduced Philadelphia to mezzotint engraving where he faithfully rendered oil paintings such as this one. This made Civil War battle scenes available to the public and thus solidified public memory of events such as the battle of Gettysburg. Within a decade of the Civil War's end, the Historical Society would acquire portraits of ten generals, eight from Pennsylvania and six distinguished at Gettysburg.

casualty rate was ghastly—seven times that in World War II—and for every soldier killed in battle, four died from camp diseases like pneumonia and dysentery. But it was the paraphernalia of the Union army that people treasured, and the Historical Society gathered a bounteous harvest over the years—some 315 Civil War objects. The society has never participated actively in the love affair that so many Americans have had with guns. The strong Quaker influence in the society alone would have made that unlikely. But now the society collected, passively for the most part, what was valued by its donors. Hence Civil War mementos entered its collections: bullets, bayonets, and cartridge boxes; ragged flags and regimental standards; portraits of officers and battlefield photographs.

Some of the most collectible of the war memorabilia were presentation weapons, the elaborately decorated swords and guns presented to war heroes, such as General George G. Meade. In Meade, Philadelphia found a genuine hometown hero. Commander of the Union forces at Gettysburg in the summer of 1863, he out-generaled Robert E. Lee in the three-day battle that halted the Confederate advance. He remained the commander of the Army of the Potomac until the surrender of Lee at Appomattox. Philadelphians showed their gratitude for the victory by presenting Meade with several ceremonial weapons, among them a sword and scabbard, and a bronze medal.

Meade lived on in the memory of the Historical Society's leaders for many years, symbolizing for them the valiant struggle to preserve the Union (Figure 105). Forty-five years after the Civil War ended, the society held a lavish banquet to commemorate the ninety-fifth anniversary of Meade's birth. This was five years before the customary centennial marker, but the earlier date was chosen because only a few of the society's officers who had served under Meade were still alive. Eight officers, including three lieutenant generals of the army, spoke at the banquet on New Year's Eve in 1910, which was attended by military and naval officers, politicians, industrialists, lawyers, and journalists—but not by enlisted men who had survived the war and the intervening years.

Many veterans carefully preserved their dress uniforms and weapons and, for many years, wore them at patriotic parades. At the first "Grand Review," held in late May 1865 in Washington, 150,000 Union soldiers, holding aloft tattered banners, paraded up Pennsylvania Avenue to the Capitol. The *Philadelphia Inquirer* applauded: "We have had wars but no reviews. We planted our flag over the steeps of Mexico, but came home separately, like folks from church. We saved our original boundaries from British graspingness but thought it useless to do any congratulatory parading. We redeemed our age of Independence, but our forefathers melted away." The Grand Review in Washington did not begin the ritualizing of male warrior heroism, but it was the first event to do this on a national scale. Yet it was white warrior heroism that marched up Pennsylvania Avenue. Black regiments, observed the *Philadelphia Inquirer*, "can afford to wait, their time will yet come."[24]

Two weeks later, Philadelphia held its own Grand Review to memorialize the city's many regiments. But only white regiments marched, to judge by the account in the history of the city published by J. Thomas Scharf and Thompson Westcott twenty years later.[25] On July 4, 1866 the city staged another gala celebration in a sea of flags, a military procession that outdid anything the city had known. From these processions of uniformed Civil War veterans came ritualized Grand Reviews, spawning local veteran societies that brought officers and enlisted men together for the first time, soon to be linked nationally by the Grand Army of the Republic (GAR).

Only when the veterans were long in their graves did their children, grandchildren, and great-grandchildren begin to donate their uniforms, regimental flags, and weapons to the Historical Society, Atwater Kent, Masonic Temple, and other museums. Descendants of Civil War soldiers donated military memorabilia to the Historical Society in the late nineteenth century and have continued to do so down to the present. Such was the case with the dress coat and chapeau of Charles H. Pile, the assistant surgeon of the Union navy, given by his relatives in 1938, and the presentation sword and scabbard of Lt. Colonel John Hampton Gardiner, donated in 1989 by his great-grandson.

Presentation swords and scabbards and dress uniforms were reminders of the heroic aspects of war, but collectors and museumgoers, decades after the war ended, developed a fascination with the common tools of war as well. Americans fought the Civil War with deadly accurate, rapid-loading rifled shoulder-arms, as well as with rifled artillery. The U.S. Army's Springfield rifle, now to be seen in many museums and historical societies,

FIGURE 105. Thomas Hicks, *Meade at Gettysburg*, oil, 1876, The Civil War Library and Museum. Hicks, painter of this portrait of General George Meade, was born in Bucks County and was a cousin of Edward Hicks, whose primitive paintings of *The Peaceable Kingdom* became the most popular images of Quaker Pennsylvania.

was one of the first guns to be mass-produced with fully interchangeable parts, and it became the principal weapon of the war. Knapsacks, canteens, bayonets, camp knives, and other such mundane paraphernalia of war gradually filled shelves at collecting institutions.

The patriotic fervor perpetuated by the Grand Army of the Republic, which had forty posts in Philadelphia by the 1870s, almost by necessity required museums devoted entirely to the Civil War. Thus, the Military Order of the Loyal Legion of the United States, an officers' organization, created the Civil War Library and Museum in Philadelphia in 1888. Deluged with what the veterans brought home, it built a huge weapons collection, including a pike used by John Brown in his Harpers Ferry attack, Ulysses S. Grant's dress uniform, Jefferson Davis's dressing gown, the largest collection of military escutcheons in the nation, the mounted head of Old Baldy, General Meade's warhorse, and a roomful of Lincoln memorabilia. Other Civil War veterans later established the Grand Army of the Republic Civil War Museum and Library in the Frankford section of the city. The museum collected relics of the war as well as books, though not until 1985 was the public able to view such items as General Meade's battered campaign hat, a pillowslip stained with the blood of the dying President Lincoln, and a small section of the Andersonville stockade, recovered from the Georgia prison where hundreds of Philadelphians died of exposure and starvation.

The Historical Society's involvement in the Gettysburg Battlefield Monument, the first Civil War monument to martial glory, patched over a deep political rift that had paralyzed the society. Less than three months after the ghastly battle of July 1-3, 1863, a meeting of Historical Society members "rocked with applause" when their leaders resolved to approve the proposed plan to "secure and perpetuate the Battle grounds at Gettysburg." Naturally, none of the society's Democratic members, who still supported slavery and conciliation with the South, were appointed to a special committee. In less than a month, the committee gathered subscriptions to purchase the battlefield, started to record oral histories from battlefield survivors, authorized the selection of a historian "to write a full and correct History of that battle," and arranged for Historical Society members to participate in the forthcoming ceremonies opening the National Cemetery at Gettysburg.[26]

The Urban Homefront

Economic and social mobilization at home was essential for what became the nation's first total or "modern" war, so called because it involved almost everyone. One British journalist believed that history had never seen so much "a woman's war" as the Civil War, and this was surely true considering that women were as important as men in the marshaling of human and material resources. Women served in multiple roles—as nurses, spies, munitions and textile factory workers, stitchers of bandages and clothing, fundraisers, government office workers, camp followers, supervisors of farms and businesses stripped of male managers, and—in at least several hundred cases—combatants disguised as men. All this raised women's confidence in the multiple roles they could play while breaking down rigid gender categories. The war was hardly over before a Philadelphia publisher was advertising *Woman's Work in the Civil War: A Record of Heroism, Patriotism, and Patience* (1867), a compilation of accounts by Mary C. Vaughan and Dr. Linus P. Brockett. In flowery language, the book wove stories of traditional womanly qualities of sacrifice, suffering, generosity, and patience with untraditional qualities of brute strength and willingness to challenge male authority. Like the war itself, the book chipped away at the wall separating the masculine battlefield from the feminine homefront (Figure 106).

Northern activists organized relief organizations to make up for deficiencies in the army quartermaster and medical corps, and these groups involved women in war as never before. No other city, claimed the first book on women's war work, "furnished so many faithful workers in the hospitals, the Refreshment Saloons, the Soldiers' Homes and Reading-rooms, and no other was half so well represented in the field, camp, and general hospitals at the 'front.'"[27] The Christian Commission and its sister institution, the U.S. Sanitary Commission—forerunners of the Red Cross—raised money and collected medical supplies and hospital provisions from across the nation. As part of this private war relief agency, Philadelphia's Christian Commission volunteers staffed the Second Corps field hospital at Gettysburg. By war's end, a Sanitary Commission male official wrote that "the supplies . . . were almost universally collected, assorted, despatched, and re-collected, re-assorted, and re-despatched by women, representing . . . every grade of society in the Republic."[28]

Geography made Philadelphia the hospital center of the Union, for it was the northern city most closely connected to the South by railroad, and it was in the South that most of the Union soldiers were injured. A medical center since the colonial period, Philadelphia now sprouted military and civilian hospitals set up for emergency use; one was in an old tavern. In 1862, benevolent Philadelphians established the Citizens Volunteer Hospital (Figure 107). It served thirty thousand soldiers in its first year and more in the next. But with casualties pouring in from the front and these volunteer sites proving inadequate, the federal government built two huge temporary facilities in the city. The largest of them was Mower Hospital in Chestnut Hill. With four thousand beds, it was the largest complex of medical buildings in the world at the time. At the height of the war, the city contained twenty-four military hospitals. More than 150,000 soldiers and sailors recuperated—or died of wounds—in Philadelphia.

Extending the public roles they had established earlier in benevolent and reform associations, women volunteers helped care for the returning wounded in private and government hospitals. Philadelphia women were in great demand as nurses, laundresses, and cooks in the hospitals, and this gave new wage work for women in the lower classes. Women were often at the side of the wounded and dying, even on the battlefields, and this contributed to the professionalization of nursing after the war. One of these army nurses and cooks was Mary Morris Husband, granddaughter of Robert Morris, the well-known politician and financier of the Revolution. The well-heeled wife of a Philadelphia

FIGURE 106. *Women and Children in Encampment of Thirty-first Pennsylvania Infantry*, photograph, 1862, Library of Congress. This family picture at an encampment of the Thirty-First Pennsylvania Infantry near Washington gives an unusual picture of the mingling of homefront and battlefront. As in the American Revolution, "regimental women" accompanied their husbands in the field to cook, launder, nurse, and sometimes clean guns and tend cattle. They got no pay, only subsistence. The woman here is surrounded with kitchen and washing utensils while members of the regiment stand in the background.

lawyer, she spent months at field hospitals in 1863, tending the wounded and dying brought off the crimson soil at Antietam, Fredericksburg, and Chancellorsville. Husband became a hero to "her boys" and was as popular and well known in many Pennsylvania regiments as General Meade.[29]

Because Philadelphia was a major port and railroad hub just north of the Mason-Dixon Line, it became a vital staging area for the Union army during the war. Here northern troops were mobilized for transport by rail to the front, and the same trains that took new recruits to battle brought back the wounded. Cheering the troops on the

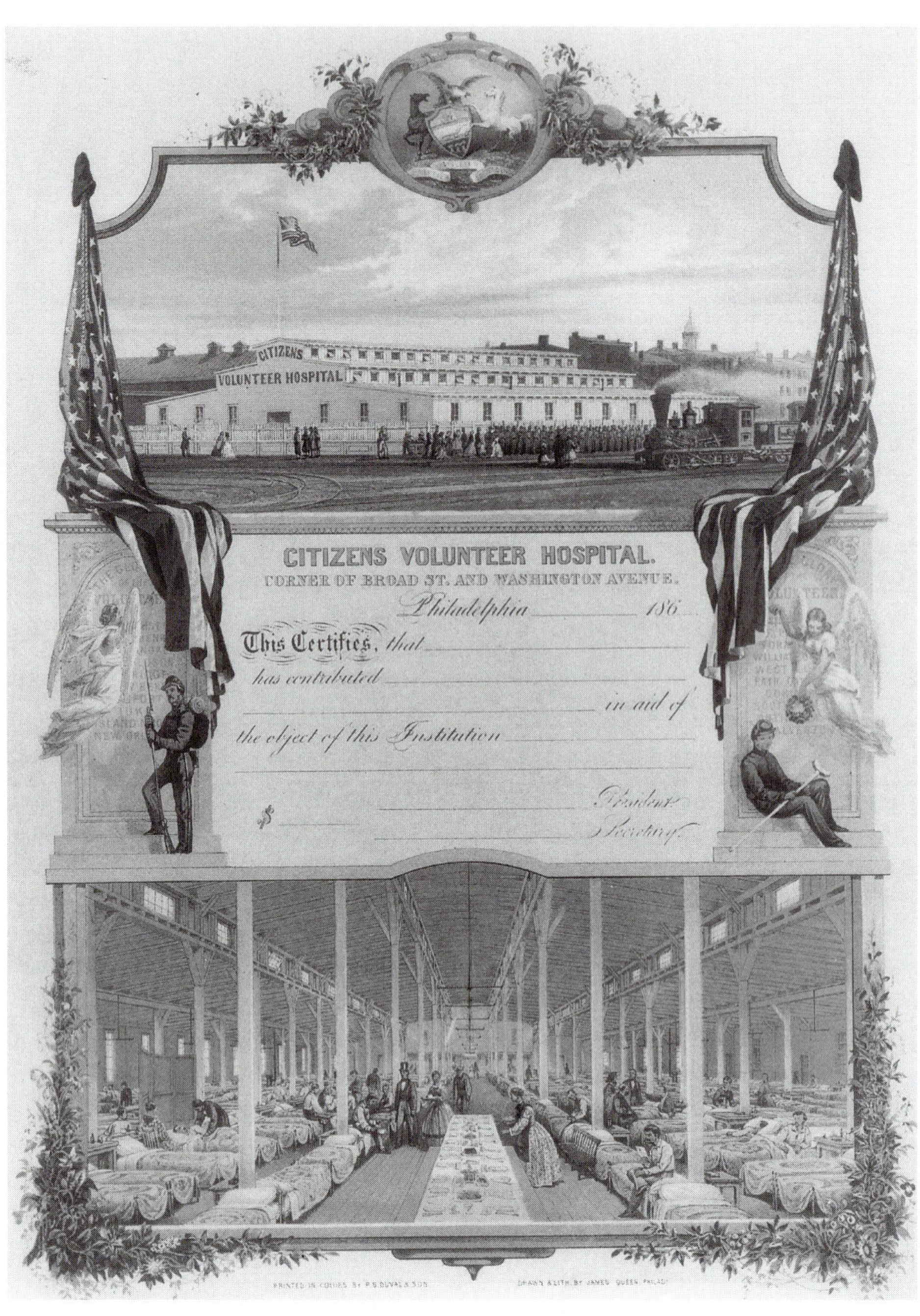

CITIZENS VOLUNTEER HOSPITAL.

CORNER OF BROAD ST. AND WASHINGTON AVENUE.

Philadelphia ________ *186*

This Certifies, *that* ________

has contributed ________

________ *in aid of*

the object of this Institution ________

____

$ ________ ________ *President*

________ *Secretary*

FIGURE 107. Citizens Volunteer Hospital contribution certificate, c. 1863, LCP. The Citizens Volunteer Hospital was one of many private hospitals that supplemented the military hospitals in Philadelphia. Warehouses, taverns, workshops, even Germantown's town hall were converted into temporary hospitals. The Library Company also acquired photographs of the interior of Mower Hospital to add to its rich Civil War collection.

FIGURE 108. Robert Newell, *Interior View of the Union Volunteer Refreshment Saloon*, lithograph, c. 1864, LCP. The Philadelphia Zouave Corps is shown here in the Union Refreshment Saloon before departing by railroad to the front. Well-dressed businessmen in the foreground are ready to provide a send-off. The saloon took its name from an old cooper shop on Otsego Street fitted out with rough tables. As it flourished, it became more comfortable and efficient, with volunteers able to feed a thousand soldiers and sailors in an hour. Other volunteers set up a Soldiers' Reading Room, with several thousand books and magazines, and taught at improvised night schools.

way south were the women of the volunteer refreshment saloons, where soldiers could wash, rest, and be fed a thousand at a time. The idea originated in 1861 with a Philadelphia grocer, Barzilai S. Brown. Soon the city became famous among northern troops for the generosity of those who organized and served in these huge refreshment centers. "Nowhere that I have been," wrote one soldier, "are soldiers treated with so much consideration and respect as there. . . . All soldiers have a great love for [Philadelphia]. Every tired & hungry regiment that has marched through there, has been rested and fed, and treated with every attention which the kind hearts of the Quaker City could suggest."[30]

The two main facilities, the Cooper Shop Saloon, and the Union Saloon (Figure 108), operated entirely with volunteer labor and contributions raised from bazaars, fairs, and balls. They served 1.3 million meals to hungry soldiers on their way through Philadelphia to the front. Both saloons were located near the Southwark docks, the debarkation staging area. A Vermont volunteer, returning from the Virginia battlefield, described "a

FIGURE 109. P. S. Duval, *Buildings of the Great Central Fair*, colored lithograph, 1864, LCP. The extensive papers of the Philadelphia Association of the U.S. Sanitary Commission related to the Great Central Fair were given to the Historical Society shortly after the war, perhaps because of the involvement of Historical Society members. Extensive collateral papers from the Fair's recording secretary, Horace H. Furness—son of the city's abolitionist Unitarian minister, Historical Society member, and Shakespearean scholar—were given to the HSP by his grandson, Fairman Rogers Furness. Charles J. Stillé, to become president of the Historical Society in 1879, wrote the official book on the Great Central Fair for the U.S. Sanitary Commission.

glorious supper . . . good enough for a first class hotel" that awaited him at the saloon in September 1863.[31]

Philadelphia's spirit of benevolence and voluntarism peaked in 1864 with the Great Central Fair, held to raise money for the revenue-starved U.S. Sanitary Commission, which aided sick and wounded soldiers and sailors. Over $1.5 million was raised to bolster the commission's dwindling funds. Hundreds of Philadelphians served on a maze of seventy-seven committees procuring everything from wagons and heavy-wheeled vehicles to canned fruits to umbrellas, parasols, and canes. This committee work brought together people who previously had served only their own group, whether religious, ethnic, or trade-related. Thousands of individuals made cash or labor contributions and donated items for sale at the fair. Nearly every Philadelphian, it seemed, was involved one way or another. The fair drew on and strengthened patriotic fervor. In the process, the line between the public and private lives of women became thoroughly blurred. Ignoring all the "formalities of social intercourse," wrote *Our Daily Fare*, the fair's newspaper, women cajoled visitors into buying more than they intended, acting "the part of amateur sales-women" and showing "that ladies can do a'most anything."[32] In forty days, workers erected a complex of buildings covering Logan Square, with a main building stretching 540 feet in length (Figure 109).

More than a quarter million visitors, including President Lincoln and his wife, attended the fair during its three-week duration. They browsed in the block-long art gallery; partook of the lavish entertainment that included an all-star baseball game, opera performances, and American Indians performing traditional dances; and, most important, bought thousands of donated articles that ranged from parrots "well accustomed to low company," with vocabularies to match, to heirlooms, farm products, five gallons of water from the Amazon River, and a donkey said to have served in the War of 1812. Among the most popular items sold were the "Flora McFlimsey" dolls, named after a character in a well-known 1859 poem, who after repeated trips to Europe to buy dresses still had "nothing to wear." They were probably exhibited in the Children's Department of the Fair, which displayed a sign reading "Every child who buys a toy, Heals the wound of some brave boy." Flora McFlimsey of Madison Square sold for $250, complete with traveling accessories, corsets with boning, ice skates, parasol, calling cards, riding habit, toothbrush, steamer trunk, toiletries, top hat, and a wealth of dresses, gloves, and hats.

The Historical Society and the Library Company enthusiastically participated in the Central Fair, as did most other Philadelphia organizations. The fair gave the Historical Society a golden opportunity for what it had been attempting with limited success for forty years—putting before the public a worshipful evocation of Pennsylvania's founder and a comforting recollection of a more peaceful period. While helping to raise money for a good cause, the Historical Society had a captive classroom. Before, it had been a small society of prosperous white gentlemen who had privately collected manuscripts, pamphlets, books, portraits, and artifacts while reading historical papers to one another in meetings where the attendance did not often exceed a few dozen. Now they had the prospect of putting before thousands of visitors to the Great Central Fair whatever they chose from their collections.

Adopting John F. Watson's belief in the almost mystical power of ancient objects owned by heroic figures to connect people to the past, the committee happily agreed to recreate William Penn's parlor at Pennsbury. The William Penn Parlor Committee, which included Historical Society members and their wives, assembled many of the society's treasures (Figure 110), supplemented by artifacts lent by private owners, the Pennsylvania Hospital, the city, and the Library Company. On the walls of the parlor hung paintings of the young Penn in armor and Inman's painting of Penn at Shackamaxon, commissioned by the Penn Society more than forty years before; portraits of his sons; one of Admiral Penn, his father; portraits of Philadelphia's first two mayors; Peter Cooper's 1720 painting of the city; and a painting of Penn's grave in Buckinghamshire. Penn's chair, gate-leg table, razor and shaving bowl, looking-glass and candlesticks, and other curios were arranged decorously to remind Pennsylvania visitors, in the midst of a national crisis, of their roots in an era of peace and harmony. The Library Company lent William Penn's desk and tall clock to complete the parlor. To focus visitors' attention on Penn's amicable relations with the Indians, the exhibit included the two Hesselius paintings of Lapowinsa and Tishcohan, the Lenape chiefs; the famous peace treaty wampum belt; Benjamin West's much admired painting of Penn's treaty with the Indians; and Penn's first two letters to the Lenape chiefs, with the memorable language—"I have great Love and Regard towards you, and I desire to win and gain your Love and friendship by

FIGURE 110. William Penn parlor at Sanitary Commission Fair, 1864, HSP. This view of the William Penn parlor is one of a large series of stereoscopic pictures created for sale as souvenirs at the Great Central Fair. William Penn's William and Mary secretary desk shown here entered the collections of the Library Company very circuitously. When the contents of Pennsbury Manor were sold after the American Revolution by Penn's grandson, Quaker Peter Worrall acquired it. From there it passed to the Quaker abolitionist George Dillwyn and then to another Quaker, Burlington, New Jersey silversmith Nathaniel Coleman. Just after the founding of the Historical Society, John F. Watson described it as "in very old & unsightly condition." But Watson's friend, Library Company librarian John Jay Smith, acquired it from Coleman and later gave it to the Loganian Library.

a Kind, Just, and Peaceable Life." Other relics—Indian headdresses, bows and arrows; a mantelpiece from Carpenter's Hall, and antique furniture—completed the furnishings.[33]

This re-creation of Penn's parlor was the Historical Society's first attempt at using artifacts in the service of cultivating historical consciousness and unifying the public. It is not possible, for an era before public opinion polls, to measure the impact of this attempt to restore Penn to public memory. But something can be surmised from many diaries, in an era when diary keeping increased, that rapturously described daily trips to the fair. One Historical Society member called it a "miracle of American spirit, energy, & beauty."[34] Beyond that, the display led to one very tangible reward for the Historical Society. William M. Tilghman, a Philadelphia lawyer, had found among the papers of his family the first deed to William Penn from the Lenape tribe, dated July 15, 1682, for a huge tract of land in what would become Bucks County. Tilghman donated the deed to the fair as a fundraising item, and its purchaser then donated it to the Historical Society in 1867.

While upper- and middle-class women did volunteer work in hospitals, refreshment saloons, and fairs, working-class women went into the factories, mainly as "government sewing women." Seamstresses at the Schuylkill Arsenal on Gray's Ferry Road met part of the constant demand for additional uniforms. The arsenal offered employment to women whose husbands were away fighting and to war widows. But unable to meet the demand for uniforms, the government soon resorted to private contractors who put out piecework to women working at home. They sewed by hand, and their employers paid them pitifully low wages. As the conflict wore on, they protested loudly, pointing bitterly to the reduction of their rates by a quarter while inflation drove up the cost of living. "We are not willing that the Government should be used by base hearted contractors for selfish purposes," declared the women after a large meeting at Temperance Hall in 1861, "and we will not submit to the starvation prices offered by these men."[35] The sewing women were still fighting for a living wage three years later, finally resorting to direct appeals to President Lincoln.

While government sewing women suffered, Philadelphia's textile entrepreneurs made ample profits simply by adapting their existing plants to supply government contracts. Horstmann Brothers did not even need to change their products; they only had to expand the range of military goods they sold, since they had been a regular federal supplier well before the war. Other Philadelphia contractors also flourished by converting their factories to wartime needs. Alfred Jenks & Son refitted their Bridesburg machine works from a textile machinery plant into a rifle factory. In another conversion, Henry Disston & Sons transformed their saw works into a saber factory. Along the Delaware waterfront, William Cramp & Sons built many ships for the Union navy; the greatest of them was the U.S.S. *New Ironsides*, the largest ship in the Union fleet. But the greatest profits of all accrued to the railroads and railroad locomotive builders. The insatiable demand for railroad equipment to transport men, weapons, and supplies drove profits up for M. W. Baldwin and Company's Locomotive Works and allowed for great capital expansion as well. The same was true for the other locomotive manufacturers, the Pennsylvania Railroad, and the Philadelphia-Wilmington-Baltimore line.

Philadelphian Jay Cooke made war profits in another way. A banker and financier, he initiated a daring approach to selling U.S. bonds to pay for the war. As the government's fiscal agent, Cooke appealed directly to working people to invest their savings instead of looking to banks and wealthy individuals to lend the government money. To make his pitch, he used an army of subagents, colorful posters, and newspaper advertisements. Cooke raised hundreds of millions of dollars in bonds and made himself a tidy fortune doing it. He lived in regal splendor at Ogontz, his house in the northern suburbs. But eight years after the war ended, Cooke overextended himself and plunged into bankruptcy, touching off a financial panic and the deep national depression of 1873-77.

Reconstructing Philadelphia

Postwar reconstruction was a northern as well as a southern problem. In Philadelphia, as in the rest of the nation, the war had created tremendous rifts within families and communities. Moreover, the war created bitterness over charges of profiteering, exploitation of labor, and continued racial discrimination. Prewar attitudes and problems were not dissolved by war but continued into the postwar period and, in some cases, intensified.

Philadelphians celebrated the fall of Richmond on April 3, 1865, with bell and cannon, bunting and flags, bonfires and fireworks. Six days later, they celebrated again at news of the Appomattox Courthouse surrender of General Lee. But on April 15 revelry turned to grief as the city learned of President's Lincoln's assassination. Within hours, black crèpe hung from thousands of public and private buildings. "I felt as tho I had lost a personal friend," one Philadelphian wrote in his diary. A week after the president's death, Lincoln's funeral train arrived in Philadelphia, where a military contingent, including Philadelphia's African American Twenty-Second Regiment, which had fought at Richmond, escorted the body to Independence Hall while a funeral procession several miles in length followed behind. Some 85,000 people filed past the coffin. The site associated with the nation's founding now became the venue for giving homage to the fallen leader of the traumatic struggle to preserve the union. "Tonight," reported the *Philadelphia Bulletin*, Lincoln's body "will rest at the feet of the statue of the most illustrious of the early Apostles of American freedom; it will be surrounded with the effigies of the great representative men who gave power and glory to the United States."[36]

While long remembering the "Great Emancipator," Philadelphians had difficulty dissolving racial hostility. Indeed, race remained Philadelphia's greatest postwar problem. White Philadelphians had celebrated Lincoln's Emancipation Proclamation issued on January 1, 1863, but many of them regarded it, as did Lincoln, primarily as a means of securing the Union. In fact, the Proclamation did not apply to the states loyal to the Union where slavery still existed. White Philadelphians understood that if the North won the war, thousands of freed bondspeople would seek a new life in the cities of the North, and the idea of a large black citizenry unsettled them. The Union League, formed to bolster support for Lincoln and the Republican Party, took the part of the emancipated slaves, but, like most white abolitionists before them, they were far from ready to offer social and political equality to African Americans. The league arranged for the publication of a lithograph that showed an idealized version of a former slave family rejoicing at the prospect of working for wages and sending their children to public school. But the reality for African Americans in the city at war's end was that they still had no right to vote or hold political office. Though numbering more than 25,000, just one of the black Philadelphians held a government job—as messenger for the city's Department of Health.

The Republican Party's skittishness toward the racial issue became apparent when the Democrats, in the wake of the Emancipation Proclamation, charged Republican politicians with seeking "Negro equality." In Democratic Party propaganda, the abolition of slavery would lead inevitably to racial intermarriage because African American men, they charged, regarded access to white women as part of their newly gained rights. Stung with charges that Lincoln's party was promoting the "amalgamation" of blacks and whites, which in fact William Lloyd Garrison, Wendell Phillips, and a few others believed would not ruin the country, the Republicans insisted, to the horror of black Philadelphians, that they did not believe in the equality of the races (Figure 111).

DEMOCRATIC Catechism

OF NEGRO EQUALITY.

July 4th, 1863.

Who said that all men are created equal? Thomas Jefferson, the Father of Democracy.

Who gave negroes the right of suffrage in New York? The Democratic party.

Who presided over the Convention which gave this privilege to negroes? Martin Van Buren, a Democrat.

Who married a negro woman, and by her had mulatto children? Richard M. Johnson, a good Democrat.

Who elected Richard M. Johnson Vice President of the United States? The Democratic party.

If President Van Buren had died, and Richard M. Johnson had become President, who would have become the Democratic mistress of the White House? This same negro woman.

Who made the negro a citizen of the State of Maine? The Democratic party.

Who enacted a similar law in Massachusetts? The Democratic party.

Who gave the negro a right to vote in New Hampshire? The Democratic party.

Who permitted every colored person owning $250 in New York to become a voter? A General Assembly, purely Democratic.

Who repealed the laws of Ohio which required negroes to give bonds and security before settling in that State? The Democratic party.

Who made mulattoes legal voters in Ohio? The Supreme Court of which Reuben Wood was Chief Justice.

What became of Reuben Wood? The Democratic party elected him Governor three times, and he is still a leader of the Democratic party.

Who helped to give free negroes the right to vote in Tennessee, under her Constitution of 1796? General Jackson.

Was General Jackson a good Democrat? He generally passed as such.

Who, with the above facts, and many others, staring them in the face, are continually whining about "negro suffrage" and negro equality? The Democratic party.

All these things were done by Democrats, and yet they deny being in favor of negro equality, and charge it upon the Republicans—just like the thief who cries "stop thief" the loudest.

N. B.—Send your Democratic friend one of these Valuable Documents, Sold Wholesale and Retail at Johnson's, No. 7 North Tenth Street, Philadelphia, Pa.

FIGURE III. *Democratic Catechism of Negro Equality*, lithograph, 1863, LCP. The election of 1864 produced an effusion of racist broadsides and led to the invention of the word "miscegenation" by two New York City Democratic press journalists. In this broadside, the Republicans tried to shift the shoe onto the Democrats' foot. However, the consistently racist positions of Pennsylvania's Democrats made them largely immune to broadsides of this kind.

OCTAVIUS V. CATTO.—[PHOTOGRAPHED BY MESSRS. BROADBENT & PHILLIPS, PHILADELPHIA.]

FIGURE 112. *Octavius V. Catto, Harper's Weekly*, October 28, 1871, LCP. Octavius Catto, son of a black Presbyterian minister, became the head of the male section of the Institute for Colored Youth, a private black academy established by Philadelphia Quakers. Handsome and athletic, Catto was a leading figure in the Equal Rights League, established in 1864. In this capacity, he led passive resistance sit-in tactics to break streetcar companies' refusal to allow black passengers. By filling up streetcars and refusing to get off, the league forced conductors and policemen to throw them off bodily, thus bringing the issue before the public for a test of conscience.

Whether Philadelphians had the resolve to reconstruct their race relations turned from a theoretical question to an immediate issue when black veterans returning from the war challenged the segregated streetcar system in Philadelphia. A few years earlier, in 1859, William Still, the successful coal merchant, black abolitionist leader, and historian of the Underground Railroad, had started a campaign to desegregate streetcars. To combat racial prejudice, Still helped organize the Social, Cultural, and Statistical Association of Colored People of Philadelphia in 1860. Late in 1861, Still convinced the association to circulate a desegregation petition among sympathetic white business leaders and clergymen. By mid-1862, 369 prominent Philadelphians had signed, yet the city took no action while the war dragged on.

By 1864, the situation had become intolerable to Philadelphia's black citizens. Black soldiers could not travel on leave from Camp William Penn northwest of the city to their homes. When black women tried to use the streetcars to visit their wounded sons and husbands in the military hospitals, conductors threatened they would take them to the depot and whitewash them. One sailor, who had escaped slavery and was a hero of the siege of Charleston, was not permitted to use the streetcar to reach his ship, then undergoing repairs in the Navy Yard. In these circumstances, younger, more militant black leaders, like the schoolteacher Octavius V. Catto, organized a mass meeting of African Americans in March 1864; anticipating the sit-ins of the 1960s, they agreed on direct action to force the hand of streetcar company owners (Figure 112). Nine months later, several streetcar lines agreed to open their cars to black Philadelphians, and several others agreed to run separate cars for African Americans. They also decided to poll white passengers on the question, "Shall colored persons be allowed to ride in all the cars?" On the day in 1865 that Congress adopted the Thirteenth Amendment, which abolished slavery, the city's streetcar companies announced that their passengers had voted in a referendum against desegregating the cars. Only state legislation ended streetcar segregation in 1867.

When Congress proposed the Fifteenth Amendment in 1869, forbidding any state from depriving male citizens from voting on the grounds of "race, color, or previous condition of servitude," Philadelphia's troubled attempts at reconstruction turned violent. Black Philadelphians knew that Pennsylvania's legislature ratified the Fifteenth Amendment with reluctance; nonetheless they celebrated the amendment with parades and bonfires. So virulent was the opposition of white Philadelphians to black voters that federal troops were sent to the city to protect African Americans who dared go to the polls on election day. To avoid flying bricks—"Irish Confetti," as they called it—black voters turned out at four in the morning. In 1871, with no federal troops on hand and the election of a mayor and city council on the ballot, whites mobbed black voters, killing three and wounding dozens. One of the victims was Octavius V. Catto, one of the first black Philadelphians to volunteer for the U.S. Colored Infantry in 1863. The first black Philadelphian elected to the Franklin Institute, he was feared by white racists as a brilliant young black leader. Stalked on his way to vote, he was murdered in cold blood by a pistol-wielding assailant. Not until six years later, after African Americans' repeated insistence on justice, was anyone brought to trial for his murder or for that of the other victims. All-white juries acquitted the defendants.[37]

Catto's murder deeply wounded black Philadelphians, who had lost a bright young leader and a dedicated conservator of their history. White Philadelphians went on staging boisterous Fourth of July parades, at which marching veterans in Civil War uniforms celebrated the American Revolution and the triumph of the Union. They took their stand on local issues as if the war had nothing to do with creating a biracial democracy in their city. However, black Philadelphia voters reminded William Stokley, the Republican mayoral candidate, that they had helped elect him in 1871. Recognizing the importance of the black vote, Stokley helped African Americans form their own political clubs through which a handful of municipal patronage jobs could be channeled. The Republican machine also named schools for Catto and James Forten; this was a powerful symbolic step in perpetuating the memory of the city's black leaders. The solid African American support for the Republican Party held firm thereafter, although a few black leaders led a brief revolt after the city's prosecution of Catto's murderer resulted in acquittal.[38]

Apart from politics, but never untouched by it, the work of restoring public memory of Philadelphia's better past became part of the Reconstruction era. By itself, the Civil War enormously intensified the thirst for local and national traditions that would bind together the shattered, blood-drenched nation. In a city whose merchants, manufacturers, and bankers were deeply vested in reestablishing commercial connections to the South, rituals of public reconciliation assumed more than casual importance. The Historical Society, which had reorganized itself during the war, was the moving force in 1867 in restoring to Independence Hall the chair of John Hancock and the inkstand and table used for signing the Declaration of Independence. All these had migrated to Harrisburg when the state capital moved there at the beginning of the century. Now, with much ceremony, the Historical Society's president placed "these priceless and sacred memorials" in their proper place, with Pennsylvania's governor, Supreme Court justices, Civil War officers, descendants of the signers of the Declaration of Independence, and survivors of the War of 1812 in attendance.[39]

While contributing to the revival of feelings for eighteenth-century virtues and accomplishments, the Historical Society and the Library Company were reconstructing themselves. After the war, the Historical Society's holdings began to grow rapidly. From a mere 3,500 volumes acquired by 1854, along with about 100 bound volumes of manuscripts, the collection doubled in the next decade and grew to 12,000 by 1872, though this paled by comparison to the incomparable holdings of the Library Company, which shelved more than 64,000 volumes by 1856 and 100,000 by 1876. Still renting space on the third floor of the Athenaeum, the Historical Society began absorbing the historical materials of its landlord into its collections.

Following a fabulous bequest of some seventy thousand books and pamphlets in 1868, the society began to receive a steady stream of newspapers, manuscripts, books, pamphlets, and artifacts. For the first time, it developed a policy of "intensive, elective and systematic acquisition, instead of relying on lucky findings and fortuitous gifts." In 1872, the society moved into the first building of which they had sole occupancy, the Pennsylvania Hospital's "Picture Building," so called because it had been built to display Benjamin West's famous painting *Christ Healing the Sick*. With a dynamic new president, John William Wallace, the Society now "teemed with new enterprises and larger outlooks," as a later president and its first historian wrote.[40] Trained as a lawyer, Wallace was an ardent historian himself, tracing the early history of printing in Philadelphia and reminding the society's 600 members that the history of colonial Pennsylvania had yet to be written.

With the Historical Society on the rise, the Library Company had a crisis of identity occasioned by the bequest of $1 million from James Rush in 1869. "Studious, somewhat misanthropic, and definitely eccentric," Rush had intended the money to pay for a new library building that the directors were planning to erect in the central part of the city; but on his deathbed he suddenly decided it had to be build in South Philadelphia instead. The Library Company's 969 members were deeply torn, because this decision would move the library far away from the central city, where most of them lived. But by a razor-thin majority, the members voted to accept the Rush bequest containing this provision. Accordingly, a huge Parthenon-like Ridgway Building was erected at Broad and Christian streets, though it was hated by many members and eventually used, after another new building was erected at Juniper and Locust, mostly as a storage house and fireproof sepulcher for rare books.[41]

In his will, Rush also tried to solve the old anomaly the Library Company had lived with for many decades—a privately controlled institution functioning as a public library. Rush hated what he regarded as over-collecting in a country whose print culture had expanded exponentially. He likened a library trying "to keep up with the progress of our country, collecting too many books," with "an avaricious man who accumulates money to the ruin of both his modesty and his intellect." For him, it was the quality of the books on the shelves, not the quantity of books acquired for "the amusement of the public," that counted. Why be the custodian of "an ambitious store of inferior printed paper . . . and crowd out the highest number of worthless books"?

Rush's criticism was too harsh for many of the Library Company's members, and the policy of withdrawing from the public library role was not strictly followed. But gradually, the Library Company adopted a "books of permanent value" philosophy. What made this approach sensible at the time was that several public libraries had been established to serve the needs of a growing and increasingly diverse city: the Apprentices Library, founded in 1820 to cater especially to younger readers; and the Mercantile Library, founded in 1821, which avowedly collected popular material but was not entirely public because it charged members initiation fees and annual contributions. By 1870, the Mercantile Library had more than 56,000 volumes and more than 6,500 members, making it easier for the Library Company to withdraw from its public library role. Eleven years later, the Library Company's librarian, soon to become a founder of the American Library Association, was proselytizing that there could be no better way to celebrate the

FIGURE 113. Independence Hall celebration for unveiling of Washington monument, July 5, 1869, *Harper's Weekly*, July 24, 1869, LCP. A *Harper's Weekly* illustrator depicted the celebrants at Independence Hall, when a new statue of George Washington was unveiled. Just five weeks before, a monument to Washington and Lafayette designed by John Sartain was dedicated in Monument Cemetery. In 1884, a giant obelisk memorializing Washington was raised in Laurel Hill Cemetery, laid out in 1836 as a prototype of a parklike urban cemetery removed from the grime and noise of the industrial city.

impending two hundredth birthday of the arrival of William Penn than "to establish a free public library in the city of Philadelphia."[42]

James Rush would have applauded the Library Company's retreat from serving the public in the era of reconstruction, and he probably would have loved the cold, isolated, and unpopulated dinosaur built in South Philadelphia. But he would not have liked some of the material that began to pour into the library through the generosity of a band of antiquarians who lovingly assembled troves of material that he had no use for: newspapers, playbills, broadsides, scrapbooks, ephemera of all kinds, and what Rush disparagingly called "every-day novels, mind-tainting reviews, controversial politics, scribblings of poetry and prose, biographies of unknown names." Yet these were the materials, from Philadelphians such as John McAllister, Henry D. Gilpin, Mary Rebecca Darby Smith, its own librarian, Lloyd P. Smith, Charles A. Poulson, and several descendants of James Logan, that propelled the Library Company forward in collecting pre-1880 materials and that, ever since, have made it a rival of the Historical Society as a Philadelphia history archive.

The uses of monuments and processions to galvanize public sentiment continued in the late 1860s and early 1870s. The creation of Decoration Day (later Memorial Day) in 1868 gave the public an annual occasion to remember and revere the dead and wounded of the Civil War. Processions of veterans turning out in their army and navy uniforms became a spring patriotic ritual. The unveiling on July 8, 1869 of a life-size statute of George Washington (Figure 113)—a gift from the Citizen's Washington Monument Fund, which had been struggling since 1810 "to establish a permanent memorial of their respect for the memory of the late Father of his Country"—continued this enshrinement of deceased heroes.[43] A thirty-three-foot statue to Edwin M. Stanton, Lincoln's secretary of war, soon went up and another for Lincoln was erected in Fairmount Park in 1870. Soldiers' monuments also arose—at Broad and Girard Streets, in the University of Pennsylvania's chapel, in Cedar Hill Cemetery, at Girard College, and in Germantown.

While using remembrances of an immaculate colonial and revolutionary past to unify deeply divided Americans, cultural leaders found it impossible in Philadelphia, as elsewhere, to keep patriotism and politics separate. In local elections after Lee's surrender at Appomattox Courthouse, Philadelphians continued the rhetorical violence and brawling as Reconstruction politics in Washington kept the nation in turmoil. Returning veterans, who could not afford partisan politics when fighting in the trenches at Gettysburg and Antietam, resumed their local political battles. To warm up for the Republican National Convention in October 1868, men in Civil War uniforms converged on the city for a convention of soldiers and sailors, "the most remarkable affair of this kind that ever occurred in the Quaker city," according to *Harper's Illustrated Weekly*.[44] The point they were making was clear: the party of Lincoln had saved the Union. Struggling under charges that their pro-southern Copperhead wing had nearly lost the war, Democrats countered with demonstrative processions of their own, whose uniformed soldiers and sailors tried to show that *their* contributions to the Union victory were as important as those of Republicans.

Monuments and commemorative occasions organized by whites had limited appeal to black Philadelphians, for by 1870 Reconstruction was proceeding badly in the South and white memory-keeping, as before the Civil War, largely ignored African Americans. Just as they had adopted January 1 or August 1 as their Fourth of July before the Civil War, because these were milestones in the dismantlement of slavery, African Americans found commemorative occasions that spoke to their most basic concern. Just before the end of the war, on November 1, 1864, African Americans and white abolitionists culminated "a grand demonstration" commemorating the emancipation of slaves in Maryland with 154

FIGURE 114. Transparency in Commemoration of Emancipation in Maryland, 1864, LCP. The *Press* called the immense transparency pictured here "the largest and one of the most imposing ever displayed to a public view." The scene at the top shows the storming of Port Hudson, a rebel stronghold on the Mississippi River where black troops carried the day. Below the transparency are portraits of Union generals, admirals, and politicians.

gasjets illuminating an enormous transparency, twenty-four feet wide, in front of the headquarters of the Supervisory Committee for Recruiting Colored Regiments. A crowd of 10,000 heard speeches from Boston abolitionist Wendell Phillips, Robert Purvis, and officers of the U.S. Colored Troops while marveling at the gas-lit painting of African American valor during the Civil War and the heroes of black history—Benjamin Banneker, James Forten, Lucretia Mott, and others (Figure 114).

Passage of the Fifteenth Amendment, guaranteeing African Americans the same political rights enjoyed by whites, provided an occasion for a new holiday. Determined "to show their calumniators that they were capable of getting up as imposing a demonstration as was ever witnessed in Philadelphia," black Philadelphians held a mass meeting in February 1870 to plan a celebration of the new milestone, ratified ten months before. Their festive celebration on April 26, 1870 indeed showed they had "been preparing on a scale of unparalleled splendor." Octavius Catto, eighteen months before his murder, received a banner at the mansion of the Union League. Then, Chief Marshal Thomas Charnock led a lengthy procession through the streets. At an evening meeting at Horticultural Hall, the black artist David Bustill Bowser presided over a massive audience that applauded speeches by Frederick Douglass, Robert Purvis, Jacob C. White, Jr., and others. Frederick Douglass gave an emotional oration that pronounced the end of an era and the beginning of a new one: "I say for me, I am no longer a black man. At last! at last! at last! I find myself not only a man, but a man among men. I find myself not a man of color but a citizen."[45]

That reconstructing race relations in Philadelphia was not on the minds of many whites became apparent in a sickening attack on the day's festive procession. For many decades, black Philadelphians had faced violence when they claimed equal right to public spaces. But the creation of an effective police force after the consolidation of 1854 seemed to settle this issue. On this day, however, the police were strangely unable to stop the "dastardly attack," as the *Press* called it, by a "mob of 'roughs,'" organized by "the scholars of the Democratic Party," that lay in wait for the procession and attacked the paraders with eggs, decayed vegetables, stones, and brickbats as the procession reached Fifth and Race Streets on its way to Independence Hall. The attacks on the African American celebration did not deter the marchers from attending their churches after the procession, where the black clergy dwelled on black Philadelphians' long historical travail—their Philadelphia history as they understood it.

Philadelphia's German Americans were as eager as black Philadelphians to celebrate an alternative historical consciousness. Visitors to the Sanitary Commission's Great Central Fair in 1864 had occasion to see the Pennsylvania German kitchen with a huge banner announcing, "Grant's Up to Schnitz." And just a few months after the African American jubilee observing the Fifteenth Amendment, the great Prussian victory at Sedan in September 1870, ending the Franco-Prussian War, gave the city's large German population an opportunity to express their love of homeland and cherish their own history. In a massive torchlight parade, described as "one of the half-dozen particularly noteworthy parades . . . since the close of the war of the Rebellion," German Americans staged a procession nine miles long that climaxed at Penn Square with speeches and festivities.[46]

By this time, Philadelphia was struggling to reorganize its economy after the end of war contracting and to repair the torn fabric of bitter wartime politics. Only a few years remained before the centennial of the nation's birth would be upon them. In 1873, the Franklin Institute and the Academy of Fine Arts stole a march on the revitalized Historical Society by being the first to memorialize Congress to sponsor an international exposition in Philadelphia in 1876 to celebrate the nation's one hundredth birthday. But the Historical Society, along with the Philosophical Society and Library Company, would soon become enthusiastic partners in the endeavor.

Chapter 8

WORKSHOP OF THE WORLD, SCHOOLHOUSE OF HISTORY

From a population of about 725,000 in 1875, Philadelphia grew to 1.3 million inhabitants by 1900 (Figure 115). The first large contingents of immigrants, including Italians, Greeks, Poles, Hungarians, Ukrainians, Lithuanians, Latvians, and Russians, added new layers to the religious and ethnic diversity of a city fast becoming a sprawling industrial giant. As established white Protestant families migrated en masse to new suburbs, facilitated by a commuter rail system, newcomers resettled the vacated neighborhoods, crowded themselves into split-up houses and subdivided lots, and converted churches to reflect their own religious practices. In a multitude of workplaces, the skills of the city's artisans and factory operatives, the products of its factories and foundries, and the innovating spirit of its investors, inventors, and managers earned Philadelphia the title of "workshop of the world." In a building boom fueled by population growth and rising wages, the city's promoters proudly called Philadelphia "the city of homes," the place where the modestly successful could purchase their own hearth.

Its growth and strength—and, of course, its history—made Philadelphia the perfect site for a world's fair celebrating how much the nation had achieved in one hundred years of independence. But the Centennial Exposition of 1876, which drew an unheard-of ten million visitors, was only the first of a series of commemorative celebrations in the last quarter of the nineteenth century. Mingling civic pride and patriotism with carefully managed invocations of the past, city organizers intended to heal old wounds while Americanizing immigrants flowing in from southern and eastern Europe. In an era when the Historical Society and other cultural institutions overcame Civil War paralysis and gathered momentum, Philadelphia became an out-of-doors schoolhouse of American history. But the presentation of the past made by institutional leaders, colored by their class position and social outlook, was challenged by those who had claims of their own to assert. Just as much as their social superiors, black Philadelphia leaders, women reformers and suffragists, labor organizers, and religious minority leaders wanted to etch *their* history in the consciousness of the general public. In the late nineteenth century, this would become apparent in a rapid succession of centennial and bicentennial celebrations at which the display of history was put to full use.

FIGURE 115. *The City of Philadelphia,* colored lithograph, Currier and Ives, HSP. With its population approaching three-quarters of a million inhabitants, Philadelphia on the eve of its Centennial Exposition in 1876 was the nation's second largest city. Lithographs such as the one portrayed here sold well because householders could take a natural pride in gracing their parlors with this proof of Philadelphia's growth, an overview that showed not the slightest clue of the city's festering problems of poverty, crime, and violence. This view looks east across the Schuylkill River with the Art Gallery and Main Hall of the Centennial Exposition at the lower left.

The Centennial Exposition

More than three years of careful planning and a tremendous burst of construction to erect 249 buildings for the nation's hundredth birthday party gave Philadelphia the opportunity to demonstrate its muscularity and organizational genius. The Centennial Exposition married the old practice of rollicking local fairs with the new idea of international expositions: the host nation advertised its cultural and industrial accomplishments, while other countries were invited to show their best face. Fifty nations built pavilions in Fairmount Park, displaying British machines, Japanese art, and Canadian wheat. But this was mainly an American party, celebrating history, promoting patriotism, and, even more, vaunting the new age of machines and technology.[1]

The buildings of the Exposition were spectacular in themselves, and some stood as monuments to the American faith in the inventiveness of the untrained person. The Main (Industrial) Building, built as a temporary structure, covered twenty-one acres and was at the time the largest building in the world. With its iron framework and massive use of glass to give a light and airy atmosphere, it stretched for more than one-third of a

FIGURE 116. Theodore R. Davis, *The Centennial Balloon View of the Grounds*, engraving, FLP. This view of the Centennial grounds in Fairmount Park from a balloon gives a sense of what Chief Engineer Hermann Schwarzmann accomplished in less than two years. Workers transformed fields, ravines, and swamps into a landscaped botanical garden and installed seventeen miles of walks, a double-track railroad, three telegraph systems, and a water works that had a daily pumping capacity of six million gallons.

mile. The two permanent buildings, Memorial Hall and Horticultural Hall, along with thirty-two others, were designed by twenty-nine-year-old German immigrant Hermann J. Schwarzmann. Without professional training, he created masterpieces in iron and glass. Five main exhibit halls, nine foreign government buildings, seventeen state buildings, and dozens of private buildings (including a Bible pavilion and even a burial casket building) were interspersed with dozens of restaurants, cigar pavilions, beer gardens, and popcorn stands, all spread over 236 acres in Fairmount Park, where 500,000 cubic yards of earth had been moved and 20,000 trees and shrubs planted. Elevated railroads and rolling chairs pushed by men in cadet uniforms and straw hats whisked the people who poured through 106 gates—on most days more than 100,000—around the vast fairgrounds (Figure 116).

Technology was a main feature of the exposition. It was conspicuously on display in the Main Building and Machinery Hall but evident throughout the spacious grounds. When the Exposition opened on May 10, 1876, President Ulysses Grant and Emperor Dom Pedro of Brazil, prince of the Houses of Bourbon, Braganza, and Hapsburg, threw the switch on the gigantic seven-hundred-ton Corliss steam engine, equipped with a thirty-foot flywheel that supplied power to some 800 other machines at the fair, con-

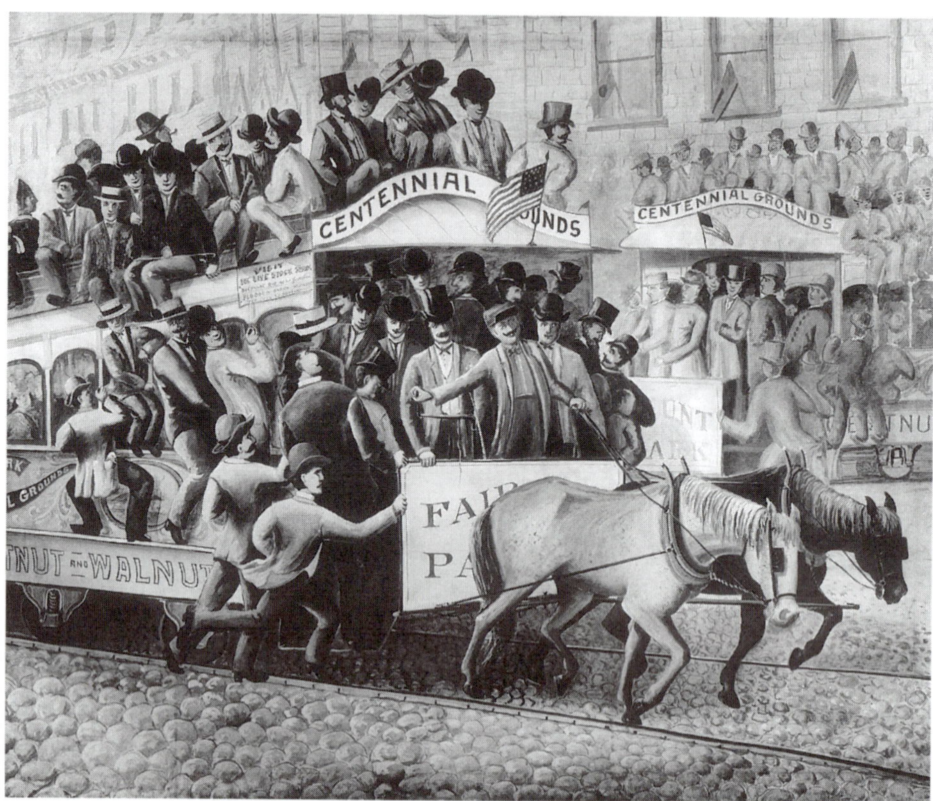

FIGURE 117. Edward S. Haley, *Street Car Travel*, oil, HSP. The crowded horse-drawn streetcar in this painting by Haley, a sign painter for the Chestnut and Walnut Street Line, gives a sense of the rush-hour exuberance of crowds making their way to the Centennial Exposition in Fairmount Park. The Historical Society acquired this painting by gift in 1919. Haley's skill, which shows in the painting's vivacity, never translated into success as a portrait, landscape, or genre artist, just as in the case of the African American artist and fellow sign-painter David Bustill Bowser.

nected by an elaborate system of shafts, wheels, and belts. The crowd cheered and threw their hats in the air as thirteen acres of machinery began to spin cotton, print newspapers, saw logs, make shoes, lithograph wallpaper, and pump water. William Dean Howells, the journalist and novelist, called the giant Corliss engine "an athlete of steel and iron with not a superfluous ounce of metal on it," and next to the American flag, it became the most celebrated artifact of the Exposition. Nobody remarked that the honored guest, Emperor Dom Pedro, ruled the greatest slave regime in the world.

There was no shortage of other machinery to dazzle the huge crowds. They marveled at Alexander Graham Bell's new telephone; Thomas Edison's quadruplex telegraph, which could transmit several messages simultaneously; George Westinghouse's railroad airbrake; and George Pullman's palace car. For the ordinary household, there were a stool with wheels for teaching infants to walk, an automatic baby feeder, a gas-heated flatiron operated by a foot bellows, and a host of other marvels. The German commissioner was so impressed with the quality and efficiency of the American-built machinery that he wrote *Letters from Philadelphia* to urge Germans to study the American designs rather than concentrate simply on mass production of cheap machines.

The Centennial Exposition also gave Philadelphia's manufacturers and artisans a chance to tout their wares and skills. Dozens of companies, such as the Wayne Iron and Steel Works, showed off their products. During this period of growing industrial strife, labor organizations displayed their craft consciousness with emblems such as the Leather Dressers' Centennial Badge, with the motto "By Industry We Thrive."

Philadelphians turned out in masses to attend the exposition, and travelers from around the country and abroad flocked to see the spectacular array of exhibits. When exhausted with exhibit-going, they listened to band music and orations and drank in many forms of popular entertainment, including a display of Wisconsin's war eagle, "Old Abe," who had followed a Union regiment through thirty-six battles and skirmishes in the Civil War. The opening-day crowd of 186,000 was claimed to be the "largest ever assembled on the North American continent." One reporter described the hotels and roominghouses that had sprung up near the fairgrounds "as full as rabbit warrens [with] politicians of every hue and cry, and clergymen of every light and shade, doctors of great and little pills, merchants, lawyers, thieves, farmers, bankers, gamblers, showmen, shopkeepers, and every known class of man in the country."[2] The bemused Japanese commissioner to the Exposition marveled at the American way of celebrating: "The first day crowds come like sheep, run here, run there, run everywhere. One man start, one thousand follow. Nobody can see anything, nobody can do anything. All rush, push, tear, shout, make plenty noise, say damn great many times, get very tired, and go home."[3] Before the Exposition closed on November 10, more than one of every five Americans, most of them paying the fifty-cent admission charge, had rushed, pushed, and made plenty of noise (Figure 117).

The Centennial Exposition's organizers knew they had a rare opportunity to educate as well as entice and entertain—in fact, to fashion or remake public memory. In an opening day address, the president of the Centennial Board of Finance emphasized that the exposition "is but a school; the more thoroughly its lessons are learned, the greater will be the gain."[4] The main lesson to be learned concerned pride in the nation's new industrial technology—in the ingenuity it demonstrated and the prosperity it promised. Yet other lessons bore on the nation's early history, its revolutionary heroes, and its constitutional system of government. Public memory-making of a presumably less divided past had much to contribute in 1876 to a nation recovering from the carnage of the Civil War. In truth, the Centennial Exposition wore several faces; in them, the accomplishments and the problems of the host city—and the nation—could be read by observant visitors. The Exposition celebrated a country reunited, but it could not disguise the political and social tensions that still existed, both between North and South and within sections, states, and cities. Also, no amount of oratorical puffery or nighttime fireworks could sweep away the awareness that the country was yet in the throes of a debilitating international depression that had begun in 1873 and that Philadelphia was reeling under double-digit unemployment. Nor could it keep from the headlines the murderous struggle on the Great Plains, where the U.S. Army was battling the Sioux in a conflict that climaxed on June 26, 1876, just six weeks after the Exposition opened its gates, when Crazy Horse and Sitting Bull led two thousand warriors forward to rout General George Custer's Seventh Cavalry. Any Centennial visitor reading the morning newspapers also knew that a series of sensational murder trials were being held about one hundred miles from Philadelphia in Pottsville, where twenty Irish coal miners were being tried and convicted for killing mine foremen and coal company operators targeted by poor anthracite miners as their foulest exploiters.

Hoping that the Exposition would bind the nation's wounds, and mindful of Philadelphia's long history of anti-Catholic and antiblack hostility, its organizers eagerly made overtures to various groups who wanted to memorialize particular histories. Presbyterians had no difficulty in obtaining space to erect the John Witherspoon Memorial, which would educate visitors about Witherspoon's role as the late colonial president of their intellectual seat, the College of New Jersey, and as a signer of the Declaration of Independence. Philadelphia Italians raised money to erect a colossal statue of Columbus to remind visitors of the American debt to one of their own. Not to be trumped, Philadelphia Germans emptied pockets to erect a huge statue of Alexander von Humboldt. B'nai Brith, the Jewish social service and reform society that had established two lodges in Philadelphia, erected on a twelve-foot pedestal a tribute to Religious Liberty, symbolized by an eight-foot armor-clad female figure with scrolls representing equality and humanity in one hand, the burning torch of religion in the other. The Catholic Total Abstinence Union, founded just four years before, financed the gigantic Centennial Fountain, with Moses as the central figure, looking down on four nine-foot marble statues of Catholic heroes: Commodore John Barry, proudly called "father of the American Navy"; Charles Carroll, Maryland signer of the Declaration of Independence; his cousin, Archbishop John Carroll, who had served as a commissioner to Canada during the Revolutionary War; and Father Theobald Matthew, a contemporary Catholic temperance leader. Life-size medallion heads of other Catholic revolutionary heroes decorated the facing of the marble basin washed by the central fountain: Lafayette; French admiral Count de Grasse; Polish patriots Pulaski and Kosciuzko; Stephen Moylan, commander of the celebrated Moylan's Dragoons; and merchant George Meade, grandfather of the Civil War Union hero who had helped clothe the starving army at Valley Forge. Also rescued from oblivion was the Penobscot chief Orono, a convert to Catholicism who held a commission in the Continental army.

While white religious and ethnic groups welcomed opportunities to enshrine their heroes' contributions to a glorious past, Native Americans and African Americans found it much more difficult to remind visitors of *their* role in the nation's history. Some Indian chiefs wanted to come to the Centennial and possibly meet with President Grant to express their grievances, while others saw a chance simply to present themselves as custodians of venerable societies. But most Indians were then on government-run reservations, and Congress's refusal to appropriate money for the Exposition thwarted

FIGURE 118. *An Indian Carnival: Philadelphia Street Scene on the Night of the Fourth of July, Illustrated London News*, July 29, 1876, LCP. The illustrator for *Illustrated London News* captured a scene at the July 4, 1876 torchlight parade that shows the kind of mummery that was becoming famous in the city at the beginning of the twentieth century. The procession lasted from 9 P.M. until 2 A.M. No sources yet discovered indicate the identity of the Indian impersonators or whether they were trying to convey more than a carnival spectacle.

the plans of the Bureau of Indian Affairs to coordinate a living display of Native Americans that might promote better understanding between the two cultures. A small number of Native Americans did appear and made an encampment in Fairmount Park, but the Sioux decimation of Custer's troops at Little Big Horn in June 1876 made the welcome of Indians of any tribe a delicate matter.[5] Rather, Indians were mostly represented in exhibits mounted by the Smithsonian Institution that emphasized the "savage" past and more "civilized" present condition of the Native Americans. But consistent with the Social Darwinism that children were learning from their textbooks, the main theme was that, in the hierarchy of the branches of humankind, the Indians were leftovers from a chaotic, stormy epoch of human beginnings and a people chiefly useful as reminders of how far European peoples had progressed. Writing in the *Atlantic Monthly* after visiting the Indian exhibits, William Dean Howells related that "the red man, as he appears in effigy and in photograph in this collection, is a hideous demon, whose malign traits can hardly inspire any emotion softer than abhorrence."[6] On the night of July 4, at a massive torchlight procession through the city, fairgoers saw Indians impersonated by costumed whites in outfits seemingly imported directly from a New Orleans Mardi Gras (Figure 118).

Long before the Exposition opened, African American leaders had seen a rare opportunity to dissolve racial prejudice and neutralize the toxic effect of textbook descriptions of the nation's black populace as a degraded and nearly irredeemable people. The African Methodist Episcopal Church's *Christian Recorder*, centered in Philadelphia, had lobbied as early as 1872 for bringing to the public's notice the African Americans' blood sacrifices, inventions, and massive uncompensated labor that had helped build the nation. "We have done something," wrote the *Recorder*, "and should not that something be felt and seen during the Centennial Celebration? Let us be up and doing. . . . Let us claim that our labor of the past has added something to the glory of the country."[7] A year later, Philadelphia's black leader, Robert Purvis, fumed, "We have been hypocrites and liars with respect to our real history long enough." July 4, 1876, would be the appropriate day to seal black America's entitlement to historical remembrance by revealing "that it was an incontestable fact that the blood of a negro [Crispus Attucks] was the first shed for liberty in the Revolution and that blacks had taken an active part in the War of 1812 and in our late civil war for freedom."[8] Then in 1875, black leaders convening in Cincinnati, including Philadelphia's B. W. Arnett and Henry McNeal Turner, planned an elaborate, eighteen-volume "Centennial Tribute to the Negro" that would "let the coming generation know our true history." They also appointed a committee to urge upon the Centennial commissioners "the necessity of having the productions of the colored race represented," particularly the "religious, literary, educational and mechanical interest of the Negro," and to commission Edmonia Lewis, the famous Indian-black sculptress, to design two statues, one of a black Cleopatra, the other of Richard Allen.

Memorializing Allen in words and marble became a key part of reaching out to both the black masses who needed heroes of their own to emulate and the white masses whose respect might be gained if they saw that Allen deserved a place in the national pantheon. Rankling at news that Philadelphia's Irish Catholics were raising money for a fountain that would call attention to their heroes who had contributed to creating the American nation, Benjamin T. Tanner, editor of the *Christian Recorder*, asked, "Why can't we *as a Church*, have a hand in the great Centennial?" Pushing for an Allen monument, black church leaders urged observances in 1875 of Allen's natal day in February.[9]

Although African Methodist Episcopal church leaders had to work hard to quash internal differences over whether they could afford the expenditure of scarce dollars for the monument (Figure 119), they faced greater resistance from the Exposition's director general, who was willing to allocate space for the Allen monument but insisted that it must be removed, unlike the other statues being erected, within thirty days of the exposition's closing. This issue was resolved only when the trustees of Mother Bethel Church agreed to provide a permanent site for the statue. Making the best of clearly unfair treatment, the black Methodist leaders used the dedication of the Allen monument site in June 1876 to hammer home the point that African Americans deserved a place in the generally

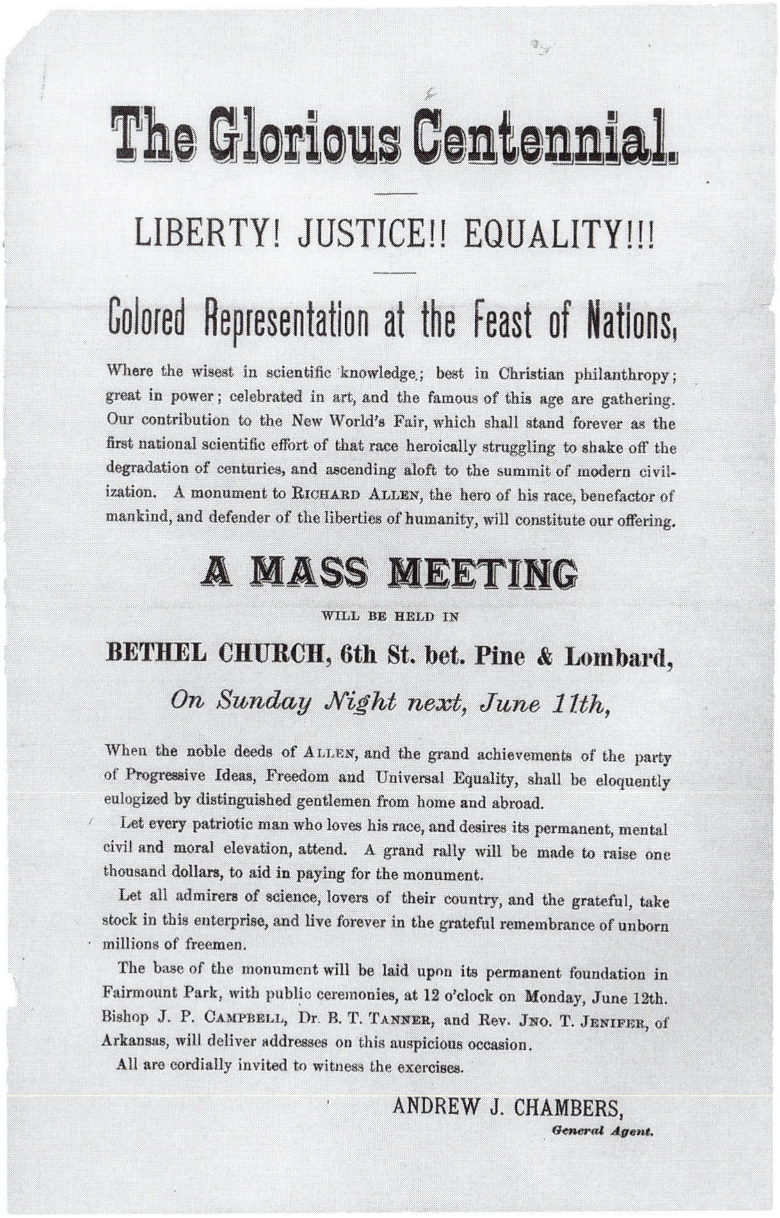

The Glorious Centennial.

LIBERTY! JUSTICE!! EQUALITY!!!

Colored Representation at the Feast of Nations,

Where the wisest in scientific knowledge; best in Christian philanthropy; great in power; celebrated in art, and the famous of this age are gathering. Our contribution to the New World's Fair, which shall stand forever as the first national scientific effort of that race heroically struggling to shake off the degradation of centuries, and ascending aloft to the summit of modern civilization. A monument to RICHARD ALLEN, the hero of his race, benefactor of mankind, and defender of the liberties of humanity, will constitute our offering.

A MASS MEETING

WILL BE HELD IN

BETHEL CHURCH, 6th St. bet. Pine & Lombard,

On Sunday Night next, June 11th,

When the noble deeds of ALLEN, and the grand achievements of the party of Progressive Ideas, Freedom and Universal Equality, shall be eloquently eulogized by distinguished gentlemen from home and abroad.

Let every patriotic man who loves his race, and desires its permanent, mental civil and moral elevation, attend. A grand rally will be made to raise one thousand dollars, to aid in paying for the monument.

Let all admirers of science, lovers of their country, and the grateful, take stock in this enterprise, and live forever in the grateful remembrance of unborn millions of freemen.

The base of the monument will be laid upon its permanent foundation in Fairmount Park, with public ceremonies, at 12 o'clock on Monday, June 12th. Bishop J. P. CAMPBELL, Dr. B. T. TANNER, and Rev. JNO. T. JENIFER, of Arkansas, will deliver addresses on this auspicious occasion.

All are cordially invited to witness the exercises.

ANDREW J. CHAMBERS,
General Agent.

FIGURE 119. Broadside for a Mass Meeting at Bethel Church, June 1876, HSP. Black Philadelphians, urged by the city's ministers to demonstrate the "effort of that race heroically struggling to shake off the degradation of centuries, and ascending aloft to the summit of modern civilization," raised much of the money for the Richard Allen monument. Money came from scores of other black Methodist churches, especially in the South, where ministers were recruiting thousands of new members after the Civil War.

white story line of American history. "With a history written in blood and baptised in tears, we are here to-day," orated John T. Jenifer, later to become a historian of the African Methodist Episcopal Church, "upon the soil where we have suffered; here to-day with those by whom we have been degraded . . . here to-day to show that the spirit of our fathers has not expired; but with a purpose grander than that which built the Pyramids or founded Carthage, we come to make our contributions to the New World's Fair." Stung by the Exposition organizers' attempts to promote sectional reconciliation when the Ku Klux Klan was rising to "redeem" the South from northern carpetbaggers, Jenifer sharply criticized the growing antiblack violence in the South and the federal government's "weakness" in doing little to stop "the fruits of wanton prejudice, hatred and hellish passions." But his culminating comments were optimistic. Giving black Americans a central role in the unfolding of American history, one that would allow African Americans to think historically about how their labor built the nation rather than about the humiliation of slavery, he looked forward to the next centennial in 1976, where he foresaw "color lines . . . wiped out, caste . . . gone; the American citizen, white or black, will be honored and loved, and mind and moral excellence will be the measure of the man."[10]

The movement to establish a monument for Richard Allen was set back when much of the marble pedestal, carved in Cincinnati, was destroyed as the railroad car transporting it to Philadelphia crashed while crossing the Delaware River in Lehigh Valley. But the bust of Allen survived and was presented in November, just before the Exposition closed. A few weeks later, the national black leader John Mercer Langston addressed a throng of some two thousand worshipers at Bethel Church. "All nations, all races of men delight to honor their mighty dead," remarked Langston. Then, noting that this was the first monument erected by African Americans to honor one of their own, he reminded his audience that "two hundred and forty-five years of enslavement ill prepares our people for incurring the outlay connected with such work, while our leading men have been denied those opportunities and responsibilities which, developing character and purpose, make large personal achievement and personal distinction possible."[11] In the years that followed, the monument figured importantly in annual celebrations honoring Allen birthday.

Sources for determining how black Philadelphians regarded the Centennial Exposition are virtually unrecoverable. But we can imagine that most African Americans wanted as much as anyone else to enjoy the festivities and be regarded as part of the celebration of nationhood. However, when at least one-third of the city's black adults were unemployed, many of them Civil War veterans, it was surely galling that jobs were rarely available in constructing the two hundred buildings. Nearly ten million visitors saw African Americans represented only as shoeshine boys, gardeners, waiters, janitors, and an occasional messenger. Nor could black Philadelphians have been pleased by the prominence of the "Southern Restaurant," a concession granted to a white Atlanta businessman, where, as the *Centennial Exposition Guide* told readers, they could see "a band of old-time plantation 'darkies' who will sing their quaint melodies and strum the banjo before visitors of every clime." The *Guide* assured readers that this nostalgic representation of happy slaves "will be one of the most interesting sights in the Exhibition."[12] In *Song of the Centennial*, Joaquin Miller, the Exposition's official balladeer, completed the picture of the carefree and contented African American:

> A new and black brother, half troubadour,
> A stray piece of midnight comes grinning on deck.
> The black man has mounted a keg. From his throne
> He thrums his banjo, Come! Let us alone.
> *The Negro Sings*
> "Gwine down to de Quaker ball,
> We white folks and de niggers all,
> Gwine to dat Centeni-awl.
> Oh fight for de Union!"[13]

But of the hundreds of exhibits and events, organizers paid heed to African Americans' heritage in only a few instances, such as the statue of the *Freed Slave* in Memorial Hall (carved by Francesco Pezzicar of Trieste); Edmonia Lewis's sculpture *Death of Cleopatra*; and Edward Bannister's *Under the Oaks*, the only painting by an African American. Other displays included one from the Republic of Liberia to which some Philadelphia blacks had immigrated in the previous generation; and in the performance of a Philadelphia Negro Militia drill team (Figure 120). On the eve of the mammoth July Fourth festivities, Forney's Philadelphia *Press* lamented "that the great show of the American people's industry and independence will close with the one link in the chain of its complete history left out. Although the chains of slavery have been broken . . . and the negro stands before the law a freeman, . . . yet the prejudice against him, the results of his previous condition, have prevented him from taking any part or having a prominent part of this marvelous undertaking . . . save that of a menial, the water-drawers and hat-takers, to the assembled races now to be found there."[14]

While African Americans struggled to remind visitors of their role in building the nation, Philadelphia's genteel white women found it easier to influence the face the Exposition presented to the public in relation to the role of women. But even so, more radical women had to use "guerrilla tactics" to put their demands for gender equality before the public. Like a play within a play, the struggle for attention by radical suffragists and labor unionists operated within a larger effort to expand women's sphere and commend female efforts to offset male domination outside the home.

When the all-male Centennial Board of Finance appointed the Women's Centennial Executive Committee in 1873, it did not anticipate how far a dependent body might go beyond its intended functions. Appreciative of the energetic efforts of Philadelphia's women in staging the Great Central Fair in 1864, the men believed women could build widespread enthusiasm for the Exposition and raise much-needed revenue through subscriptions to Centennial stock. With the great-granddaughter of Benjamin Franklin serving as president, the Women's Committee more than exceeded the men's expecta-

FIGURE 120. *Negro Militia After Drill, Illustrated London News,* May 13, 1876, LCP. The African American unit depicted was probably the Delaney Guards, composed of veterans from the black regiments raised in Philadelphia in 1863-64. Some of the remnants of the U.S. Colored Troops marched in the opening ceremonies on May 10 and at the July 4 torchlight procession in Philadelphia, but few newspapers commented on this.

tions. Much like her grandmother, Benjamin Franklin's daughter, who had gone into the streets to raise money to clothe George Washington's tattered army, Elizabeth Duane Gillespie led a female army through the city's neighborhoods to sell subscriptions for the stock and obtain signatures for raising $1 million. Within two days, Gillespie's army had 82,000 signatures and soon had generated letters of support from all over the nation that convinced Congress to lend $1.5 million to the Exposition's organizers.

The Women's Committee was also charged with mounting exhibits for the Main Building that would display the products of women's labor. But the women's insistence that foreign nations should be widely invited to exhibit, lest the exposition become a narrowly conceived affair, ironically turned to their disadvantage. Foreign exhibitors came forward in such numbers that the Exposition's director general, just eleven months before opening day, informed the women that little room was left in the Main Building for their exhibits. Though angry at this last-minute decision, Gillespie's committee rose enthusiastically to the challenge. In four months they raised more than $31,000 to erect the one-acre Woman's Pavilion, the first at any world's fair (Figure 121). Gillespie became what one executive committee member called the "imperial wizard, the arch-tycoon" of the Exposition.[15]

The unexpected exclusion of the women's exhibits from the Main Building galva-

FIGURE 121. Woman's Pavilion, Centennial Exposition, photograph, LCP. The Woman's Pavilion was built in the shape of a cross. In the background of the photograph is the New Jersey building. Pointing ominously at the Woman's Pavilion is a revolutionary war cannon. It is tempting to speculate on the positioning of the cannon, a male weapon to project power, but I have found no contemporary comment on this. Gillespie later regretted that the contract for designing the building was given to Hermann J. Schwarzmann rather than to Emma Kimball, an accomplished architect in Lowell, Massachusetts.

nized the women to reach Centennial visitors with a message of women's achievements, their potential, and their dissatisfaction with the world of male power and privilege. A separate building gave them far more space to display women's achievements in arts and crafts, medicine and science, literature and education, philanthropy, and especially industry—all designed to build women's confidence and promote economic and intellectual self-sufficiency. Among some seventy-four patented inventions on display, many of them showcasing not only females' mechanical ingenuity but also the desire to decrease the burdens of household labor, were a dishwasher, a stocking darner, a life-preserving mattress, a lunch-warmer, and a self-heating gas iron. The *New Century for Women*, a weekly newspaper written, set in type, and printed entirely by women in the Woman's Pavilion, contained comments on the inspirational displays. "I know many mothers, who since visiting the Women's Department," wrote one correspondent, "have determined to seek out the 'bent' of their daughters' abilities and to educate them, as well as their boys, to be self-supporting."[16]

Elizabeth Gillespie and her colleagues on the Women's Committee belonged to Philadelphia's upper class, and this status put boundaries around their concern for opening new opportunities for women and breaking down the barriers of inequality. In raising additional money to publish a women's journal, publishing a national cookbook, and sponsoring a kindergarten and a series of symphony concerts at the Exposition, they promoted professional and entrepreneurial opportunities for women of the middle and upper classes. As close as they came to noticing the work and contributions of ordinary women were the living displays by Swedish and Norwegian peasants, more quaint and exotic than respectful. Publicizing the problems of wage-earning women caught at the bottom of society hardly fit the upbeat tone of the pavilion, though Gillespie did insist in *New Century* that women should receive equal pay for equal work. But the Centennial's women leaders appealed mainly to females situated far above the waged women in domestic or factory jobs, the women who, as "Miss Emily Faithful" pointed out, "will get what they have always got—that kind [of work] men do not want to do themselves . . . hard work, rough work, poorly paid work, hopeless work."[17]

While critical of the patriarchal order that kept women in subordinate positions, the Women's Committee were not ready to embrace the demands for women's suffrage echoing around the country. On receiving an exhibit from the National Woman Suffrage Association displaying the "Protests of Women Against Taxation Without Representation," they tucked it in a place where the public could hardly find it. This infuriated Susan B. Anthony, Elizabeth Cady Stanton, Philadelphia's Lucretia Mott, and other women of the Suffrage Association, who argued that their exhibit, if prominently placed, would teach a multitude of citizens that the political and legal slavery suffered by half the population was "as much a sin and as truly unworthy when committed against women as committed by George III against the Colonies."[18]

Going beyond the Women's Committee in attacking the bastions of male privilege, and carrying their history lessons for the nation far beyond the efforts of African Americans to obtain recognition of their history, the radical suffragists held fundraising and protest meetings around the country before the Exposition opened. Declaring that "to women this government is not a Republic, but a hateful oligarchy of sex," they called for a mass protest in Philadelphia and urged women across the country to meet on July 4 to "declare themselves free and independent, no longer bound to obey laws in whose making they have had no voice, and . . . to demand justice for the women of this land." Throughout the Centennial summer and fall—at Philadelphia churches, meeting halls, and the headquarters they established on Chestnut Street near the construction site of the city's massive new City Hall—they insisted that "the women of this nation in 1876 have greater cause for discontent, rebellion, and revolution than our fathers of 1776."[19]

After the Centennial's male organizers denied officers of the Suffrage Association a place on the Fourth of July program in Independence Square, Susan B. Anthony took dramatic action. As the acting Vice President of the United States, a grandson of Richard Henry Lee, concluded his reading of the Declaration of Independence, Anthony pressed forward through the crowd of 50,000 and mounted the platform. She thrust a copy of a

Woman's Declaration of Rights and also *Articles of Impeachment Against the United States* into the hands of the nonplussed vice president (Figure 122). Anthony strode off the stage as the flustered Centennial chairman shouted, "Order, order!" Then, with her cohorts, she passed out copies of the *Woman's Declaration*, climbed onto a bandstand across from Independence Hall, and addressed a cheering throng of women. "While the nation is buoyant with patriotism, and all hearts are attuned to praise," she read from the declaration, "it is with sorrow we come to strike the one discordant note. . . . We cannot forget, even in this glad hour," she told the crowd, "that while all men of every race, and clime, and condition have been invested with the full rights of citizenship under our hospitable flag, all women still suffer the degradation of disenfranchisement."[20] In this dramatic incident women seized the sacred space of Independence Square in order to publicize Independence Hall not as an edifice representing the nation's commitment to liberty and equality but as a symbol of the nation's unrealized ideals.

From Independence Square the women marched to the First Unitarian Church, where the convention of the Suffrage Association had gathered to demand equality before the law for American women. But equal rights were not to come during the Centennial celebrations—or for a long time thereafter. When rain forced the closing ceremonies inside in the Main Building on November 10, 1876, creating a shortage of seats, officials had the final say by refusing to honor women's tickets.

Neither the women of the Centennial Women's Committee nor the men of the governing board were oblivious to the labor strife accompanying the nation's rise to industrial colossus, and both groups hoped that the Exposition would spread faith in American progress while dampening discontent from below. They hoped to reach workingmen, whose rush to trade unions in a volatile period of depression threatened the house of capital far more than women suffragists. Bringing laboring Americans to the Centennial, some corporate leaders maintained, would open their eyes to "a test of two systems, one the poorly paid, poorly fed and uneducated cheap labor of the old world, against the intelligent, contented, protected labor of the new."[21] But this was a hard sell, because much of the American labor force knew they were poorly paid, poorly fed, and undereducated just as in the Old World. Still, thousands came on excursions organized by the railroads, textile factory owners, and coal mining companies. To encourage them, the Exposition organizers experimented with keeping the fair open after 6 P.M., the end of the 10-hour work day, and set aside a "poor man's day" with reduced admission rates.

Historians have found no way to gauge working-class participation in the Exposition, but it is likely that the costs of travel, admission, and absence from work made visits nearly impossible for the large numbers who lived in poverty or at its edge. For those who did come—most of them probably lived in the city or nearby—the Centennial Exposition offered much that was unabashedly patriotic and designed to evoke nostalgia for a presumably more placid and unified past. Indeed, through the summer of 1876 the city was awash in the rhetoric of patriotism. Philadelphians bedecked their city—and themselves—with flags, ribbons, banners, bunting, and streamers in red, white, and blue. Even dogs and horses sported the nation's colors. Among the most popular exhibits was the

☞ Editors Please Copy.

All persons in unison with the views of the following protest, are requested to circulate for signatures. Ask those of both men and women.

Send by June 20th, to care E. M. Davis, 333 Walnut Street, Philadelphia.

1876.

PROTEST.

National Woman Suffrage Association.

To the Men of the United States in Celebration of the Nation's Centennial Birth-day, July 4th, 1876.

One century ago the walls of Independence Hall echoed to that famous "Declaration" of our Fathers, that startled the world from its old dreams of authority, and proclaimed the individual above all principalities and powers.

The revolutionary heroes of '76 asserted and re-asserted these great truths, :

"All men are created free and equal, with certain inalienable rights to life, liberty, and the pursuit of happiness;"—"taxation without representation is tyranny;"—"no just government can be framed without the consent of the governed."

Such were the fundamental principles of the experiment of government they proposed to try in the new world. Such are the grand doctrines taught their sons and daughters through the century; the texts for our Fourth of July orations; the mottoes for our banners; the songs for our national music. Individual rights, individual conscience and judgment are our great American ideas, the cardinal points of our faith in church and in State, the soul of our republican government.

Through prolonged discussion, hot debate, and bloody conflict on the battle-field, the men of this generation have secured for their sex, white and black, rich and poor, native and foreign born, the liberty of self-government, and it well befits them to celebrate the centennial birth-day of such sacred rights.

But the mothers, wives and daughters of this republic have no lot nor part in this grand jubilee; they stand to-day where their fathers did when subjects of King George; "slaves" according to the definition of Benjamin Franklin, "having no voice in the laws and rulers that govern them."

Women are denied the right of self-government; the most ignorant and degraded classes of men are their rulers.

Women are denied a right of trial by a jury of their peers; men, foreign and native are their judges and jurors.

Women are taxed without represention, governed without their consent, and now Kings, Emperors and Czars from the despotisms of the old world are invited here to behold the worst form of aristocracy the sun ever shone upon, "an aristocracy of sex."

Our rulers may learn a lesson of justice from the very government they repudiated a century ago. In England women may occupy the highest political position, fill many offices, and vote on a property qualification at all municipal elections, while here the political status of the daughters of the pilgrims, is lower than that of the paupers from the old world who land on our shores to vote our taxes and governors.

In view of such degradation of one-half our people, citizens of a Republic, WE PROTEST before the assembled nations of the world against the centennial celebration, as an occasion for *National* rejoicing, as only through equal, impartial suffrage can a genuine republican form of government be realized.

With pride we may point the world to our magnificent domain, our numberless railroads, our boundless lakes and rivers, our vast forests, and exhaustless mines, our progress in the arts and sciences, our inventions in mechanical and agricultural implements, but in human rights how false to our theory of government we still remain.

The enfranchisement of 20,000,000 of women, is the only act of justice that in its magnanimity and magnitude is worthy the occasion you propose to celebrate, the crowning glory of the great events of the century.

NAMES.	NAMES.

FIGURE 122. National Woman Suffrage Association petition, 1876, FLP. Much in the mode of revolutionary declarations against importing British tea, women at the Centennial passed out this Protest of the National Woman Suffrage Association in order to solicit signatures at the bottom. How many signatures were obtained is not known. Note at the top that "editors"—newspaper editors—were requested to print this protest in their columns. None did so as far as I have been able to tell.

"New England kitchen," a reconstructed colonial hearth with cooking utensils tended by women appropriately clad in colonial costumes.

Veneration for the Founding Fathers was everywhere, and Washington's image was especially in evidence, emblazoned on doilies, beer bottles, candy, bars of soap, vases, trivets, and souvenir handkerchiefs. Nobody could walk very far without seeing a statue of Washington, including one in Memorial Hall—the *Apotheosis of Washington* by an Italian sculptor, in which a legless version of the Pater Patriae perched on a gigantic eagle about to waft him aloft with the Constitution in hand. Washington even arose from the dead. In a working model of his tomb, nine feet tall, toy soldiers saluted the nation's first president at regular intervals as he arose from the sepulcher. A silk memento ribbon boasted the nation's growth from three to forty million in its first century and recalled famous revolutionary battles. A centennial chair went the final step with a woven silk portrait of Washington covering the backrest, revolutionary rifles and patriot soldiers for back and front stiles respectively, and an elaborately carved eagle and seal of the nation atop the back.

In all the attention to Washington, other colonial leaders and Founding Fathers were surprisingly eclipsed, including Philadelphia's William Penn, Benjamin Franklin, Benjamin Rush, James Wilson, and Robert Morris. Of the combative Thomas Paine not a trace could be found since the Exposition's managers, at federal, state, and local levels, were interested in purveying symbols of unity for a divided society. Neither Paine nor the radical architects of Pennsylvania's 1776 constitution could fit that mold. Even Washington the battlefield leader and Washington the president in the tumultuous era of the French and Haitian revolutions yielded to a domesticated, depoliticized Washington.

Apart from souvenirs of every description emblazoned with Washington's image, fairgoers saw the great man most intimately through the exhibits of the U.S. Patent Office. By arranging displays of Washington's military field gear and household items alongside dazzling examples of ingenious machines, the Patent Office balanced history and technology (Figure 123). The exhibit of Washington items earlier acquired from the general's adopted son turned out to be one of the most popular exhibits at the Exposition. The public loved the sense of intimacy they felt with the great hero by gazing at his waistcoat thrown over a chair, the folding cot spread with his blankets, the portable camp table laid for tea with salt and butter boxes and tin plates, and his rumpled regimental uniform worn when he resigned his commission to return to farming at Mount Vernon. One visitor exclaimed: "Oh what feelings I did feel as I see that coat and vest that George had button up so many times over true patriotism, truthfulness, and honor. When I see the bed he had slept on, the little round table he had eat on [sic], . . . the belluses he had blowed the fire with in cold storms and discouragements. . . . Why they all rousted up my mind so, that I told Josiah I must see Independence Hall before I slept, or I wouldn't answer for the consequences."[22]

The Historical Society wanted fervently to be involved in the Centennial Exposition, and it seemed that this would happen when one of its councillors, Frank Marx Etting, became both the key figure in a campaign to restore Independence Hall to its 1776 ap-

FIGURE 123. "Washington Relics," in *Frank Leslie's Illustrated Historical Register of the Centennial Exposition*, LCP. Wildly popular, Washington relics such as the ones portrayed here gave the public a more human, personable quasi-deity, compressing the distance between 1776 and 1876 and muffling the radical character of the American Revolution.

pearance and the chief of the Centennial's history department. While cognizant of the Centennial organizers' goal of celebrating a century of progress and pointing forward to greater triumphs, Etting and the Historical Society knew they were now presented with an opportunity to fuse the past with the present and future by refreshing public memory about the golden colonial and revolutionary age. They even proposed that Independence Hall should "be appropriately given up to the Historical Society of Pennsylvania to receive its valuable collection and [serve] as a general hall for its meetings."[23] As it happened, what at first seemed an opportune occasion to realize the dreams of John Jay Smith and John F. Watson turned into a depressing disappointment.

The Historical Society had enthusiastically joined city and state officials in urging the federal government to authorize a grand celebration of the nation's one hundredth birthday in Philadelphia. Plans were soon afoot to restore the badly neglected Independence Hall under Etting's direction, and the society's collections (along with those of the Library Company) were opened to an army of newspaper and magazine editors, artists, historians, and others associated with planning the Exposition.

Descended from German immigrants, Etting had become recording secretary of the Historical Society in 1855 at age twenty-two, just a year after graduating from the University of Pennsylvania. In 1859 he became a Historical Society councillor, the first Jew elected to this position. When war broke out in 1861, Etting eagerly joined the army and after the war served eight additional years as the U.S. Army's paymaster and disburser of Reconstruction funds. All the while he had developed a fascination for autographs and historical materials. Now it was time to become the John F. Watson of the postwar era.

Etting turned the restoration of Independence Hall and the staging of historical exhibits on the colonial and revolutionary periods into a master plan for rehabilitating historical memory with a fervor matching his pro-northern Civil War passion. When Philadelphia voters decided in 1870 to erect a new city hall in Penn Square rather than Independence Square, the road was paved for Etting to rehabilitate Independence Hall, so that "the American people shall come to Philadelphia in 1876 to see how faithfully we have kept the sacred charge entrusted to us by our grandfathers."[24] To the question posed, "What will they [Philadelphians] be able to show the pilgrims who throng from all parts of the country to this 'American Mecca?'" Etting had a definitive answer: exactly what history-minded members of old Philadelphia families had the expertise to recreate—Philadelphia of 1776 as they imagined it. And in this recreation material objects would assume the utmost importance. "The actuality . . . of our Founders is already losing itself in the mists of the past," explained Etting. "So long, however, as we can preserve the material objects left to us which those great men saw, used, or even touched the thrill of vitality may still be transmitted unbroken." If the public could see the Treaty Elm of 1682, a letter written by William Penn, the residence of Washington in Philadelphia in 1776, or the walking stick of Ben Franklin, these "talismans with which to conjure up forms and figures, and endow them with life," would "annihilate distance in time as in space."[25]

Appointed chairman of the Committee on Restoration of Independence Hall, Etting began his crusade to restore the sacred chambers in which the Declaration and the Constitution had been written. First, the hallowed chamber would have to be cleansed of the layers of history deposited on what was a kind of city museum. Declaring that the Assembly Room had been turned into "a storehouse, a lumber-room for every variety of trash," Etting started cleaning house. But he ran into opposition when his house cleaning extended to vetting the portrait gallery established in 1854, mostly from Peale's collection and augmented with likenesses of Civil War heroes such as Lincoln, Grant, and local Union army generals. Etting insisted Peale's portrait of the Mohawk chief Joseph Brant must go, for "Brant, the savage, above all others in Pennsylvania history, [was] damned to eternal infamy." So, too, Red Jacket, the Iroquois chief, must go. Etting also scheduled for removal what he called "the vilest daub and caricature of General Jackson (unfit for a tavern sign)" and Peale's painting of Thomas Paine, "an obscure political agitator doing duty for Charles Lee, of Revolutionary notoriety."[26] These portraits would be replaced by likenesses of the signers of the Declaration and revolutionary statesmen and officers, such as the presidents of the Continental Congresses. The Assembly Room would be refurnished with as many "Declaration chairs" as Etting could find. He also persuaded the state to send back from Harrisburg a table and a silver ink stand believed to have been used in signing the Declaration of Independence. In the former Pennsylvania Supreme Court room, he began assembling portraits and artifacts relating to early Pennsylvania history, along with portraits of signers of the Constitution of 1787 and Benjamin West's painting of Penn signing the mythical treaty of peace with Indian chiefs at the Shackamaxon Treaty Elm, which a private owner had donated to the city.

A true crusader, Etting found no minutiae connected to his restoration of Independence Hall unworthy of his attention. But his obsessiveness and high-handedness in proclaiming his omniscience on how history should be presented to the public led to cascading attacks from the press and city officials. "A man named Etting," sputtered a city newspaper, "seems to have taken a lease of Independence Hall, and the appurtenances thereto, for his own special glory and benefit, and that of a few high-toned ladies,"[27] Newspapermen questioned Etting's democratic instincts when he banned reporters from the organizational meeting of the Board of Lady Managers, which he had commissioned. Etting and his friends, charged another newspaper, operated "by virtue of their own self-assumption," acting as if they were "not only the bonafide owners of Independence Hall but the original authors of the Declaration and the head and shoulders of the Centennial."[28] Democrats were outraged that the portrait of Andrew Jackson had been removed and stored in the cellar. Others believed that Lincoln and Grant disappeared because Etting, with family connections in the South, wanted to ruffle no feathers of southern visitors to the Centennial. Worse yet, Etting installed portraits of all the British monarchs from Charles II, who granted Penn his charter to the colony, to George III.

For Etting, press critics and city council enemies proved how municipal corruption and boss politics stood in the way of enshrining the Founding Fathers and restoring the historical memory of past greatness so badly needed by the nation. Rather than bending to his critics, he audaciously proposed that the city government turn over control of Independence Hall as a national shrine to the Historical Society and the Philosophical Society. This suggestion only confirmed what his detractors suspected—that he was "unfit to occupy the position from the rude manner in which he invariably dealt with citizens who [had] business relations with him."[29] Out of patience with Etting, both city councils dismissed him as chairman of the Independence Hall Restoration Committee ten days after the gala July Fourth ceremonies at Independence Hall. The committee itself was soon dissolved. It was a stinging rebuke by a new breed of city politicians determined to displace the representative of Philadelphia's old families and a leading light of the Historical Society.

Yet Etting's restored rooms of Independence Hall remained as he refurnished them for many years, as did the exhibits he mounted, British monarchs and all. Etting basked in accomplishments rendered in the name of a historical authenticity that raised goose bumps, he hoped, on the skin of visitors who entered the secular sanctuary. No doubt, he took satisfaction that Independence Hall now stood in most minds as the nation's greatest symbol of liberty and equality. However, Etting's dismissal must have given the Historical Society councillors pause about the perils of exercising a personal ownership of history, even in the name of promoting patriotism.

Despite its firing of Etting on July 14, 1876, Philadelphia's Select Council agreed heartily with him on one element of the celebration honoring the American Revolution on its hundredth birthday—the remembrance of Tom Paine. Etting had banished Bass Otis's painting of Paine from the Assembly Room, but he did install his likeness in the adjoining room dedicated to Pennsylvania history, where "miscellaneous" portraits were hung. However, the Select Council, when presented with a pedestal and bust of Paine donated by the National Liberal League in October 1876 for Independence Hall's National Museum, overruled the Common Council by a 27-4 vote. Pungent attacks on Paine's character, including charges of his treachery in attacking Washington's morals, convinced most council members that the author of *Common Sense* and the *Crisis Papers* was not a fit personage for public veneration. Not until 1905, after several attempts of the donors to reverse this decision, did the city accept the bust, but only after the inscription on the pedestal was changed to read that it had been presented by "the Patriots of America" rather than "the Liberals of America."[30]

Etting's falling out with city officials over restoring Independence Hall still left him as chairman of the Centennial's Department of History. This position invested him with even greater power to shape the historical memory of millions of visitors. As the letters Etting left to the Historical Society show, he tirelessly solicited artifacts, manuscripts, and ephemera from around the country. There will be "object teaching, extended History object teaching, and patriot object teaching too," he wrote, as he canvassed for items from here, there, and everywhere. He must have portraits of Samuel Adams and James Otis from Harvard University; he must have a replica of Roger Williams's old church in Salem, Massachusetts; he must have precious books and documents from the American Antiquarian Society. But here, too, Etting ran into a series of mishaps that left him frustrated and embittered. Many turned down his requests, wary of lending rare materials and not even sure that Philadelphia had the best claim to staging the Centennial Exposition. Moreover, the Department of History was established only on March 4, 1876—a mere two months before the gala opening. Nonetheless, objects began to arrive by April, only for Etting to find that the space allotted for his history displays were "unceremoniously" cut back so severely that the four thousand square feet he had been promised was now reduced to a mere forty square feet. John Sartain, Philadelphia's eminent lithographer and chairman of the Exposition's Bureau of Art, made this decision because the call for the display of artworks from all over the world was overwhelming. Etting bellowed to the head of the Exposition about this "enormity," and he was surely justified in claiming that it was now "utterly impossible to exhibit the collections promised or any collection in keeping with the character of the event." Precious relics and memorials of Washington, sputtered Etting, would be "lost . . . by the surroundings of inferior art."[31]

Etting flayed Sartain in a barrage of angry letters, but his bare-fisted method of fighting did not alter the outcome. In fact, Sartain and Etting were locked in a contest not only for space but also for how the past should be portrayed. Sartain wanted fine paintings—and he wanted them to include historical panoramas, such as the burning of the capital by the British in the War of 1812 and the battle of Bull Run. But Etting found this "entirely inconsistent with the fraternal and international good feeling intended to be fostered" by the Exposition; he had earlier decided that historical exhibits should show nothing after the War of 1812 for fear of risking the "censure of reviving battle scenes [and] recollections of our unfortunate civil war." Etting lost on both counts, and when Exposition director A. J. Goshorn backed up Sartain's arguments about the primacy of art over history, Etting quickly resigned his post.[32] However, Etting did get the Pennsylvania Academy of Fine Arts to display some of the colonial and revolutionary portraits he had gathered as "an addenda to and part of the National History Museum of Independence Hall."[33] But the vast majority of Centennial visitors spent their time in Fairmount Park, not at the Broad Street building of the Pennsylvania Academy.

One last chance to mold the public's memory of Philadelphia's past lay in the possibility of history exhibits for the Pennsylvania Educational Hall. But the members of the Pennsylvania Board of Centennial Managers were soon as frustrated as Etting. Because the state legislature did not provide "the requisite means to provide a collective representation of the history, resources, and capabilities of the state," they were hopelessly hamstrung. "'Where are your exhibits?' was frequently asked at the Pennsylvania Building," the board later divulged, in its two-volume report. Other state buildings—West Virginia, Kansas, and Colorado, for example—"were admirable schools wherein to study the history and resources of those States." Philadelphia repositories "would cheerfully have yielded rich and rare contributions" such as "historic paintings; portraits of the Colonial and State Governors, . . . and other distinguished personages of the past; specimens of ancient fabrics and handiwork; ancestral relics; Indian curiosities; and quaint old records and manuscripts, with which our public archives abound."[34] But weeks went by and the opening day approached; "the appropriation came too late," reported the Pennsylvania Board of Managers, "to prepare and organize a collection." So visitors thronging the Pennsylvania Building found aisles filled with mining, metallurgy, manufacturing, agricultural, and horticultural exhibits—almost all mounted by private companies angling for new customers. Some art was displayed, and various schools and colleges mounted exhibits. About as close as the Historical Society came toward using history to add "new strength to the bonds which unite the United States" was to lend its old Ephrata press to a Philadelphia manufacturer of printing presses who wanted to display it to show the marvels of modern presses.

The efforts of the Historical Society to ensure that Washington and his era would not slip away in the public memory mirrored Etting's upper-class attitudes of the day, but the Historical Society avoided the contention sparked by Etting's brusque manner and his disdain for city officials. For the public, the Historical Society put one of its members, the young, spell-binding Henry Armitt Brown, on the speakers' circuit with a new style of oratory "especially fit for the centennial season—that of descriptive historical narration as a basis for appeals to patriotism."[35] Brown stressed the heroic, especially stories about the exploits and intellectual gifts of the fabled leaders of the Revolution, though recapturing little of the multifarious experience and the contending agendas of different groups of Americans at the time. For a more select audience, the society published a series of biographical sketches of the signers of the Declaration of Independence in its new publication, *Pennsylvania Magazine of History and Biography*, which first appeared in 1877. Along with these were many sketches of Continental officers and militia generals. Always the focus was on the great man, not the common man, and hardly ever on women of any social position. Interspersed were Revolutionary War diaries acquired by the Historical Society and church records that were primarily of genealogical interest at the time but, much later, part of the stuff of social history.

The World's Workshop

When their months-long birthday party was over, most Philadelphians could feel proud of their city and their newly acquired cosmopolitanism, although they could hardly be complacent in an era when the growth of industry, swelling immigration, and the rise of conflict between capital and labor presented new problems. Imagining the colonial and revolutionary past in heroic hues might inspire patriotism, but that by itself provided no specific way to cope with current problems or push forward into uncharted waters. "Safe and sound, prosperous and potbellied, this was the image Philadelphia liked to present," it has been said of this era. The reality was entirely different, however, for the self-image promoted by the affluent had little to do with the seething life of new immigrants, old working-class families, and southern blacks moving north (Figure 124).[36]

Beneath the buoyant spirit of the Centennial Exposition churned a city of industrial producers and consumers. Visitors walking from the fairgrounds would have found no single, unified Philadelphia but a conglomeration of neighborhoods, reaching out from the old commercial downtown to the new streetcar and railroad suburbs. By the 1880s, waves of new immigrants—mostly from eastern and southern Europe rather than from England, Ireland, and Germany—were reconfiguring old neighborhoods and creating new ones. A city whose immigrants had been predominantly northern European Christians became home by 1905 to 100,000 Jews, two-thirds of them from Russia. The tide of Jewish immigrants changed the character of the city's Jewish population. The small German Jewish contingent of pre-Civil War days, by now fully incorporated into the city's business and cultural life, kept their distance from the new arrivals. By 1895, forty-five synagogues had sprung up south of Spruce Street, many of them established in formerly Protestant churches.[37] Near the teeming Jewish neighborhoods, Italian immigrants, mostly from southern Italy and Sicily, learned the ways of America. Their num-

FIGURE 124. *Scene in St. Mary St., South Philadelphia*, woodcut, 1875, in Edward Strahan, *A Century After: Picturesque Glimpses of Philadelphia and Pennsylvania*, LCP. Though Strahan was a booster in his *Picturesque Glimpses*, published for Centennial Exposition visitors, he included candid descriptions of the "phases of social life" where "all that the words squalor, filth, misery, and degradation can convey" could be found in Philadelphia. The text accompanying this scene described "bad young darkeys chucking bad young white girls under the chin (white girls having pitchers of beer); darkeys in the door, on the cellar-door, on the coal-box, under the lamp-post, around the corner, laughing, whooping, cursing, blaspheming; darkeys, darkeys everywhere."

FIGURE 125. *616 Pemberton Street*, photograph, c. 1900, Urban Archives, Temple University. This photograph of four dilapidated houses behind an old frame building in South Philadelphia shows the crowded, debris-filled conditions typical of immigrant neighborhoods at the turn of the twentieth century. The Progressive reformers studying the city's immigrant and blue-collar neighborhoods used photographs as an important weapon in their fight to improve living conditions for the poor while instilling in them American middle-class values.

ber had reached nearly 80,000 by 1910, and no construction site in the city was without Italian masons, bricklayers, and laborers. Smaller groups of Hungarians, Poles, Greeks, and Chinese added to the city's linguistic and ethnic diversity (Figure 125).

Many of the Jewish and Italian immigrants mingled closely with Philadelphia's black citizens, who since the early nineteenth century had huddled in the neighborhoods in Southwark and farther west in what became the Seventh Ward. More than sixty-two thousand African Americans lived in Philadelphia by 1900—the largest number in any northern city. Three years earlier, according to the survey by the young sociologist W. E. B. Du Bois, Philadelphia's black community had fifty-five churches, several hundred mutual aid associations, and six newspapers or church publications.

Old and new black Philadelphians interacted daily with newcomers who spoke different languages and worshiped differently. It was not unusual to find equal numbers of black and Jewish students in the schools around Lombard Street in the 1890s. But on work sites, it was a different matter. Deeply ingrained attitudes among white Philadelphians kept most blacks out of the better-paying industrial and municipal jobs, confining the majority to manual and domestic labor. Nonetheless, a black middle class, as well as a large number of black artisans, pursued careers within the black community. Occasionally, the color line was broken, as when Philadelphia's Frederick W. Taylor, the famous student of the scientific management of labor, hired two hundred African Americans to work with his white steelmakers at Midvale Steel Company in 1886, or when John Wanamaker promoted one of his black postal employees to run the city's second-largest postal substation, which operated out of Philadelphia's greatest emporium.[38]

In late nineteenth-century Philadelphia, awash with new immigrants, public schools struggled to teach "American ways." African Americans, radical women, resolute reformers, and immigrants themselves could take little comfort in what their children learned from history textbooks. Textbooks applauded the end of slavery but generally portrayed freed African Americans as inherently uncivilized and therefore incapable of earning an equal status with whites. As for the equality of the sexes in law or women's entitlement to economic and social advancement, such an idea was "invisible in nineteenth-century American schoolbooks," where the ideal woman, as in earlier periods, "has not interests or ambitions of her own" and "spends her life in happy submission to the will of others."[39] The radical Paine, because he attacked Christianity, became a villain of the revolutionary era, second only to the traitorous Benedict Arnold.

Like all immigrants in all ages and places, the newcomers imbibed many of the lessons dispensed from above, for often this was the way to get ahead in a new land. Yet in their neighborhoods and at home, the immigrants read ethnic newspapers, attended ethnic churches, served their traditional cuisine, and gathered to feast, dance, and banter on holidays particular to their group. "A *mensch* in the street, but a Jew at home" went the common expression. The idea of a melting pot in which ethnic traditions and Old World ways would be boiled out or blended was always more a metaphor than a reality, and by the early twentieth century the idea itself was attacked by those who saw that one of America's greatest assets was the distinctiveness of each of the many pieces in its cultural mosaic.

Philadelphia's late nineteenth-century workshops, foundries, factories, and mills turned out a staggering array of manufactured goods—more than any other American city. Iron and steel and textiles continued to underpin the local economy. Giant industrial firms such as Baldwin Locomotive, which manufactured steam locomotives for the nation's railroads and for Mexico, Australia, Russia, Palestine, Japan, Brazil, and African nations as well, employed thousands of skilled workers. In the new age of iron ships, Cramp and Sons Shipyards supplied the world with ships, from merchant ships to J. P. Morgan's regal yacht *Corsair* to warships such as the U.S.S. *Maine* (and warships for Turkey, Russia, and Japan as well). Stetson hats, Disston saws, and textiles of all sorts, from elaborate rugs to hosiery, reached markets worldwide.[40]

Yet the majority of Philadelphians still worked in small factories and shops or even in their homes. The city's promoters emphasized the heavy industry that made Philadelphia seem like the German Ruhr or English Midlands of America. But the economic strength of the city actually lay in the large variety of its specialty firms. As late as 1900, customized foundry work, saddle and harness making, cigar rolling, and upholstered furniture were still done mainly in small shops with only a few workers.[41]

The late nineteenth and early twentieth centuries marked the era of greatest industrial strife in the nation's history, and Philadelphia saw its share, though trade unionism made less headway than in many other centers of industry. The Knights of Labor attracted immigrant cigar makers, brewers, and trolley-car conductors in the 1880s, and socialist unions recruited thousands of textile and garment workers, especially immigrants from eastern Europe. In 1895, street railway workers paralyzed the city at the height of the Christmas season during a week-long strike that turned violent. They won a small wage increase but, more important, the limitation of the working day to twelve hours. Far larger was the huge textile strike of 1903, when more than 100,000 workers, demanding a fifty-five-hour week, shut down the industry locally. More than 10,000 of the textile workers were children, many only ten years old. Seventy-eight-year-old Mary Harris Jones ("Mother Jones") made national headlines in July 1903, when she marched 125 miles with a band of impoverished children from the textile mills of Kensington all the way to the lawn of President Theodore Roosevelt's mansion in Oyster Bay, Long Island, to demand support for laws prohibiting child labor.[42]

One of the reasons labor militancy never reached the pitch in Philadelphia that roiled other industrial cities was the unusual availability of modestly priced row houses. Its population burgeoning and its industry thriving, workers sought housing within walking distance of their jobs, and Philadelphia became a city of loosely connected factory-based urban villages. Kensington, Manayunk, Frankford, Nicetown, Tacony, and dozens of other communities—each with its own markets, shops, business district, and flavorful identity—contained thousands of row houses. A "model Philadelphia house," somewhat upgraded from what was within the range of most workers, made an appearance at Chicago's Columbian Exposition in 1893.

Weaving the city together by the late nineteenth century were the street railways, with horse-car lines giving way to cable cars in the 1880s and then, beginning in 1892, to electric trolleys. The network of street railway lines—264 miles of them by 1880—allowed more and more workers to buy modest row houses away from factory sites and commute to work. And nothing promoted the idea of social mobility better than the streetcar lines, because their two most important entrepreneurs, Peter Arrell Brown Widener and William Lukens Elkins, had started out, respectively, as a butcher boy in a meat shop and a clerk in a grocery store. Between them, Widener and Elkins bought up dozens of the small traction companies that had popped up after the Civil War and, by the 1880s, had consolidated and extended them into the immensely profitable Philadelphia Rapid Transit Company.

The streetcars also took people from their row house neighborhoods in two directions: into center city to shop at new consumer emporiums such as the palatial John Wanamaker's, where nearly anything could be purchased and always in the most fashionable style; and outward to the new amusement and baseball parks, built on the periphery to encourage real estate development but only viable because of the shorter work weeks and enhanced living wages that gave ordinary city dwellers the leisure time and wherewithal to go to them.[43]

Modern industrialization required a new type of citizen who worked differently, thought differently, and lived differently from the urban dwellers of pre-Civil War days. Punctuality and diligence become new virtues taught in the home, in the schools, and on the playgrounds. Employers stressed the importance of time saving and being on time, and employees, taking the lessons to heart, countered with demands for overtime, time and a half, and free time. Time became a commodity to be spent, saved, or wasted in an era when carefully regulated workdays and work weeks gave rise to the idea of the weekend, vacations, leisure time, and off-the-workplace activities.

Of course, leisure time was most available to the upper class, who beginning in the 1880s built baronial estates featuring craggy Victorian castles of stone to the west and northwest of the city. They used their leisure and money to establish clubs, especially for cricket, lawn tennis, yachting, and golf; to engage in philanthropic enterprises; and to cultivate the arts. Two of today's most important institutions owe their rise to the philanthropists' largesse in the late nineteenth century. The Philadelphia Museum, later the Philadelphia Museum of Art, was founded in 1877 and by the end of the century had become a distinguished institution. Huge bequests from William Pepper, one of the city's wealthiest lawyers, and the transit mogul Peter Widener launched the Free Library of Philadelphia in 1891. This provided a public library filled with immigrant newspapers, magazines, children's books, and popular novels—the very materials that the privately controlled Library Company mostly stayed away from after Rush's bequest of 1869. In the last third of the nineteenth century, the Library Company built its specialized collections, of tremendous value to historians and literary scholars, from harvests gathered by a generation of book collector and antiquarian benefactors. But for the immigrants pouring into the city, the Library Company had little to offer. The Free Library, established much later than the great public libraries in New York, Baltimore, and Boston, finally began to fill a much-needed gap. Gathering momentum in the twentieth century, it also became an important repository of historical materials that disclosed the city's early history, becoming a junior partner of the Historical Society, Philosophical Society, and Library Company in holdings of prints, photographs, pamphlets, ephemera, and rare books. Especially in collecting colonial-period furniture, silver, fabrics, ceramics, and paintings, the Art Museum became a treasure house for researchers trying to recapture the material culture of the city's first century, or at least life as it was lived at the top and upper middle echelons.

Partly as a result of their largesse and partly because everywhere in the nation the rise of heavy industry created a new demand for highly skilled engineers, managers, scientists, and lawyers, the era after the Centennial Exposition of 1876 witnessed the rapid development of a modern system of higher education. The University of Pennsylvania, still a small and parochial academy at the end of the Civil War, moved to West Philadelphia in 1872. Under the leadership of Charles J. Stillé, the descendant of a Swedish immigrant and president of the Historical Society from 1892 to 1899, and William Pepper, a descendant of a German immigrant, the university grew into a distinguished institution with notable professional schools of law and medicine. In the western and southwestern suburbs arose Bryn Mawr, Haverford, and Swarthmore, all Quaker institutions that became strongholds of social reformers.[44]

Meanwhile, the golden-tongued Baptist evangelist Russell H. Conwell converted a fortune made on a single lecture—his "Acres of Diamonds" speech that made money-making a holy quest—into a showpiece "workingman's university." Chartered in 1888, Temple University opened the doors of higher education in the decades that followed to those who would never have been able to afford the University of Pennsylvania. Also designed for the children of the working class—and for both sexes—was Drexel Institute. Founded in 1892 by financier Anthony J. Drexel, it was committed to technical education and hence partook of the same spirit, originating with Benjamin Franklin, that led to the creation of the Franklin Institute many years before.

Commemorating Penn

While the Centennial Exposition of 1876 fed the pride of Americans in their technological ingenuity and industrial progress, and while its foreign exhibits broadened the masses' appreciation of people from distant cultures, it also led to a burst of organizational talent directed at cultivating the public memory of Philadelphia's past. In part, this was a local application of the broader "colonial revival" that swept the country in the late nineteenth century. In part it was the coincidence of a number of signal dates that provided opportunities for commemoration, pageantry, monument building, oration, and history-book publishing. Within little more than a decade, Philadelphians would be treated to lavish celebrations of the one hundredth anniversary of the Valley Forge encampment (1878), the bicentennial of the founding of Pennsylvania (1882), the bicentennial of German arrival (1883), and the centennial of the writing of the Constitution (1887).

FRANK LESLIE'S
ILLUSTRATED
NEWSPAPER

Entered according to the Act of Congress, in the year 1878, by Frank Leslie, in the Office of the Librarian of Congress at Washington.

No. 1,188—Vol. XLVI.] NEW YORK, JULY 6, 1878. [Price 10 Cents. $4.00 Yearly. 13 Weeks, $1.00.

EXERCISES IN THE HUGE TENT.

THE MILITARY HEADQUARTERS.

REVIEW OF THE MILITARY ORGANIZATIONS BY MAJOR-GENERAL W. S. HANCOCK, U. S. A.

PENNSYLVANIA.—CELEBRATION OF THE ONE HUNDREDTH ANNIVERSARY OF THE EVACUATION OF VALLEY FORGE, JUNE 19TH.

FIGURE 126. Front page of *Frank Leslie's Illustrated Newspaper*, July 6, 1878, LCP. Though women were the main organizers of the Valley Forge celebration, only men appeared on the platform from which the Historical Society of Pennsylvania's Henry Armitt Brown gave the oration to the assembled masses under the canvas. Reviewing the military grand display was Major General Winfield S. Hancock, the Civil War hero at Gettysburg's Cemetery Ridge.

Forging ahead of all other cultural institutions in the city in endeavoring to refurbish public memory, the Historical Society provided leadership and historical materials for several of these efforts. But the Historical Society could not gain a monopoly on the memory of Philadelphia's history. In the background, as had been the case in earlier eras, subaltern parts of Philadelphia's diverse population presented counter-narratives of their own and held their own commemorations to preserve the memory of still largely unrecognized heroes and hidden chapters of the city's history. And in the monstrous 1882 bicentennial celebration marking Penn's arrival, the Historical Society's putative role was eclipsed by a diverse group whose attempts to commercialize the past with carnivalesque presentations showed how difficult it was to maintain a stable, unitary memory of the past.

In the post-Centennial years, the councillors of the Historical Society acquired more clout than ever before to shape the educational and cultural efflorescence of the city. The councillors were eminent clubmen, and their collecting tastes reflected it. There was not much about the new immigrants, the new row house neighborhoods, the swelling black population, the new rhythms of labor, or the popular culture of their city that interested them. If anything, the new waves of migrants and immigrants, the intense confrontations between labor and capital in the 1870s and 1880s, the new assertiveness of women's suffrage reformers, the rise of newly monied men (many of them immigrants)—indeed, the entire character of the new industrial order—deepened their conviction that the Historical Society's greatest mission was to celebrate the past, to use history to resist change and provide a sheet anchor for political and social stability. Probably never in Philadelphia's history has one of its cultural institutions tried harder to shape historical consciousness than did the Historical Society in the last quarter of the nineteenth century.

Little more than a year after the closing of the Centennial Exposition on November 10, 1876, a group of patriotic and historically minded ladies from Philadelphia and its suburbs gathered to form the Centennial and Memorial Association of Valley Forge to enshrine Washington's winter headquarters during the dark days of the Revolution (Figure 126). A small semi-centenary celebration had been held in June 1828, but now the patriotic women devised much more ambitious plans.[45] Purchasing the old stone farmhouse that a local mill owner had rented to Washington, along with the surrounding property, the women created a memorial park and planned a commemoration for June 1878. About 30,000 people competed for space in a gigantic tent on a hot summer day, where they listened to orations and military music and then watched Civil War veterans reenact the encampment of Washington's army, which had been spruced up and whipped into shape by the dour Baron von Steuben. Then the reenactors broke camp to march off to pursue the British withdrawing from Philadelphia. Though the mock execution of John Smith by Powhatan and his rescue by the nubile Pocahontas had been reenacted four times a day at the Great Central Fair in 1864, thrilling audiences who watched faux Indians "dancing and screaming in anticipation of his [Smith's] fate," the Valley Forge historical enactment was the first outdoor mass scene seen by Philadelphians. It became an inspiration for historical enactments to follow.

It is likely that the success of the Valley Forge reenactment animated the organizers of the much more elaborate bicentennial of Philadelphia's founding in 1882. If the singular focus on George Washington at the Centennial Exposition seemed to have diverted attention from Philadelphia's founder, the conveners of the Bi-Centennial Association intended to make up for this, at least in principle. But their interests were actually less about using the past as a guide for the future than about turning history into a carnival that would attract a million visitors and provide a bonanza for downtown businesses. Philadelphia had not celebrated its centennial in 1782, but now it did so ebulliently, with historical pageantry that displeased many yet quickly spawned costume balls and colonial teas sponsored by fast-growing Protestant white patriotic and hereditary societies.

Though the Historical Society might logically have organized the William Penn bicentennial, it was the leaders of the Masonic Temple, working with publishers and corporate leaders, who formed the Bi-Centennial Association. The *Keystone*, the temple's weekly newspaper, publicized the effort most fully. None of the Historical Society's councillors and officers were involved, and the minutes of its council are entirely silent on the gala six-day festivities. Quakers were also as uninvolved as the Historical Society.

What the Masons had in mind was apparent months before the October Penn festivities. Preparing for the 150th anniversary of Freemasonry in Pennsylvania in June 1882, planned as a warmup celebration for the week-long Penn festivities, the Masons affirmed that "We live in an era of celebrations. . . . Men delight to revive the past . . . to pay honor to their founders. . . . It brings before us the great men of the past, who are, to the majority of persons, mere shadows. . . . When we honor the founders, when we contemplate their genius and study their work, we drink at the fountain's source. . . . We associate with the giants of early days. The chasm of time is spanned, the present and past are linked together, the continuity of history is established."[46]

This stirring call in May 1882 for cultivating historical memory of a past with untarnished heroes slipped quickly away as the Mason-led Bi-Centennial Association went into feverish planning. After its first few meetings, the association decided "that several days should be given up to parades, entertainments, meetings, and other forms of popular demonstration." In this spirit, the association appointed a general manager, Alexander P. Colesberry, a lawyer who began to arrange bicycle races, a Schuylkill River regatta, and other carnival events. "How should a people celebrate their Bi-Centennial?" asked the Masons' newspaper, a month before the elaborate Penn festivities were scheduled to begin. "Mainly, we say, with processions and parades. . . . A state anniversary is a people's anniversary, and we should study to please the people." With these bows to Philadelphia's highly diverse people, the Masons promised to deliver "great pageants . . . [that] all can enjoy—street parades, exhibiting the development of our industries, our progress in the arts, living and moving historical pictures, closing with a muster of the people's military."[47]

The "living and moving historical pictures" arranged by the Bi-Centennial Association, as it turned out, included twenty-seven parade floats imported from that year's

New Orleans Mardi Gras. The people would see "Illustrious Women Rulers of World History" (including Zenobia, Sappho, Cleopatra, Queen Elizabeth, Joan of Arc, and Napoleon's beautiful hapless Empress Josephine) and a series of exotic tableaux portraying "The Ramayana—Ancient Hindu Epic of the East." To be sure, they would also see ten floats depicting scenes from Pennsylvania history, such as Penn's mythical treaty meeting with the Indians and the last delivery of beaver skins, the battles at Bushy Run and Germantown, and Washington's encampment at Valley Forge. But in the planning of the Bi-Centennial Association, historical consciousness of Philadelphia's founding was becoming a footnote to the commercialization of chapters of history that had nothing to do with Penn, the Quakers, or the city's first century.

The monster celebration began on Sunday, October 22, a day set aside for special church services remembering Penn and the city's founders. Though the city was bedecked more gaily than for the Centennial Exposition six years before, signs of discord appeared even in the churches. People of "different temperaments and temperance views," reported *Harper's Weekly*, were reading history differently. One side, inspired by a clergyman who gave a sermon in "the shadow of the 'treaty elm'" on the first day of the festival, objected to any celebration of Penn, "bicentennially or otherwise," because the Quaker proprietor, it was claimed, was the first colonist in the new colony of Pennsylvania "to undermine the morality of the Indian by giving him rum." Should Penn and the Quakers be memorialized for treaties where the colony's founder obtained grants for the land on which Philadelphia and its outlying regions were located if history proved they had driven "a shrewd bargain after he had muddled the heads" of Indian chiefs?[48]

The pageantry began the next day, October 23, at Chester, downriver from the city. Costumed Quakers, Swedes, and Indians (from the Chester Dramatic Association) took their places as a vast crowd assembled to witness the landing of Penn and his party from the *Welcome*. After Indian chief "Bear's Meat" greeted Penn, the costumed Lenape chief, Tamanend, welcomed "the great white chief" ashore. In an invented scene resembling Montezuma's vision of Cortes's arrival in Mexico, Tamanend told Penn he had had a vision many summers ago. "He dreamed he saw these hills and valleys covered with white man, many as the sand on the shore, but he saw no Lenape. At first his heart was hot within him. Then it became as the heart of a little child. It was the will of the Manitou. The Lenape will go back to their homes near the setting sun when that time comes. The stranger is welcome. It is the wind of the Manitou that has blown his canoe. He is welcome. It is enough."[49]

Few in the audience likely gave much thought to this concocted story of historical inevitability, in which Native Americans believed that a cosmic plan was at work impelling them westward; most probably saw what the *New York Times* reported as "a curious jumble of history, realism, and beer," with the Indians "taken bodily from Cooper's novels." Expressing skepticism about presenting historical dramas "in the public street," the *Times* observed, "It is easy enough to dress up a man so that he may bear some resemblance to the portraits of William Penn, but it is another thing to exhibit him to the public and to induce people to accept him as a faithful representative of the great Quaker."[50] The *Times*

FIGURE 127. William Penn's arrival on the *Welcome*, *Harper's Weekly*, November 4, 1882, LCP. The illustrator depicted William Penn alighting from the *Welcome* while his Quaker friends get ready to disembark and sailors in jailbird outfits secure the lines. In something of a public relations coup, the Penn bicentennial organizers also got front-page coverage in *Frank Leslie's Illustrated Newspaper*, showing the crowd breaking through the police lines as dignitaries stood ready to welcome the Penn reenactor in a broad-brimmed Quaker hat.

reporter may have been unduly cynical in arguing that "an anachronism in an omnibus on the balcony of a hotel cannot command the approval of the unimaginative person" and that the impersonator of William Penn would be lucky if he left the commemorative festivities "without the painful recollection that he has been jeered at and hooted." But he may also have been alluding to the fact that Penn had been played by a twenty-one-year-old who arrived at the Chester reenactment of Penn's landing so plied with "the firewater of the pale-face" that "he could only fall, with a vacuous smile, upon the neck of the nearest savage, and utter incoherent communications in his ear."[51]

Sober or not, a procession following the ceremony for Penn's landing featured waves of parading firemen, members of beneficial and temperance societies and the Improved Order of Red Men (a patriotic society that had been appropriating history for two generations), Civil War veterans, and unionized tradesmen. Back in Philadelphia, German singing societies staged a torchlight parade through the city. At midnight the Liberty Bell struck two hundred times.

On Tuesday, October 23, as nearly one million visitors jammed the city, the latter-day Penn sailed up the Delaware on a replica of the *Welcome,* manned by "gaudily-uniformed British officers," thus presenting an entirely fabricated version of a late seventeenth-century merchantman's crew. Discordant notes were already being observed in the press: having Penn stand in the stern sheets with hat in hand—"a plain inconsistency since no Quaker even unbonnets except to God"; or the necessity of a last-minute construction of a miniature Blue Anchor tavern, where Penn was said to have had his first lunch because two contemporary tavern keepers, each of whom claimed to own the authentic Blue Anchor Tavern, had fought so nastily that the celebration leaders gave up on using a real building. Penn's "Unquakerlike outfit" and the suits of fifty other faux Quakers dressed up as "perfect Cavaliers" were also criticized, though the costume maker, A. R. Van Horn, father of the Penn impersonator, assured the press that Penn's "gorgeous suit" festooned with bronzed silver and the outfits of the other Quakers "were strictly historical," because seventeenth-century Friends wanted to display their high rank "in order to avoid being mistaken for persons of the lower classes."[52]

Such caviling paled by comparison to the debacle at the landing of Penn in Philadelphia on the morning of October 23. Awaiting the arrival of the *Welcome* at the Dock Street wharf were the costumed Lasse Cock, the Swede who served as interpreter in 1682; other Swedes, Dutch, and Quakers; and a delegation of Indian chiefs. In the streets thousands of spectators waited impatiently for the *Welcome* to heave into view. Caught in fog shrouding the Delaware River, the converted Danish boat was long overdue as the police struggled to hold back the massive crowd from the wharfside, where the welcoming party waited. When Penn finally stepped ashore (Figure 127), reported the *Press*, masses of people broke through the police cables "as though fired through a catapult." Trying to contain the melee, the police engaged in "a fierce battle with the heaving mob, and clubs were frequently used on the heads of the more turbulent." Through it all, "Iquation," the chief of the Narragansetts (inexplicably hundreds of miles south of his home) tried valiantly to accept Penn's promise of peace and good will. But the mob boiled up into "a pandemonium of exclamations of pain and anger as the helpless people were hurled from wave to wave of the surging throng and thrown back like bagatelles." Not to be denied, the mob overran the seven wigwams erected at Second and Dock Streets and stamped out the brightly burning council fires. "The wigwams went down like wisps of straw and the Indian village was quickly overrun with a writhing mass of humanity," lamented the *Press*. The fake Indians, "jostled about with rude violence," reacted "by turning on the crowd with their wooden tomahawks." Even the Quaker impersonators "forgot they were men of peace and likewise turned back the torrent of humanity."[53]

The "harsh and uproarious welcome," the *Public Ledger* noted, "entirely demoralized those in charge of the show." For a *Harper's Weekly* reporter, the Philadelphians seemed "to be moved rather by the desire to celebrate than to celebrate any particular thing." Historical Society leaders apparently agreed. The reenactment of Penn's landing at Chester and the disaster the next day in Philadelphia, where "weak women were crushed, children were trampled upon, and only by a miracle was loss of life averted," must have convinced them that they had made the right decision to "decline to countenance the festivities upon which Philadelphia has just lavished itself."[54] They were convinced that

WILLIAM PENN RECEIVING THE CHARTER FROM CHARLES II.
OFFICIAL PROGRAMME
— OF THE —
BI-CENTENNIAL CELEBRATION
— of the —
FOUNDING
with
an historical
sketch and guide
to Philadelphia.
Published by authority
of the
Bi-Centennial
Association

FIGURE 128. Official Program, Penn Bi-Centennial Commemoration, LCP. The Penn Bicentennial Association published 40,000 copies of the souvenir program shown here. The program included sketches of each of the thirty-seven tableaux in the grand procession on the evening of October 26. *Harper's Weekly* reported that the procession was "alleged to have been twelve miles or five hours long." The program featured a full-page view of the Masonic Temple. Included also were smaller photographs of the Union League, Library Company, and Mercantile Library but not of the Historical Society.

Penn had landed in Philadelphia not on October 24 but on November 8; this technicality aside, they were disgusted with the carnivalesque plans for rendering history. Withdrawing from the entire affair, Historical Society members scheduled a decorous dinner on November 8, during which they heard the lecture "Penn, Franklin, and Pennsylvania in Their Relation to Our Form of Government." Quakers contented themselves simply by publishing a memorial volume, *Passages from the Life and Writing of William Penn*.

Despite the morning's havoc, the Bi-Centennial Association leaders regrouped for the massive afternoon procession. The fake Indians "soon recovered their spirits" and "resumed their shouting and yelling." The faux Dutch and Swedes astonished the crowd by using earthy English to exclaim on "their rough reception on Dock Street."[55] Twenty thousand men marched in the parade, which took about four hours to pass a given checkpoint. Quaker pacifism was set aside as federal and state military units, along with plenty of Civil War regiments, thrilled the crowd. Eighty-five painted and feathered non-Indian men from the Improved Order of Red Men danced along the parade route in the third division, along with fifty faux "Quakers" impersonated by members of the Knights of the Golden Eagle. In the fourth division, some 4,000-5,000 additional "Indians" with white skins pranced along with floats depicting "curious and picturesque tableaux of life in the forests prior to the advent of the whites."[56] Then came 4,500 entirely sober members of the Catholic Total Abstinence societies. Fireworks that night in Fairmount Park were cut short when an exploding shell killed six people and injured many others.

For those still ready for more entertainment, October 26 was Trades Day, given over to another parade of 20,000 marchers, mostly workingmen from factories, shops, and mills. But more entertaining was the nighttime "mystic pageant," where a reported 150,000 onlookers gaped at a bewildering program of thirty-seven "historical and mythical tableaux" illuminated by calcium and hydrocarbon lights (Figure 128). It is very difficult, perhaps impossible, to measure the impress of such historical presentations on the public mind. But the *Press* called it "a brilliant pageant" and "a scene never to be forgotten." Certainly, the world's "illustrious women" and the tableaux from the *Ramayana*—"Valmiki and Brahma," "The Nuptials," "The Crime," "The Abduction," "Kabhanda," "The Coronation," "The Purification," and "The Descent"—were visually more exciting than the ten Pennsylvania history floats. Some noted that the Battle of Bushy Run showed Indians as "murderous looking wretches [wearing] all sorts of feathers and other adornments" with "human scalps at the belt of the warriors." As for the long history of African Americans in the city, there was only one float, cryptically titled "Pennsylvania—A Re-united Country," which showed a slave at the feet of the Goddess of Liberty, casting off broken shackles.

The final day of the extravaganza, October 27, was designated Military Day, and here the motives of the organizers were clear: to preserve the memory of blood sacrifices and express gratitude for the war heroes who preserved the Union. Fifteen thousand men, about half of them Grand Army of the Republic (GAR) members, marched through a pouring rain, led by Civil War major general and former governor John F. Hartranft. Behind them marched the Masonic Knights Templar; the Improved Order of Red Men; the Knights of the Golden Eagle; Irish, Welsh, Scottish, German, and other ethnic societies; and temperance societies. All were eager participants in the parades and pageantry, many dressing up as Indians and Quakers. Missing were Philadelphia's women suffragists and African Americans. Later, fifteen hundred girls from local schools provided the largest vocal concert ever heard in the city. Prizes were awarded to the Welsh singers.

Despite debate and acrimony, the Masons congratulated themselves for their key role in staging the Penn bicentennial: "From the origin of the movement to its close we were intimately connected with it, actively and constantly engaged in popularizing it, and in devising and developing such plans as should . . . give delight to the mass of our citizens." Philadelphia journalists were satisfied that the name of William Penn, "almost forgotten by the commonwealth which he had founded," was now "securely fixed in the hearts of the teeming population." To the organizers, the gigantic turnout was proof that the city, two hundred years after its founding, was "sound, prosperous, and progressive," with all of its people enjoying "the substantial comforts and happiness . . . never surpassed by any other city of which history makes record."[57]

If Historical Society and Library Company leaders deplored the cheap commercialism of the Penn bicentennial, they could at least take comfort in the interest it raised in rescuing the forlorn and dilapidated Laetitia Penn House. Recent research has proved that Penn never lived there; moreover, the house was not built until about 1713, twelve years after Penn left Philadelphia, never to return.[58] But as part of the post-Civil War effort to heal war wounds by looking backward to an era now depicted as glorious and unified, the salvaging of the Laetitia Penn House was an important moment. Dismantled timber by timber and brick by brick, it was reconstructed and refurbished as a house museum in Fairmount Park (Figure 129).

However, even as this rescue mission went forward, preservationists lost another battle. The London Coffee House, scene of so many commercial transactions and revolutionary meetings (and the site of slave sales in Philadelphia for many decades), had stood at the corner of Front and Market Streets since 1702, on land purchased from Laetitia Penn. From 1813 to 1883, the Ulrich brothers and their descendants sold tobacco, pipes, cigars, and snuff, at retail and wholesale, from the premises (Figure 130). But once the Ulrichs decided to sell the property, its prime commercial location put the cost of conserving it far beyond the means of the preservationists. It fell to wrecking crews in 1883, simultaneous with the salvaging of the Laetitia Penn House, one block away.

Multiple Histories

Whether a raised historical consciousness could unify Philadelphians through a common appreciation of their ancestors' attempts to build a city of brotherly love was debatable, but it was unarguable that the massive commemorations brought money into the city. The Masons had proved this in 1882. Twelve months later, Philadelphia's citizens of Ger-

FIGURE 129. Laetitia Penn House in Fairmount Park, Athenaeum. Reclaiming the Laetitia Penn house in 1883 was an important victory for preservationists. It became an icon, displayed on postcards, newspaper carriers' Christmas greetings to customers, and memorabilia. Today the house is shuttered, closed to the public, and sits in lonely disrepair opposite the Philadelphia Zoo.

man extraction held their own bicentennial, marking the arrival in 1683 of Daniel Pastorius and his band of followers from Crefeld, Germany. But this affair was more high-toned; its sober German organizers eschewed the kind of fictitious reenactments and carnivalesque tableaux of the previous year. The festivities opened on Saturday night, October 6, with a vocal and instrumental concert of German selections at the Academy of Music, while commemorative services were held at the city's Jewish synagogues. Worshipers thronged German churches of all denominations on Sunday morning. Monday was the culminating day of the jubilee, with a Broad Street procession that included tableaux representing Germania, German immigrant farmers and artisans surrounding William Penn, freedom of the press featuring John Peter Zenger, and the Emancipation of the Slaves, with a special bow to the four Germantown residents protesting slavery in 1684. Ten thousand men of the German singing societies; GAR regiments; the Bavarian Society; and tradesmen—bakers dispensing freshly baked bread from a mounted oven, brewers providing a steady stream of free beer, butchers making sandwiches passed out to the celebrants, blacksmiths hammering iron in their wagons, and many others—paraded up Broad Street. This commemoration much more to its liking, the Historical Society became involved, with Samuel Pennypacker, a councillor soon to be vice president, giving one of the orations that compared the careers of William Penn and Daniel Pastorius.

FIGURE 130. James E. McClees, *Old London Coffee-House*, salt print, 1858, LCP. For John F. Watson, John Jay Smith, John McAllister, Jr., and other collectors, Philadelphia's ancient buildings refreshed their mental connection to a vanishing past, allowing them, as Watson put it in a letter to McAllister, to "evoke spirits . . . from the vasty deep of olden time."

If Germans could celebrate their history in 1883, African Americans had reason to hold commemorations in the following year. On September 29, 1884, thousands of black Philadelphians paraded to observe the centennial of black Masonry. Richard Allen and Absalom Jones had been leaders of black Masonry a century before, after Prince Hall established the first African American lodge in Boston. But this parade was not for the city but for themselves, just as the Poles had paraded four years before to celebrate the semicentennial of the Polish Revolution. Black Philadelphians had little money for elaborate planning and float building, and doubtless they had no illusions that more than a few native-born whites, let alone Italians, Irish, Germans, and Russians, would turn out to watch their procession. Yet the black Masons made their claim on public space and demonstrated a ceremonial life of their own. Pride of place showed itself in the refusal of Boston's black Masons to participate, since they regarded their city as the birthplace of black Masonry.

While staging centennial and bicentennial celebrations, Philadelphia, like other cities, enshrined some of its heroes in a flurry of statue building in the 1880s. The selection of those deemed fit for incarnation provides additional evidence of how the public memory of the past was constructed in the afterglow of the Centennial Exposition of 1876. As a part of the 1882 Penn commemoration, the Bi-Centennial Association intended to erect a monument to William Penn, and this was accomplished in 1883 when the statue was placed along a pathway overlooking Wissahickon Creek. But the first monument erected by the Bi-Centennial Association was a monumental bronze statue of Morton McMichael. At the heavily-traveled approach to the Girard Avenue bridge leading to Fairmount Park, Philadelphians could now see the former Philadelphia sheriff, Union League founder, and recently deceased newspaper publisher who had been elected as the first Republican mayor in 1865. Though McMichael was the hero of the new business interests that had displaced the old Philadelphia elite after the Civil War and was the favorite of native-born, white Philadelphians, his three-year term as mayor had ended in 1868 with little indication that he would be worth bronzing. Still, for the first time, a Philadelphia mayor was held up for public veneration—in this case by a group of business leaders whose announced intention was to celebrate the colonial and revolutionary past.

Other monuments sprang up in the closing years of the century. The Germantown GAR post raised money for a Civil War Soldiers' and Sailors' Monument, erected in Market Square in 1883. Other Civil War monuments rose in 1884 and 1887, with equestrian statues of Major General John Fulton Reynolds, killed at Gettysburg, and Major General George Gordon Meade. In 1897, the long delayed plans of the Society of the Cincinnati of Pennsylvania, first launched in 1810, culminated in the unveiling of a massive monument to Washington. In the same year, General Ulysses S. Grant received statuary recognition; two years later, in 1899, Justus C. Strawbridge, department store magnate, commissioned a huge bronze statue of a seated Benjamin Franklin. Installed at Ninth and Chestnut Streets, it was donated by the city to the University of Pennsylvania in 1938.

FIGURE 131. Alexander Calder, *William Penn*, 1886, FLP. The immigrant son of a Scottish tombstone cutter, Calder was angered by the positioning of his Penn statue so that it faced northeast instead of south. This made it nearly impossible to see Penn's face clearly except in early morning light. Calder believed that his Penn in bronze had been condemned to an "eternal silhouette" because Philadelphia's architect did not like the statue.

In this era of statue building, by far the most monumental of all was Alexander Milne Calder's thirty-six-foot-high William Penn, designed to surmount the gargantuan new City Hall, which had taken twenty-three years to complete (Figure 131). As early as 1875, the Historical Society had advised the commissioners of public buildings on how to clothe Penn realistically at the point of his arrival in Philadelphia in 1682, and Calder followed their advice faithfully. "What we want," Calder explained, "is William Penn as he is known to Philadelphians; not a theoretical one or a fine English gentleman."[59] In the bronze statue, Penn holds the charter from Charles II in his left hand and seems to gesture toward Penn Treaty Park, where legend held that he signed the treaty with the Lenape.

In 1884, just after the Historical Society had proudly moved into the Patterson mansion on Locust Street, the site of the society ever since, Hampton L. Carson, a councillor and later its president, urged careful planning for the centennial of the Constitution in 1887. Perfectly in keeping with the Historical Society's continuing emphasis on political and constitutional history and on the white leaders of the past, Carson called for reflective veneration of the "masterpiece of master minds," which contained "the best thoughts of statesmen trained in the best schools." "Surely," he argued, "there can be no higher patriotic duty for any of us to perform than to study with reverence the deeds of that day." Carson himself became the secretary of the Constitution Centennial Commission, acquired a major role in shaping the celebration, and edited an elaborate two-volume *History of the Celebration*, in which he wrote of how the commission hoped to inspire "a great awakening of patriotism"—and, as it turned out, smooth over all discontinuities in the historical record.[60]

The Historical Society was well positioned to participate in orchestrating the 1887 Constitution Centennial. For nearly twenty years, first under the vigorous leadership of John William Wallace, a legal scholar and former reporter of the U.S. Supreme Court, the society had followed his dictum that it was "not founded in the tastes of antiquaries, but in the philosophy of statesmanship."[61] Consistent with this mission, which aligned it with a nation beginning its ascent to global eminence, the Historical Society acquired materials almost exclusively that illuminated the colonial and revolutionary periods. By the 1880s, supported by generous bequests, the society was able to move beyond adding incrementally to its collections. With Brinton Coxe and Charles J. Stillé serving as presidents from 1884 to 1899, the Historical Society acquired huge amounts of material that established it as one of the premier manuscript, pamphlet, and newspaper repositories in the country (Figure 132). In 1885, it acquired the Athenaeum's fabulous collection of colonial and early national newspapers, as well as two valuable eighteenth-century pamphlet collections assembled by Benjamin Franklin and Mathew Carey.

Occasionally something came to the Historical Society that historians could use to uncover Philadelphia's social history, such as William Winner's paintings of "Crazy Nora" the Irish bag woman, and the Pie Man. But the main effort was to build on what had been acquired in the previous decades: materials relating to William Penn and the early Quakers; famous men of the colonial, revolutionary, and early national period; militaria; legal and legislative records; and documents relating to the British administration of the colonies. The directors of the Historical Society, as well as those of other cultural institutions, still had little interest in working-class unions, much less blue collar day-to-day life, so to the present day its collections—with the exception of its photographic archives—provide historians with relatively little material for uncovering this chapter of the city's past. Instead, the Historical Society's efforts in the late nineteenth century, like those of other historical societies, were part of a national effort among elites to promote

FIGURE 132. Isaac L. Williams, *The Historical Society of Pennsylvania, Spruce Street Hall*, oil, 1884, HSP. Williams's painting gives a good picture of the patrician atmosphere that the Historical Society's members treasured. The library was in the "Picture Building" that the society occupied from 1872 to 1884 on the grounds of the Pennsylvania Hospital. Just after Williams finished this painting, the Society purchased the mansion of General Robert Patterson at Thirteenth and Locust Streets, only a short distance from where the Library Company's newly built Victorian structure had opened its doors four years before. The Library Company's librarian, Lloyd Pearsall Smith, inspired Historical Society members at their opening ceremonies with a speech about how the two institutions were fighting as one "against the Kingdom of darkness and ignorance and obscurantism, resisting the modern Goths and Vandals, and constituting one mighty citadel of thought."

a greater loyalty to the state—all the more urgent in a nation they perceived to be teeming with militant workers, assertive "new" women, aspiring black Americans, and strangely garbed new immigrants speaking unfamiliar tongues.

In planning the hundredth birthday party of the Constitution, Carson and his colleagues had no intention of replicating the carnivalesque character of the Penn bicentennial, which had played to the lowest common denominator and invited unruliness in the city's highly diverse and poorly schooled population. As part of creating a modern nationalism, they wanted to nurture a worshipful stance toward the glorious past, a more elevated public taste, and a deeper loyalty of the masses to the state. With Historical Society members fully involved, the centennial Constitution birthday party was thoroughly upbeat, sedate, and carefully controlled as compared to the stagy, commercialized, and boisterous Penn bicentennial five years before. The event is a good example of how cultivated intellectuals and businessmen tried to elicit mass participation—at least to some extent—while carefully shaping and regulating public celebrations.

The Centennial Commission cast its net broadly, enlisting governors from most of the states and involving commercial, financial, and professional leaders rather than city politicians. Supported by state-appropriated and private funds, it planned a decidedly tasteful three-day affair, with two lengthy, carefully managed processions rather than a week of pageantry, athletic contests, historical reenactments, fireworks, and spontaneous street theater. Though the commission claimed its goal was "to make this affair . . . a representative meeting of every class of people . . . who have contributed to [the nation's] advancement and prosperity, morally, intellectually, and materially," the planning was done by subcommissions narrowly drawn from genteel whites. The Citizens Committee of 361 persons contained no women and not a single black Philadelphian—nor for that matter, any representative of the Italian, Polish, Irish, Russian, Lithuanian, or Greek subcommunities.[62] The Centennial Commission pulled out all stops to obtain the presence of many dignitaries, from President Grover Cleveland and his wife to aging Civil War generals, "a regular 'blue-book' of names of men famous the nation over," as *Harper's Weekly* expressed it.[63] These events, the commission believed, would help to create an aura of civic unity and social harmony. They believed the need for this was very great, because they were organizing the celebration amid "the great upheaval," as labor historians call the year 1886. In Chicago, on May 1, 1886, a general strike led to a confrontation between police and workers in Haymarket Square. Philadelphia's workers were not as involved as those in other cities in the massive nationwide strikes of that year. But as the Centennial opened, newspapers carried screaming headlines about the convictions of the Haymarket anarchists, now scheduled for execution, and ominous bulletins about 20,000 striking anthracite miners a day's journey from Philadelphia.

People *did* come to see the celebrations. A local population of more than a million, along with about 500,000 visitors, who slept on park benches and grassy parks when rooms ran out, flocked to see the two processions advertised to end all processions. The first, a civic and industrial procession, was reportedly fourteen miles long, "excelling everything of its kind since the great Washington review at the close of the [revolutionary] war."[64] Philadelphia's civic, religious, educational, benevolent, trades, and commercial organizations turned out by the thousands, with 21,029 paraders, 2,106 musicians, 2,099 horses, and 497 mammoth floats: mounted locomotives, a model of the first steamship to cross the Atlantic, fully rigged whale boats, the Carpenters' Company replica of the Grand Federal Edifice that had been pulled through the streets in 1788, Conestoga wagons, firemen "of the old school," costumed German peasants and Italian nobles, pugilists battling on horse-drawn stages, and some people "going to bed and others just arising" (Figure 133). Many floats commemorated the American Revolution with tableaux recalling the minutemen at the Battle of Lexington, the Declaration of Independence, Valley Forge, the surrender at Yorktown, and George Washington and his generals. The press applauded. "A great fair on wheels," crowed the *Press*. "A marching object lesson teaching vividly how much the nation has grown during the century of the world's great-

FIGURE 133. Frederick Gutekunst, float at the Constitution Centennial, 1889, in Carson's *History of the Celebration*, LCP. Colonel A. Loudon Snowden, grand marshal and organizer of the civic and industry procession, told many commercial proposers of floats that he would not allow the parade to "degenerate into a mere medium of advertising." But he had to make choices in the end and favored displays that would show advancement in the nation's industrial and commercial strength. Those with plenty of money to spend on crowd-pleasing floats, such as Gutekunst, the city's prominent portrait photographer, got Snowden's approval. The Pennsylvania Railroad, with thirteen floats and two bands, and the Baldwin Locomotive Company took the prize for free advertising. More modestly, reported *Harper's Weekly*, "sidewalk hucksters amassed small fortunes selling little imitations of the cracked old 'Liberty Bell' and other devices of a patriotic nature."

est advancement."[65] The second parade, on the following day, was a military display with 23,722 marchers—the largest in the nation's history—from the army, the navy, and the marine corps but especially from the National Guard and GAR veterans. Putting men on parade in their military outfits was hardly conducive to discussions of constitutional issues but exactly fit the purposes of the Centennial organizers.

The reigning spirit of the Centennial was to lavish praise on the Constitution and gloss over any of the conflict that attended its creation and ratification. The rhetoric was all about handing down to posterity remembrances of greatness. Historical Society councillor Hampton Carson, addressing the first meeting of governors at Carpenters' Hall, reminded them that they were now "standing in this temple of liberty, with our hands upon the horns of the altar and our hearts quickened with celestial fire," so "we can go forth without fear to meet the responsibilities of the century to come." Reminding Philadelphians about how, in 1876, they had assembled in the city "like worshippers before a shrine, to bow in reverence and return devout thanks to God for the spirit which inspired the fathers of the republic," the Centennial Commission summoned citizens again to "the Mecca of America," where "every lover of free government, every student of the political achievements of mankind, every citizen who values the blessings of liberty" should gather. The commission invited almost any group or organization to participate in what they hoped would be a celebration evincing not even the slightest sign of fissures in the city of brotherly love. Fearful of anarchist labor leaders, however, they steered clear of those who, as Hampton Carson put it, "carry the red flag and refuse to recognize the flag of the United States."[66]

Of particular interest to Centennial organizers in their attempt to show a unified America was an elaborate display showing the accomplishments of the nearby Carlisle Industrial Indian School. Founded only eight years before by a Civil War Union officer, the boarding school was a centerpiece of Protestant Christianity's attempts in the 1880s to rescue the remaining Indian people from what it regarded as a corrupt and broken-down reservation system—and from "savagery." Philadelphia had been at the center of new programs to incorporate Indians into American society through total assimilation, to be achieved by dismantling the reservation system and bringing up a new generation of Native American children in strictly run schools where the Indianness of youngsters was to be leached out. In 1879, as the Carlisle boarding school was established in an abandoned army barracks, Amelia Stone Quinton and Mary Bonney of Philadelphia launched the Women's National Indian Association to further this cause. Three years later, Philadelphia's tireless reformer Herbert Welsh organized the Indians Rights Association, committed to "educate the Indian race and so prepare it for gradual absorption into ours."[67]

For Hampton Carson and the Centennial Commission leaders, the Carlisle Indian school display was "doubtless the greatest 'object-lesson' ever attempted to be inculcated by a processional display." Central to the lesson were the 642 students from 38 tribes, marching smartly in crisp uniforms and clasping slates and schoolbooks. Following them were five horse-drawn floats, each with its own didactic portrayal (Figure 134). The first float reproduced Benjamin West's painting of the legendary treaty between Penn and the Lenape chiefs at Shackamaxon (even though the Historical Society knew this was a mythical event). The side of the float reproduced the famous wampum belt showing a Quaker clasping hands with an Indian. Atop the second float was an Indian camp featuring a teepee; on the side were words from President Cleveland's inaugural address: "I would rather have my administration marked by a sound and honorable Indian policy than by anything else." The third float showed Indian children doing blackboard exer-

FIGURE 134. Carlisle Indian School parade float at Constitution Centennial, *Harper's Weekly*, September 24, 1887, LCP. Here the second of five floats of the U.S. Industrial School, known as the Carlisle Indian School, passes under the main ceremonial arch on Broad Street. The *Press* described the "large detachment of tame young Indians in civilized coats and trousers and nine mounted heavily built and wild redskins who arrived from the plains early in the morning." The new City Hall tower appears in the background without the statue of William Penn atop it, still awaiting placement.

cises in a schoolroom with signs proclaiming that 12,316 Indian children attended white schools while 34,561 were still "growing up in ignorance and barbarism."[68] Floats four and five showed Indian boys learning trades, from tinsmithing to carpentry.

The Centennial Commission's desire to display the nation's efforts to "civilize" the Indians could not be dramatized forcefully without the presence of "savage" Indians ready to scalp the nearest parade onlooker. But producing these Indians caused some problems. The official history of the Centennial found it sufficient to say that "ten wild Indians directly from their homes in the Indian Territory, belonging to the Cheyenne and Arapahoe tribes," headed the Indian procession under the charge of "an authorized trader of the Cheyenne and Arapahoe Agency." But the *Press* told a different story. Little Chief, Wolf Face, Man-on-a-Cloud, Black Coyote, White Snake, Bear Father, and the others were not at all interested in playing foil to Carlisle students, many of whom were members of their own tribes. Tense negotiations over getting "wild" Indians to act wildly broke down but were finally resolved with a compromise—the reservation Indians would ride their horses, look fierce, wear feathered headdress and war paint, and wave tomahawks and guns—which at least approximated what urban easterners took to be wild Indian behavior.[69]

Editors declared the pantomime exhibit of wild Indians and tamed schoolchildren an enormous success. The official history of the Centennial pridefully excerpted a *Brooklyn Eagle* account that described how the "fierce-visaged" braves, "savages from scalp-lock to moccasin," were followed by neatly uniformed slate-bearing students marching "steady as soldiers"—a new breed of braves who "will sweep these old warriors and savages out of existence forever." "It was grand, it was inspiring, it was sublime, it was Christian," cried the *Eagle*. "I never in all my life saw such an object-lesson," exclaimed the reporter. "Ahead were the savages, 'exceeding fierce,' possessed with seven times seven devils, and then these boys and girls clothed in their right minds, sitting at the feet of the Prince of Peace." Here was the solution to the "much-discussed 'Indian problem'—the rescue of a race by a Christian nation."[70]

The attempt to include the city's African Americans, in contrast to the 1876 or 1882 celebrations, signified that even the all-white male Centennial organizers and their Citizens Committee were eager to heal Philadelphia. But, as it turned out, certain long-standing racial rifts could not be mended by a parade. Colonel A. Loudon Snowden, chair of the committee to organize the civic and industrial parade, wrote black leaders in New York, Philadelphia, and Washington a month before the Centennial was scheduled to open to invite them to participate. Former postmaster general and superintendent of the U.S. Mint, Snowden proposed two parade floats. One was to show an old log cabin set in corn and cotton fields, where slaves would be working under the direction of a white overseer brandishing his bullwhip. Some of the field hands, counseled Snowden, "should be selected singers . . . [who] might render such melodies as are associated with the cotton plantations of the South." The second float, representing a century of black progress, would show prosperous black Americans grouped in "a parlor scene showing the highest refinement and taste."[71]

Though most black leaders wanted to participate in the parade, their meeting "of the people at large" turned them against Snowden's idea of two floats contrasting conditions in 1787 and 1887. Some of the people may have objected to the parlor scene, with its misleading message of black prosperity, for the vast majority of African Americans in Philadelphia, as elsewhere, were frozen out of industrial employment and were desperately poor. But more explicitly, "a great majority" was opposed to reviving memories of the past with a float showing a menacing white overseer cracking his bullwhip at slaves. Snowden was "greatly disappointed" at the rebuff of his "pet idea" and was lukewarm to black leaders' suggestion that "we are willing to mix in with the industrial departments according to our several businesses."[72]

In debating the issue of participating in the parade, black Philadelphians were at a crossroads on the matter of self-identity and historical remembrance. As their leaders told Colonel Snowden, many felt that "we don't care longer to be a distinctive people in a cosmopolitan country." Yet many had celebrated their distinctiveness just seven months before, when they observed the one hundredth birthday of the Free African Society, from which came Richard Allen's Mother Bethel Church and Absalom Jones's St. Thomas African Episcopal Church. Many had read the special homage paid to Allen in the Philadelphia-published *Christian Recorder*, which compared the black founding father with Moses, Martin Luther, George Whitefield, George Washington, and Thomas Jefferson. Others were reading the new editions of Allen's autobiography and a pamphlet entitled *Richard Allen's Place in History*. And just a week before Snowden's proposal arrived, 125 black Philadelphians organized by William Still had gone by special train to Chester to gather with several hundred other African Americans for the annual celebration of West Indian emancipation in 1834.[73]

At the last minute, with the support of Christopher Perry, the editor and publisher of the city's only black newspaper, the *Philadelphia Tribune*, a three-float "Colored People's Display" was hastily pulled together. The first float depicted slavery days but with only a slave cabin in a cotton field. Hampton Carson's history of the Centennial noted that "the slaves were absent" because not a single black Philadelphian, "even with the offer of a liberal pecuniary," was willing to appear on the float as a slave. The history of slavery was watered down to four terse labels on the float: "No personal freedom," "No schools and no colleges," "No hope of advancement," and "But little personal property held by us." In the second float, Snowden's idea for showing parlor-room prosperity for African Americans in 1887 was entirely scrapped in favor of a school scene with sixty-five boys and girls at their desks with banners telling what Hampton Carson called "the glad story of the present time": "Emancipation," "Enfranchisement," "Entitled to full political rights and privileges," "Material wealth of the colored people South, $150,000,000," and "Material wealth of the colored people North, $35,000,000." Carson's writeup of the float complained that Snowden's hope to show black prosperity had been thwarted by "the unwillingness of leading men of color to undertake a work which would have been of the highest credit and advantage to their race." Instead, grumbled Carson, they banished the elegant parlor scene, substituted a schoolroom scene, and put together a third float, titled "Industry," which portrayed a more realistic view of the upper limits of what was possible for black Philadelphians. On the third float, real-life black artisans—a brick mason, saddle and harness maker, stove repairman, bookbinder, shoemaker, tailor, house painter, paperhanger, watchmaker, and house carpenter—plied their trades.[74]

All the while, Philadelphia's African Americans were collecting historical materials that the city's white institutions ignored in order to hold fast to a black past. Lacking a building or even an organization, civic leaders such as William Dorsey and Robert M. Adger, Jr. painstakingly clipped magazines and newspapers to fill scrapbooks with material relating to African American life. Also carefully gathered were black church and music concert programs, photographs, and other ephemeral material; wood carvings, clay sculpture, sketches, and paintings by black artists; and records of early black churches, schools, and beneficial societies going back to the 1820s. Not lawyers, corporate leaders, and doctors—because they had little opportunity to become so—but janitors, postal clerks, and messengers formed the American Negro Historical Society a decade after the Constitution Centennial festivities in order to pool their resources. Unlike Historical Society leaders, Dorsey collected *everything*—news items about burglars as well as bankers, the ugly as well as the noble. Rather than shaping memory by filtering out unwanted images at the source, he collected anything relating to black life, thus allowing historians many decades later to reconstruct the lives of black Philadelphians at all levels of urban society after the Civil War.

History-conscious black Philadelphians made no attempt to crash or spoil the thoroughly white Centennial party, but white women with history firmly in mind did—though much more quietly than in 1876. In fact, there was a sharp difference between the feminist uproar created midway through the 1876 Exposition, during the ceremonies at Independence Hall, and the discreet protest at President Cleveland's public reception at City Hall on the last day of the Centennial. Neither Elizabeth Cady Stanton nor Susan B. Anthony of the National Woman's Suffrage Association made it their business to appear, leaving the matter in the hands of Lillie Devereux Blake of New York, who wrote a draft of the protest and quietly handed it to President Cleveland without saying a word to the crowd about the contents of the protest.[75]

The protest itself, at least in its wording, was not at all timid. It reminded the Centennial organizers and the nation's president that amid "the pomps and glories of this celebration," half of the American people "who obey the laws . . . are unjustly denied all place or part in the body politic." Pointing out that the Constitution's preamble claimed that it was established by "the people of the United States," the protest charged that the Constitution's words "have been falsified for a hundred years" by men who have perpetrated "a century of injustice." In conclusion, the protest demanded that the states set aside "a cruel and unwarranted discrimination" and end "a despotism under which one-half of the citizens are held in a condition of political slavery."

Though the language was strong, the body language employed by the suffragists was weak. Nobody mounted a platform, as had Susan B. Anthony in 1876, to read the protest before a cheering crowd. Nobody opened an office of the Suffrage Association to continue broadcasting the main message. Philadelphia newspapers hardly took notice of the protest, nor did the city's women it appears. The *Woman's Journal* deplored a week later "the event that did not transpire," a reference not to the decorous delivery of the protest to President Cleveland but to the male organizers of the Centennial who might have used the occasion to begin "the end of the subjection of women." In failing to act, even symbolically, while celebrating "the great deed of dead heroes," the men "left no great deed of their own to be celebrated now or hereafter." Lillie Devereux Blake contributed her own account of her encounter with President Cleveland and noted that the Centennial organizers had invited not a single woman to "participate in any of the public observances."[76]

Part of the explanation for the pallid women's protest may be that discouragement had already set in. Earlier in 1887, the Senate passed the Edmonds-Tucker Act, taking away woman's suffrage legislated by the government of the Utah Territory in 1870, and defeated a constitutional amendment for woman's suffrage. Radical suffragists were beginning to lose faith in American democracy, even questioning whether the vote for women would do much to reform government corruption and robber baron capitalism. But the weakness of the protest was also testimony to the determination of the Centennial organizers to contain and control all signs of disunion. Lillie Blake's Presentation Committee was denied entrance to the public reception at City Hall. She finally got in, leaving her colleagues behind, only because, as she wrote, "I was accompanied by a representative of the press, who persuaded the guardian at the door to admit us both."[77]

For an era not yet introduced to public opinion polls, it is not easy to measure the effect of the Constitution centennial processions as a memory-making affair, but it seems likely that its impact was minimal. Hampton Carson was a tireless cheerleader of patriotism and churned out eloquent if not spine-tingling prose, even though the organizer of the civic, industrial, and military parades complained that "the great difficulty I encountered on the threshold of my labors was the entire absence of any public interest in the celebration."[78] Through plenty of publicity, the festooning of the city in the nation's colors, and the participation of groups such as the Sons of Italy and the Catholic abstinence societies, most of the city turned out for the parades. But watching a seven-hour parade dominated by marching bands and military units was unlikely to bring about serious discussion of the Constitution and American history.

The Centennial's largest effect was probably on Philadelphia's hereditary elite and cultural leaders. Judging by what they attempted in the years that followed, it deepened their conviction about the need to sponsor civic celebrations that promoted American power and progress and drew the entire city into gigantic processions as a way of submerging distinct ethnic, racial, and class celebrations and demonstrations. In this management of memory, Anglo-Saxon roots and the veneration of Founding Fathers must take precedence.[79] This seemed apparent five years after the Constitution Centennial, when twenty-eight members of the Historical Society founded the Genealogical Society of Pennsylvania. Restricting inclusion to members of the Historical Society, the Genealogical Society poured energy into building the genealogical collections that would show the lineage of wealthy, white, and early arrived Philadelphians and vouch for their pedigrees. When writing the history of the Historical Society in the 1920s, Hampton Carson, its president from 1921 to his death in 1929, gave testimony to the emphasis on genealogy that continued unabated for half a century. Carson filled his history with elaborate sketches of the family background of each society president, emphasizing family connections to the founders of Pennsylvania and the nation. "In this way," wrote Carson, "the unity of our history as a colony, a state, a municipality, and as a nation becomes apparent."[80]

This belief that historical memory would nourish sacred values, that remembrances of the dead white heroes would sustain a country of immigrants, remained the core of the Historical Society's self-identity. But beyond its doors for the remainder of the century, others worked to keep alive their own histories and present them to the American people at large. In 1888, speaking at the twenty-sixth anniversary of the abolition of slavery in the nation's capital, Frederick Douglass reminded the audience that the nation might well forget about slavery—because whites wanted to put sectional carnage behind them and African Americans did not want to dwell on the nightmare of life in chains. The nation "may shut its eyes to the past, and frown upon any who may do otherwise," Douglass warned, "but the colored people of this country are bound to keep the past in lively memory till justice shall be done them."[81] In black Philadelphia, Douglass's words must have resonated among many, as did his faith that history would serve to make a better future. White cultural leaders agreed in principle, but the history of the city they purveyed was far different.

Chapter 9

RESTORING MEMORY

Half a century after the Historical Society played a leading role in orchestrating the 1887 Constitution Centennial celebration, its executive council listened raptly to a report from a special committee on the society's past, present, and future. Chairing the committee was Edward Carey Gardiner, great-great-grandson of Mathew Carey, the publisher and avid collector who was to give the society a blockbuster collection of papers from the extended Carey family of printers, publishers, and politicians. In a "Declaration of Faith," Gardiner's committee expressed its "growing conviction that historical societies in America . . . had been blown off their course and their forces scattered by the contrary winds of narrowed interests, preoccupation with antiquarian subjects, jealous competition with each other, . . . and a reluctance to accept improved methods or new interpretations."[1] Among the members of the committee were Conyers Read, a Tudor England historian at the University of Pennsylvania; R. Norris Williams, 2d, descendant of one of Philadelphia's oldest Quaker families and soon to become president of the Historical Society; Joseph Carson, son of the society's president from 1921 to 1924; and Julian P. Boyd, who had assumed the librarian's position four years earlier at age thirty-two.

Boyd was the mainspring behind the electrifying new mission statement that promised to recalibrate the mechanisms of memory-making. A South Carolinian by birth and upbringing and the son of a small-town railroad telegrapher, Boyd had been urging the society's patrician council members for four years to move from a white gentlemen's club to a professional scholarly society—and, in the process, democratize its collecting policies and make itself more accessible to the public. Boyd had come to the Historical Society in 1934, after a meteoric rise in the increasingly professionalized ranks of historians. After completing a year of graduate training in history at the University of Pennsylvania in 1928, he left to become editor of the Susquehannah Company Papers at the Wyoming Historical and Genealogical Society in Wilkes-Barre, a project that put him in close touch with lives of ordinary frontiersmen in eighteenth-century Pennsylvania. In 1932, he moved to Ticonderoga to become director of the New York State Historical Association's headquarters house. Backed by Herman V. Ames, the University of Pennsylvania's early American historian, Boyd was hired as the Historical Society's assistant librarian in 1934. In the following year, he became its head librarian.

Before reaching the Historical Society, Boyd had developed progressive ideas about historical scholarship and its practice at the nation's historical societies. At Penn, he became close to Roy Nichols, a young, recently hired radical. Together, in 1928, they published an outline for "the social and economic history of the United States," an effort to shift attention from political leadership as the motivating force in the unfolding of the American past to something akin to Henry Mercer's argument at the Bucks County Historical Society that the work of ordinary Americans propelled society forward and gave it its definition. Boyd may also have been influenced in his first year as assistant librarian by an unusual person who came through the Historical Society's doors bearing gifts. Leon Gardiner, a black Philadelphia printer and custodian of most of the American Negro Historical Society collections, had seen most of his organization's founders—Jacob White, Jr., William Dorsey, W. Carl Bolivar, Robert Adger, and others—pass away. This was the group that had challenged the white monopoly on telling the nation's story by vowing that "no country can tell its history truthfully until all its scrolls are unrolled."[2] Despairing in the depths of the Depression that the next generation could sustain their efforts, some of the remaining members of the Negro Historical Society claimed parts of the collections, and some dispersed materials to Wellesley College and Cheyney State College. But Gardiner brought much of the Negro Historical Society's material to the Historical Society of Pennsylvania, where the young southerner was about to become head librarian. The Historical Society had never had a black member, though many of its members were friends of the city's black community, and this is probably why Gardiner, with few options, brought the materials to 1300 Locust Street. It seems likely that, combing through the rich trove of materials—autograph material from Benjamin Banneker and Frederick Douglass but also the stuff of everyday life, such as early black church records; schedules of the Philadelphia Pythians, a black baseball club; records of black benevolent societies and schools—Boyd's enthusiasm for a history of all the people was reenforced.

This certainly became apparent five years later, when Boyd maneuvered the Historical Society's council into a top-to-bottom reconsideration of its mission. Drafting the "Statement of Policy and Declaration of Faith" for the newly formed Committee on Objectives, Boyd wrote: "This declaration of faith and of purpose is grounded upon certain compelling assumptions. It implies a belief in the value and dignity of the incomparable story of America, a delight in its variant voices from all lands blending into a common voice of hope and promise. It means a deep concern for the life of the people as well as a desire to record the actions of their leaders." Then Boyd sought the council's endorsement for a statement that few of the nation's historical society and museum leaders would have accepted: that the polyglot character of American society was one of its sturdiest qualities and that in a democracy no satisfactory history could be fashioned until it took account of all its constituent parts. "It means," wrote Boyd, "that here in Pennsylvania—from the beginning the most cosmopolitan and democratic of all the States—history concerns itself with the Finns and Swedes, the Dutch and English, the Scots-Irish and Germans, the Negroes and Slavs, without regard to their status, their beliefs, their color, their accent." In sharp contrast to the reigning interest among the society's members, who had always regarded the Historical Society as an ultra-patriotic organization of Philadelphia's elite, Boyd continued: "It means a broad and intelligent interest in the fundamental unit in society, the family, and not a mere concern for the compilation of genealogical tables."[3]

In the statement of policy that followed these bold populist words, Boyd redefined the Historical Society's mission as gathering and presenting materials that reflected "the history of the whole community and not merely a portion of it." Behind these words, however reasonable they seem to our sensibilities today, lay a profound difference between the traditional collecting policies of the Historical Society and the emerging viewpoints and values of professional historians. Boyd urged that the society's acquisition policy should be conducted on "an inclusive rather than a highly selective basis," the latter phrase referring to the viewpoints and values of the Historical Society's founders and funders for more than a century. Now the society would make "a systematic effort" to obtain materials from "all phases of history, all periods, and all population elements," with the guiding criterion that materials should be viewed as valuable for their "significance in throwing new light on historical processes . . . rather than rarity or sentimental associational values."[4]

Boyd's policy statement also pledged that "the Society should uphold a broad definition of history and high standards of scholarship in all its functions," a clarion call for reorienting the *Pennsylvania Magazine of History and Biography* so that scholarly history would distinctly outweigh genealogically driven biography. Further, the society's members "should be representative of the whole community; its publications should not neglect any of these categories; its lectures and public activities should be addressed to the interests not of particular groups or even to the present membership but should adhere to an ideal that might appeal to a much larger potential membership." In effect, this policy would democratize the society and give new emphasis to its public history role.

That Boyd was able to gather the support of the council, most of them descended from Historical Society founders, who decidedly had *not* been interested in the "whole community" or in *all* periods, or believed the membership should include *all* elements of Philadelphia's diverse population, is remarkable in itself. How did Boyd corral those who controlled his salary and tenure with his breathtaking departure from the philosophy that had animated the Historical Society since its founding? How did he obtain what was, in effect, a confession that the society's narrow conception of itself had produced a smug, cocoonlike insulation from the larger society? The answer, as Sally Griffith has made clear in her recent history of the Historical Society, lies in the erosion of the society's membership and financial base during the Depression and an aging leadership that had left it nearly rudderless in recent years. Now, despite sharp disagreements within the council, the councillors deferred to Boyd's professionalism, his boundless energy, and his impressive agenda for raising the prestige of the Historical Society as one of the nation's most important cultural institutions. But only briefly. Within months of the issue of the *Pennsylvania Magazine of History and Biography* that reprinted the "Declaration of Faith" and "Statement of Policy," controversy resurfaced as key councillors of the society tried to regain an upper hand over their insistent young librarian, who argued that he could not turn the society into a truly scholarly enterprise without authority to direct its daily operations, in effect shearing the council's president of much of his power and leaving him only as the "titular" chief executive. When the skirmishing intensified in 1939, threatening his visionary program, Boyd decamped, moving north to accept the position of head librarian at Princeton University.[5]

Having acceded grudgingly to new principles, practices, and programs, the Historical Society leaders, no longer goaded by Boyd, confronted a world at war, first hot, then cold. By itself, World War II made it impossible to implement the bold plans for reorganization and outreach. The Cold War that followed deferred implementation of the 1939 program because academic historians and librarians, as well as the society's well-heeled leaders, began reimagining American history in ways that nearly snuffed out the embers of a multiethnic, democratic history that Boyd had stirred up. The so-called consensus school of American history, which held sway for two decades after 1945, smoothed over the rough spots in the American historical record, minimized conflict among different groups, and found little of interest to study in the history of racial minorities, women, labor, or laboring people. Where Boyd had seen a new era in which Americans would rethink their history more democratically, the consensus mentality of the post-1945 generation played to the old siren patriotism of Americans returning to a history neatly packaged and attractively wrapped, as at Colonial Williamsburg, where no slaves could be seen, no weeds grew in the gardens, and the only enemy at the nation's birth took the form of a nasty English lion.[6]

Yet much of Julian Boyd's dream was put into place by his successors. Indeed, historical societies and museums all over the nation began to adopt his rationale and agenda in the 1970s, changing their collecting policies, exhibition planning, governance, interpretive stances, outreach, and service to precollegiate schools. This time, the effort was enormously assisted by a development that seemed hardly imaginable during the 1930s—money, lots of it, from the National Endowments for the Humanities and Arts, as well as from a variety of foundations and corporations newly interested in history and culture. Chief among the factors responsible for turning on the fiscal faucet were the Cold War superpower clashes that led the Eisenhower, Kennedy, Johnson, and Nixon administrations to subsidize the arts and humanities as a way of defusing "charges of soulless materialism" hurled by America's Communist enemies.[7]

The era of protest in the 1960s and 1970s made obvious the sense of injury and exclusion felt by large groups who regarded Philadelphia's cultural institutions—the Free Library and Atwater Kent Museum excepted—as distant precincts run for and by the elite, the memory managers whose highly selective stories of the past had rarely encompassed the experiences and contributions of most Philadelphians. That changed markedly as institutional leaders came to see connectedness to the community as an essential test of their value. Part of their institutions' future would depend on doing what they had been best at: collecting materials allowing scholars and the public at large to see American history, literature, and culture through the lenses of the most advantaged. But, simultaneously, they began to take satisfaction in enabling the historically forgotten—or those who wrote about them—to recapture their stories. Because the American Philo-

FIGURE 135. John Neagle, *Thomas Ustick Walter*, oil, 1835, Athenaeum. Among the 30,000 Thomas Walter manuscripts acquired by the Athenaeum in 1983 was a receipt for $180 from Neagle for this painting and one of Walter's wife. Only the most revered paintings of Charles Willson Peale would fetch this much at an auction of his portrait collection nearly twenty years later.

sophical Society, the Library Company, and the Historical Society of Pennsylvania are primarily repositories of books and manuscripts, and therefore essentially centers of research, their ability to reach out to the community has taken the form of changing their collecting priorities to accommodate new scholarly interests while mounting small exhibits, symposia, and lecture programs for a wider audience. Object-centered museums—for example, the Atwater Kent and new museums such as the African American Museum, the Balch Institute of Ethnic Studies, and the Independence Seaport Museum—have built-in advantages for staging exhibits that can reach out to the city's diverse people, stimulate their memory of who built Philadelphia, and remind them that historical memory has been a constructed and contested affair since the beginning.

Inside the boardrooms of Philadelphia's cultural institutions by the late 1960s, reformulated policies governing collecting and exhibiting began to restore public memory of disparaged groups and forgotten chapters of the city's history. In varying degrees, the museums, historical societies, and libraries have proved what the director of the Cleveland Museum of Art said nearly twenty-five years ago: "Museums are inventions of men, not inevitable, eternal, ideal, nor divine. They exist for the things we put in them, and they change as each generation chooses how to see and use those things."[8]

Among the city's most venerable institutions—the Library Company, Philosophical Society, Athenaeum, and Historical Society—change occurred in various ways and at different paces. Both the Athenaeum and the Philosophical Society have reinvented themselves. For more than a century, the Athenaeum had provided its cultured shareholders with newspapers, magazines, and other reading material—"all varieties of doctrine and opinion, political and religious," as its founder remarked in 1847. "In the newspaper room, you will find the principal political journals from the chief places of this country and Europe; Whig and Democrat, Abolition, Radical and Conservative."[9] But the years had treated the Athenaeum badly. Its membership shrinking and its founding vision compromised, the library teetered on the brink of extinction by the 1960s. Then it acquired a new life by entirely redefining itself as a scholarly library of nineteenth-century architecture and related design. Winning grants from the National Endowments for the Arts and Humanities and the Pennsylvania Historical and Museum Commission, the Athenaeum rebuilt its crumbling landmark and, by 1978, was mounting scholarly exhibits, first on the work of John Notman (1810-65), a noted Philadelphia architect; and then on Thomas Ustick Walter, the city's famed designer of the U.S. Capitol, Girard College, Moyamensing Prison, and Andalusia, Nicholas Biddle's Delaware River country seat (Figure 135). Four years after this exhibit in 1979, the Athenaeum acquired by purchase about five hundred architectural drawings by Walter along with 30,000 pages of his manuscripts, all stored away in the bunkhouse of a Colorado horse ranch where his descendants live.

Under the directorship of Roger W. Moss for more than three decades, the Athenaeum has rebuilt its shareholder ranks and mounted public programs—exhibits, symposia, and lectures. This is an example of a private institution serving a public role. Today it houses 180,000 architectural drawings and 50,000 historical photographs connected to the work of some two thousand nineteenth-century architects and master builders. No longer, as in its early years, can shareholders read a variety of religious and political newspapers, a function gladly relinquished to the Free Library.

The American Philosophical Society did not have to reinvent itself to survive, but in the twentieth century it revitalized itself and refined its mission. At the dawn of the twentieth century, the society had become increasingly a social club without particular national or international distinction. But for the next half century, it established itself as a coordinator of important scholarly projects in science, linguistics, and history. In 1904-5, the society published an eight-volume edition of the Lewis and Clark Expedition, built out of the materials Jefferson had given to the society in 1817. In 1906, the society staged an elaborate commemoration for the bicentennial of Benjamin Franklin's birth and then published a hefty volume of essays from a conference on Franklin. Then, in the 1930s, the Philosophical Society tried to parley the expertise of its elected members into an outreach program, using radio and public lectures to "promote useful knowledge," in Franklin's terse mission phrase. This attempt to become a "clearing house of knowledge" or a "knowledge bureau" did not succeed, although a broadened publication program did serve the scholarly public well.

After World War II, the Philosophical Society found its modern métier, first as a national research center for studying the history of science and early American history, and second as a partner and facilitator in the publication of major projects such as modern multivolume editions of the papers of Benjamin Franklin and the papers of Charles Willson Peale and his family. Earning foundation support, the society has also been a major dispenser of grants for scholarly research, including one in Native American languages and ethnohistory. Coupled with this, the society since 1980 has collaborated with other institutions to stage national exhibitions, to offer opportunities for the professional development of local public school teachers, and to cosponsor public affairs symposia and lectures broadcast by local radio and television to the public.

The bulk of the Society's manuscript and rare book accessions in the past half century have been in linguistics, anthropology, and the history of science, but its early affection for its founder and his era has not been forgotten. The purchase of a large collection of Franklin materials in 1936 from a descendant solidified the society's claim as the archival center of Frankliniana. The enormous collection of papers acquired over several decades, beginning in 1945, from one of Franklin's comrades-in-arms, Charles Willson Peale, further strengthened the Society's materials on the revolutionary and early national periods. As late as 1971, the acquisition of an important collection of materials relating to Thomas Paine, Franklin's young protégé on the eve of the American Revolution, continued this assembling of Philadelphia historical materials (Figure 136).[10]

It was fitting that the long-hidden bust of Tom Paine, after many peregrinations, found its final resting place in the office of the Philosophical Society's librarian, Edward C. Carter II. The city had dawdled for years in accepting the bust of Paine but finally, in 1905, accessioned it and put it on display on the second floor of Independence Hall. Paine vanished once again, however, in 1931, after the city's Art Commission ruled that the bust was not taken from real life and was therefore inappropriate to exhibit. Richard Gimbel tried to rectify this situation. In 1937, convinced that Philadelphia "has too long ignored one of its greatest citizens," he almost singlehandedly staged a bicentennial celebration of Paine's birth. Using the Edgar Allan Poe House on North Seventh Street, which he had purchased and restored, Gimbel displayed his collection of Paine pamphlets, books, manuscripts, and cartoons to promote the remembrance of a man he asserted "was the first to suggest justice to women, public education for the poor, a practical plan for international peace to quarantine belligerent nations, protection of dumb animals, and international copyright." For two decades, Gimbel beleaguered Philadelphia's mayors with requests to bring Paine's bust back to public view, finally achieving a partial victory in 1954, when the Art Commission reversed its 1931 decision.

FIGURE 136. *Tom Paine's Nightly Pests*, hand-colored engraving, Richard Gimbel Collection, APS. Philadelphians have had a hard time remembering Tom Paine's key role in the coming of the American Revolution and the Revolution's course in the city, because many found him too ambiguous, if not obnoxious, to fit into an immaculate conception story of the nation's birth. The grandson of one of the city's premier merchandisers, Richard Gimbel, spent many years collecting Paine materials and presented his Paine collection to the Philosophical Society in 1971. Included is a rich assemblage of anti-Paine cartoons, most of them produced in London. In the cartoon shown here, Paine's guardian angels on the headboard of his straw bed are Charles J. Fox on the left and Dr. Joseph Priestley on the right—both part of the radical party in English politics. Paine's many sins, in the view of conservative Anglo-America, are listed, including libels, scurrilities, falsehoods, perjuries, rebellions, and treason. Punishments for this include corporal pain, contempt, detestation, and extinction from society.

But Paine could still not come up from the cellar at Independence Hall, because the national shrine by this time had become the property of the National Park Service, which was restoring it to its eighteenth-century form and furnishing it only as it then existed. Nor was the Park Service, dependent on congressional appropriations, willing to risk a political firefight if it displayed Paine at the height of the Cold War. All the while, Philadelphians argued whether Paine was what Theodore Roosevelt had called a "dirty little atheist" or a far-seeing radical reformer whose values went to the essence of American democracy. Paine finally saw sunlight again in 1967, when the Philosophical Society agreed to give a permanent home to the great propagandist, who had been elected one of

FIGURE 137. Male and female black Quaker dolls, Atwater Kent Museum. Some white Philadelphians began to shed their racial prejudices during Reconstruction, although the city as a whole remained a segregationist bastion. It was at this time that black dolls such as these became common. Black dolls had been made in the United States and Europe as early as 1830, probably on a limited commercial basis. White boy dolls are as infrequently found in this era as black boy dolls.

their members in 1785. His bust has stood in the librarian's office ever since, hardly before the public view but at least out of the basement and available for members of the Thomas Paine Association to gaze at and pose beside for photographs.[11] His memory is assured mostly through the Philosophical Society's Gimbel Collection of Thomas Paine, which attracts scholars from all over the world.

Only a few blocks from where Tom Paine lived when he wrote *Common Sense*, the Atwater Kent Museum of Philadelphia History, from its establishment in 1937, has always privileged what other collecting institutions generally scoffed at—the residue of everyday life. From shop signs to kitchenware to craftsmen's tools, its 80,000 objects, along with a sizeable print and photograph collection, are especially rich in the period from the 1870s to the present. After World War II, occupying the old Franklin Institute building on Seventh Street near Market, the museum became a kind of drop-off point for countless Philadelphia families emptying their cellars and attics. This was both a curator's dream and a curator's nightmare, because every donated artifact is "a gift that eats," requiring preservation, restoration, and space.[12] Thus every institution must impose some limit on how much it can collect. But some of the items coming over the transom were indeed extraordinary, though the public will have to wait for a long time before the museum will have appropriate exhibiting space to present more than fragments of the city's rich history. For example, descendants of David Bustill Bowser have made gifts of some of his gorgeously painted commercial signs and fireman's parade helmets. Also coming to the museum from the Friends Historical Society, which could no longer exhibit or maintain modern preservationist methods, was a fabulous collection of fabrics, clothing, and dolls, reminding people of how Quakers dressed and played from before the Revolution to the early twentieth century (Figure 137).

In 1998, the Atwater Kent Museum entered into a contractual relationship with the Historical Society of Pennsylvania, agreeing to assume a guardianship role over some 600,000 museum objects that the Historical Society decided it could no longer house, exhibit, or make accessible to scholars. Drawing on hundreds of these priceless remains of material culture from the first two centuries of Philadelphia's history, the Historical Society mounted its most successful exhibit—Visions and Revisions: Finding Philadelphia's Past—which occupied most of the first floor from 1991 to 1999.[13] However, to prop up its sagging finances, the Historical Society sold one of its most famous portraits, John Singleton Copley's painting of Thomas Mifflin and Sarah Mifflin, to the Philadelphia Museum of Art in 1999 for $4.5 million while redefining itself strictly as a temple for scholarly and genealogical research. Then the society warehoused its museum collections and struck an agreement that the Atwater Kent Museum would serve as custodian of the paintings and artifact collection while seeking enlarged exhibit space to display these invaluable materials in the future.

To abandon exhibits and public programs that had been energetically pursued since the 1982 tricentennial of Penn's arrival and thought by most sister institutions as instrumental in gaining government and foundation support involved great risks. Historical societies and rare book libraries as much as museums, warns the former head of Chicago's Field Museum of Natural History, "are more than repositories; they are places where collections are interpreted for the public through exhibits and related educational programs."[14] Institutions that resist "changing from offering a passive venue for the already educated to being an active center of learning for a public of diverse educational and cultural backgrounds" will risk the loss of support from foundations and the community at large. The Smithsonian Institution's Stephen Weil believes that whether a large historical society, a campus-based museum of natural history, or a small private art gallery, America's cultural institutions must shift their "principal focus outward to concentrate on providing a variety of primarily educational services to the public and will measure [their] success by the overarching criterion of whether [they are] actually able to provide those services in demonstrably effective ways.[15]

By what means the Historical Society can negotiate itself out of the difficult position it has chosen to occupy remains to be seen. Nonetheless, its collecting policies have broadened in ways that would have pleased Julian Boyd. Since the 1970s the society has acquired by gift and purchase a wide variety of source materials that allow historians to explore the rhythms and character of life at the lower and middle levels of Philadelphia society, including eighteenth-century poor tax records, nineteenth-century journals of militia units such as the Washington Grays, diaries of black and white Philadelphia women during the Civil War, letters from enlisted men on the battlefields of the Civil War and World Wars I and II, 20,000 photographs from the *Philadelphia Record*'s morgue, and voluminous records of such organizations as the Philadelphia-centered Indian Rights Association, the most important nongovernmental group established in 1882 to which Native Americans could turn for support and protection.

In collecting materials necessary for remembering how Philadelphians at all levels made history, the Library Company had a running start because it benefitted immensely from a series of antiquarian benefactors, such as Pierre-Eugène Du Simitière and John McAllister, Jr., who from before the American Revolution to after the Civil War collected ephemera that seemed useless to the city's aristocracy. By the end of the nineteenth century, the library received its last great collections of pamphlets, scrapbooks, and other ephemera. Well into the twentieth century it followed a "books of great worth" collecting policy. But the Library Company struggled financially during the Depression and nearly collapsed. Then, in the 1950s, reviving under its new librarian, Edwin Wolf II, it redefined itself as a scholarly research library. By the early 1970s, its leaders rethought their collecting priorities. "Everybody is *talking* about Negro history," wrote Wolf in 1970, "so we decided to *do* something about it." With funding from the Ford Foundation, the Library Company catalogued its holdings on European accounts of Africa, the slave trade and abolitionism, slave narratives and material related to free black communities, and literature about and by African Americans. All this material had been classified previously by politics, autobiography, travel, and other categories. "By seeing this material in a new way, by recovering the common thread that linked these diverse books, a subject collection of surprising strength was formed." The resulting catalogue became a standard bibliography of Afroamericana. The nation's oldest library now aggressively sought out materials by and about African Americans—books, pamphlets, newspapers, broadsides, playbills, lithographs, indeed *anything* that would enable scholars to deepen our understanding of the crucial role of race in the nation's history.[16]

With John Van Horne succeeding Wolf as librarian in 1985, an interest in African American materials became a designated collecting priority. The addition of more than two thousand books and others materials since then have made the Library Company a magnet for scholars from around the world interested in what has been a sizzling history topic for several decades. On a parallel path, the Library Company moved to strengthen its collections in another cutting edge area—women's studies, a field created only three decades ago. Spurred by the International Year of the Woman in 1973, it held a pioneering exhibit on the vast array of gender-related materials it already had and persistently built its Women's History Collection. By the late 1990s, at least half of all purchased materials directly or indirectly bear on women's history.[17] Even the finger-wagging of the crusty James Rush in 1869 about banning pulp fiction from the library's shelves lost its force as its curators realized how much insight into women's lives and concerns, especially those who refused to follow the feminine gender norms of the Victorian era, could be derived from popular novels. For example, Mrs. E. D. E. N. Southworth, thought a "trashy" writer by earlier Library Company directors, was one of the most widely read

American female authors of the nineteenth century, and the Library Company has since added her many novels to its shelves.

In 2000, in an example of success breeding success, the Library Company acquired by gift and purchase the most important collection of pre-1801 imprints in private hands. By securing the collection of Michael Zinman, a New York collector, the Library Company in a single stroke captured about 7,800 books, pamphlets, and broadsides—a fabulous hoard of rare materials. Included were some 4,500 titles of pre-1801 imprints not previously owned by the Library Company, three-quarters of them printed in New England. As the new millennium begins, a Philadelphia institution with a brilliant but predominately mid-Atlantic reputation addressed a regional collecting bias and thereby turned itself into a national and international center for research in the entire breadth of early American history.

Much of memory-making depends on the materials collected and preserved by museums, libraries, historical societies, and public archives, and we have seen how difficult it has been in Philadelphia to impose a benign and sanitized tableau of history on a varied population in a vast industrial city. Today, the process of producing history and restoring memory continues—and it is happening in many sites outside academe. In what is now a far more complex and democratic process, historical reenactors from all walks of life create their own versions of the past. Crowding in on public spaces, a terrain once dominated by city officials, historical societies, and museums, muralists from ethnic communities are creating public displays that administer visual doses for curing historical amnesia about groups and events for which professional historians bear the responsibility for enormous silences.[18]

In Philadelphia, for example, thousands of people pass by a mural at Chestnut and Ninth Streets that was unveiled in July 2000 on the side of the old I. Goldberg building. The mural recalls Philadelphia's Underground Railroad of the 1850s and celebrates a group of radical abolitionists who were reviled by most of the city's population 150 years ago (Figure 138). Standing tall in vivid hues is Harriet Tubman, the "stationmaster" who helped thousands of "passengers" throw off their chains and stealthily make their way north to Philadelphia. Honored places to the right and left of Tubman are occupied by railroad "conductors" William Still and Lucretia Mott, whose names are inscribed in medallions. Both were known to all Philadelphians at the time and to many historians since: Mott as the inextinguishable voice of woman's suffrage, abolition, and world peace; Still as a leading antislavery activist, the leader of the movement to desegregate the city's streetcars, and the chronicler of oral testimonies of slaves fleeing the South who made their way to Philadelphia. Until now, both had been largely forgotten by the twentieth-century public because textbooks, movies, television, and the popular press have given them short shrift. Inscribed on the mural's honor roll are the names of nine other Philadelphia antislavery activists, all but forgotten: Passmore Williamson, Robert Purvis, J. Miller McKim, Richard Allen, Charles and Joseph Bustill, Isaac Hopper, Henrietta Bowers Duterte, and Samuel Johnson and family. Nearly every Philadelphian knew them in the 1850s, because they were heroes for some and targets of abuse for others; they were

FIGURE 138. *The Philadelphia Underground Railroad Network*, mural, Ninth and Chestnut Streets, City of Philadelphia. Murals in public places, especially in highly multiethnic cities, have become an important way for minority groups to present their own understandings of their history. In this mural, the artist worked with Charles Blockson, African American historian and director of the Afroamerican Archive at Temple University, to create an honor roll of Underground Railroad figures.

the unsettling and unrepentant leaders who insisted that America could be true to itself only if it abolished slavery and made radical changes in race relations.

How this mural came to grace Philadelphia's downtown commercial district is a story in itself about how memory is restored and how the recapturing of lost history usually involves a fight, if not protracted negotiation. The inspiration for commemorating these freedom fighters, more than a century after all went to their graves, came from Susanne Nicholson, an artist and wife of the chairman of the Republican National Committee. Fascinated with the story of the Underground Railroad as an example of bravery and community action, she believed that bringing it back to memory was a perfect way to thank the city for graciously hosting the Republican National Convention of July 2000. Finding money and a sponsoring partner to paint the mural was not a problem. General Motors and General Motors Assistance Corporation, already involved in supporting urban historical murals, promised funding. The Republic National Committee agreed to sponsor the historical tableau as a copartner with the Philadelphia Mural Arts Program.

That left the choice of a site. The ideal location seemed to be 6300 Germantown Avenue—at the Johnson House, which still bears the scars from the Battle of Germantown in 1777 and served as one of the Underground Railroad stations where "passengers" could hide, rest, and gather strength before trekking farther north. When Philadelphia's Jane Golden, director of the Mural Arts Program, held community meetings to discuss this proposal, she was met with unbridled enthusiasm from black Germantowners, although "shockingly offensive" opposition, as she describes it, from white neighbors who saw no merit in celebrating this chapter of African American history at the Johnson House. Golden located several other Germantown Avenue sites, including Ernie's Gym, but white opposition was so fierce that she despaired that the project could go forward.[19]

Only six weeks before the convention in Philadelphia, Golden spotted a building at Ninth and Chestnut Streets owned by the Pennsylvania Manufacturers' Association. She quickly navigated through a tangle of legal complications to obtain all the necessary clearances. Working against the clock, Sam Donovan, a Philadelphia artist, completed the mural just before the convention began. Schoolchildren enlisted to help paint the lower parts of the mural were learning for the first time that long ago a dedicated band of Philadelphians helped thousands of people throw off slavery's shackles as they followed the North Star to William Penn's city. At the unveiling ceremonies on July 28, 2000, the great-grandniece of William Still, accompanied by many members of her family, read movingly from her ancestor's *The Underground Railroad*, the compendium of stories by runaway slaves who reached Philadelphia, carefully recorded by Still over a period of years and finally published in 1872. People attending looked up at the words on the mural: "Philadelphians, men and women, young and old, from all races, religions, and walks of life, kept the freedom train rolling." Tubman, Still, Mott, and their compatriots now command public space in the city of brotherly love.

Much about Philadelphia's history remains to be written and much still needs to be remembered. Not all the scrolls are yet unrolled. But what we remember today is far more than could have been imagined a half century ago. The property in history has been redistributed as collecting institutions have broadened their vision about what is collectible and as the access to the means of producing stories about the past has widened greatly. This trend unsettles many people, leading even to pronouncements about "the end of history" and the irreparable shattering of a what is imagined to have been a coherent, unified story about the past. These are the worried cries of those who formerly monopolized the production of history or those who yearn today for the spotless version of the American story that they learned as schoolchildren or those who fatuously pretend that a partial and biased history was a unifying and commonly accepted version of the national story. But the Philadelphia story, as it has emerged in our generation, is nonetheless inspiring for all its new messiness. Indeed, if it is now streaked with contradictions, ambiguities, and paradoxes, it is much more like life itself as a rich mixture of Philadelphians lived it over the past three centuries.

ABBREVIATIONS

APS	American Philosophical Society
FLP	Free Library of Philadelphia
HSP	Historical Society of Pennsylvania
INHP	Independence National Historic Park
LCP	Library Company of Philadelphia
PAFA	Pennsylvania Academy of Fine Arts
PMA	Philadelphia Museum of Art
PMHB	*Pennsylvania Magazine of History and Biography*
TAPS	*Transactions of the American Philosophical Society*

NOTES

Introduction

1. Quoted in Hampton L. Carson, *History of the Historical Society of Pennsylvania*, 2 vols. (Philadelphia: Historical Society of Pennsylvania, 1940), 1: 36. For a fascinating study of Independence Hall's many lives, see Charlene Mires, *Memories Lost and Found: Independence Hall in American History and Imagination* (Philadelphia: University of Pennsylvania Press, forthcoming).
2. Charlene Mires, "Memories Lost and Found: Independence Hall in American History and Imagination," Ph.D. dissertation, Temple University, 1997, 59.
3. For a discussion of the widespread desire to unburden the new nation from the past, see David Lowenthal, *The Past Is a Foreign Country* (Cambridge: Cambridge University Press, 1985), 110-14.
4. John L. Cotter, Daniel G. Roberts, and Michael Parrington, *The Buried Past: An Archaeological History of Philadelphia* (Philadelphia: University of Pennsylvania Press, 1993), 91.
5. *Philadelphia Aurora*, February 10, 1816, quoted in Mires, "Memories Lost and Found," 63.
6. *Philadelphia Union*, June 6, 10, 1818, published in Isaac V. Brown, ed., *Memoirs of the Rev. Robert Finley* (New Brunswick, N.J.: Terhune and Letson, 1819), 313-45.
7. Edgar W. Brandon, ed., *Lafayette, Guest of the Nation: A Contemporary Account of the Triumphal Tour of General Lafayette in the United States in 1824-1825*, 2 vols. (Oxford, Ohio: Oxford Historical Press, 1950-94), 2: 58-97 reprints most of the Philadelphia press coverage.
8. Quoted in Mires, "Memories Lost and Found," 76. For the Lafayette tour, see Stanley J. Idzerda, Anne C. Loveland, and Marc H. Miller, *Lafayette, Hero of Two Worlds: The Art and Pageantry of His Farewell Tour of America, 1824-1825* (Hanover, N.H.: Queens Museum, 1989).
9. Mires, "Memories Lost and Found," 71.
10. Many studies of public memory have emerged in recent years. Among the most valuable are Benedict Anderson, *Imagined Communities: Reflections on the Origin and Spread of Nationalism* (London: Verso, 1983); Lowenthal, *The Past Is a Foreign Country*; Michael Kammen, *Mystic Chords of Memory: The Transformation of Tradition in American Culture* (New York: Knopf, 1991); Eric Hobsbawm and Terence Ranger, eds., *The Invention of Tradition* (Cambridge: Cambridge University Press, 1983); Raphael Samuels, *Theatres of Memory: Past and Present in Contemporary Culture* (London: Verso, 1994); Paul Connerton, *How Societies Remember* (Cambridge: Cambridge University Press, 1989); Michel-Rolph Trouillot, *Silencing the Past: Power and the Production of History* (Boston: Beacon Press, 1995); Jacques Le Goff, *History and Memory* (New York: Columbia University Press, 1992); John Bodnar, *Remaking America: Public Memory, Commemoration, and Patriotism in the Twentieth Century* (Princeton, N.J.: Princeton University Press, 1992); and Daniel L. Schacter, *Searching for Memory: The Brain, the Mind, and the Past* (New York: Basic Books, 1996).
11. Quoted in Mires, "Memories Lost and Found," 75.
12. Roberts Vaux to John F. Watson, in Carson, *History of the Historical Society of Pennsylvania*, 1: 46-47.
13. For essays on the creation and the significance of the exhibit, see Gary B. Nash, "Behind

the Velvet Curtain: Academic History, Historical Societies, and the Presentation of the Past," *PMHB* 114 (1990): 3-26; Barbara Clark Smith, "The Authority of History: The Changing Public Face of the Historical Society of Pennsylvania," *PMHB* 114 (1990): 37-66; and Emma J. Lapsansky, "Patriotism, Values, and Continuity: Museum Collecting and 'Connectedness,'" *PMHB* 114 (1990): 67-82. For a variety of reflections on public presentations of history, see Jo Blatti, ed., *Past Meets Present: Essays About Historic Interpretation and Public Audiences* (Washington, D.C.: Smithsonian Institution Press, 1987); Warren Leon and Roy Rosenzweig, eds., *History Museums in the United States: A Critical Assessment* (Urbana: University of Illinois Press, 1989); Michael Frisch, *A Shared Authority: Essays on the Craft and Meaning of Oral and Public History* (Albany: State University of New York Press, 1990); Susan Porter Benson, Stephen Brier, and Roy Rosenzweig, eds., *Presenting the Past: Essays on History and the Public* (Philadelphia: Temple University Press, 1986); and Ivan Karp, Christine Mullen Kreamer, and Steven D. Lavine, eds., *Museums and Communities: The Politics of Public Culture* (Washington, D.C.: Smithsonian Institution Press, 1992).

14. J. H. Plumb, *The Death of the Past* (London: Macmillan, 1969).
15. John Fanning Watson, *Annals of Philadelphia and Pennsylvania in Olden Times*, rev. ed., 2 vols. (Philadelphia: E. Thomas, 1857), 1: 590.
16. Trouillot, *Silencing the Past*, 47.
17. Ibid., 29.
18. For marketing history, see David Lowenthal, *Possessed by the Past: The Heritage Crusade and the Spoils of History* (New York: Free Press, 1996), and Mike Wallace, *Mickey Mouse History and Other Essays on American Memory* (Philadelphia: Temple University Press, 1996).
19. For a recent study of remembering and marketing history in one community, see John Seelye, *Memory's Nation: The Place of Plymouth Rock* (Chapel Hill: University of North Carolina Press, 1998).

Chapter 1

1. Penn to Robert Turner, August 25, 1681, in *The Papers of William Penn*, ed. Richard S. Dunn and Mary Maples Dunn, 5 vols. (Philadelphia: University of Pennsylvania Press, 1982-86), 2: 110. Philadelphia's colonial history is treated in Gary B. Nash, *Quakers and Politics: Pennsylvania, 1681-1726* (Princeton, N.J.: Princeton University Press, 1968), and Edwin Blaine Bronner, *William Penn's Holy Experiment: The Founding of Pennsylvania, 1681-1701* (New York: Temple University Publications/Columbia University Press, 1962).
2. For a succinct history of the Library Company see Edwin Wolf, *"At the Instance of Benjamin Franklin": A Brief History of the Library Company of Philadelphia*, rev. ed. (Philadelphia: LCP, 1995).
3. Quoted in J. Stephen Catlett, ed., *A New Guide to the Collections in the Library of the American Philosophical Society* (Philadelphia: APS, 1987), xiii; Edward C. Carter II provides a short history of the Philosophical Society in *"One Grand Pursuit": A Brief History of the American Philosophical Society's First 250 Years, 1743-1993* (Philadelphia: APS, 1993).
4. Hampton L. Carson, *A History of the Historical Society of Pennsylvania*, 2 vols. (Philadelphia: HSP, 1940), 1: 43.
5. Jacob Duché, quoted in Austin K. Gray, *Benjamin Franklin's Library: A Short Account of the Library Company of Philadelphia* (New York: Macmillan, 1936), 20.
6. George Maurice Abbot, *A Short History of the Library Company of Philadelphia* (Philadelphia: LCP, 1913), 24.

7. Quoted from *Poulson's American Daily Advertiser*, December 10, 1824, in Carson, *History of the Historical Society of Pennsylvania*, 1: 46-47.
8. Among the many modern biographies of Penn, the most durable is Catherine Owens Peare, *William Penn: A Biography* (Philadelphia: J. B. Lippincott, 1957). Other excellent specialized studies include Joseph E. Illick, *William Penn the Politician: His Relations with the English Government* (Ithaca, N.Y.: Cornell University Press, 1965), and Mary Maples Dunn, *William Penn: Politics and Conscience* (Princeton, N.J.: Princeton University Press, 1967).
9. The essays in Jack Lindsey et al., *Worldly Goods: The Arts of Early Pennsylvania, 1680-1758* (Philadelphia: PMA, 1999) provide an excellent introduction to the material culture of upper-class Philadelphians in the colonial era.
10. Mary Maples Dunn, "The Personality of William Penn," in *The World of William Penn*, ed. Richard S. Dunn and Mary Maples Dunn (Philadelphia: University of Pennsylvania Press, 1986), 3.
11. Ministering Quaker women are studied in Rebecca Larson, *Daughters of Light: Quaker Women Preaching and Prophesying in the Colonies and Abroad, 1700-1775* (New York: Knopf, 1999).
12. *The America of 1750: Peter Kalm's Travels in North America*, ed. Adolph B. Benson, 2 vols. (New York: Dover, 1964), 1: 33; Penn to John Tillotson, January 29, 1667, quoted in Harry Emerson Wildes, *William Penn* (New York: Macmillan, 1974), 74.
13. Penn to unknown correspondent, July 1681, quoted in Nash, *Quakers and Politics*, 10.
14. Frederick B. Tolles, ed., "William Penn on Public and Private Affairs," *PMHB* 80 (1956), 246.
15. Penn to the Kings of the Indians, October 1681, in *Papers of William Penn*, 2:128. Pennsylvania's early Indian relations are covered extensively in Anthony F. C. Wallace, *King of the Delawares: Teedyuscung, 1700-1763* (Philadelphia: University of Pennsylvania Press, 1949), and James H. Merrell, *Into the American Woods: Negotiators on the Pennsylvania Frontier* (New York: W.W. Norton, 1999).
16. *Papers of William Penn*, 2: 128.
17. "Secretary Logan's Conference with the Indians," June 27, 1720, in "Presentation to the Historical Society of Pennsylvania of the Belt of Wampum, Delivered by the Indians to William Penn . . .," *Memoirs of the Historical Society of Pennsylvania* 6 (1858): 256.
18. Quoted in Carson, *History of the Historical Society of Pennsylvania*, 1: 246.
19. *Papers of William* Penn, 2:128.
20. For West's career as a painter see Ann Uhry Abrams, *The Valiant Hero: Benjamin West and Grand-Style History Painting* (Washington, D.C.: Smithsonian Institution Press, 1985).
21. Merrell's *Into the American Woods* provides extensive background to the "Paxton Boys" massacre.
22. Edwin Wolf 2nd and Marie Elena Korey, eds., *Quarter of a Millennium: The Library Company of Philadelphia, 1731-1981: A Selection of Books, Manuscripts, Maps, Prints, Drawings, and Paintings* (Philadelphia: LCP, 1981), 3.
23. For interethnic relations in early Pennsylvania, see Sally Schwartz, *"A Mixed Multitude": The Struggle for Toleration in Colonial Pennsylvania* (New York: New York University Press, 1987).
24. Stephanie Grauman Wolf's *Urban Village: Population, Community, and Family Structure in Germantown, Pennsylvania, 1683-1800* (Princeton, N.J.: Princeton University Press, 1976) is the indispensable book on Germans in early Philadelphia. A fine study of German immigrants is Aaron Spencer Fogleman, *Hopeful Journeys: German Immigration, Settlement, and Political Culture in Colonial America, 1717-1775* (Philadelphia: University of Pennsylvania Press, 1996).

25. For an introduction to the material culture of German-Americans in early Pennsylvania held by the Philadelphia Museum of Art, see Beatrice B. Garvan, *The Pennsylvania German Collection* (Philadelphia: PMA, 1982).
26. Wolf, *Brief History of the Library Company*, 7
27. The early history of Africans in Philadelphia is covered in Gary B. Nash, "Slaves and Slaveowners in Colonial Philadelphia," *William and Mary Quarterly* 3rd ser. 30 (1973): 223-56.
28. John Fanning Watson, *Annals of Philadelphia and Pennsylvania in Olden Times*, 3 vols., rev. ed. (Philadelphia: E.S. Stuart, 1900), 2: 261.
29. *Eccentric Biography; or Memoirs of Remarkable Female Characters, Ancient and Modern* (Worcester, Mass.: Isaiah Thomas Jr., 1804), 9-11.
30. For the significance of runaway advertisements, see Billy G. Smith and Richard Wojtowicz, *Blacks Who Stole Themselves: Advertisements for Runaways in the* Pennsylvania Gazette, *1728-1790* (Philadelphia: University of Pennsylvania Press, 1989).

Chapter 2

1. For two examples of Georgian grandeur, see Nicholas B. Wainwright, *Colonial Grandeur in Philadelphia: The House and Furniture of General John Cadwalader* (Philadelphia: HSP, 1964), and George B. Tatum, *Philadelphia Georgian: The City House of Samuel Powel and Some of Its Eighteenth-Century Neighbors* (Middletown, Conn: Wesleyan University Press, 1976).
2. Frederick Tolles's *Meeting House and Counting House: The Quaker Merchants of Colonial Pennsylvania, 1682-1763* (Chapel Hill: University of North Carolina Press, 1948) is a classic study. Thomas Doerflinger's *A Vigorous Spirit of Enterprise: Merchants and Economic Development in Revolutionary Philadelphia* (New York: W.W. Norton, 1986) is a deep study of the merchant community in the late colonial era.
3. Doerflinger, *Vigorous Spirit*, chapter 1.
4. Karin A. Wulf, *Not All Wives: Women of Colonial Philadelphia* (Ithaca, N.Y.: Cornell University Press, 2001) is the fullest study of the city's colonial women.
5. Indentured servitude in Philadelphia has been closely studied by Sharon Salinger, *"To Serve Well and Faithfully": Labor and Indentured Servants in Pennsylvania, 1682-1800* (New York: Cambridge University Press, 1987).
6. Quoted in Roger W. Moss, *The American Country House* (New York: Henry Holt, 1990), 82.
7. Ibid., 79.
8. Quoted in Gary B. Nash, *The Urban Crucible: Social Change, Political Consciousness, and the Origins of the American Revolution* (Cambridge, Mass.: Harvard University Press, 1979), 239. Atlantic basin mariners are brought to life by Marcus Rediker, *Between the Devil and the Deep Blue Sea: Merchant Seamen, Pirates, and the Anglo-American Maritime World, 1700-1750* (Cambridge, Mass.: Harvard University Press, 1987).
9. The role of African Americans in early maritime history is traced in Jeffrey Bolster, *Black Jacks: African American Seamen in the Age of Sail* (Cambridge, Mass.: Harvard University Press, 1997).
10. Especially notable among many studies of Philadelphia's artisans is Billy G. Smith, *The "Lower Sort": Philadelphia's Laboring People, 1750-1800* (Ithaca, N.Y.: Cornell University Press, 1990), and Ronald Schultz, *The Republic of Labor: Philadelphia Artisans and the Politics of Class, 1720-1830* (New York: Oxford University Press, 1993).

11. I have studied the values and lives of Philadelphia's artisans in *The Urban Crucible.*
12. John L. Cotter, Daniel G. Robert, and Michael Parrington, *The Buried Past: An Archaeological History of Philadelphia* (Philadelphia: University of Pennsylvania Press, 1993), 102.
13. Richard L. Bushman explores the meaning of houses and their furnishings at different levels in *The Refinement of America: Persons, Houses, Cities* (New York: Knopf, 1992).
14. Quoted in Steven Conn, *Museums and American Intellectual Life, 1876-1926* (Chicago: University of Chicago Press, 1998), 166.
15. Quoted in ibid., 172, 166.
16. Quoted in ibid., 168.
17. Wulf, *Not All Wives* is the fullest study of women retailers and enterprisers.
18. Laurel Thatcher Ulrich, *Goodwives: Image and Reality in the Lives of Women in Northern New England, 1650-1750* (New York: Oxford University Press, 1980), 34.
19. Jane C. Nylander, *Our Own Snug Fireside: Images of the New England Home, 1760-1860* (New York: Knopf, 1993).
20. William Smith, Jr., *The History of the Province of New-York* (1757), quoted in Cary Carson, Ronald Hoffman, and Peter J. Albert, eds., *Of Consuming Interest: The Style of Life in the Eighteenth Century* (Charlottesville: University Press of Virginia, 1994), 25.
21. Bushman, *The Refinement of America,* 182.
22. Quoted in ibid., 21.
23. John Smith Diary, quoted in Gary B. Nash, "Poverty and Poor Relief in Pre-Revolutionary Philadelphia," *William and Mary Quarterly* 3rd ser. 33 (1976): 6. An important study of poverty in early Philadelphia is John K. Alexander, *Render Them Submissive: Responses to Poverty in Philadelphia, 1760-1800* (Amherst: University of Massachusetts Press, 1980).
24. *Pennsylvania Gazette,* January 7, 1762.
25. Wulf, *Not All Wives* is the latest of new studies on Philadelphia women in the colonial era. Also important is Lisa W. Wilson, *Life After Death: Widows in Pennsylvania, 1750-1850* (Philadelphia: Temple University Press, 1992), and Patricia Cleary, "'She Will Be in the Shop': Women's Sphere of Trade in Eighteenth-Century Philadelphia and New York," *PMHB* 119 (1995): 181-202.
26. Elizabeth Drinker, *The Diary of Elizabeth Drinker: The Life Cycle of an Eighteenth-Century Woman,* ed. Elaine Foreman Crane, 3 vols. (Boston: Northeastern University Press, 1993), and Milcah Martha Moore, *Milcah Martha Moore's Book: A Commonplace Book from Revolutionary America* , ed. Catherine L. Blecki and Karin A. Wulf (University Park: Penn State University Press, 1997).
27. Studies of Franklin are legion. The most accessible is Esmond Wright, *Franklin of Philadelphia* (Cambridge, Mass.: Harvard University Press, 1986).
28. Quoted in Charles Eames and Ray Eames, *The World of Franklin and Jefferson: The American Revolution Bicentennial Administration Exhibition* (New York: n.p., 1976), 44.
29. Studies of Quaker antislavery in Philadelphia include Jean R. Soderlund, *Quakers and Slavery: A Divided Spirit* (Princeton, N.J.: Princeton University Press, 1985), and Gary B. Nash and Jean R. Soderlund, *Freedom by Degrees: Emancipation in Pennsylvania and Its Aftermath* (New York: Oxford University Press, 1991).

Chapter 3

1. Thomas Paine, *Common Sense and Other Political Writings*, ed. Nelson F. Adkins (Indianapolis: Bobbs-Merrill, 1953), 51.
2. For Philadelphia's role in the coming of the Revolution, see David Hawke, *In the Midst of Revolution: The Politics of Confrontation in Colonial America* (Philadelphia: University of Pennsylvania Press, 1961), and Richard Alan Ryerson, *The Revolution Is Now Begun: The Radical Committees of Philadelphia, 1765-1776* (Philadelphia: University of Pennsylvania Press, 1978).
3. The best account of the Quakers' travails is Jack D. Marietta, *The Reformation of American Quakerism, 1748-1783* (Philadelphia: University of Pennsylvania Press, 1984).
4. Franklin's troubled relationship with his son and the career of his grandson is well told in Willard Sterne Randall, *A Little Revenge: Benjamin Franklin and His Son* (Boston: Little Brown, 1984).
5. Watson to Rawle, September 16, 1826, quoted in Deborah Waters, "Philadelphia's Boswell: John Fanning Watson," *PMHB* 98 (1974): 15.
6. Hampton L. Carson, *History of the Historical Society of Pennsylvania*, 2 vols. (Philadelphia: HSP, 1940) 1: 110.
7. Quoted in John C. Miller, *Origins of the American Revolution* (Boston: Little, Brown, 1948), 460.
8. Quoted in Gary B. Nash, "The Transformation of Urban Politics, 1700-1765," *Journal of American History* 60 (1973): 628.
9. The dynamics of boycotting are explored in Gary B. Nash, *The Urban Crucible: Social Change, Political Consciousness, and the Origins of the American Revolution* (Cambridge, Mass.: Harvard University Press, 1979), and in Ryerson, *The Revolution Is Now Begun.*
10. Quoted in Edwin Wolf, 2nd and Marie Elena Korey, eds., *Quarter of a Millennium: The Library Company of Philadelphia, 1731-1981* (Philadelphia: LCP, 1981) 50. The central role of taverns in revolutionary politics is explored in chapter 5 of Peter Thompson, *Rum Punch and Revolution: Taverngoing and Public Life in Eighteenth-Century Philadelphia* (Philadelphia: University of Pennsylvania Press, 1999).
11. For tea and politics, see Ryerson, *The Revolution Is Now Begun*, ch. 2.
12. *Diary and Autobiography of John Adams*, ed. L. H. Butterfield, 4 vols. (New York: Atheneum, 1974), 2: 117.
13. Paine's role in Philadelphia politics is ably discussed in Eric Foner, *Tom Paine and Revolutionary America* (New York: Oxford University Press, 1976).
14. The story of the many lives of Independence Hall is the subject of Charlene Mires's forthcoming *Memories Lost and Found: Independence Hall in American History and Imagination.*
15. Loyalism in Philadelphia and its hinterland is fully explored in Anne M. Ousterhout, *A State Divided: Opposition in Pennsylvania to the American Revolution* (New York: Greenwood Press, 1987).
16. The campaign for Philadelphia is most fully covered in David G. Martin, *The Philadelphia Campaign: June 1777-July 1778* (Conshohocken, Pa.: Combined Books, 1993).
17. The black Philadelphians' revolutionary experience is explored in chapter 2 of Gary B. Nash, *Forging Freedom: The Formation of Philadelphia's Black Community, 1720-1840* (Cambridge, Mass.: Harvard University Press, 1988).
18. The extraordinary life of Joseph Brant is portrayed in Isabel Thompson Kelsay, *Joseph Brant,*

1743-1807: Man of Two Worlds (Syracuse, N.Y.: Syracuse University Press, 1984). Colonel Adam Hubley's journal was published in *PMHB* 33 (1909).

19. *The Selected Papers of Charles Willson Peale and His Family*, ed. Lillian B. Miller and Sidney Hart (New Haven, Conn.: Yale University Press, 1983-), 1: 402. A lively biography of Peale is Charles Coleman Sellers, *Charles Willson Peale* (New York: Charles Scribner's Sons, 1969).
20. Quoted in Edgar P. Richardson, Brooke Hindle, and Lillian Miller, *Charles Willson Peale and His World* (New York: Abrams, 1982), 180.
21. Linda K. Kerber explores the role of Philadelphia women in *Women of the Republic: Intellect and Ideology in Revolutionary America* (Chapel Hill: University of North Carolina Press, 1980).
22. Quoted in Mary Beth Norton, *Liberty's Daughters: The Revolutionary Experience of American Women, 1750-1800* (Boston: Little, Brown, 1980), 190.
23. The poem is included in the scrapbook version of the *Annals of Philadelphia* at the Library Company and is reproduced in *Milcah Martha Moore's Book: A Commonplace Book from Revolutionary America*, ed. Catherine La Courreye Blecki and Karin A. Wulf (University Park: Pennsylvania State University Press, 1997), 52.
24. Lewis Burd Walker's "The Life of Margaret Shippen, Wife of Benedict Arnold" was published in ten chapters in *PMHB* 24-26 (1900-1902).
25. *The Continental Almanac* (Philadelphia: Francis Bailey, 1781).
26. For a full treatment of the radical constitution and the role of Philadelphia's lower classes, see Steven Rosswurm, *Arms, Country, and Class: The Philadelphia Militia and the "Lower Sort" During the American Revolution*, 1775-1783 (New Brunswick, N.J.: Rutgers University Press, 1987), quoted passage p. 104.
27. Rush is quoted in David Freeman Hawke's fine biography, *Benjamin Rush: Revolutionary Gadfly* (Indianapolis: Bobbs-Merrill, 1971), 197. The fullest study of the 1776 Pennsylvania constitution is J. Paul Selsam, *The Pennsylvania Constitution of 1776: A Study in Revolutionary Democracy* (Philadelphia: University of Pennsylvania Press, 1936).
28. Robert Proud, "On the Violation of Established Order . . . ," *PMHB* 13 (1889): 435-56.
29. Quoted in Nash, *Forging Freedom*, 60.
30. *Freedom's Journal*, September 21, 1781.
31. Marietta, *Reformation of American Quakerism*, ch. 6.
32. Rosswurm, *Arms, Country, and Class*; chapter 7 treats the Fort Wilson riot fully.
33. Lyman Butterfield, ed., *The Letters of Benjamin Rush*, 2 vols. (Princeton, N.J.: Princeton University Press, 1951), 1: 243-44.
34. Quoted in Page Smith, *A New Age Now Begins: A People's History of the American Revolution*, 2 vols.(New York: Penguin Books, 1976), 2: 1783.
35. Sarah J. Purcell, *Sealed with Blood: National Identity and Public Memory of the Revolutionary War, 1775-1825* (Philadelphia: University of Pennsylvania Press, 2002). The Society of the Cincinnati is treated fully by Minor Myers, Jr., *Liberty Without Anarchy: A History of the Society of the Cincinnati* (Charlottesville: University Press of Virginia, 1983).
36. E. Wayne Carp, *To Starve the Army at Pleasure: Continental Army Administration and American Political Culture, 1775-1783* (Chapel Hill: University of North Carolina Press, 1984), covers the mutiny in detail.

Chapter 4

1. Quoted in David Freeman Hawke, *Benjamin Rush: Revolutionary Gadfly* (Indianapolis: Bobbs-Merrill, 1971), 346. A full account of Philadelphia's involvement in opposing and ratifying the Constitution is Saul Cornell, *Anti-Federalism and the Dissenting Tradition in America, 1788-1828* (Chapel Hill: University of North Carolina Press, 1999).
2. A now-standard work on creating the Constitution of 1787 is Gordon S. Wood, *The Creation of the American Republic, 1776-1787* (Chapel Hill: University of North Carolina Press, 1969).
3. Max Farrand, ed., *Records of the Federal Convention of 1787*, 4 vols. (New Haven, Conn.: Yale University Press, 1911), 4: 75.
4. The activities of the Pennsylvania Abolition Society after the Revolution are treated at length in Gary B. Nash and Jean R. Soderlund, *Freedom by Degrees: Emancipation in Pennsylvania and Its Aftermath* (New York: Oxford University Press, 1991).
5. The "Centinel" essays, and many other Philadelphia ones, pro and con, on ratifying the Constitution are in Merrill Jensen, *The Documentary History of the Ratification of the Constitution*; vol. 2: *Ratification of the Constitution by the States; Pennsylvania* (Madison: State Historical Society of Wisconsin, 1976).
6. David Waldstreicher, *In the Midst of Perpetual Fetes: The Making of American Nationalism, 1776-1820* (Chapel Hill: University of North Carolina Press, 1997), 18.
7. For an exploration of holiday-making in Philadelphia in the era of the early republic, see Simon P. Newman, *Parades and the Politics of the Street: Festive Culture in the Early American Republic* (Philadelphia: University of Pennsylvania Press, 1997), and Albrecht Koschnik, "Political Conflict and Public Contest: Rituals of National Celebration in Philadelphia, 1788-1815," *PMHB* 118 (1994): 209-48.
8. Krimmel's genre painting is perceptively discussed in Annelise Harding, *John Lewis Krimmel: Genre Artist of the Early Republic* (Winterthur, Del.: Winterthur Publications, 1994).
9. Quoted in Gary B. Nash, *Forging Freedom: The Formation of Philadelphia's Black Community, 1720-1840* (Cambridge, Mass.: Harvard University Press, 1988), 181.
10. Quoted in Mark Thistlethwaite, "The Artist as Interpreter of American History," *In This Academy: The Pennsylvania Academy of the Fine Arts, 1805-1976* (Philadelphia: PAFA, 1976), 105.
11. For the cult of Washington, see Michael Kammen, *A Season of Youth: The American Revolution and the Historical Imagination* (New York: Knopf, 1978). Mathew Carey and other Philadelphia printers of this era are ably discussed in Rosalind Remer, *Printers and Men of Capital: Philadelphia Book Publishers in the New Republic* (Philadelphia: University of Pennsylvania Press, 1996).
12. A general account of Philadelphia as the federal city is Richard G. Miller, *Philadelphia—The Federalist City: A Study of Urban Politics, 1789-1801* (Port Washington, N.Y.: Kennikat Press, 1976).
13. Quoted in Bray Hammond, *Banks and Politics in America: From the Revolution to the Civil War* (Princeton, N.J.: Princeton University Press, 1957), 54.
14. Quoted in Frederick E. Hoxie, ed., *Encyclopedia of North American Indians* (Boston: Houghton Mifflin, 1996), 532. For Indian policy in the early republic see Anthony F. C. Wallace, *Jefferson and the Indians: The Tragic Fate of the First Americans* (Cambridge, Mass.: Harvard University Press, 1999).

15. Gary B. Nash, "Reverberations of Haiti in the American North: Black Saint Dominguans in Philadelphia," *Pennsylvania History*, Special Supplement 65 (1998): 44-73.
16. Quoted in Nash, *Forging Freedom*, 124. The classic study of the yellow fever crisis of 1793 is J. H. Powell, *Bring Out Your Dead: The Great Plague of Yellow Fever in Philadelphia in 1793* (Philadelphia: University of Pennsylvania Press, 1949; reprint 1993). More recent work can be found in J. Worth Estes and Billy G. Smith, eds., *A Melancholy Scene of Devastation: The Public Response to the 1793 Philadelphia Yellow Fever Epidemic* (Philadelphia: College of Physicians of Philadelphia and LCP, 1997).
17. Quoted in Dennis Clark, *The Irish in Philadelphia: Ten Generations of Urban Experience* (Philadelphia: Temple University Press, 1973), 15.
18. The fullest account of the radical Irish immigrants is Robert J. Twomey, *Jacobins and Jeffersonians: Anglo-American Radicalism in the United States, 1790-1820* (New York: Garland, 1989).
19. *Gazette of the United States*, May 10, 1792; Russell F. Weigley, ed., *Philadelphia: A 300-Year History* (New York: W.W. Norton, 1982), 194.
20. John Adams, *The Works of John Adams*, ed. Charles Francis Adams, 10 vols. (Boston: Little, Brown, 1850-56), 9: 279.
21. Quoted in Charles Coleman Sellers, *Charles Willson Peale* (New York: Charles Scribner's Sons, 1969), 276. For the Whiskey Rebellion, see Thomas P. Slaughter, *The Whiskey Rebellion: Epilogue to the American Revolution* (New York: Oxford University Press, 1986).
22. The Alien and Sedition acts are extensively treated in James Morton Smith, *Freedom's Fetters: The Alien and Sedition Laws and American Civil Liberties* (Ithaca, N.Y.: Cornell University Press, 1956). Bache and his newspaper are treated in James Tagg, *Benjamin Franklin Bache and the Philadelphia* Aurora (Philadelphia: University of Pennsylvania Press, 1991).
23. Quoted in Susan Branson, "Politics and Gender: The Political Consciousness of Philadelphia Women in the 1790s," unpublished ms., 57, and treated also in Linda K. Kerber, *Women of the Republic: Intellect and Ideology in Revolutionary America* (Chapel Hill: University of North Carolina Press, 1980), 222.
24. Quoted in Branson, "Politics and Gender," 3.
25. For Peale's long, fascinating career, see Charles Sellers's biography of his ancestor cited above in n.21; also valuable are Edgar P. Richardson, Brooke Hindle, and Lillian B. Miller, *Charles Willson Peale and His World* (New York: Abrams, 1982); Lillian B. Miller and David C. Ward, eds., *New Perspectives on Charles Willson Peale* (Pittsburgh: University of Pittsburgh Press, 1991); and the beautifully edited *The Selected Papers of Charles Willson Peale and His Family*, ed. Lillian Miller and Sidney Hart, 6 vols. (New Haven, Conn.: Yale University Press, 1983-2000).
26. Peale is quoted in Sellers, *Charles Willson Peale*, 191.
27. Kenneth Silverman, *A Cultural History of the American Revolution* (New York: Thomas Y. Crowell, 1976), 429.
28. For sharply contrasting views of Peale's museum, see Charles Coleman Sellers, *Mr. Peale's Museum: Charles Willson Peale and the First Popular Museum of Natural Science and Art* (New York: W.W. Norton, 1980), and David R. Bingham, *Public Culture in the Early Republic: Peale's Museum and Its Audience* (Washington, D.C.: Smithsonian Institution Press, 1995).
29. Quoted in Bingham, *Public Culture in the Early Republic*, 122.
30. Sidney Hart to Gary B. Nash, May 17, 2000. The quote about Peale as a "Furious Whig" is from Sellers, *Mr. Peale's Museum*, 8.
31. On the Philadelphia work of Latrobe, Strickland, Haviland, and Walter, see Theo B. White

et al., *Philadelphia Architecture in the Nineteenth Century* (Philadelphia: University of Pennsylvania Press, 1953). The quote is from *The Correspondence and Miscellaneous Papers of Benjamin Henry Latrobe*, ed. John C. Van Horne, 3 vols. (New Haven, Conn.: Yale University Press, 1988), 3: 76.

32. Hampton L. Carson, *A History of the Historical Society of Pennsylvania*, 2 vols. (Philadelphia: HSP, 1940), 1: 32.

Chapter 5

1. The best account of Irish immigrants in Philadelphia is Dennis Clark, *The Irish in Philadelphia: Ten Generations of Urban Experience* (Philadelphia: Temple University Press, 1973).
2. Environmental and spatial rearrangements of the nineteenth-century city are treated in William W. Cutler, III and Howard Gillette, Jr., eds., *The Divided Metropolis: Social and Spatial Dimensions of Philadelphia, 1800-1975* (Westport, Conn.: Greenwood Press, 1980).
3. Black Philadelphians in the antebellum era are studied by Emma Lapsansky, *Neighborhoods in Transition: William Penn's Dream and Urban Reality* (New York: Garland, 1994); Gary B. Nash, *Forging Freedom: The Formation of Philadelphia's Black Community, 1720-1840* (Cambridge, Mass.: Harvard University Press, 1988); and Julie Winch, *Philadelphia's Black Elite: Activism, Accommodation, and the Struggle for Autonomy, 1787-1848* (Philadelphia: Temple University Press, 1988), 369.
4. Edward Needles, *Ten Years' Progress*, quoted in Theodore Hershberg, ed., *Philadelphia: Work, Space, Family, and Group Experience in the Nineteenth Century* (New York: Oxford University Press, 1981), 369.
5. Forten's leading role in the antebellum years is chronicled in Nash, *Forging Freedom* and Winch, *Philadelphia's Black Elite*. See also Julie Winch, *A Gentleman of Color: The Life of James Forten* (New York, Oxford University Press, 2002).
6. The excavation of the African Baptist Church cemetery and the analysis of skeletal remains described in the subsequent paragraph is detailed in John L. Cotter, Daniel G. Roberts, and Michael Parrington, *The Buried Past: An Archaeological History of Philadelphia* (Philadelphia: University of Pennsylvania Press, 1993), 284-87.
7. Philip Scranton, *Proprietary Capitalism: The Textile Manufacture at Philadelphia, 1800-1885* (Cambridge: Cambridge University Press, 1983), xi.
8. Ibid., 268. For a full study of Manayunk in the early years, see Cynthia J. Shelton, *The Mills of Manayunk: Industrialization and Social Conflict in the Philadelphia Region, 1787-1837* (Baltimore: Johns Hopkins University Press, 1986).
9. Bruce Sinclair, *Philadelphia's Philosopher Mechanics: A History of the Franklin Institute, 1824-1865* (Baltimore: Johns Hopkins University Press, 1974), 108.
10. Locomotive building in Philadelphia is the subject of John K. Brown, *The Baldwin Locomotive Works, 1831-1915* (Baltimore: Johns Hopkins University Press, 1995).
11. Thomas R. Heinrich, *Ships for the Seven Seas: Philadelphia's Shipbuilding in the Age of Industrial Capitalism* (Baltimore: Johns Hopkins University Press, 1997) is a comprehensive study of nineteenth-century shipbuilding in Philadelphia.
12. Building the expanding city's infrastructure is treated in Sam Bass Warner Jr., *The Private City: Philadelphia in Three Periods of Its Growth* (Philadelphia: University of Pennsylvania Press, 1968; second edition 1987).
13. Nicholas B. Wainwright, "Augustus Kollner: Artist," *PMHB* 84 (1960): 325-51.

14. Among the most important books on antebellum labor are Scranton, *Proprietary Capitalism*; Shelton, *Mills of Manayunk*; Bruce Laurie, *Working People of Philadelphia, 1800-1850* (Phila-delphia: Temple University Press, 1980); Ronald Schultz, *The Republic of Labor: Philadelphia Artisans and the Politics of Class, 1720-1830* (New York: Oxford University Press, 1993); Allen F. David and Mark H. Haller, eds., *The Peoples of Philadelphia: A History of Ethnic Groups and Lower-Class Life, 1790-1940* (Philadelphia: Temple University Press, 1973; reprint Philadelphia: University of Pennsylvania Press, 1998); and Laura Rigal, *The American Manufactory: Art, Labor, and the World of Things in the Early Republic* (Princeton, N.J.: Princeton University Press, 1998).
15. *The Mysteries and Miseries of Philadelphia . . . ; A Sketch of the Most Degraded Classes in the City* (Philadelphia: n.p., 1853), 12.
16. James W. Alexander, *The American Mechanic and Workingman* (1847; rev. ed. Philadelphia, 1867), 197.
17. Lewis H. Arky, "The Mechanics Union of Trade Associations and the Formation of the Philadelphia Workingmen's Movement," *PMHB* 86 (1952): 142-76; the quote is from *National Gazette*, June 14, 1827.
18. *United States Gazette*, June 4, 1835.
19. *Public Ledger*, August 29, 1842, quoted in Elizabeth M. Geffen, "Violence in Philadelphia in the 1840's and 1850's," *Pennsylvania History* 36 (1969): 398.
20. George Lippard, *George Lippard, Prophet of Protest: Writings of an American Radical*, ed. David S. Reynolds (New York: Peter Lang, 1986), 4.
21. Lippard, "Jesus and the Poor" (1848), ibid., 55.
22. *Quaker City*, June 30, 1849, quoted in Roger Butterfield, "George Lippard and His Secret Brotherhood," *PMHB* 79 (1955): 286.
23. *Quaker City*, September 29, 1849, quoted in Lippard, *George Lippard*, 219.
24. *Quaker City*, May 12, 1849, ibid., 5.
25. Edwin Wolf, 2d and Marie Elena Korey, *Quarter of a Millennium: The Library Company of Philadelphia, 1731-1981* (Philadelphia: LCP, 1981), 239.
26. James Green to Gary B. Nash, June 12, 2000.
27. Newspaper clipping from unidentified Philadelphia newspaper, Mathew Carey Scrapbooks, Miscellaneous, 10: 31, LCP.
28. The mounting racial conflict in the 1830s is covered in Nash, *Forging Freedom*, and in Winch, *Philadelphia's Black Elite*.
29. Diary of Augustus James Pleasonton, 1838-1844, HSP.
30. *Pennsylvania Freeman*, August 1842.
31. *The Liberator*, September 9, 1842, quoted in Herbert Aptheker, ed., *A Documentary History of the Negro People in the United States*, 2 vols. (New York: Citadel Press, 1951), 1: 220.
32. Quoted in Nick Salvatore, *We All Got History: The Memory Books of Amos Webber* (New York: Times Books, 1996), 24.
33. Michael Feldberg, *The Philadelphia Riots of 1844: A Study in Ethnic Conflict* (New York: Greenwood Press, 1975) is the most comprehensive study of the antebellum riots. Warner's *Private City* also has a valuable analysis. For Bishop Kendrick, see Joseph L. J. Kirlin, *Catholicity in Philadelphia from the Earliest Missionaries down to the Present Time* (Philadelphia: John Joseph McVey, 1909).
34. Quoted in Hugh J. Nolan, *The Most Reverend Francis Patrick Kendrick, Third Bishop of Philadelphia, 1830-1851* (Washington, D.C.: Catholic University of America, 1948), 304.

35. *Native American*, May 7, 1844; *Public Ledger*, May 8, 1844, quoted in Feldman, *Philadelphia Riots of 1844*, 109, 108.
36. *Spirit of the Times*, July 9, 1844.
37. Jean Barth Toll and Mildred S. Gillam, eds., *Invisible Philadelphia: Community through Voluntary Organizations* (Philadelphia: Atwater Kent Museum, 1995), 880.
38. Kirlin, *Catholicity in Philadelphia*, 304.
39. Quoted in Feldberg, *Philadelphia Riots of 1844*, 129.
40. Joseph Sill Diaries, HSP, 8: 4, 262, quoted in Elizabeth M. Geffen, "Joseph Sill and His Diary," *PMHB* 94 (1970): 317-18.

Chapter 6

1. Charles Godfrey Leland, *Memoirs* (New York: D. Appleton, 1893), 216.
2. The most comprehensive study of antebellum violence is Michael Feldberg, *The Philadelphia Riots of 1844: A Study of Ethnic Conflict* (Westport, Conn.: Greenwood Press, 1975).
3. Quoted in Elizabeth M. Geffen, "Violence in Philadelphia in the 1840's and 1850's," *Pennsylvania History* 36 (1969): 405.
4. Many scholars examine these problems in *Philadelphia: Work, Space, Family, and Group Experience in the Nineteenth Century: Essays Toward an Interdisciplinary History of the City*, ed. Theodore Hershberg (New York: Oxford University Press, 1981).
5. Alexis de Tocqueville, *The Republic of the United States of America and Its Political Institutions, Reviewed and Examined*, trans. Henry Reeves, 2 vols. (New York: A. S. Barnes, 1863), 1: 332.
6. Lee's career is discussed and her famous *The Life and Religious Experience of Jarena Lee* republished in William L. Andrews, ed., *Sisters of the Spirit: Three Black Women's Autobiographies of the Nineteenth Century* (Bloomington: Indiana University Press, 1986).
7. Harry C. Silcox, "Delay and Neglect: Negro Public Education in Antebellum Philadelphia," *PMHB* 97 (1973): 463.
8. Roger Lane, *William Dorsey's Philadelphia and Ours: On the Past and Future of the Black City in America* (New York: Oxford University Press, 1991), 137.
9. Quoted in Bruce Laurie, *Working People of Philadelphia, 1800-1850* (Philadelphia: Temple University Press, 1980), 41.
10. Quoted in Donald Yaccavone, "The Transformation of the Black Temperance Movement, 1827-1854," *Journal of the Early Republic* 8 (1988): 295.
11. Michael Meranze, *Laboratories of Virtue: Punishment, Revolution, and Authority in Philadelphia, 1760-1835* (Chapel Hill: University of North Carolina Press, 1996), 3.
12. Norman Johnston, *Eastern State Penitentiary: Crucible of Good Intentions* (Philadelphia: PMA, 1994). The quotation from Dickens is on 58.
13. Quoted in Meranze, *Laboratories of Virtue*, 278.
14. Frederick B. Tolles, "Lucretia Coffin Mott," in *Notable American Women: A Biographical Dictionary*, ed. Edward T. James et al., 3 vols. (Cambridge, Mass: Harvard University Press, 1971), 2: 592. Almost every aspect of women's involvement in reform movements can be explored through biographies of Mott, including Otelia Cromwell, *Lucretia Mott* (Cambridge, Mass: Harvard University Press, 1958) and Margaret Hope Bacon, *Valiant Friend: The Life of Lucretia Mott* (New York: Walker, 1980).

15. For the background on the Seneca Falls Convention and the text of the Declaration, see Bradford Miller, *Returning to Seneca Falls: The First Woman's Rights Convention and Its Meaning for Men and Women Today* (New York: Lindisfarne Press, 1995).

16. Paul S. Boyer, "Sarah Josepha Buell Hale," in *Notable American Women*, 2: 111. A fine biography of Hale and her work is Patricia Okker, *Our Sister Editors: Sarah J. Hale and the Tradition of Nineteenth-Century American Women Editors* (Athens: University of Georgia Press, 1995).

17. Quoted in Russell F. Weigley, ed., *Philadelphia: A 300-Year History* (New York: W.W. Norton, 1982), 336.

18. Quoted in Lloyd C. M. Hare, *The Greatest American Woman, Lucretia Mott* (New York: American Historical Society, 1937), 83.

19. Quoted in P. J. Staudenraus, *The American Colonization Movement, 1816-1865* (New York: Columbia University Press, 1961), 125.

20. Quoted in ibid., 128.

21. Gurley, quoted in ibid., 125-26.

22. Edward S. Abdy, *Journal of a Residence and Tour in the United States...* (1835), 3: 321, quoted in Julie Winch, *Philadelphia's Black Elite: Activism, Accommodation, and the Struggle for Autonomy, 1787-1848* (Philadelphia: Temple University Press, 1988), 46.

23. Samuel J. May, *Some Recollections of Our Antislavery Conflict* (Boston: Fields, Osgood, 1869), quoted in Gary B. Nash, *Forging Freedom: The Formation of Philadelphia's Black Community* (Cambridge, Mass.: Harvard University Press, 1988), 276.

24. Quoted in Elizabeth M. Geffen, "Philadelphia Protestantism and Social Reform," *Pennsylvania History* 30 (1963): 197.

25. Butler's Philadelphia career and his mass slave sale in 1859 is chronicled in Malcolm Bell, Jr., *Major Butler's Legacy: Five Generations of a Slaveholding Family* (Athens: University of Georgia Press, 1987).

26. Two important studies of the Hicksite movement are Robert W. Doherty, *The Hicksite Separation: A Sociological Analysis of Religious Schism in Early Nineteenth-Century America* (New Brunswick, N.J.: Rutgers University Press, 1967), and H. Larry Ingle, *Quakers in Conflict: The Hicksite Reformation* (Knoxville: University of Tennessee Press, 1986).

27. Ingle, *Quakers in Conflict*, 146, 134.

28. Hampton L. Carson, *A History of the Historical Society of Pennsylvania*, 2 vols. (Philadelphia: HSP, 1940), 1: 158.

29. Elizabeth M. Geffen, *Philadelphia Unitarianism, 1796-1861* (Philadelphia: University of Pennsylvania Press, 1961), 190; the second quote is from Geffen, "William Henry Furness, Philadelphia Antislavery Preacher," *PMHB* 82 (1958): 269.

30. Joseph Sturge, *A Visit to the United States in 1841...* (London: Hamilton, Adams, 1841), 40.

31. Purvis's important role as a black leader in Philadelphia is covered in Winch, *Philadelphia's Black Elite.*

32. Howard Jones, *Mutiny on the Amistad: The Saga of a Slave Revolt and Its Impact on American Abolition, Law, and Diplomacy* (New York: Oxford University Press, 1987).

33. *National Anti-Slavery Standard*, April 29, 1841.

34. Ibid.

35. The Christiana "riot," as it came to be called, is analyzed in Jonathan Katz, *Resistance at Christiana: The Fugitive Slave Rebellion, Christiana, Pennsylvania; A Documentary Account* (New York:

Thomas Y. Crowell, 1974), and Thomas P. Slaughter, *Bloody Dawn: The Christiana Riot and Racial Violence in the Antebellum North* (New York: Oxford University Press, 1991).

36. William Dusinberre, *Civil War Issues in Philadelphia, 1856-1865* (Philadelphia: University of Pennsylvania Press, 1965), 86.
37. *Public Ledger*, December 2, 1859, reported the meeting fully.
38. The description of Forrest is quoted in Ellis Paxson Oberholtzer, *The Literary History of Philadelphia* (Philadelphia: George W. Jacobs, 1906), 243. For a history of antebellum Philadelphia theater, see Arthur H. Wilson, *A History of the Philadelphia Theater, 1835 to 1855* (Philadelphia: University of Pennsylvania Press, 1935).
39. Philip Lapsansky, "Afro-Americana: Inventing Black Folks," *1997 Annual Report of the Library Company of Philadelphia* (Philadelphia: LCP, 1998), 29-46. I am indebted to Lapsansky for information on Robert Douglass, Jr.'s illuminated transparencies of Washington crossing the Delaware.
40. Street theater is incisively treated in Susan G. Davis, *Parades and Power: Street Theatre in Nineteenth-Century Philadelphia* (Philadelphia: Temple University Press, 1986).
41. Quoted in ibid., 82, 94, from *Democratic Press*, May 19, 1825, and *Pennsylvania Gazette*, May 21, 1833.
42. Quoted in Milo Naeve, *John Lewis Krimmel: An Artist in Federal America* (Newark: University of Delaware Press, 1987), 46.
43. Carson, *History of the Historical Society of Pennsylvania*, 1: 46.
44. Doris Devine Fanelli, *History of the Portrait Collection, Independence National Historical Park*, Transactions of the American Philosophical Society, forthcoming, ch. 1, pp. 2-3.
45. Watson to J. Francis Fisher, quoted in Deborah Waters, "John Fanning Watson: Philadelphia's Boswell," *PMHB* 98 (1974): 39-41.
46. Waters, "Philadelphia's Boswell," 34-35.
47. Quoted in ibid., 24.
48. The Lyon incident is fully analyzed in Laura Rigal, *The American Manufactory: Art, Labor, and the World of Things in the Early Republic* (Princeton, N.J.: Princeton University Press, 1998), ch. 6.
49. Joseph Sill Diary, Historical Society of Pennsylvania, III, 344, quoted in Elizabeth M. Geffen, "Joseph Sill and His Diary," *PMHB* 94 (1970): 289.
50. The anti-Catholic riots are discussed fully in Michael Feldberg, *The Philadelphia Riots of 1844: A Study in Ethnic Conflict* (New York: Greenwood Press, 1975), and Sam Bass Warner, Jr., *The Private City: Philadelphia in Three Periods of Growth* (Philadelphia: University of Pennsylvania Press, 1968; 2nd ed. 1987), ch. 7.
51. Quoted in Susan Stitt, "The Historical Society of Pennsylvania: The First Forty Years, 1824-1864," in *Historical Consciousness in the Early Republic: The Origins of State Historical Societies, Museums and Collections, 1791-1861*, ed. H. G. Jones (Chapel Hill: North Caroliniana Society, 1995), 59.
52. Carson, *History of the Historical Society of Pennsylvania*, 1: 69.
53. John Fanning Watson, *Annals of Philadelphia and Pennsylvania in the Olden Time*, 3 vols. (Philadelphia: E. S. Stuart, 1900), 1: 163
54. Ibid., 1: 419.
55. Quoted in Charles Peterson, "Carpenters' Hall," *Historic Philadelphia: From the Founding Until*

the Early Nineteenth Century, Transactions of the American Philosophical Society 43, pt. 1 (Philadelphia: APS, 1953), 113.

56. Introduction to John Jay Smith and John Fanning Watson, comps., *American Historical and Literary Curiosities* (Philadelphia: National Publishing, 1849),
57. George Lippard, *Thomas Paine: Author-Soldier of the American Revolution* (Philadelphia: n.p., 1852), 1-2.
58. Whitfield Bell, *The Bust of Thomas Paine* (Philadelphia: APS, 1974), 8.
59. David S. Reynolds, *George Lippard* (Boston: Twayne Publishers, 1982), 66.
60. Quoted from Lippard, *Legends of Mexico* (1847), quoted in ibid., 66.
61. David S. Reynolds, *George Lippard: Prophet of Protest: Writings of an American Radical, 1822-1854* (New York: Peter Lang, 1986), 116-17.
62. Lippard, *Thomas Paine*, 2.
63. George Lippard, *Quaker City; or The Monks of Monk Hall* (Philadelphia, 1876), 3: 462.
64. *Pennsylvania Freeman*, December 24, 1846, January 3, 1850.
65. *The Celebration of the Eighty-third Anniversary of the Declaration of American Independence by the Banneker Institute*... (Philadelphia, 1859), in *Autobiography of Dr. William Henry Johnson* (1900; repr. New York: Haskell House, 1970), 219-30.
66. Lippard, *Thomas Paine*, 2.
67. Fanelli, *History of the Portrait Collection*, chapter 2, 11. Fanelli tells the full story of the city's purchase of most of Peale's paintings.

Chapter 7

1. William Dusinberre, *Civil War Issues in Philadelphia, 1856-1865* (Philadelphia: University of Pennsylvania Press, 1965), 88.
2. *Proceedings of the Great Union Meeting, Philadelphia, December 7, 1859* (Philadelphia, n.d.), quoted in Elizabeth M. Geffen, *Philadelphia Unitarianism, 1796-1861* (Philadelphia: University of Pennsylvania Press,1961), 232.
3. *Proceedings of the Great Union Meeting*, 43.
4. Hampton L. Carson, *A History of the Historical Society of Pennsylvania*, 2 vols. (Philadelphia: HSP, 1940), 1: 237.
5. Minutes of Council, March 9, 1863, HSP Archives.
6. Carson, *History of the Historical Society of Pennsylvania*, 1: 310-11.
7. Fanny Kemble Wister, ed., "Sarah Butler Wister's Civil War Diary," *PMHB* 102 (1978): 271-327; the quoted passage is on 277.
8. Quoted in George E. Stephens, *Voice of Thunder: The Civil War Letters of George E. Stephens*, ed. Donald Yacovone (Urbana: University of Illinois Press, 1997), 15. For the political tension and violence that wracked Philadelphia on the eve of Civil War, see Dusinberre, *Civil War Issues*.
9. Recruitment in the city is addressed in J. Matthew Gallman, *Mastering Wartime: A Social History of Philadelphia During the Civil War* (Cambridge: Cambridge University Press, 1990; rep. Philadelphia: University of Pennsylvania Press, 2000).
10. George Wolff Fahnestock Diaries, August 9, 10, 12, 1863, HSP.

11. Quoted from *Christian Recorder* in James M. McPherson, *The Negro's Civil War: How American Negroes Felt and Acted During the War for the Union* (New York: Pantheon, 1965), 181.
12. Frederick Douglass, *The Frederick Douglass Papers*, ser. 1, *Speeches, Debates, and Interviews*, ed. John W. Blassingame, 5 vols. (New Haven, Conn.: Yale University Press, 1979–92), 3: 592.
13. *Philadelphia Ledger*, June 25, 1863.
14. William Wells Brown, quoted in Russell F. Weigley, ed., *Philadelphia: A 300-Year History* (New York: W.W. Norton, 1982), 363.
15. Charles Biddle, *Speech of Charles Biddle, Delivered in the House of Representatives . . .* (Washington, D.C., 1862), quoted in Nicholas B. Wainwright, "The Loyal Opposition in Civil War Philadelphia," *PMHB* 88 (1964): 296; Charles Ingersoll, *A Letter to a Friend in a Slave State . . .* (Philadelphia, 1862), quoted in ibid., 297.
16. *Address of the Democratic State Central Committee . . .* (Philadelphia, 1862), quoted in ibid., 298.
17. *Constitution and By-laws of the Central Democratic Club . . .* (Philadelphia, 1863), 1–2.
18. Ingersoll's address, reported in the *Press*, January 9, 1863, is quoted in Wainwright, "Loyal Opposition," 299; Fisher's comment is in *A Philadelphia Perspective: The Diary of Sidney George Fisher Covering the Years 1834-1871*, ed. Nicholas B. Wainwright (Philadelphia: HSP, 1967), 444.
19. Quoted in Wainwright, "Loyal Opposition," 307.
20. Quoted in ibid., 313.
21. The role of the Union League is treated in Maxwell Whiteman, *Gentlemen in Crisis: The First Century of the Union League of Philadelphia, 1862-1962* (Philadelphia: Union League of Philadelphia, 1975).
22. Allan Nevins, quoted in Gallman, *Mastering Wartime*, 115.
23. R. J. M. Blackett, ed., *Thomas Morris Chester, Black Civil War Correspondent* (Baton Rouge: Louisiana State University Press, 1989).
24. *Philadelphia Inquirer*, May 25, 26, 1865, quoted in Cecilia Elizabeth O'Leary, *To Die For: The Paradox of American Patriotism* (Princeton, N.J.: Princeton University Press, 1999), 31, 33.
25. J. Thomas Scharf and Thompson Westcott, *History of Philadelphia, 1609-1884*, 3 vols. (Philadelphia: J.H. Everts, 1884).
26. Carson, *History of the Historical Society of Pennsylvania*, 1: 306–7.
27. Linus P. Brockett and Mary C. Vaughan, *Woman's Work in the Civil War: A Record of Heroism, Patriotism and Patience* (Philadelphia: Ziegler, McCurdy, 1867), 596.
28. Quoted in Jeanie Attie, "War Work and Domesticity in the North," in *Divided Houses: Gender and the Civil War*, ed. Catherine Clinton and Nina Silber (New York: Oxford University Press, 1992), 257.
29. For a study of Civil War nursing, see Jane E. Schultz, "The Inhospitable Hospital: Gender and Professionalism in Civil War Medicine," *Signs* 17 (1992): 363–92.
30. Quoted in Gallman, *Mastering Wartime*, 117.
31. Quoted in ibid., 127.
32. Quoted in ibid., 153.
33. For a complete description of articles in the Penn parlor, see *Memorial of the William Penn Parlor, in the Great Central Fair* (Philadelphia: James B. Rodgers, 1864).
34. Sydney George Fisher, June 11, 1864, in Wainwright, ed., *A Philadelphia Perspective*, 473.
35. *Philadelphia Public Ledger*, September 4, 1861, quoted in Gallman, *Mastering Wartime*, 242.
36. Fisher, April 15, 1865, in *A Philadelphia Perspective*, 492; *Philadelphia Bulletin*, April 22, 1865.
37. For the streetcar desegregation controversy and the murder of Catto, see Harry C. Silcox,

"Nineteenth-Century Philadelphia Black Militant: Octavius V. Catto (1839-1871)," *Pennsylvania History* 44 (1977): 53-76; for the broader context of racial violence, see Roger Lane, *Roots of Violence in Black Philadelphia, 1860-1940* (Cambridge, Mass.: Harvard University Press, 1986).

38. For African American life after the Civil War, see Roger Lane's masterful *William Dorsey's Philadelphia and Ours: On the Past and Future of the Black City in America* (New York: Oxford University Press, 1991).
39. Carson, *History of the Historical Society of Pennsylvania*, 1: 333.
40. Ibid., 2: 1; 1: 374.
41. Edwin Wolf, *"At the Instance of Benjamin Franklin": A Brief History of the Library Company of Philadelphia*, rev. ed. (Philadelphia: LCP, 1995), 57.
42. Quoted in Donald G. Davis, Jr. and Jeannette Woodward, "Lloyd Pearsall Smith," *American National Biography*, ed. John A. Garraty and Mark C. Carnes, 24 vols. (New York: Oxford University Press, 1999), 20: 246.
43. Carson, *History of the Historical Society of Pennsylvania*, 1: 43.
44. *Harper's Weekly*, October 17, 1868.
45. The *Press*, April 27, 28, 1870.
46. Scharf and Westcott, *History of Philadelphia*, 1: 836-37.

Chapter 8

1. Among many books on the Centennial Exposition, especially important are Robert W. Rydell, *All the World's a Fair: Visions of Empire at American International Exhibitions, 1876-1916* (Chicago: University of Chicago Press, 1984); John Maass, *The Glorious Enterprise: The Centennial Exhibition of 1876 and J. J. Schwarzmann, Architect-in-Chief* (Watkins Glen, N.Y.: American Life Foundation, 1973); Robert Post, ed., *A Centennial Exhibition* (Washington, D.C.: Smithsonian Institution Press, 1976), and Dee Brown, *Year of the Century, 1876* (New York: Scribner, 1966).
2. Quoted in Maass, *Glorious Enterprise*, 112. The opening day crowd, reported in the *New York Herald*, is given in Russell Weigley, ed., *Philadelphia: A 300-Year History* (New York: W.W. Norton, 1982), 466.
3. Quoted in Weigley, ed., *Philadelphia*, 466.
4. J. S. Ingram, *The Centennial Exposition, Described and Illustrated Being a Concise and Graphic Description of This Grand Enterprise* (Philadelphia: Hubbard Brothers, 1876), 78.
5. The Indian encampment is described in the *Press*, April 3, 1876.
6. William Dean Howells, "A Sennight of the Centennial," *Atlantic Monthly* 38 (1876): 103, quoted in Robert W. Rydell, "All the World's a Fair: America's International Expositions, 1876-1916," Ph.D. dissertation, UCLA, 1980, 47.
7. *Christian Recorder*, March 16, 1872, quoted in Mitch Kachun, "Before the Eyes of All Nations: African-American Identity and Historical Memory at the Centennial Exposition of 1876," *Pennsylvania History* 65 (1998): 309.
8. The *Press*, May 14, 1873, quoted in Philip S. Foner, "Black Participation in the Centennial of 1876," *Phylon* 39 (1978): 284.
9. *Christian Recorder*, March 5, 1874. The struggle to erect a monument to Allen is best told in Kachun, "Before the Eyes of All Nations," 309-23.

10. *Press*, June 13, 1876, quoted in Kachun, "Before the Eyes of All Nations," 316-17.
11. John Mercer Langston, *Freedom and Citizenship: Selected Lectures and Addresses* (1883; reprint Miami: Mnemosyne Publishing, 1969), 127.
12. Quoted in Rydell, "All the World's a Fair," 52.
13. Frank Leslie, *Illustrated Historical Register of the Centennial Exposition* (New York: Frank Leslie, 1876), 128.
14. Quoted in Foner, "Black Participation in the Centennial of 1876," 289.
15. Quoted in Brown, *Year of the Century*, 139; for a full exploration of the Women's Committee, see Mary Frances Cordato, "Toward a New Century: Women and the Philadelphia Centennial Exhibition, 1876," *PMHB* 107 (1983): 113-35.
16. *New Century for Women*, August 26, 1876.
17. Ibid., August 5, 1876.
18. *Woman's Journal*, January 8, 1876, quoted in Cordato, "Towards a New Century," 130.
19. Quoted in Brown, *Year of the Century*, 145.
20. *Evening Bulletin*, July 5, 1876.
21. *Evening Bulletin*, April 18, 1874, quoted in Rydell, "All the World's a Fair," 59.
22. Quoted in Karal Ann Marling, *George Washington Slept Here: Colonial Revivals and American Culture, 1876-1986* (Cambridge, Mass: Harvard University Press, 1988), 30.
23. Minutes of Historical Society Council, October 17, 1873, HSP.
24. *The Public Buildings: An Appeal to the Legislature to Prevent the Desecration of Independence Square* (Philadelphia, 1870), quoted in Charlene Mires, "Memories Lost and Found: Independence Hall in American History and Imagination," Ph.D. dissertation, Temple University, 1997, 122.
25. Frank Etting, *An Historical Account of the Old State House of Pennsylvania* (Boston: J.R. Osgood, 1876), 1-2.
26. Ibid., 166.
27. "Boss Etting the Restorer," *Sunday Times*, July 6, 1873, quoted in Mires, "Memories Lost and Found," 133.
28. *Philadelphia Inquirer*, October 27, 1873, quoted in Doris Fanelli, *The Independence Hall Historical Museum Collection*, Transactions of the American Philosophical Society (Philadelphia: APS, forthcoming), ch. 2, p. 27.
29. Quoted in ibid., ch. 2, p. 38.
30. Whitfield J. Bell, Jr., *The Bust of Thomas Paine* (Philadelphia: APS, 1974), 15-16.
31. Etting to Goshorn, May 1, 1876, Etting Papers, HSP.
32. Etting to Goshorn, May 5, 1876, Etting Papers; for Sartain's side of the story, see his *Reminiscences of a Very Old Man, 1808-1897* (New York: D. Appleton, 1899), 266-67.
33. Etting to Charles Francis Adams, May 18, 1876, Etting Papers, HSP.
34. *Pennsylvania and the Centennial Exposition: Comprising the Preliminary and Final Reports of the Pennsylvania Board of Centennial Managers . . .* , 2 vols. (Philadelphia: Gillin and Nagle, 1878), 1: 59-61.
35. Hampton L. Carson, *History of the Historical Society of Pennsylvania*, 2 vols. (Philadelphia, HSP, 1940), 1: 379.
36. Weigley, ed., *Philadelphia*, 474.
37. Murray Friedman, *Jewish Life in Philadelphia, 1830-1940* (Philadelphia: ISHI Publications, 1983).
38. The best study of Philadelphia's black community in the late nineteenth century is Roger

Lane, *William Dorsey's Philadelphia and Our Own: On the Past and Future of the Black City in America* (New York: Oxford University Press, 1991).

39. Ruth Miller Elson, *Guardians of Virtue: American Schoolbooks of the Nineteenth Century* (Lincoln: University of Nebraska Press, 1964), 301, 303.

40. Two important studies of large-scale manufacturing in the late nineteenth-century city are John K. Brown, *The Baldwin Locomotive Works, 1831-1915* (Baltimore: Johns Hopkins University Press, 1995), and Thomas R. Heinrich, *Ships for the Seven Seas: Philadelphia Shipbuilding in the Age of Industrial Capitalism* (Baltimore: Johns Hopkins University Press, 1997).

41. For small manufacturing, see Philip Scranton, *Endless Novelty: Specialty Production and American Industrialization, 1865-1925* (Princeton, N.J.: Princeton University Press, 1997).

42. The labor history of the city in the late nineteenth century is best explored by Walter Licht, *Getting Work: Philadelphia, 1840-1950* (Cambridge, Mass: Harvard University Press, 1992; reprint Philadelphia: University of Pennsylvania Press, 1999).

43. Sam Bass Warner, Jr.'s *The Private City: Philadelphia in Three Periods of Its Growth* (Philadelphia: University of Pennsylvania Press, 1968; second edition 1987) gives a good picture of the streetcar culture of the late nineteenth century.

44. For Quakers and Quaker institutions in this era, see Philip S. Benjamin, *The Philadelphia Quakers in the Industrial Age, 1865-1920* (Philadelphia: Temple University Press, 1976).

45. Frank H. Taylor, *Valley Forge: A Chronicle of American Heroism* (Philadelphia: J.W. Nagle, 1905) gives full details on this commemoration.

46. *Keystone*, May 20, 1882.

47. *Keystone*, September 16, 1882.

48. *Harper's Weekly*, November 4, 1882.

49. A full account is in the *Press*, October 23, 1882.

50. *New York Times*, October 25, 1882.

51. *Harper's Weekly*, November 4, 1882.

52. The *Press*, October 18, 19, 1882.

53. Ibid., October 19, 1882.

54. *Harper's Weekly*, November 8, 1882.

55. *Public Ledger*, October 25, 1882.

56. Scharf and Westcott, *History of Philadelphia*, 1: 852. For the growing identification of fraternal societies with American Indians, see Philip J. Deloria, *Playing Indian* (New Haven, Conn.: Yale University Press, 1998).

57. The first quote is from *Keystone*, November 4, 1882; the second and third are from Scharf and Westcott, *History of Philadelphia*, 1: 850, 852.

58. The Laetitia Penn House is discussed in John L. Cotter et al., *The Buried Past: An Archaeological History of Philadelphia* (Philadelphia: University of Pennsylvania Press, 1993), 80-81.

59. Calder quoted in Penny Balkin Bach, *Public Art in Philadelphia* (Philadelphia: Temple University Press, 1992), 204.

60. Carson, *History of the Historical Society of Pennsylvania*, 2: 19; 1: 261.

61. Ibid., 1: 373.

62. Hampton L. Carson, ed., *History of the Celebration of the One Hundredth Anniversary of . . . the Constitution of the United States*, 2 vols. (Philadelphia: J.B. Lippincott, 1889), 1: 323, for quotation; the list of committee members is on 307-10.

63. *Harper's Weekly*, September 24, 1887.

64. Ibid., September 24, 1887.
65. The *Press*, September 16, 1887.
66. Carson, *History of the Celebration*, 1: 269, 296–97, 323.
67. Frederick E. Hoxie, *A Final Promise: The Campaign to Assimilate the Indians, 1880-1920* (Cambridge: Cambridge University Press, 1984), 12.
68. Carson, *History of the Celebration*, 2: 39, 41.
69. Ibid., 2: 40; *Press*, September 16, 1887.
70. Carson, *History of the Celebration*, 2: 42.
71. Snowden's letter of August 12, 1887 is in ibid., 1: 184-85; a report of the meeting with black Philadelphia leaders is in the *Press*, September 16, 1887.
72. Carson, *History of the Celebration*, 2: 42.
73. *Press*, August 5, 1887.
74. Carson, *History of the Celebration*, 2: 71.
75. *Woman's Journal*, September 24, 1887. See also Katherine Devereux Blake and Margaret Louis Wallace, *Champion of Women: The Life of Lillie Devereux Blake* (New York: Fleming H. Revell, 1943).
76. *Woman's Journal*, September 24, 1887.
77. Ibid.
78. Carson, *History of the Celebration*, 2: 429.
79. For an incisive discussion of this see David Glassberg, *American Historical Pageantry: The Uses of Tradition in the Early Twentieth Century* (Chapel Hill: University of North Carolina Press, 1990).
80. Carson, *History of the Historical Society of Pennsylvania*, 1: xv. The rise of genealogical and patriotic societies in this era is traced in Wallace Evan Davies, *Patriotism on Parade: The Story of Veteran's and Hereditary Organizations in America, 1783-1900* (Cambridge, Mass: Harvard University Press, 1955). For the broader context of the Historical Society's sense of mission, see John Bodnar, *Remaking America: Public Memory, Commemoration, and Patriotism in the Twentieth Century* (Princeton, N.J.: Princeton University Press, 1992).
81. Quoted in David Blight, *Frederick Douglass' Civil War: Keeping Faith in Jubilee* (Baton Rouge: Louisiana State University Press, 1989), 224.

Chapter 9

1. Julian P. Boyd, "A Statement of Policy by the Historical Society of Pennsylvania," *PMHB* 64 (1940): 153.
2. Quoted in Willard Gatewood, *Aristocrats of Color: The Black Elite, 1880-1920* (Bloomington: Indiana University Press, 1990), 216.
3. Boyd, "A Statement of Policy," 154.
4. Ibid., 162.
5. Sally Griffith, *Serving History in a Changing World: The Historical Society of Pennsylvania in the Twentieth Century* (Philadelphia: HSP, 2001), chapter 3.
6. For the development of Colonial Williamsburg, see Mike Wallace, "Visiting the Past: History Museums in the United States," in *Mickey Mouse History and Other Essays on American Memory* (Philadelphia: Temple University Press, 1996), 3-32.
7. Neil Harris,"The Divided House of the American Art Museum," *Daedalus* 128 (1999): 40.

8. Quoted by Stephen E. Weil, "From Being *About* Something to Being *for* Somebody: The Ongoing Transformation of the American Museum," ibid., 229-30.
9. Thomas I. Wharton, *Address Delivered at the Opening of the New Hall of the Athenaeum of Philadelphia* (Philadelphia: J.C. Clark, 1847), quoted in Roger W. Moss, *Philadelphia Victorian: The Building of the Athenaeum* (Philadelphia: Athenaeum of Philadelphia, 1998), 4.
10. The recent history of the Philosophical Society can be followed in Edward C. Carter II, *"One Grand Pursuit": A Brief History of the American Philosophical Society's First 250 Years, 1743-1993* (Philadelphia: APS, 1993), and J. Stephen Catlett, ed., *A New Guide to the Collections in the Library of the American Philosophical Society* (Philadelphia: APS, 1987).
11. Whitfield Bell, *The Bust of Thomas Paine* (Philadelphia: APS, 1974), 15-23. The quotation from Richard Gimbel, "Tom Paine's Nightly Pests," is on 16.
12. For this phrase and a detailed explanation, see Douglas Greenberg, "'History Is a Luxury': Mrs. Thatcher, Mr. Disney, and (Public) History," *Reviews in American History* 26 (1998): 294-311.
13. I tell the story of creating this exhibit in "Behind the Velvet Curtain: Academic History, Historical Societies, and the Presentation of the Past," *PMHB* 114 (1991): 3-36.
14. Willard L. Boyd, "Museums as Centers of Controversy," *Daedalus* 128 (1999): 199.
15. Weil, "From Being *About* Something," 229-30.
16. Edwin Wolf, *"At the Instance of Benjamin Franklin": A Brief History of the Library Company of Philadelphia*, rev. ed. (Philadelphia: LCP, 1995), 92-94; also see *An African American Miscellany: Selections from a Quarter Century of Collecting, 1970-1995* (Philadelphia: LCP, 1996).
17. James Green to Gary B. Nash, June 12, 2000; see also *Women, 1500-1900: A Joint Exhibition of Books and Manuscripts, Prints, Photo and Ephemera from the Collections of the Historical Society of Pennsylvania and the Library Company of Philadelphia* (Philadelphia: LCP, 1974).
18. For African American murals that recapture lost chapters of the past, see James Prigoff and Robin J. Dunitz, *Walls of Heritage, Walls of Pride: African American Murals* (Rohnert Park, Calif.: Pomegranate Communications, 2000).
19. Details on the struggle to find a site for the Underground Railroad mural were related to the author by Jane Golden on November 15, 2000, and by Susanne Nicholson on November 28, 2000.

ACKNOWLEDGMENTS

A number of friends, colleagues, and students have provided valuable criticisms and assistance while this book moved from one draft to another. Al Young, retired from Northern Illinois University and always generous with his time, provided important comments and suggestions on an early draft. So did Allen Davis of Temple University. Peter Wood at Duke University and Roger Lane at Haverford College took much time out of their crowded schedules to furnish detailed criticisms of later drafts. Richard Dunn and Dan Richter at the McNeil Center for Early American Studies at the University of Pennsylvania, Doug Greenberg at the Chicago Historical Society, and Sidney Hart at the Charles Willson Peale Papers also made valuable suggestions. Bob Lockhart, my editor at the University of Pennsylvania Press, was a shrewd and sympathetic commentator as the manuscript went through several drafts.

For discussions of institutional history, I am indebted to Ted Carter and Whitfield Bell at the American Philosophical Society; Roger Moss at the Athenaeum of Philadelphia; John Van Horne, Phil Lapsansky, and Jim Green at the Library Company of Philadelphia; and Jeffrey Ray and Ken Finkel at the Atwater Kent Museum of Philadelphia History. Three scholars generously allowed me to read unpublished chapters of the Philadelphia stories they are telling: Sally Griffith's fine history of the modern Historical Society of Pennsylvania, Charlene Mires's scintillating history of Independence Hall in myth and reality, and Doris Fanelli's scrupulous history of the Independence Hall portrait collection. All three provided inspiration and precious insights. Morris Vogel of Temple University and Howard Gillette, Jr. of Rutgers University, Camden generously gave me an opportunity to try out some ideas about memory-making in Philadelphia at the inaugural Frederic M. Miller lecture.

A very different version of this book was first drafted as part of the exhibit at the Historical Society of Pennsylvania titled "Finding Philadelphia: Visions and Revisions." In its first form, it was a work of collaboration with two talented curators, Liz Jarvis and David Cassedy, who were key figures in mounting the HSP exhibit. Their names would have appeared on the title page if the book had been published at that time. But now the book has taken a very different form. Nonetheless, I am greatly indebted to them for their scholarly meticulousness, their insights into the material and artistic culture of historic Philadelphia, and their friendship in our many months of working together. They are still part of the creation of this book.

For research assistance—finding books, tracking down footnotes, combing newspapers, and running scholarly errands—I thank three talented graduate students at UCLA: Samantha Holtkamp Gervase, Kelly Lytle, and Shauna Mulvihill. All will be heard from before long in the history profession.

Librarians and curators, those unheralded and invaluable professionals who stand behind so much of the work of historians, deserve special thanks. I am indebted to those who helped me at the Research Library at the University of California, Los Angeles, the Masonic Temple in Philadelphia, the American Philosophical Society, the Free Library of Philadelphia, the Philadelphia Museum of Art, the Pennsylvania Academy of Fine Arts, the Balch Institute of Ethnic Studies, the Historical Society of Pennsylvania, the Athenaeum of Philadelphia, the Atwater Kent Museum of Philadelphia, and the Library Company of Philadelphia. Special thanks go to Jim Green, Phil Lapsansky, Erika Piola, Sarah Weatherwax, Cornelia S. King, and Nicole H. Scalessa, consummate librarians, archivists, and curators at the Library Company of Philadelphia who make every scholarly trip to Philadelphia the ultimate busman's holiday.

For traveler's rest, traffic in ideas, and companionship, I thank Vern and Betsy Stanton and Peter and Gail Hearn. Every research trip to Philadelphia provided a chance to refresh our lifelong friendship.

This book is dedicated to my sister and brother, Carol H. Knowlton, Ralph Clarke Nash, Jr., and their spouses. We grew up in Philadelphia together—or at least just across City Line. They stayed east and I went west. But the hold of Philadelphia on me proved enduring. Though out of the Main Line, I continued to find explorations of Philadelphia's history an important part of my scholarly life.

INDEX

PERMISSIONS

Permission to reproduce images in this volume is gratefully acknowledged as follows. Included are citations for sources quoted in the captions.

1. Trumbull, *The Declaration of Independence 4 July 1776*. Yale University Art Gallery, Trumbull collection. Quote from Doris Devine Fanelli, *History of the Portrait Collection, Independence National Historical Park* (Philadelphia: APS, 2001), 11.
2. Raphaelle Peale, *Absalom Jones*. Delaware Art Museum. Gift of Absalom Jones School.
3. *General LaFayette's arrival at Independence Hall*. Courtesy of Winterthur Museum.
4. Place, drawings of Hannah and William Penn. Historical Society of Pennsylvania.
5. William Penn gateleg table. Philadelphia Museum of Art. Purchased with the Thomas Skeleton Harrison Fund.
6. Holme, *A Mapp of the Improved Part of Pensilvania*. Library Company of Philadelphia.
7. Great Belt of Wampum. Historical Society of Pennsylvania.
8. West, *Penn's Treaty with the Indians*. Courtesy of the Pennsylvania Academy of the Fine Arts, Philadelphia. Gift of Mrs. Sarah Harrison (The Joseph Harrison, Jr. Collection).
9. Jigsaw puzzle of Penn's Treaty with the Indians. Library Company of Philadelphia.
10. Hesselius, *Tishcohan*. Historical Society of Pennsylvania.
11. *The Paxton Expedition*. Library Company of Philadelphia.
12. Pennsylvania German painted chest. Mercer Museum of the Bucks County Historical Society.
13. Mortality bill. Library Company of Philadelphia.
14. *Portrait of Black Alice*. Library Company of Philadelphia. *Eccentric Biography; or Memoirs of Remarkable Female Characters, Ancient and Modern* (Worcester, Mass.: Isaiah Thomas, 1804).
15. Slave harness and weathervane. Historical Society of Pennsylvania.
16. Slave advertisement. Historical Society of Pennsylvania.
17. Cooper, *Southeast Prospect of the City of Philadelphia*. Library Company of Philadelphia.
18. Scull and Heap, *An East Prospect of the City of Philadelphia*. Library Company of Philadelphia.
19. 1772 Philadelphia tax list. Historical Society of Pennsylvania.
20. W. L. Breton, *The London Coffee House*. Library Company of Philadelphia.
21. Iron stoveplate with German inscription. Philadelphia Museum of Art.
22. Birch, *Preparation for War to Defend Commerce*. Library Company of Philadelphia.
23. Interior of Mercer Museum. Mercer Museum of the Bucks County Historical Society.
24. Woman's pocket. Philadelphia Museum of Art.
25. Dining room setting. Philadelphia Museum of Art.
26. Rebecca Jones sampler. Courtesy of The Atwater Kent Museum.
27. Richardson coffeepot. Philadelphia Museum of Art. Gift of Mrs. Louise Hoffman.
28. Manuscript relief roll. Historical Society of Pennsylvania.
29. *A View of the House of Employment*. Library Company of Philadelphia.

30. West, *Benjamin Franklin Drawing Electricity from the Sky*. Philadelphia Museum of Art. Gift of Mr. and Mrs. Wharton Sinkler.
31. Dawkins, *Benjamin Lay*. Haverford College.
32. Astronomical clock. American Philosophical Society.
33. Henry, *Cliveden During the Battle of Germantown*. Photograph courtesy of Cliveden of the National Trust, Inc.
34. *Magna Britania*. Library Company of Philadelphia.
35. *To the Delaware Pilots*. Library Company of Philadelphia.
36. Savage, *Congress Voting Independence*. Historical Society of Pennsylvania.
37. First Battalion recruitment broadside. Library Company of Philadelphia.
38. Charles Willson Peale, *Joseph Brant*. Independence National Historical Park. Quote from Charles Coleman Sellers, "Portraits and Miniatures by Charles Willson Peale," *TAPS* 42, Pt. 1 (1952): 41.
39. Rothermel, *State House on the Day of the Battle of Germantown*. Courtesy of the Pennsylvania Academy of the Fine Arts. Bequest of Henry C. Gibson.
40. *Sentiments of an American Woman*. Library Company of Philadelphia. Quote from Linda K. Kerber, *Women of the Republic* (Chapel Hill: University of North Carolina Press, 1980), 104-5.
41. Charles Willson Peale, *A Representation of the Figures Exhibited and Paraded*. Historical Society of Pennsylvania. Anthony Sharp, *The Continental Almanac for the Year of Our Lord...* (Philadelphia: Francis Bailey, 1781). Quotes from Samuel Rowland Fisher, *Journal of Samuel Rowland Fisher of Philadelphia, 1779-1781* (Philadelphia, 1928).
42. *Committee-Room*. Library Company of Philadelphia.
43. Birch, *Second Street North from Market Street with Christ Church*. Library Company of Philadelphia.
44. Svinin, *Night Life in Philadelphia—An Oyster Barrow in Front of the Chestnut Street Theatre*. Metropolitan Museum of Art.
45. Banner of Philadelphia tobacconists. Library Company of Philadelphia.
46. Trenchard, *East View of Gray's Ferry*. Library Company of Philadelphia.
47. Birch, *High Street, from the Country Market-place Philadelphia*. Library Company of Philadelphia.
48. Krimmel, *Fourth of July in Centre Square*. Courtesy of the Pennsylvania Academy of the Fine Arts, Philadelphia. Pennsylvania Academy purchase (from the estate of Paul Beck, Jr.).
49. Liverpool pitcher. Philadelphia Museum of Art. Bequest of R. Wistar Harvey
50. Charles Willson Peale, *George Washington at Princeton*. Courtesy of the Pennsylvania Academy of the Fine Arts, Philadelphia. Gift of Maria McKean Allen and Phebe Warren Downes through the bequest of their mother, Elizabeth Wharton McKean.
51. Jennings, *Liberty Displaying the Arts and Sciences*. Library Company of Philadelphia.
52. *View of Con[gre]ss on Way to Philadelphia*. Historical Society of Pennsylvania.
53. Birch, *Colonel Frederick Muhlenberg escorting the Indians*. Library Company of Philadelphia.
54. Pages from *Census Directory*. Library Company of Philadelphia.
55. Indenture of Lundy. Pennsylvania Abolition Society Indenture Book D. Historical Society of Pennsylvania.
56. *A Peep into the Antifederal Club*. Library Company of Philadelphia.
57. *Porcupine, in Colours Just Portrayed*. Historical Society of Pennsylvania.
58. Charles Willson Peale, *The Artist in His Museum*. Courtesy of the Pennsylvania Academy

of the Fine Arts, Philadelphia. Gift of Mrs. Sarah Harrison (The Joseph Harrison, Jr. Collection).

59. Charles Willson Peale, *Yarrow Mamout*. Historical Society of Pennsylvania.
60. Charles, *A Boxing Match*. Library Company of Philadelphia.
61. Wild, *Panorama of Philadelphia*. Library Company of Philadelphia.
62. Kollner, *The Draymen*. Free Library of Philadelphia. From Kollner, *Common Sights in Town & Country* (Philadelphia: American Sunday-School Union, 1850).
63. Birch, *Gaol in Walnut Street, Philadelphia*. Library Company of Philadelphia.
64. First African Baptist Church Cemetery Excavation Plan. Courtesy of the Redevelopment Authority of the City of Philadelphia and John Milner Associates.
65. Sinclair, *Morris Iron Works*. Historical Society of Pennsylvania.
66. Kennedy, *First Passenger Train to Reading*. Historical Society of Pennsylvania.
67. Baldwin's Lodge Alley shop. Smithsonian Institution, Transportation Collection.
68. Kollner trade card. Courtesy of The Atwater Kent Museum.
69. Wild, *Manyunk, Near Philaelphia*. Library Company of Philadelphia.
70. Hugg after Krimmel, *White's Great Cattle Show*. Philadelphia Museum of Art.
71. *George Lippard*. Marian S. Carson Collection of Americana, U.S. Library of Congress (LC-USZC4-6548).
72. Wild (presumably), *Destruction by Fire of Pennsylvania Hall*. Library Company of Philadelphia.
73. Robinson, *View of the City of Brotherly Love*. Historical Society of Pennsylvania.
74. Magee, *Death of George Shiffler*. Library Company of Philadelphia.
75. Buchholtzer, *Riot in Philadelphia*. Free Library of Philadelphia.
76. Duval, *Bird's Eye View of Philadelphia*. Historical Society of Pennsylvania.
77. Traubel, *Der Brantweins Drache*. Library Company of Philadelphia.
78. Duval, lithograph of Cowperthwaite drawing. Library Company of Philadelphia.
79. Women's Room at the Library Company. Library Company of Philadelphia. George Maurice Abbott, *A Short History of the Library Company, compiled from the Minutes, together with some Personal Reminiscences* (Philadelphia: LCP, 1913), 61.
80. List of slaves sold at auction. Wister Family Papers. Historical Society of Pennsylvania. Quote from Q. K. Philander Doesticks, *Great Auction of Slaves at Savannah, Georgia* (New York: American Anti-Slavery Society, 1859).
81. Gutekunst photograph. Friends Historical Library of Swarthmore College.
82. Sartain, mezzotint after Jocelyn. Library Company of Philadelphia.
83. *The Rescue of Jane Johnson and Her Children*. Library Company of Philadelphia. Engraving in William Still, *The Underground Railroad: A Record of Facts, Authentic Narratives, Letters, &c. . . .* (Philadelphia: Porter and Coates, 1872).
84. Magee, *Forcing Slavery Down the Throat of a Freesoiler*. U.S. Library of Congress (LC-USZ62-92043).
85. Bowser, *John Brown*. Historical Society of Pennsylvania.
86. Clay, *The Elopement*. From *Tregear's Black Jokes: Being a Series of Laughable Caricatures on the March of Manners Amongst the Blacks* (London: G.S. Tregear, 1834). Turner, *The Negro in Pennsylvania, Slavery—Servitude—Freedom, 1639-1861*(Washington, D.C.: American Historical Association, 1912).
87. Clay, *The Nation's Bulwark*. Library Company of Philadelphia.

88. Krimmel, *Election Day in Philadelphia.* Winterthur Museum.
89. Hoffy, *Frank Johnson.* Historical Society of Pennsylvania.
90. Inman, *William Penn.* Independence National Historical Park. Quote from George G. Foster, "Philadelphia in Slices," *PMHB* 93 (1969): 69.
91. Breton, *The Slate House of PENN.* The Athenaeum of Philadelphia.
92. Brown, *The Gold and Silver Artificers in Civic Procession.* Library Company of Philadelphia.
93. Neagle, *Pat Lyon at the Forge,* oil, 1829. Courtesy of the Pennsylvania Academy of the Fine Arts, Philadelphia. Gift of the Lyon family. *The Locksmith of Philadelphia* (New York: Carlton and Phillips, 1854).
94. Native American Republican Association certificate. U.S. Library of Congress (LC-USZ62-90660).
95. Handkerchief, Germantown Print Works. Swarthmore College Peace Collection.
96. Rosenthal, *Interior View of Independence Hall.* Library Company of Philadelphia.
97. *Chestnut Street.* Free Library of Philadelphia.
98. *Rally for the Defence of the City.* Library Company of Philadelphia.
99. Duval, *Soldiers of Camp "William Penn".* Library Company of Philadelphia. Quote from George Fahnestock diary, Historical Society of Pennsylvania.
100. Nast, *Philadelphia Recruitment Rally.* Library Company of Philadelphia.
101. Sartain, *Young America Crushing Rebellion and Sedition.* Historical Society of Pennsylvania.
102. Cavada, *Battle of Fredricksburg.* Historical Society of Pennsylvania. *Libby Life: Experiences of a Prisoner of War in Richmond, Va., 1863-64* (Philadelphia: J.B. Lippincott, 1864).
103. Russell, *Stone Wall at Fredericksburg.* Historical Society of Pennsylvania.
104. Sartain, *Battle of Gettysburg.* Library Company of Philadelphia.
105. Thomas Hicks, *Meade at Gettysburg.* The Civil War Library and Museum.
106. *Women and Children in Encampment.* U.S. Library of Congress (LC-B8171-2405).
107. Membership Certificate, Citizens Volunteer Hospital. Library Company of Philadelphia.
108. Newell, *Interior View of the Union Volunteer Refreshment Saloon.* Library Company of Philadelphia.
109. Duval, *Buildings of the Great Central Fair.* Library Company of Philadelphia. Charles J. Stillé, *Memorial of the Great Central Fair for the U.S. Sanitary Commission, Held at Philadelphia, June 1864* (Philadelphia: The Commission, 1864).
110. William Penn parlor. Historical Society of Pennsylvania.
111. *Democratic Catechism of Negro Equality.* Library Company of Philadelphia.
112. *Octavius Catto.* Library Company of Philadelphia.
113. Independence Hall celebration. Library Company of Philadelphia.
114. Commemoration of Emancipation in Maryland. Library Company of Philadelphia.
115. Panoramic view of Philadelphia. Historical Society of Pennsylvania.
116. Davis, *Centennial Balloon View.* Free Library of Philadelphia
117. Haley, *Street Car Travel.* Historical Society of Pennsylvania.
118. *An Indian Carnival.* Library Company of Philadelphia.
119. Broadside for Mass Meeting. Historical Society of Pennsylvania.
120. *Negro Militia After Drill.* Library Company of Philadelphia.
121. Woman's Pavilion, Centennial Exposition. Library Company of Philadelphia.
122. National Woman Suffrage Association petition. Free Library of Philadelphia.
123. "Washington Relics." Library Company of Philadelphia. Frank H. Norton, ed., *Frank Leslie's*

Illustrated Historical Register of the Centennial Exposition (New York: Frank Leslie's Publishing House, 1877), 113.

124. *Scene in St. Mary St.* Library Company of Philadelphia. Edward Strahan, *A Century After: Picturesque Glimpses of Philadelphia and Pennsylvania . . .* (Philadelphia: Allen, Lane, and Scott, 1875).
125. *616 Pemberton Street.* Urban Archives, Temple University.
126. *Frank Leslie's Illustrated Newspaper.* Library Company of Philadelphia.
127. Penn's arrival on the *Welcome.* Library Company of Philadelphia.
128. Program, Penn Bi-centennial Commemoration. Library Company of Philadelphia. Quote from *Harper's Weekly* (November 4, 1882).
129. Laetitia Penn House. The Athenaeum of Philadelphia.
130. McClees, *Old London Coffee-House.* Library Company of Philadelphia. Quote from Deborah Waters, "John Fanning Watson: Philadelphia's Boswell," *PMHB* 98 (1974): 49.
131. Calder, *William Penn.* Free Library of Philadelphia.
132. Williams, *Historical Society Library in 1884.* Historical Society of Pennsylvania. Quote from Hampton L. Carson, *History of the Historical Society of Pennsylvania* (Philadelphia: Historical Society of Pennsylvania, 1940), 2:14.
133. Gutekunst, *Float at Constitution Centennial.* Quote from Hampton L. Carson, ed., *History of the Celebration of the One Hundredth Anniversary of . . . the Constitution of the United States,* 2 vols. (Philadelphia: J.B. Lippincott, 1889), 1:150. Snowden quote, 2:177. *Harper's Weekly* quote, September 24, 1887.
134. Carlisle Indian School parade float. Library Company of Philadelphia.
135. Nagle, *Thomas Ustick Walter.* The Athenaeum of Philadelphia.
136. *Tom Paine's Nightly Pests.* Richard Gimbel Collection, American Philosophical Society.
137. Black Quaker dolls. Courtesy of The Atwater Kent Museum.
138. Philadelphia Underground Railroad mural. City of Philadelphia Department of Recreation, Mural Arts Program. Photo Jack Ramsdale.